WHERE
TO FIND IT
IN THE
BIBLE

WHERE TO FIND IT
IN THE
BIBLE

Ken Anderson

Illustrated by John Hayes

THOMAS NELSON
Since 1798

NASHVILLE   DALLAS   MEXICO CITY   RIO DE JANEIRO   BEIJING

*Dedicated to
staff, associates and friends
in the ministry of InterComm.*

PREFACE

My lengthening ministry as a Christian writer and audiovisual producer has long involved constant dependence upon the Bible as a content resource. Concordances helped me locate specific words, verses, and passages.

But where do you look for Bible verses dealing with today's contemporary topics? How do you locate Scripture on topics such as credit cards, diet, race, networking, computers, women's rights, and politics?

I saw the need for a topical resource where, unlike a traditional concordance, the descriptive references used everyday speech rather than verbatim Scripture or fancy theological language. I developed a card file, elementary at first, then expanded.

"This should be in a book," a friend said one day. The end result is this combination of traditional and contemporary words, topics, and phrases with relevant Scripture references. You will find it equally useful for personal study of the Scriptures as well as for teaching and sermon preparation.

My wife and family teamed with me in the development of the final manuscript, making our "camaraderie" entry even more apt. The crew included two preteen grandsons who also diligently looked up verses to ensure the references are correct.

My God bless you as you use *Where to Find It in the Bible* to enrich your life and service.

Ken Anderson

Note: Unless otherwise specified, topics refer to content of all Bible versions. Specific references are designated as follows:

AB	Amplified Bible
Berk.	Berkeley Version
CEV	Contemporary English Version
GNB	Good News Bible
KJV	King James Version
LB	Living Bible
NASB	New American Standard Bible
NIV	New International Version
NKJV	New King James Version
NRSV	New Revised Standard Version
RSV	Revised Standard Version

ABILITY

Lost skill, Genesis 4:9–12.
Building Tower of Babel, Genesis 11:1–6.
"Special ability," Genesis 47:6.
Talent, ability from God, Exodus 4:10–12; 6:30.
Not by strength alone, 1 Samuel 2:9.
Ability gives confidence, 1 Samuel 17:32–37.
Great ability, 1 Chronicles 26:6 (NKJV).
Jewish ability ridiculed, Nehemiah 4:1–10.
Skillful writer, Psalm 45:1.
Race not to swift, strong, Ecclesiastes 9:11.
Large, small shields, Jeremiah 46:3.
Strength, ability fail, Amos 2:14–16.
Ability of Jesus, Mark 6:2–6.
Discredited ability, John 5:31–38.
God given ability, Acts 6:8.
Confident of ability, 2 Corinthians 11:5–6.

ABORTION

Accidental abortion, Exodus 21:22–25.
Abortion desired, Job 3:11–16 (Berk., AB).
"Womb to tomb," Job 10:19 (CEV).
Fetus in God's care, Isaiah 44:2 (CEV).
Desiring abortion, Jeremiah 20:17 (CEV).
Fearfully, wonderfully made, Psalm 139:13–14 (Berk.).
Fetus development, Ecclesiastes 11:5 (NKJV, AB).
Abortive spiritual birth, 1 Corinthians 15:7 (Berk.).

ABSTINENCE

Abstinence prior to worship, Exodus 19:14–15; Leviticus 10:8.
Sexual abstinence, Numbers 30:3–12 (Berk.); 1 Thessalonians 4:3–4.
Marital continence, Exodus 19:15; 1 Corinthians 7:1–5.
Requirement for priests, Leviticus 10:9.
Clean, unclean animals for food, Leviticus 11:1–47.
Abstaining from fruit of grapes, Numbers 6:2–4.
Military sexual abstinence, 1 Samuel 21:1–5.
Covenant to avoid lust, Job 31:1.
Avoid temptation for wine, Proverbs 23:31.
Political leaders to abstain, Proverbs 31:4.
Abstaining from affection, Ecclesiastes 3:5.
Total abstinence, Jeremiah 35:5–8.

Daniel, the king's wine, Daniel 1:5, 8 (LB).
Nazarites forced to imbibe, Amos 2:12.
Example of John the Baptist, Luke 1:15.
Lifelong abstinence, Luke 7:33 (LB).
Abstain from idolatrous food, Acts 15:20.
Abstaining from meat, Romans 14:23; 1 Corinthians 8:1–13; 1 Timothy 4:3.
Abstinence from evil, 1 Thessalonians 5:22; 1 Peter 2:11.
Drinking wine, 1 Timothy 5:23.

ABSURD

Sheer absurdity, 1 Corinthians 1:18 (AB).

ABUSE

Moral perversion, Genesis 19:5–9, 31–38.
Authority abused, Numbers 20:10–13.
Corrupted ordinances, 1 Samuel 2:12–17; 1 Corinthians 11:17–22.
Perverting truth, 2 Peter 2:10–22.

ACCOMPLISHMENT

Creator's accomplishment, Genesis 1:10, 12, 18, 21, 25, 31.
Wonders performed by God's power, Exodus 34:10.
Wanting to share honors, Judges 12:1–3.
Work rewarded, Psalm 62:12.
Giving God glory, Psalm 118:23.
Delight in one's work, Ecclesiastes 2:10.
End better than beginning, Ecclesiastes 7:8.
God sees all, rewards good, Jeremiah 32:19.
Beyond belief, Habakkuk 1:5.
Vine, fruit, John 15:1–8.
Giving glory to the Lord, Romans 15:18–19.
Success belongs to God, 1 Corinthians 3:7.
Runner, prize, 1 Corinthians 9:24–27.
No one has what it takes, 2 Corinthians 2:16.
Let the Lord commend, 2 Corinthians 10:17–18.
Pride in good work, Galatians 6:4 (CEV, LB).

ACCOUNTANT

Temple accounts, 2 Chronicles 34:14 (LB).

ACCUSATION
Penalty for false accusation, Deuteronomy 19:16–19.
False accusation, 1 Samuel 13:14; Nehemiah 6:7; Job 2:5; 22:6; Jeremiah 37:13; Matthew 5:11; 27:12; Luke 6:7; 1 Peter 3:16.
Accusation, innocence, 1 Samuel 22:11–15.
Accusing the accuser, 1 Kings 18:16–18.
Satanic tirade, Job 1:6–12.
Assuming guilt, Job 6:29 (LB).
Crushing words, Job 19:2.
Ruthless witnesses, Psalm 35:11 (CEV).
Restoring what was not stolen, Psalm 69:4.
No reason for accusation, Proverbs 3:30.
Accusation against God, Jeremiah 4:10.
False charges, Daniel 6:5–24.
Satan the accuser, Zechariah 3:1–2.
Silence of Jesus, Matthew 26:57–67; 27:12–14.
Answering one, avoiding another, Matthew 27:11–14.
Jesus accused by family, Mark 3:20–21, 31–32.
Conflicting false accusations, Mark 14:56.
Accused by servant girl, Mark 14:66–69.
Given words for response, Luke 12:11–12.
Alleged blasphemy, John 5:18.
Moses as accuser, John 5:45.
Woman caught in adultery, John 8:3–11.
Trumped up charge, John 8:12–13 (LB).
Produce fruit, John 15:16 (LB).
Stephen's death, Acts 6:8 to 7:60.
Jealous backlash, Acts 16:16–24.
Unproved accusation, Acts 25:7.
Accuser guilty of same sin, Romans 2:1.
Need for two or three witnesses, 1 Timothy 5:19.

ACTION
"Tarried long enough," Deuteronomy 1:6 (Berk.).
"Take action," Ezra 10:4 (NRSV).
Defiled by one's actions, Psalm 106:39.
Time ripe for divine action, Psalm 119:126 (Berk.).
Path of righteous, way of wicked, Proverbs 4:18–19.
Hasty speech, Proverbs 29:20.
Words put into action, Isaiah 48:3.
Deeds, motives likened to eggs, Isaiah 59:4–5.
Time to act, Ezekiel 24:14.
Louder than words, Matthew 11:2–5.
Tree known by fruit, Matthew 12:33–35.

"Dressed for action," Luke 12:35 (NRSV).
Inner change validated, Luke 19:8–9.
Sowing and reaping, Galatians 6:7–10.
Committed speech, actions, Colossians 3:17.
Truth put into action, James 1:22–25.
Minds ready for action, 1 Peter 1:13 (GNB, NRSV).

ADDICTION
Master and slave, 2 Peter 2:19.

AD LIB
Given right words, Isaiah 50:4 (CEV).

ADMIT
King Saul admitted David's righteousness, 1 Samuel 24:16–17.
Admitting many sins, Psalm 25:11.
Admission of God's superior power, Daniel 3:28–30.

ADOLESCENCE
Ignorant generation, Judges 2:10.
Sacrifice of daughter, Judges 11:30–40.
Boy ministering in temple, 1 Samuel 2:18.
Juvenile kings, 2 Kings 21:1; 22:1.
Covenant to avoid lust, Job 31:1.
Child's service, Jeremiah 1:4–7.
Hard labor for boys, Lamentations 5:13.
Puberty described, Ezekiel 16:7–8.
God's message to children, Joel 1:1–3.
Holy Spirit, youth, Joel 2:28.
Boy with evil spirit, Mark 9:14–29.
Dying 12-year-old girl, Luke 8:41–56.

ADOPTION
Adopted children, Genesis 15:3; 48:5; Exodus 2:10; Esther 2:7.
Selected as nation, Deuteronomy 14:1–2.
Becoming God's children, Psalm 27:10 (AB); John 1:12; Romans 8:15; 2 Corinthians 6:18; Galatians 4:3–7.

ADULTERY
Foiled adulteress, Genesis 39:7–20.
Seventh commandment, Exodus 20:14.
Neighborhood relationship, Leviticus 20:10.
Defiled engagement, Deuteronomy 22:23–24 (GNB).

Cover of darkness, Job 24:15.
Repentant adulterer, Psalm 51:1–19.
Foolish adultery, Proverbs 6:32 (NRSV).
Folly of simpleton, Proverbs 7:6–23.
Profuse adultery, Jeremiah 3:6.
Adulterous wood, stone, Jeremiah 3:9.
Iniquity in heart, mind, Ezekiel 6:9; Matthew 5:27–28.
Wife's infidelity, Ezekiel 16:32.
"Worn out by adultery," Ezekiel 23:43 (NIV).
Instruction to marry adulterous woman, Hosea 1:2–3.

ADVANTAGE
Taking advantage, Job 6:27.
Revenge for taking advantage, Proverbs 22:22–23.

ADVERTISING
Ancient billboards, Deuteronomy 27:2–8.
Signboard, Mark 15:26 (LB).

ADVICE
Advice leads to tragedy, Genesis 37:14–20.
Father-in-law's advice, Exodus 18:13–27.
Good advice, 1 Kings 12:1–11.
Elder's advice, 1 Kings 12:1–11.
Search for advice, 1 Chronicles 13:1.
Good advice spurned, 2 Chronicles 10:1–19.
Royal advisors, Esther 1:13.
Advisor needing advice, Job 4:3–6.
Open to advice, Job 6:24.

ADVERTISING

Voices of experience, Job 8:8–10.
National guidance, Proverbs 11:14.
Fools spurn counsel, Proverbs 12:15.
Failed plans, Proverbs 15:22.
Accumulated advice gives wisdom, Proverbs 19:20.
Value of good advice, Proverbs 24:5–6.
Avoid father's advice, Ezekiel 20:18.
Advice from Pilate's wife, Matthew 27:19.
Paul's parting counsel, Acts 20:25–28.

AFFECTION
Frustrated grandfather, Genesis 31:28.
Turning to rejected brother, Judges 11:1–10.
Daughter-in-law's affection, Ruth 1:14–18.
David, Jonathan, 1 Samuel 18:1–4; 19:1–6; 20:17, 41;
   23:18; 2 Samuel 1:26.
Kiss of death, 2 Samuel 20:9–10.
Our Lord's enduring love, Psalm 136:1–26.
Superficial affection, Proverbs 20:6.
Embrace with propriety, Ecclesiastes 3:5.
Everlasting love, Jeremiah 31:3.
False affection, Matthew 26:47–48.
Betrayal kiss, Mark 14:44–45.
Command to love, John 13:34; 15:12.
Love expressed through anguish, 2 Corinthians 2:4.
Deep spiritual affection, 1 Thessalonians 2:7–12.
Love each other deeply, 1 Peter 4:8.
Kiss of love, 1 Peter 5:14.
Love in the truth, 3 John 1.
Love dearly, tenderly, Revelation 3:19.

AFFLUENCE
Wealth, power, envy, Genesis 26:12–18.
God-given ability to produce wealth, Deuteronomy
   8:18.
Spiritual test, Deuteronomy 28:47–48.
Affluent in-law, Ruth 2:1.
Divine simplicity, 2 Samuel 7:1–7.
Wisdom preferred to wealth, 1 Kings 3:1–15.
Overwhelming royal affluence, 1 Kings 10:4–5.
Solomon's wealth, 1 Kings 10:23.
Downfall of wicked wealth, Job 27:16–17.
Wealth, bribery, Job 36:18–19.
Lending money without interest, Psalm 15:5.
Eternal wealth, Psalm 19:8–11.

Trusting the Lord, Psalm 20:7.
Earth belongs to God, Psalm 24:1–2.
Short-lived prosperity, Psalm 37:35–36.
Transient wealth, Psalm 39:6.
Wealth gained hurting others, Psalm 52:7.
Envying the affluent, Psalm 73:3–28.
Greatest wealth, Psalm 119:14.
Worthless wealth at day of wrath, Proverbs 11:4.
Untrustworthy wealth, Proverbs 11:28.
Pretense of wealth, Proverbs 13:7.
Little with faith, much with turmoil, Proverbs 15:16.
Simple food in peace, quiet, Proverbs 17:1.
Character needed to handle wealth, Proverbs 19:10.
Rich, poor have common origin, Proverbs 22:2.
Emptiness of success, affluence, Ecclesiastes 2:4–11.
Unsatisfied with wealth, Ecclesiastes 4:8.
Perils of national prosperity, Isaiah 2:7–8.
Ruined rich, Isaiah 5:17.
No desire for silver, gold, Isaiah 13:17.
Potential harm of wealth, power, Jeremiah 5:27–28.
Wealth given away in judgment, Jeremiah 17:3.
Boasting, trusting in wealth, Jeremiah 48:7; 49:4.
Lost luster, Lamentations 4:1.
Worth weight in gold, Lamentations 4:2.
Arrogant affluence, Ezekiel 16:49.
Wealth confused with righteousness, Hosea 12:8.
Wealth incites violence, Micah 6:12.
Silver, gold, dust, dirt, Zechariah 9:3.
Humility in service, Matthew 11:7–15.
Gain world, lose soul, Matthew 16:26.
Wealth hinders salvation, Matthew 19:16–26.
Jesus accused of luxury, Matthew 26:6–13.
Deceitful wealth, Mark 4:19.
Rich young man, Mark 10:17–27.
Widow's small coins, Mark 12:41–44.
Own world, lose self, Luke 9:25.
Greed over possessions, Luke 12:13–15.
Rich man, Lazarus, Luke 16:19–31.
Spiritual perils of rich man, Luke 18:24.
Wealthy Creator, poor Savior, 2 Corinthians 8:9.
Nothing at birth, nothing at death, 1 Timothy 6:6–8.
Monetary wealth, wealth of good deeds, 1 Timothy 6:11–19.
Love of money, Hebrews 13:5.
High position in reality low, James 1:10.

Clothes do not always make the man, James 2:1–5.
Sharing possessions, 1 John 3:17.
Wealth temporal, spiritual, Revelation 3:15–18.
Respect for those older, 1 Peter 5:5.

AGGRESSIVE

Demanding blessing, Genesis 32:26.
Commanded to avoid conflict, Deuteronomy 2:3–6, 19.
Eager for salvation, Mark 10:17.
Making most of opportunity, Ephesians 5:15–16; Colossians 4:5.

AGILITY

Ambidextrous soldiers, 1 Chronicles 12:1–2.
Deer feet, 2 Samuel 22:34; 1 Chronicles 12:8; Song of Songs 2:17.

AIDS *(References chosen are descriptive, not diagnostic.)*

Prevented infection spread, Numbers 5:1–4; 25:6–9.
Relevant statements, Deuteronomy 28:20, 22, 27, 34, 35, 37.
Sins of youth, Job 20:11–17 (KJV).
Young male prostitutes, Job 36:14.
Physical, social distress, Psalms 31:9–13; 38:5–11.
Loathsome disease, Psalm 38:7–11.
"Fatal disease," Psalm 41:8 (CEV).
Stalking pestilence of darkness, Psalm 91:6–8 (Berk.).
Sin-inflicted disease, Psalm 107:17.
Dreaded skin disease, Matthew 8:2–4.
Penalty for perversion, Romans 1:27 (AB).

AIR CONDITIONING

AIRCRAFT
Cloud chariot, Psalm 104:3 (Berk.).
Those who fly, Isaiah 60:8.
Suggested prophecy of aircraft, Isaiah 60:8; 31:5; Ezekiel 1:19.
High in sky, Romans 8:39 (LB).

ALCOHOL
Noah's drunkenness, Genesis 9:18–27.
Lot, daughters, Genesis 19:30–38.
Sobriety in worship, Leviticus 10:8–10 (Note "wine or beer," GNB).
Sacrificial wine, Numbers 15:5–7.
Alcohol, pregnancy, Judges 13:2–5.
Alcoholic beverage other than wine, Judges 13:7.
Drinking for good spirits, Ruth 3:7.
Unlimited drinks, Esther 1:8.
Joy beyond wine's levity, Psalm 4:7.
Wine, overeating, laziness, Proverbs 23.20–21.
Lingering over wine, Proverbs 23:30–33.
Medicinal wine, Proverbs 31:4–7; Mark 15:23; Luke 10:34; 1 Timothy 5:23.
Notorious bartenders, Isaiah 5:22.
Crying for wine, Isaiah 24:7–13.
Wine for sedation, Isaiah 24:11.
Festive wine, Isaiah 25:6.
Incapacitated by wine, Isaiah 28:1, 7.
Making poor decisions, Isaiah 28:7.
Drunk not with wine, Isaiah 51:21.
False sense of values, Isaiah 56:10–12.
Wine, divine judgment, Jeremiah 13:12–14.
Exemplary forefathers, Jeremiah 35:1–16.
False joy, Jeremiah 51:39.
Wine forbidden in temple, Ezekiel 44:21.
Weeping drunkard, Joel 1:5.
Vow forcibly broken, Amos 2:12.
Drinking women, Amos 4:1; Titus 2:3.
Abundant wine, beer predicted, Micah 2:11.
Excessive wine, Nahum 1:10.
Betrayed by wine, Habakkuk 2:5.
Intoxicating neighbors, Habakkuk 2:15.
Constant drinking, Haggai 1:6.
Avoiding fermentation, Matthew 9:17.
Storing wine, Matthew 9:17; Mark 2:22.
Changing water into wine, John 2:1–11.

Causing another to stumble, Romans 14:20–23.
Drunk from wine, filled with the Spirit, Ephesians 5:18.
Sobriety for elders, Titus 1:7.
Enslaved, 2 Peter 2:19.
Drunk with blood, Revelation 17:6.

ALIEN

Alien, stranger, Genesis 23:4 (KJV).
Aliens barred from Passover, Exodus 12:43–45.
Foreigner's debt, Deuteronomy 15:3.
Alien wife's beauty treatment, Deuteronomy 21:10–13.
Attitude toward aliens, Deuteronomy 23:7.
Half Jewish, 1 Kings 7:13, 14 (LB).
Wearing foreign clothes, Zephaniah 1:8.

ALLOWANCE

King's allowance, Jeremiah 52:34.

ALZHEIMER'S

Forgotten prosperity, Lamentations 3:17.
Precious lingering memory, Ecclesiastes 12:6–7.
"Land of forgetfulness," Psalm 88:12 (NKJV).

AMATEUR

Father, inexperienced son, 1 Chronicles 22:5; 29:1.
Amateur theology, Acts 17:18 (Berk.).
Admitted amateur status, 2 Corinthians 11:6 (GNB).

AMAZEMENT

Vindication by earthquake, Numbers 16:28–34.
Breathless queen, 1 Kings 10:4 (CEV).
"Faces aflame," Isaiah 13:8 (Berk.).
Ezekiel overwhelmed, Ezekiel 3:15.
Awesome acts of God, Joel 1:13–20.
Amazed audience, Matthew 7:28–29; 9:33; 13:54–58; Mark 1:22; 6:2.
Amazed at shallowness, Galatians 1:6 (Berk.).

AMBIDEXTROUS

Soldiers agile with either hand, 1 Chronicles 12:1–2.
Two-handed frustration, Ecclesiastes 4:6.
Ambidextrous evil, Micah 7:3.
Creative hands, Hebrews 1:10 (GNB).

AMBIGUOUS

Confused languages, Genesis 11:1–8.
Ambiguous statements, Numbers 23:27 (KJV); 2 Kings 5:25 (KJV); 1 Chronicles 26:18 (KJV).
Avoiding ambiguity, Habakkuk 2:2.
Comprehension of Jesus' followers, Luke 9:44–45.
Accused of babbling, Acts 17:18.
Trumpet's uncertain sound, 1 Corinthians 14:8.
Ambiguous gospel, Galatians 1:6–7.

AMBITION

Ambition of secular society, Genesis 11:1–4.
Campaigning for office, 2 Samuel 15:1–4.
Full obedience desired, Psalm 119:1–5.
Determination to fulfill destiny, Psalm 132:1–5.
"Make hay while sun shines," Proverbs 10:5 (LB).
Man's plans, God's purposes, Proverbs 16:1; 19:21.
Desire to exceed neighbor, Ecclesiastes 4:4.
Search for schemes, Ecclesiastes 7:29.
Seeking great things in rebellion against God, Jeremiah 45:4–5.
Indulgent mother, Matthew 20:21.
Desire for prominence, Luke 22:24.
Continual lust for more, Ephesians 4:19 (GNB, NEB).
Making most of opportunity, Ephesians 5:15–16; Colossians 4:5.
Ready to serve, witness, Ephesians 6:15.
Paul's supreme desire, Philippians 3:7–11.
Motivated to Christian lifestyle, 1 Thessalonians 4:11–12.
Goal for goodness, 2 Thessalonians 1:11 (LB).
Desire to be overseer, 1 Timothy 3:1.
Dangerous motivation toward wealth, 1 Timothy 6:9–10.
Uncertain tomorrows, James 4:13–16.

AMUSEMENT

Inappropriate laughter, Genesis 18:10–15.
Wicked revelry, Exodus 32:6.
Samson's performance, Judges 16:25.
Hand to hand matches, 2 Samuel 2:14.
Dancing children, Job 21:11–12.
Meaningless amusement, Ecclesiastes 2:1–2.
Spiritual need ignored, Isaiah 5:12.
Strumming harps, Amos 6:5.

Worship of fishing, Habakkuk 1:16.
Children playing, Zechariah 8:5.
Refusing to be amused, Matthew 11:16.

ANARCHY
Following personal whim, Deuteronomy 12:8–9.
Contempt for temple, government, Deuteronomy 17:12;
    Ezra 7:26.
Positive anarchy of ants, Proverbs 6:6–8.
Many rulers during rebellion, Proverbs 28:2.
Brother against brother, Isaiah 19:2.
Egypt's future distress, Isaiah 19:12.
People turning against each other, Isaiah 3:5–7; Zecha-
    riah 8:10.
Destructive shepherds, Jeremiah 12:10.
Every man on his own, Jeremiah 23:36.
No God, no king, Hosea 10:3.
Distorted sense of right, Amos 3:10.
Family disloyalty, Micah 7:2, 6.
Fish have no ruler, Habakkuk 1:14.
Slaves against masters, Zechariah 2:9.
Men attacking each other, Zechariah 14:13.

ANECDOTE
Illustrative anecdote, Judges 9:8–15.

ANGELS
Abraham's heavenly visitors, Genesis 18:1–10.
Amenities to angels, Genesis 19:1–4.
Angels spoken of as men, Genesis 19:1–13.
Angelic authority, Genesis 22:11–12.
Guidance by assigned angel, Genesis 24:7.
Personal angel, Genesis 24:40; Acts 12:11, 15.
Give heed to angels, Exodus 23:20–23.
Donkey, angel, Numbers 22:23–28.
Commander of the Lord's army, Joshua 5:13–15.
Angel's secret name, Judges 13:16–18.
Mistaking angel for God Himself, Judges 13:21–23.
Alluding to angels, 2 Kings 6:16.
Association with Satan, Job 1:6; 2:1.
Anonymous spirit, Job 4:15–16.
Give praise to God, Psalm 29:1.
Deliverance for those in need, Psalm 34:7.
Bread of angels, Psalm 78:25.
Role of guardian angels, Psalm 91:9–12; Exodus 23:20.

Angels obedient to the Lord, Psalm 103:20.
Soldiers destroyed by angel, Isaiah 37:36.
Angel subdued lions, Daniel 6:22.
Gabriel, Daniel, Daniel 9:20–21.
Strengthening angel, Daniel 10:15–19.
Angels, dreams, visions, Zechariah 1:7–17.
Ministry of angel to prophet, Zechariah 1:8–21 (Note continuing chapters).
Ministry following temptation, Matthew 4:11.
Agent of judgment, Matthew 13:41–42.
Children's angels, Matthew 18:10.
Angelic protection, Mark 1:12–13.
Angelic birth announcements, Luke 1:5–38.
Frightened by angel, Luke 1:11–12.
Gabriel's two assignments, Luke 1:11–38.
Firstborn's name given by angel, Luke 1:13.
Rejoicing angels, Luke 15:10.
Angelic intervention, Acts 5:17–20; 12:4–11.
Human face resembled angel, Acts 6:15.
Guided by angel, Acts 8:26.
Angel seen in vision, Acts 10:3–4.
Ministering angels, Acts 12:8–10; 27:21–25.
Possible reference to angels, 1 Corinthians 4:15.
Demons masquerade as angels, 2 Corinthians 11:14–15.
Christ superior to angels, Hebrews 1:4–8.
Status of angels, Hebrews 1:5–14.
Unaware encounter with angels, Hebrews 13:2.
Angels' curiosity, 1 Peter 1:12.
Chained angels, Jude 6.
Message delivered by angel, Revelation 1:1.
Assigned to God, Revelation 3:5.
Angel choir, Revelation 5:11–12.
Illuminating presence, Revelation 18:1.
Do not worship angels, Revelation 19:10; 22:9.
One angel versus Satan, Revelation 20:1–3.

ANGER

Murder incited by anger, Genesis 4:3–8.
Anger subsided, Genesis 27:44.
God's anger, Exodus 4:14; Numbers 11:1; 12:9; Deuteronomy 9:20; Joshua 7:1; Judges 2:14; 2 Samuel 24:1; 1 Kings 14:15; 15:29–30; 16:2, 26, 33; 22:53; 2 Kings 13:3; 17:11; 22:13; 23:19; 1 Chronicles 13:10; 2 Chron-

icles 28:25; Psalms 2:12; 7:11 (LB); Hosea 12:14; John 3:36; Romans 1:18; 2:8; Ephesians 5:6.
Red-faced anger, Exodus 11:8.
Fierce anger, Numbers 25:4.
Things done in rage, Deuteronomy 19:4–7.
Dangerous hot temper, Judges 18:25; Proverbs 22:24–25.
Angered by divine remedy, 2 Kings 5:1–12.
Memory dimmed by anger, Esther 2:1.
Flashing eyes, Job 15:12.
Debilitating anger, Proverbs 14:17; Ecclesiastes 7:9.
Gentle words, quiet anger, Proverbs 15:1; 17:27.
Controlled anger, Proverbs 16:32.
Hot-tempered man, Proverbs 19:19.
Pacified by bribery, Proverbs 21:14.
Lacking self-control, Proverbs 25:28.
Fool, wise man, Proverbs 29:11.
Anger stirs dissension, Proverbs 29:22.
Anger incited, Proverbs 30:33.
Enraged by hunger, Isaiah 8:21.
God like angry soldier, Isaiah 42:13.
Cup of God's wrath, Jeremiah 25:19–29.
Anger eliminated, Colossians 3:8; Titus 1:7.
Continual anger, Amos 1:11.
Unjustified anger, Jonah 4:4, 9.
Anger as murder, Matthew 5:21–22.
Furious opposition, Luke 6:11.
Resentment to spiritual truth, Acts 5:30–33.
Anger at sunset, Ephesians 4:26.

ANGST

What ails you? Genesis 21:17 (NKJV).
Nation in mourning, Numbers 14:39.
Royal lament, 1 Chronicles 21:17.
Remorse for disobedience, Matthew 27:3–5.

ANIMAL RIGHTS

Overworked donkey, Exodus 23:5.
Mistreated donkey, Numbers 22:27.
Hamstrung horses, 2 Samuel 8:4; 1 Chronicles 18:4.
Righteous man, animal rights, Proverbs 12:10.
Kindness to birds, Deuteronomy 22:6.
Rescued ox, Luke 14:5.

ANIMAL RIGHTS

ANNIVERSARY
Looking back many years, Deuteronomy 2:7.
Recording historic date, Nehemiah 6:15.
Important date recorded, Ezekiel 24:2.
Date to remember, Haggai 2:18.

ANNOUNCEMENT
Coming plague announced, Exodus 9:5 (LB).
Single trumpet, double trumpet, Numbers 10:1–4.
Trumpet message, 1 Samuel 13:1–3.
Royal announcement, Ezra 1:2–4.
History's premier announcement, Isaiah 9:6–7.
Advance notice, Isaiah 40:3.
Proclaiming year of Lord, Isaiah 61:1–3.
Royal decree of disobedience, Daniel 3:4–7.
Announcement preaching, Matthew 3:1–3.
"Shouting in the desert," Mark 1:3 (GNB).
Angelic announcements, Luke 1:15–38.

ANNOY
Disturbing privacy of others, Proverbs 25:17.

ANSWER
Nonverbal response, Judges 6:36–40; 1 Kings 18:37–38.
Mother's answered prayer, 1 Samuel 1:10–28.
"Time for the Lord to act," Psalm 119:126 (CEV).
Answers to unasked questions, Isaiah 65:1 (CEV).
Answer delayed ten days, Jeremiah 42:7.
Daniel looked to God for answers, Daniel 2:14–28.

Assured answer, Luke 7:18–22.
One question answered with another, Luke 20:1–8.
Patiently awaiting answers, Hebrews 6:13–14.

ANTAGONIST
"Worthless bums," Acts 17:5 (CEV).

ANTICHRIST
"Horrible thing," Daniel 12:11 (LB).
Many will claim to be Christ, Matthew 24:4–5.
Man of sin, 2 Thessalonians 2:1–11.
World deceivers, 2 John 7–11.

ANTI-SEMITISM
Persecuted Jews, Nehemiah 1:1–3.
"Decrepit Jews," Nehemiah 4:2 (Berk.).
Plot to destroy Jews, Esther 3:1–6.
Enemies of Israel, Jeremiah 30:16–17.
Mixing human blood with sacrifices, Luke 13:1.
Jews ordered out of Rome, Acts 18:1–2.

ANXIETY
Insurmountable opposition, Exodus 14:5–14.
Anxiety episode, Deuteronomy 28:66–67.
Rest in divine protection, Deuteronomy 33:12.
Command to courage, Joshua 1:9.
Counselor of distressed, discontented, 1 Samuel 22:2.
Lifted from deep waters, 2 Samuel 22:17.
Desire for peace, security, 2 Kings 20:19.
Curdled like cheese, Job 10:10.
Terrified by the Lord, Job 23:16.
Internal tension, Job 30:27.
Total trust all circumstances, Psalm 3:1–8.
Wrestling with anxiety, Psalm 13:2, 5.
Ever present Lord, Psalm 14:4–5.
Light overcomes darkness, Psalm 18:28.
Heavyhearted, Proverbs 12:25.

APATHY
Complacent women, Isaiah 32:9.
Those who pass by, Lamentations 1:12.
Heart of flesh, stone, Ezekiel 11:19.
Refusing to see, hear, Ezekiel 12:1–2.
Zion's complacency, Amos 6:1.
Neither seek nor ask, Zephaniah 1:6.

Carefree people, Zephaniah 2:15.
Hearts like flint, Zechariah 7:11–12.
Rejected invitation, Matthew 22:1–14.
Caring neither for God or man, Luke 18:1–5.

APPEARANCE
Handsome physique, Genesis 39:6–7.
Angel's description, Judges 13:6.
Outward appearance, 1 Samuel 16:7; 2 Corinthians 5:12.
Boy's appearance, 1 Samuel 16:12.
Neglecting personal appearance, 2 Samuel 19:24.
Happy heart, cheerful face, Proverbs 15:13.
Dress up, look your best, Ecclesiastes 9:8 (cev).
Prophetic description of Jesus, Isaiah 53:2.
Varied facial appearance, Ezekiel 1:10.
No wash, shave, combed hair, Daniel 10:3 (lb).
Comb hair, wash face, Matthew 6:17 (cev).
Whitewashed tombs, Matthew 23:27; John 7:24.

APPETITE
Human, animal vegetarians, Genesis 1:29–30; 2:16.
Angels with appetites, Genesis 19:1–3.
Taste for game, Genesis 25:27–28.
Esau's foolish hunger, Genesis 25:29–34.
Craving for meat, Numbers 11:4–5.
Hungry as lion, Numbers 23:24.
Physical, spiritual appetites, Deuteronomy 8:10–14.
Food as lust, Deuteronomy 12:15, 20 (kjv).
Appetite loss, 1 Samuel 1:7; 20:34; 28:23; Psalm 102:4; 107:18; Job 3:24.
Sufficient food, no complaint, Job 6:5.
Sorrow numbs appetite, Psalms 42:3; 102:9.
Sin causes appetite loss, Psalm 107:17–18.
Disciplined appetite, Proverbs 23:2.
Excessive food, drink, Proverbs 23:20.
Lazy man's appetite, Proverbs 26:15.
Bitter tastes sweet, Proverbs 27:7.
Unappeased appetites, Ecclesiastes 6:7; Isaiah 9:20.
Dream of food, Isaiah 29:8.
Hungry dogs, Isaiah 56:11.
King's lost appetite, Daniel 6:18.
Appetite for righteousness, Matthew 5:6.
Four thousand hungry people, Mark 8:1–9.
Too much concern for food, Luke 12:22, 29.

Hunger-induced trance, Acts 10:10.
Tension numbed appetite, Acts 27:33–36.
Appetite for lust, Ephesians 4:19.
Spiritual milk desired, 1 Peter 2:2–3.
Sweet mouth, sour stomach, Revelation 10:9–10.

APPRECIATION

Forgotten favor, Genesis 40:14, 23.
Unappreciated donkey, Numbers 22:21–30.
Mutual appreciation, Ruth 2:8–13.
Grateful foreigner, Ruth 2:10.
Vicarious appreciation, 2 Samuel 9:1; 10:2.
Showing no appreciation, Psalm 78:9–18.
National appreciation lacking, Psalm 106:1–43.
Gratitude for great forgiveness, Luke 7:39–50.
No thanks for service rendered, Luke 17:7–10.
Ten healed of leprosy, Luke 17:12–18.
Appreciate clergy, teachers, 1 Thessalonians 5:12–13 (CEV).

APPROVAL

People responded with one voice, Exodus 24:3.
Sandal removed, Ruth 4:7.
Authorized travel, Nehemiah 2:1–8.
Approved by strong people, Isaiah 25:3.
"The Lord's approval," Lamentations 3:37 (CEV).
God's approval of His Son, Matthew 3:17.
Pharisees' empty sincerity, Mark 12:15–17.
Approved by God, 1 Corinthians 4:5.
Approval of men or God? Galatians 1:10.
Paul's approval of followers, Colossians 4:7–17.
Approval by faith, Hebrews 11:2 (NASB, NRSV).

ARCHANGEL

Voice of resurrection, 1 Thessalonians 4:16.
Archangel versus Satan, Jude 9.

ARGUMENT

Strife among brothers, 2 Samuel 2:27–28.
Argument with God, Job 3:2–3.
Always last word, Job 16:3.
Tactful approach, Job 16:4, 6.
Winning argument, Job 32:1.
Make tumult, Psalm 2:1 (Berk.).
Cause made valid, Psalm 37:6.

Gentle words subdue anger, Proverbs 15:1.
Good counsel against argument, Proverbs 17:14.
Loving quarrels, Proverbs 17:19.
Silence elevates fool, Proverbs 17:28.
Avoiding strife brings honor, Proverbs 20:3.
Evidence turns against accuser, Proverbs 25:8.
Gentle tongue, Proverbs 25:15.
Meddling in quarrel, Proverbs 26:17.
"Present your case," Isaiah 41:21 (Berk.).
Disputing mercy, justice, Ezekiel 33:10–20.
Wisdom, tact, Daniel 2:14.
Agree with adversary, Matthew 5:25 (KJV).
Entangling words, Matthew 22:15 (Berk.).
Daring to dispute God, Romans 9:20.
Avoid dispute, Romans 14:1.
"You keep arguing," 1 Corinthians 1:11 (CEV).
Trivial disagreements, 1 Corinthians 6:2.
Paul's logic, Galatians 2:14–17.
Promoting controversies, 1 Timothy 1:3–4.
Vain argument, 1 Timothy 1:6 (AB).
Petty controversy, 2 Timothy 2:14 (AB).
Terminology, 2 Timothy 2:14, 23.
"Morbid craving for controversy," 1 Timothy 6:4 (NRSV).
"Stupid, senseless arguments," 2 Timothy 2:23 (CEV).
Gentleness in disputes, 2 Timothy 2:23–26.
Heads up all situations, 2 Timothy 4:5.
Useless topics, Titus 3:9.

ARMY

Conscription age, Numbers 26:2–4.
Army strategy, Joshua 8:6–7.
Army at full strength, Judges 9:29; Ezekiel 37:10.
Army of chosen men, 2 Samuel 6:1.
Nations' armies face divine wrath, Isaiah 34:2.
Warrior with hands tied, Jeremiah 14:9 (CEV).
Vast army, Revelation 9:16.

ARREST

Sabbath breaking arrest, Numbers 15:32–34.
City of refuge, Numbers 35:6–15.
Apprehended by speech manner, Judges 12:5–6.
Imprisoned for tax evasion, 2 Kings 17:4.
House arrest, Jeremiah 37:15; Ezekiel 3:24–25 (LB); Acts 28:16.
Refusal to arrest Jesus, John 7:45–46 (LB).

House entry, Acts 8:3.
Posting bond, Acts 17:9.
Angel to arrest, chain Satan, Revelation 20:1–3.

ARROGANCE
Arrogant gods, Exodus 18:11.
Arrogant before the Lord, 1 Samuel 2:3.
Presumed ease facing enemy, Deuteronomy 1:41–45.
Flattering lips, boastful tongue, Psalm 12:3–4.
Strutting arrogance, Psalm 12:8.
Presuming God does not hear, Psalm 59:7–8.
Arrogance brought low, Isaiah 2:17–18.
Haughty, ruthless, Isaiah 13:11.
Arrogance, insolence, Isaiah 16:6 (Berk.).
Those who do not blush, Jeremiah 6:15.
Boast only about the Lord, Jeremiah 9:23–24.
Pride, arrogance, Jeremiah 48:29.
Arrogant affluence, Ezekiel 16:49.
Israel's arrogance, Hosea 5:5.
Proud, arrogant strut, Zephaniah 3:11 (CEV).
Ironical evaluation of weak Christians, 1 Corinthians 4:8–18.
Evil queen refuses to admit sin, Revelation 18:7–8.

ARSON
Method for burning fields, Judges 14:4–5.

ART
Celestial artistry, Psalm 19:1.
Artwork destroyed, Psalm 74:6.
Engraved hearts, altars, Jeremiah 17:1.
Jerusalem sketch, Ezekiel 4:1.
Wall murals, Ezekiel 8:7–12; 23:14.

ARTHRITIS
Searing pain, Psalm 38:7.
Dry bones, Proverbs 17:22.

ARTIFICIAL
Cheap glaze, Proverbs 26:23 (GNB).
Ego displayed by teachers of law, Mark 12:38–40.
False humility, Colossians 2:18.

ARTIST
Separating light, darkness, Genesis 1:4, 17–18.
Talents provided by Holy Spirit, Exodus 31:1–5.
Chisel at work, Deuteronomy 10:1.
Man of skill, Proverbs 22:29.
Idols fashioned from firewood, Isaiah 44:15–17.
Temple decor, Ezekiel 41:17–20.

ASHAMED
Ashamed to mention Lord's name, Amos 6:10.
Hiding light, Matthew 5:15.
Judas' guilt, Matthew 27:3.
Ashamed to identify, Luke 22:53–62.

ASKING
Invitation to ask, 1 Kings 3:5.
Asking for spring rains, Zechariah 10:1.
Ask, seek, knock, Matthew 7:8; Luke 11:9.
Asking in faith, Matthew 21:22.
Assured answers, John 14:13–14; 15:7.
Asking for wisdom, James 1:5.
Confident asking, 1 John 5:14.

ASSASSINATION
Murder for pay, Deuteronomy 27:25.
Death of king, Judges 3:21.
Death of King Saul's killer, 2 Samuel 1:1–16.
Brother avenged, 2 Samuel 3:27.
Recruited to turn against king, 2 Kings 9:14–24.
King destroyed by associates, 2 Kings 12:19–20.
Slain at temple worship, 2 Kings 19:37.
Assassinated governor, Jeremiah 41:2.

ASSERTIVE
Conditions for answered prayer, Exodus 32:31–32.
Approach to God, Psalm 51:1–7.
Repetitious prayer, Luke 11:5–13.

ASSETS
Creditor takes all, Psalm 109:11.
Lavish assets, no assets, Mark 8:36.

ASSURANCE
Promise to Abram, Genesis 12:2–3; 15:1; 17:1.
Entering Egypt reassured, Genesis 46:1–4.

God's nearness, Deuteronomy 4:7.
Righteous assurance, Joshua 22:31.
Assurance of good, evil, Joshua 23:15.
Refuge, strength, Psalm 46:1–3.
"God is for me!" Psalm 56:9.
Confidence in God, not men, Isaiah 36:4–10.
No fear of danger, Isaiah 43:1–2.
Desert passage, Isaiah 43:19.
End assured from beginning, Isaiah 46:10–11.
God knows best, Isaiah 48:17–18.
Walking in dark, Isaiah 50:10.
Heaven, earth temporal, salvation eternal, Isaiah 51:6.
God fulfills promises, Jeremiah 29:10–11.
Nothing too hard for God, Jeremiah 32:27.
Daily love, faithfulness, Lamentations 3:22–24.
Assurance in fiery furnace, Daniel 3:16–17.
God's presence assured, Haggai 1:13.
Believe the Gospel, Mark 1:14–15.
Help assured, John 6:37.
Ever present Lord, Acts 2:25–28.
Assured protection, Acts 18:9–11.
Certain of erroneous belief, Acts 19:35–36.
Standing at end struggle, Ephesians 6:13.
Work begun, completed, Philippians 1:6.
Standing firm, Philippians 1:27–30.
Need fulfilled, Colossians 1:15–23.
Full comprehension, Colossians 2:2.
In-depth conviction, 1 Thessalonians 1:5.
Eternal encouragement, 2 Thessalonians 2:16–17.
Absolute confidence, 2 Timothy 1:12.
Faithful Lord, 2 Timothy 2:13.
Coming to High Priest with confidence, Hebrews 4:14–16.
God cannot lie, Hebrews 6:18–20.
Eternal guarantee, Hebrews 7:22.
Full assurance, Hebrews 10:9–23.
Perfect Savior, perfect salvation, Hebrews 10:11–14.
Obedience toward unknown objective, Hebrews 11:8.
Assurance of promises fulfilled, Hebrews 11:13.
Internal assurance, 1 John 3:24.
Shielded from evil, 1 John 5:18.
The God who keeps, provides, Jude 24–25.

ASTROLOGY

Sun, moon, stars not worshiped, Deuteronomy 4:19;
  17:2–3.
Warning against false predictions, Deuteronomy 18:10–
  12; Jeremiah 27:9.
Worship of stars, 2 Kings 21:3, 5; Zephaniah 1:5.
Zodiac constellations designed by God, Job 9:9.
Homage to sun, moon, Job 31:26–28.
"Laws of the heavens," Job 38:33 (NIV).
Astrology decried, described, Isaiah 47:10–15 (GNB,
  NRSV).
Exhumed star-worshipers' bones, Jeremiah 8:1–2.
Signs in the sky, Jeremiah 10:2 (See LB).
Silent stars, Daniel 2:1–4; 4:7; 5:7–9.
Wise astrologers, Matthew 2:1 (LB).
"Spirits of the universe," Colossians 2:8 (NRSV).

ASTRONOMY

Creation of sky, Genesis 1:8, 14–17.
Bethlehem star, Numbers 24:17; Matthew 2:1–8.
Sun, moon, stars not worshiped, Deuteronomy 4:19.
Dark stars, Job 3:9.
Sealed star light, Job 9:7.
Invisible sun, Job 37:21.
Creation's scope, Job 38:4–13, 31–33.
Sky proclaims God's glory, Psalm 19:1–6.
Created heavens, Psalm 33:6.
Ancient skies, Psalm 68:32–33.
Ageless sun, moon, Psalm 72:5, 17.
Enduring sun, moon, Psalm 89:36–37.
Moon designates seasons, Psalm 104:19.
Space cannot contain God's love, Psalm 108:4–5.
Stars numbered, named, Psalm 147:4; Isaiah 40:26.
Earth, sky show God's wisdom, Proverbs 3:19–20.
Wisdom preceded creation, Proverbs 8:24–31.
Sun, moon, stars darkened, Isaiah 13:10.
Bright moon, brighter sun, Isaiah 30:26.
Sky, stars removed, Isaiah 34:4.
Sun, moon not needed, Isaiah 60:19.
God of all nature, Jeremiah 31:35.
Christ the Creator, Colossians 1:15–17.
Morning star as gift, Revelation 2:28.
Falling stars, Revelation 6:13; 9:1.
Celestial garments, Revelation 12:1, 4.
Hailstones from sky, Revelation 16:21.

Flight of earth, sky, Revelation 20:11.
Bright morning star, Revelation 22:16.

ATHEISM
No God in Israel, 2 Kings 1:3.
Atheistic defiance, 2 Kings 18:17–25.
No God, no priest, no law, 2 Chronicles 15:3.
No room for God, Psalm 10:4 (LB, "God is dead").
Fool's voice, Psalms 14:1 (See LB, AB); 53:1.
Universal God consciousness, Ecclesiastes 3:11.
Living under other lords, Isaiah 26:13.
Judgment makes God known, Ezekiel 11:7–12.
Doubt augmented by truth, John 8:45–47.
Atheistic denial, 1 John 2:22.

ATHLETICS
Ishmael, the archer, Genesis 21:20.
Wrestling with God, Genesis 32:22–30.
Athletic physique, Genesis 39:6–7.
Hairbreadth accuracy, Judges 20:16.
A head taller, 1 Samuel 9:2.
Stature of King Saul, 1 Samuel 10:23–24.
Mighty, brave men, 1 Samuel 14:52.
Strength, agility from God, 2 Samuel 22:33–37.
Feet like deer, 2 Samuel 22:34.
Bend bronze bow, 2 Samuel 22:35.
Swift runner, Job 9:25.
Strong as bull, Psalm 92:10.
Physical strength of limited value, Psalm 147:10–11.
Swimming breast stroke, Isaiah 25:11.
Men against horses, Jeremiah 12:5.
Strong oarsmen, Ezekiel 27:26.
Disciple's foot race, John 20:4.
Runner, prize, 1 Corinthians 9:24–27.
Avoid aimless effort, 1 Corinthians 9:26.
Hindrance to good race, Galatians 5:7.
Playing according to rules, 2 Timothy 2:5.
Finishing race, 2 Timothy 4:7.
Running with perseverance, Hebrews 12:1–2.

ATTACK
Ready for enemy, Nehemiah 4:16–18.
Neighborhood watch, Proverbs 27:10.
Dangerous roads, Jeremiah 6:25.

ATTITUDE

Negative attitude, Genesis 4:3–7.
Good attitude displayed, Genesis 13:8–9.
Positive worship attitude, Leviticus 22:29.
Servant attitude, Ruth 2:13.
Food, drink, good spirits, Ruth 3:7.
Open to rebuke, 2 Samuel 16:5–12.
Childlike attitude, 1 Kings 3:7.
Boastful attitude, 1 Kings 12:13–14.
Pagan king's altered attitude, Ezra 1:1–4, 7–8; 5:8–6:12; 7:13–26.
Optimistic attitude toward trouble, Job 1:21–22.
Joyful spirit from the Lord, Job 8:21.
Serve with gladness, Psalm 100:1–2.
Rejoicing attitude, Psalm 118:24.
Positive attitude toward problems, Psalm 119:71; Proverbs 14:10.
God's attitude to proud, humble, Psalm 138:6.
Happy heart, cheerful face, Proverbs 15:13, 30; 17:22.
Pride brings destruction, Proverbs 16:18.
Hot temper, Proverbs 19:19.
Enjoying another's failure, Proverbs 24:17–18.
Hatred of life, Ecclesiastes 2:17.
Sorrow sublimates laughter, Ecclesiastes 7:3–4.
Patience versus pride, Ecclesiastes 7:8.
Positive lifestyle, Ecclesiastes 8:15.
Attitude control over anxiety, Ecclesiastes 11:10.
Evaluating desolate circumstances, Jeremiah 33:10–11.
Pride, arrogance, Jeremiah 48:29.
Bitterness, anger, Ezekiel 3:14.
Sour grapes, Jonah 4:1–11.
Attitude toward those disliked, Matthew 5:38–48.
Effect of attitudes, understanding, Matthew 13:14–15.
Nature of Kingdom of Heaven, Matthew 19:14.
"Salt" of good spiritual attitude, Mark 9:50.
True humility, Luke 7:6–7.
Violent rebuke, Acts 7:51–58.
Weak, strong evaluated, Romans 14:1–8.
More harm than good, 1 Corinthians 11:17–32.
Refresh other's spirit, 1 Corinthians 16:18.
Radiant face, 2 Corinthians 3:18.
Servant attitude, 2 Corinthians 4:5.
Making room in heart, 2 Corinthians 7:2.
Grieving Holy Spirit, Ephesians 4:30.

Attitude toward opposition, Philippians 1:15–18.
No complaining, arguing, Philippians 2:14.
Gentleness always, Philippians 4:5.
Attitude decides lifestyle, Philippians 4:8–9.
Keys to positive attitude, 1 Thessalonians 5:16–18.
Attitude toward wealth, 1 Timothy 6:17–19.
Attitude toward deserters, 2 Timothy 4:16.
Response to discipline, Hebrews 12:5–11.
Persecution, suffering, James 1:2–6.
Negative thoughts, 1 Peter 2:1.
Attitude toward suffering, 1 Peter 4:12–16.

AUTHORITY

Creator's command, Genesis 1:3, 6, 9, 14–15, 20, 24, 26.
Human authority over creation, Genesis 1:26–29.
The eternal "I am," Exodus 3:13–14.
Sovereign authority, Exodus 6:1–8, 28–29.
Moses, man with authority, Exodus 7:1–2.
Final authority, Deuteronomy 1:17.
God-given authority, Deuteronomy 2:25.
Speaking with divine authority, Leviticus 23:1–2, 9–10, 23–24.
Authority of father, husband, Numbers 30:3–16.
Prolonged authority, 1 Samuel 13:1.
Spear as authority symbol, 1 Samuel 26:7.
Power over citizens, foreigners, 2 Samuel 22:44–46.
Prophet authenticated, 1 Kings 18:10–24.
God's saving name, Psalm 54:1.
Wealth as authority symbol, Proverbs 22:7.
Fools given authority, Ecclesiastes 10:6.
God speaks, acts, Isaiah 44:24–28.
Jeremiah's reluctance to proclaim, Jeremiah 1:1–10, 17–18.
Authority of teachers, masters, Matthew 10:24.
Contrasting authority, Matthew 12:22–32.
Finger of God, Luke 11:20; Acts 3:11–16.
Jesus' obedience to authority, John 12:50.
Protective authority, John 17:11.
Jesus accused of disrespect, John 18:19–24.
Authority challenged, John 19:8–11.
Scripture as authority, Acts 18:28.
Demons unmoved by lack of authority, Acts 19:13–16.
Insulting high rank, Acts. 23:4–5.
Truth declared with power, Romans 1:4.
Relationship of men, women, 1 Corinthians 11:2–16.

Holy Spirit's witness, 1 Corinthians 12:3.
Ultimate world authority, 1 Corinthians 15:24.
Spiritual weapons, 2 Corinthians 10:1–5.
Wives, husbands, Ephesians 5:22–23.
Savior, King, Colossians 1:15–20.
Christ, Head over all, Colossians 2:9–10.
Overthrowing man of sin, 2 Thessalonians 2:8.
Desire to be overseer, 1 Timothy 3:1.
God does not lie, Titus 1:2.
Leadership with authority, Titus 2:15.
Superior to angels, Hebrews 1:3–4.
Submission to authority, 1 Peter 2:13–17.
Ministering in Lord's name, 3 John 7.
Wrong church authority, 3 John 9–10.
Authority over evil, Jude 9.
Earth's sovereign, Revelation 1:5.
Satanic authority. Revelation 13:2.
Temporary authority, Revelation 13:5.
Ten kings' one-hour reign, Revelation 17:12.
Given authority, Revelation 20:4.

AUTOGRAPH
"Here is my signature," Job 31:35 (NASB, NRSV).
Paul's signature, Colossians 4:18; 2 Thessalonians 3:17.

AVENGE
Not do unto others, Proverbs 24:29.
Love to those who cause grief, 2 Corinthians 2:5–11.
Leave revenge to God, 2 Thessalonians 1:6–7.

AWE
Standing on holy ground, Exodus 3:1–6.
Queen overwhelmed, 1 Kings 10:5.
In awe of God, Job 25:2; Isaiah 6:1–8; Ezekiel 38:20.
Awesome Lord, Psalm 47:2 (NKJV).
King, priests, prophets, Jeremiah 4:9 (NKJV).
"Gasp at the sight," Jeremiah 49:17 (LB).
Ezekiel overwhelmed, Ezekiel 3:15.
Awed by vision, Daniel 10:7–8.
Talking to God, Daniel 10:15–21.
Silent earth, Habakkuk 2:20.
Reverence to the Lord, Zechariah 2:13.
Amazed audience, Matthew 7:28–29; 9:33; 13:54–58.
Amazed disciples, Matthew 8:27.
Overwhelmed with wonder, Mark 9:15.

Terrorized awe, Luke 2:9 (AB).
Awe-stricken Pilate, John 19:8.
Contemplating Christ's glory, Ephesians 1:18–23.

AWOL
Frightened soldiers, 1 Samuel 13:7–8.

--------------------- **B** ---------------------

BABEL
Babel's heights, Jeremiah 51:53.

BACHELOR
No record of Joshua's family, Joshua 1:1.
Promises to eunuchs, Isaiah 56:3–5.
"Gift of staying single," Matthew 19:11 (CEV).
Marriage renounced, Matthew 19:12.
Bachelor's marriage counsel, 1 Corinthians 7:1–40.
Did Paul consider marriage, 1 Corinthians 9:5 (CEV).
144,000 apparent bachelors, Revelation 14:1–5.

BACKBITING
Continual backbiting, Psalm 50:20.
Tongue like storm, Proverbs 25:23.

BACKSLIDING
Causes of backsliding, Exodus 17:7; Deuteronomy
    8:11–14; Psalm 106:14; Proverbs 16:18; Mark 4:18–
    19; 1 Timothy 6:10; 2 Peter 1:9.
Good leader needed, Exodus 32:1–6.
Wayward community, Deuteronomy 13:12–18.
Egypt forbidden, Deuteronomy 17:16.
Journey never retaken, Deuteronomy 28:68.
Wayward people, Joshua 22:18.
Backsliding prone, Judges 2:18–19; Hosea 11:7.
National backsliding, Judges 10:16.
Told to seek pagan gods, Ruth 1:15.
Unrestrained backsliding, 1 Samuel 3:13.
Restoration, 1 Samuel 15:24–25.
Failure into success, 1 Kings 8:33–34.
Old age, spiritual decline, 1 Kings 11:4.
Turning away, 1 Kings 11:9.
Backslidden king, 2 Chronicles 12:1.
David's perilous experience, Psalm 73:2.

Stubborn, rebellious, Psalm 78:8.
Blessings quickly forgotten, Psalm 106:13.
Once astray, then obedient, Psalm 119:67.
Choosing evil, Psalm 125:5.
Rewards for conduct, Proverbs 14:14.
Massive backsliding, Isaiah 1:1–4.
Grieving Holy Spirit, Isaiah 63:10.
Divinely hardened hearts, Isaiah 63:17.
Backslider's dilemma, Jeremiah 3:1.
Waywardness cure, Jeremiah 3:22.
Leaders, people backslide, Jeremiah 5:3–5.
Ineffective leadership, backsliding people, Jeremiah 15:1.
Spiritual conspiracy, Jeremiah 17:13.
Repentant backslider, Jeremiah 31:19.
Wishing return to Egypt, Jeremiah 42:1–22; 43:1–7.
Inevitable judgment awaits disobedience, Jeremiah 44:15–28.
Impudent Israel, Ezekiel 2:4.
Righteous man becomes unrighteous, Ezekiel 3:20–21; 18:24–28.
Deeds of darkness, Ezekiel 8:12.
Backslider's fate, Ezekiel 18:26.
Actions betray speech, Ezekiel 33:31.
Time of refinement, Daniel 11:35.
Israel forgot God, Hosea 8:14.
Certain judgment, Hosea 9:7.
Dangerous material blessings, Hosea 13:6.
Sin, boasting, Amos 4:4–5.
Overt backsliding, Jonah 1:1–3.
Hearts like flint, Zechariah 7:11–12.
Unsavory salt, hidden lights, Matthew 5:13–16.
Serving two masters, Matthew 6:24.
Miracles, hard hearts, Matthew 11:20.
Love grown cold, Matthew 24:12.
Unfulfilled promise, Mark 14:27–31, 66–72.
Looking back, Luke 9:62; Galatians 4:9.
Backsliding disciples, John 6:66.
Shame items, Romans 6:21.
Fallen restored, Romans 11:23.
Missing mark, 1 Corinthians 4:1–21.
Wayward believers, 1 Corinthians 5:9–12.
Astonishing Galatians, Galatians 1:6–9.
Led astray, Galatians 2:13.
Weak, miserable, Galatians 4:9.

Shipwrecked faith, 1 Timothy 1:18–20.
Deserters, 2 Timothy 1:15; 4:10.
Wandering from truth, 2 Timothy 2:17–18.
Worldliness, 2 Timothy 4:9–10.
Hearts astray, Hebrews 3:10, 12.
Danger continuing sin, Hebrews 10:26–27.
Backslider restored, James 5:19–20.
Avoid former error, 1 Peter 1:14.
Backs turned, 2 Peter 2:20–22.
Straying from body, 1 John 2:18–19.
Full reward lost, 2 John 8.
Permanently listed in Book of Life, Revelation 3:2–5.
Neither cold nor hot, Revelation 3:15–16.

BAKING

Fast food, Genesis 18:6.
Bible bakers, Genesis 40:1; Jeremiah 37:21; Hosea 7:4.
Sabbath baking for Sabbath, Exodus 16:23.
Oven baked offering, Leviticus 2:4.
Ten bakers, one oven, Leviticus 26:26.
Bread loaf vitality, Judges 7:13–15.
Hot coals for baking, 1 Kings 19:6.
Raisin cakes, Isaiah 16:7.
Bakers' street, Jeremiah 37:21 (Berk.).
Unclean fuel, defiled food, Ezekiel 4:12–15.
Spiritual yeast, Matthew 13:33.

BANKER

Generous loan policy, Deuteronomy 15:7–8.
Mortgaging land, Nehemiah 5:3.
Rich versus poor, Proverbs 22:7.
Commercial centers, Ezekiel 27:12–23.
Currency values, Ezekiel 45:12.
Storing treasures, Matthew 6:19–20.
Temple money changers, Matthew 21:12; Mark 11:15;
    John 2:15.

BANKRUPTCY

Powerless, helpless, Job 6:13.
Total loss, Psalm 109:11.
Deceitful man's loss, Jeremiah 17:11.
Remembered treasures, Lamentations 1:7.
Prosperity forgotten, Lamentations 3:17.
Debtors take over, Habakkuk 2:7.

YES, I'M THE FATTED CALF! WHO WANTS TO KNOW?

BARBECUE

Fortunes restored, Zephaniah 2:7.
Insolvency, Matthew 18:21–25.

BAPTISM

Unworthy of baptism, Matthew 3:7–8.
Baptism of suffering, Matthew 20:20–24 (KJV).
Believer's baptism, Matthew 28:19; Mark 16:16; Acts
    2:38; 10:48; Galatians 3:27; Colossians 2:12.
"John the baptizer," Mark 1:4 (NRSV).
Jesus' baptism, Mark 1:9.
Baptism as witness, Luke 3:3 (LB).
Water, spirit, John 3:5.
Abundant water, John 3:23.
Jesus, disciples, John 4:1–2.
Simultaneous conversion, baptism, Acts 8:36–37.
Red Sea baptism, 1 Corinthians 10:1–2 (CEV).
Baptized for dead, 1 Corinthians 15:29.
Symbolic Ark, 1 Peter 3:20–22 (GNB).
Water, blood, 1 John 5:6 (GNB).

BARGAINING

Bargaining for a city, Genesis 18:20–33.
Bargain birthright, Genesis 25:27–34.
Life for life, Joshua 2:14.
Best price, Proverbs 20:14.
Greatest bargain, Isaiah 55:1–2.
Bad exchange, Jeremiah 2:11.
Sadistic bargaining, Matthew 14:7–10.
Judas' infamy, Matthew 26:14–16.

BARTENDER

Mixing drinks, Isaiah 5:22.

BATH
Washing traveler's feet, Genesis 18:4; 19:2.
Egyptian princess' bath, Exodus 2:5.
Ceremonial cleansing, Leviticus 14:8; 2 Kings 5:10–14.
Bathed but unclean, Numbers 19:7.
Prostitutes, chariots, 1 Kings 22:38.
Soda, soap, Jeremiah 2:22.

BEACH
"Ocean boundaries," Job 38:8 (CEV).
Waterfront audience, Matthew 13:2.
Fisherman's catch, Matthew 13:48.
Broiling fish, John 21:9.
Kneeling in sand, Acts 21:5.
Seaside miracle, Acts 28:1–6.

BEAUTICIAN
Alien wife's beauty treatment, Deuteronomy 21:10–14.
Palace procedure, Esther 2:2–13.

BEAUTY
Beauty in creation, Genesis 2:9; Psalm 19:1; Ecclesiastes 3:11.
Wife's beauty, Genesis 12:11; 1 Samuel 25:3.
Beautiful Rebekah, Genesis 24:16.
Means to personal safety, Deuteronomy 21:10–14.
Beauty, brains, 1 Samuel 25:3.
Tempting beauty, 2 Samuel 11:2.
Most beautiful women, Esther 1:11; 2:1–4.
Beauty treatment, Esther 2:8–12.
Beautiful daughters, Job 42:15.
Feminine beauty, Psalm 45:11.
Beauty skin deep, Proverbs 11:22; 31:30.
Bald women of Zion, Isaiah 3:16–17.
Jerusalem allegory, Ezekiel 16:4–14.
Nature's beauty, Hosea 14:5–6; Matthew 6:28–29.
Beautiful young women, Zechariah 9:17.
Mountain of Transfiguration, Matthew 17:1–8.
God's gift, 1 Corinthians 4:7.
Radiant face of Moses, 2 Corinthians 3:7–8.
Flowers wither, 1 Peter 1:24
Inner beauty, 1 Peter 3:3–4.

BEAUTY CONTEST
All time beauty, 1 Kings 1:3 (LB).

BEER

Fermented drink not wine, Numbers 6:3; Deuteronomy 29:6; Judges 13:7.
Bitter beer, Isaiah 24:9.

BEGGING

Children begging, Psalm 37:25; 109:10.
Handicap induced begging, Mark 10:46–52; John 9:1–12.
Beggar, rich man, Luke 16:19–31.
"Beggar's bag," Mark 6:8 (GNB).
Surprised beggar, Acts 3:1–8.

BEGINNING

God at outset, Genesis 1:1.
New calendar, Exodus 12:2.
Beginning to end, Deuteronomy 31:24.
"Spring of the day," 1 Samuel 9:26 (KJV).
Initial foundations, Psalm 102:25.
Beginning of wisdom, knowledge, Psalm 111:10; Proverbs 1:7; 9:10.
Before earth's creation, Proverbs 8:23.
Beyond comprehension, Ecclesiastes 3:11.
End contained in beginning, Isaiah 46:10.
New day dawning, Isaiah 60:1 (CEV).
Beginning of sorrows, Matthew 24:8; Mark 13:8.
Eternal Word, John 1:1.
Alpha, omega, Revelation 21:6.

BEHEADED

John the Baptist, Matthew 14:10; Mark 6:16, 27; Luke 9:9.
Beheaded martyrs, Revelation 20:4.

BELIEVER

Idols in heart, Ezekiel 14:1–11.
Weak believers, Matthew 6:30; 8:26; 14:31; 16:8; John 12:42.
Believers' potentials, Mark 9:23; 11:24; Luke 17:6; John 14:12.
Resurrection belief, John 2:22.
First believers, John 2:23.
Miracle-motivated believer, John 4:53; Acts 9:36–42.
Believers' rationale, John 7:31.
"Out of the believer's heart," John 7:38 (NRSV).

Response to Christ's message, John 8:30; 10:42.
Secret believers, John 12:42–43 (LB).
Jesus prayed for believers, John 17:6–26.
God-fearing Jews, Acts 2:5.
Jailer's belief, Acts 16:25–35.
Sincere believers, Acts 17:10–12.
Sins confessed by new believers, Acts 19:17–20.
Holy Spirit's temple, 1 Corinthians 3:16–17.
Hopeless yet believing, Romans 4:18.
Confident believer, 2 Timothy 1:12.
Faith pleases God, Hebrews 11:6.
Clean in society of deceit, Revelation 3:4, 10.
All tribes, nations, Revelation 7:9–10.

BELOVED

Sacrificing daughter, Judges 11:30–40.
Dawn of love, Ruth 3:1–18.
Beloved, barren, 1 Samuel 1:2–11.
Mutual love between friends, 1 Samuel 20:17.
Esteemed of the Lord, Isaiah 66:2.
The Lord's signet ring, Haggai 2:23.
Apple of His eye, Zechariah 2:8.
Earth marriage, Heaven relationships, Mark 12:18–27.
Mother's gentle spirit, 1 Thessalonians 2:7–8.

BETRAYAL

Captive's information about enemy, Judges 8:13–14.
Deceitful Delilah, Judges 16:15–19.
Disloyal priest, Judges 18:4–26.
Turning against friends, Job 17:5.
Close friend deceived, Psalms 41:9; 55:12–14.
Betrayed by friends, Psalm 55:20; Lamentations 1:19.
Parable of two eagles, Ezekiel 17:2–10.
Family dishonor, Micah 7:6; Matthew 10:21.
Jesus betrayed, Matthew 26:14–16, 47–50; Mark 14:43–46; Luke 22:3–6; Zechariah 11:12–13.
Peter's denial, Matthew 26:31–35, 69–75.
Implicated by bread morsel, John 13:21–27.

BEWILDERED

Walking in darkness, Psalm 82:5.
Spirit of dizziness, Isaiah 19:14.
Foolish Galatians, Galatians 4:1–5.

B

BIAS

Negative, positive, Numbers 13:17–33.

Favoring one against another, 1 Corinthians 4:6.

BIBLE

Not by bread alone, Deuteronomy 8:3; Job 23:12; Jeremiah 15:16; Matthew 4:4.

Joy, light, Psalms 19:8; 119:105, 130; Proverbs 6:23; 2 Peter 1:19.

Sweeter than honey, Psalms 19:10; 119:103.

Eternal book, Psalm 119:89; Isaiah 40:8; Matthew 5:18; 24:35; 1 Peter 1:25.

"The book of the Lord," Isaiah 34:16 (NKJV).

Beloved Bible, Psalm 119:47, 72, 97, 140.

Rain, snow, Isaiah 55:10–11.

Bible as joy, delight, Jeremiah 15:16.

Fire, hammer, Jeremiah 5:14; 23:29.

Commissioning Bible authors, Jeremiah 36:1–3; Ezekiel 1:2–3; 2 Peter 1:21.

Edible scroll, Ezekiel 3:1.

"People need every word," Matthew 4:4 (CEV).

Cleansing water, Ephesians 5:26.

Spirit's sword, Ephesians 6:17.

Important reading, Colossians 4:16.

Inspired Bible, 2 Timothy 3:16.

Dynamic Bible, Hebrews 4:12.

Milk, solid food, Hebrews 5:12; 1 Peter 2:2.

Divine mirror, James 1:23–25.

BIGOTRY

Abrasive nationalism, Esther 3:8–9.

Bigoted religious leaders, Matthew 21:15.

Well-intentioned bigotry, Mark 9:38.

Pharisee attitude, John 8:33–38.

Name-calling, John 8:48–49.

Spiritual blindness, John 9:39–41.

Presumed justification, Philippians 3:3–6.

Ignorant bigotry, 1 Timothy 1:13.

BILLBOARD

Stone billboards, Deuteronomy 27:2–8.

Calvary's sign board, Mark 15:26 (LB).

BIOGRAPHY

Thumbnail biographies, Genesis 25:12–18; Judges 10:1–5.
Limited biography, 2 Kings 15:13–15.
Beginning to end, 1 Chronicles 29:29–30.
Satan's brief biography, Isaiah 14:12–15.
Biographies of Christ, Luke 1:1–4 (LB).
Life of Jesus, John 21:25; 1 Timothy 3:16.

BIRTH CONTROL

Physical procedure, Genesis 38:8–10.
Population growth, Exodus 1:7.
Doors shut to womb, Job 3:10 (KJV).
Children a heritage, Psalm 127:3–5.
Mandate for large families, Jeremiah 29:4–6.
Nursing, pregnancy, Hosea 1:8.
Husband's option, John 1:13.

BIRTHDAY

Old Testament fathers, Genesis 11:10–26.
Birthday parties, Genesis 40:20; Matthew 14:6–11.
Remembering family birthdays, Genesis 43:33.
120th birthday, Deuteronomy 31:2 (KJV).
Family birthday celebrations, Job 1:4–5 (LB, AB).
Day of birth regretted, Job 3:1–26; Jeremiah 15:10; 20:14–18.
Birthdays all too often, Job 9:25–26.
Number of birthdays determined, Job 14:5.
Time flies, Job 16:22.
God's numberless years, Job 36:26.
Brevity of life, Psalm 39:4–5.
Counting the days, Psalm 90:12 (LB).
Morbid birthday gift, Matthew 14:6–12.
Age misunderstood, John 8:57.

BITTERNESS

Bitter fruit, Deuteronomy 32:32.
Bitterness of soul, Job 3:20; Proverbs 14:10.
Forsaking the Lord, Jeremiah 2:19.
Punished conscience, Jeremiah 4:18.
Gall of bitterness, Lamentations 3:15.
Filled with bitterness, Acts 8:23.
"Cursing and bitterness," Romans 3:14 (NIV, NKJV).
Bitterness overcome, Ephesians 4:31.

Bitter roots, Hebrews 12:15.
Bitterness harbored in heart, James 3:14.

BLACK
Black is beautiful, Song of Songs 1:5 (NRSV).
Skin, hair, Song of Songs 1:5–6; 5:11 (KJV).
Black man and the cross, Mark 15:21 (Note: Cyrene,
    North African city).

BLACKMAIL
Joseph's initial attitude to brothers, Genesis 42:1–34.
Love exploited, Judges 16:4–21.
Conniving against Daniel, Daniel 6:3–24.
Misused relationship, Matthew 26:47–50; Mark 14:43–
    46; Luke 22:47–48; John 18:1–4.

BLAME
Passing blame to others, Genesis 3:8–13.
Accepting blame, Genesis 42:21–22; 43:8–9.
Avoid blaming God, Job 1:22.

BLAME

Self-inflicted disaster, Jeremiah 44:7.
Pardon for nation's guilt, Joel 3:21.
Blamed for storm at sea, Jonah 1:10–12.
Guilt of Judas, Matthew 27:3.
Looking for something to criticize, Mark 3:2.
Blaming women, 1 Timothy 2:14.
Seeing light, walking in darkness, 2 Peter 2:21.

BLAMELESS
Blameless conduct, Psalm 119:1 (RSV).

BLESSING
Blessing, protection for Ishmael, Genesis 21:9–21.
Material blessing, Genesis 24:35;26:12; 48:15–16; Exodus 23:25; Deuteronomy 29:5; 1 Kings 3:13; Proverbs 10:22; Isaiah 30:23; Joel 2:26; Zechariah 10:1.
Parental blessing, Genesis 27:21–40; 28:1; 2 Samuel 13:25.
Benefiting from another, Genesis 39:5.
Curse becomes blessing, Deuteronomy 23:5.
Forgotten blessings, Psalm 106:7–8.
Blessing others, Joshua 14:13; Psalm 129:8.
Leadership blessing, Joshua 22:6; 1 Kings 8:14.
Blessing of pregnancy, 1 Samuel 2:20.
Household blessing, 2 Samuel 7:29.
Requirements for blessing, 1 Kings 8:56–61.
Promise, warning, 1 Kings 9:1–9.
Abundant blessing, Nehemiah 9:25; Psalm 133:3.
Righteousness brings blessing, Psalm 18:20–21.
Blessing, righteousness, Psalm 24:5.
Abundant blessings, Psalm 68:9.
Honey from the rock, Psalm 81:16.
Divine wonders, Psalm 88:10–12.
Blessing of faithfulness, Proverbs 28:20.
Blessing held in abeyance, Isaiah 1:19–20.
Forsaken source of blessing, Jeremiah 2:13.
Obedience to covenant, Jeremiah 11:1–5.
Lesser blessing forgotten, Jeremiah 16:14–15.
Blessings leading to backsliding, Hosea 13:6.
Cursed blessings, Malachi 2:2.
Good stewardship blessing, Malachi 3:8–10.
Source of blessing, Matthew 5:11–12 (Note verses 3–10).
First things first, then blessing, Matthew 6:33.
Touching Jesus, Mark 5:24–30.

Prophet, widow, Luke 4:23–26.
Discipleship blessing, Luke 18:29–30.
Touch of the Master's hand, John 2:1–11.
Desire for material blessing, Acts 1:6.
Temporal blessings, Acts 14:17.
Blessing by default, Romans 11:11–12.
Not one blessing missed, 1 Corinthians 1:7.
A blessing to others, 2 Corinthians 7:13–16.
Those who refresh, 1 Corinthians 16:18.
Illness brings blessing, Galatians 4:13–14.
Blessing to many, Philippians 1:25–26.
Every good gift, James 1:16–17.
Abundant grace, peace, 1 Peter 1:2; Jude 2.
Scripture finale, Revelation 22:21.

BLINDNESS

Instant blindness, Genesis 19:11; 2 Kings 6:18; Acts 9:8.
Blinded slave set free, Exodus 21:26.
Kindness to unsighted, Leviticus 19:14; Deuteronomy 27:18.
No blind clergy, Leviticus 21:16–23.
Healing blind, deaf, dumb, Isaiah 35:5–6.
Healed of blindness, Matthew 9:27–31; 12:22; 20:30–34; 21:14; Mark 8:22–25; 10:46–52; Luke 7:21–22; John 9:1 12.
Last healing prior to Crucifixion, Matthew 20:29–34.
Blind man's active faith, Mark 10:46–52 (CEV).
Convert's blindness, Acts 9:8.
Blindness, sorcerer, Acts 13:6–12.
Eyes that cannot see, Deuteronomy 29:4.
Leading the blind, Isaiah 42:16.
Spiritual blindness, Isaiah 59:10; Matthew 6:23; 15:14; Ephesians 4:18; 1 John 2:11.
Becoming as blind men, Zephaniah 1:17.
Darkness within, Matthew 6:23; Ephesians 4:18; 2 Peter 1:5–9.
Look, never see, Matthew 13:14 (CEV).
Blind leading blind, Matthew 15:14.
Blind worship, Matthew 23:19.
Seeing, hearing, not understanding, Luke 10:24.
Messianic blindness, John 7:25–36.
Questioning validity of Jesus, John 8:12–30.
Pagans certain of error, Acts 19:35–36.
Look, never see, Acts 28:26 (CEV).
Covenant blindness, 2 Corinthians 3:14.

Blinded by Satan, 2 Corinthians 4:1–6.
Blinded by hatred, 1 John 2:11.

BLISS

Ignorance is bliss, Ecclesiastes 1:18.

BLOOD

Food containing blood, Genesis 9:4; 1 Samuel 14:31–33.
Blood sprinkling, Exodus 12:7; 24:8; Leviticus 4:6; Numbers 19:4; Hebrews 11:28; 12:24; 1 Peter 1:2.
Identified by blood, Exodus 12:13.
Blood atonement, Exodus 30:10; Leviticus 17:11; John 6:56; 19:34; Acts 20:28; Romans 5:9; Hebrews 9:7, 14, 21–22; 1 Peter 1:18–19; 1 John 1:7; Revelation 1:5; 5:9.
Mixing human blood with sacrifices, Luke 13:1.
Nectar of judgment, Revelation 16:5–6.

BLUSH

Embarrassed Ezra, Ezra 9:6.
Blushing moon, Isaiah 24:23 (Berk.).
Not knowing how to blush, Jeremiah 6:15; 8:12.
"Do not blush," 2 Timothy 1:8 (AB).

BOASTING

Goliath's macho, 1 Samuel 17:44.
Windy mouth, Job 8:2.
Hedonistic boasting, Psalm 10:3.
Boasting about God, Psalm 44:8.
Talk is cheap, Proverbs 20:6 (GNB).
Clouds without rain, Proverbs 25:14.
Future plans, Proverbs 27:1.
Satan's taunts, Isaiah 14:12–15; Ezekiel 28:12–19.
Only reason to boast, Jeremiah 9:23–24.
"Talks-Big-Does-Nothing," Jeremiah 46:17 (CEV).
False claims, Jeremiah 48:14–20 (GNB).
Claiming to make Nile river, Ezekiel 29:9.
Boasting of hypocrisy, Amos 4:4–5 (LB).
"We did it on our own," Amos 6:13 (CEV).
Unable to live up to boasting, Matthew 26:31–35, 69–75; Mark 14:27–31, 66–72; John 13:37–38; 18:15–18, 25–27.
Truth disbelieved, John 5:31–38.
Proud sorcerer, Acts 8:9–10.
Self-confidence, 2 Corinthians 3:4 (GNB).

"Boast about us," 2 Corinthians 5:12 (NRSV).
Self-praise, commendation from the Lord, 2 Corinthians 10:13–18.
Spiritual pride, Romans 2:17–21.

BODY

Corruption after death, Genesis 3:19; Job 19:25–26; 21:23–26; Ecclesiastes 3:20; John 11:39; Acts 13:36.
Death's nearness, 1 Samuel 20:3; Psalm 103:14; Isaiah 2:22.
Demons use physical bodies, Matthew 8:31.
Human body enslaved, serving, Romans 6:19 (CEV).
Holy Spirit's temple, 1 Corinthians 3:16–17.
Resurrection bodies, 1 Corinthians 15:35–44.
Only a tent, 2 Corinthians 5:4 (AB).

BODYGUARD

Trained men, Genesis 14:14.
Without bodyguard, 1 Samuel 21:1.
"Godliness and integrity," Psalm 25:21 (LB).
Shielded by God's power, 1 Peter 1:5.

BONDAGE

Right to be set free, Leviticus 25:47–55.
Sold into bondage, Judges 4:2.

BONES

Evil bondage, Proverbs 5:22; John 8:34; Acts 8:23; Romans 6:16; 7:23.
Sold to creditors, Isaiah 50:1.
Restoration of Israel prophesied, Jeremiah 30:8–17.
Free men ruled by slaves, Lamentations 5:8.
Bound by infirmity, Luke 13:12 (KJV).
Those enslaved think they are free, John 8:31–36.
Chains increased ministry, Philippians 1:12–14.
Escape from bondage, 2 Timothy 2:26.
Bondage defined, 2 Peter 2:19.
Satan bound, Revelation 20:1–3.

BOOKS

Immutable book, Proverbs 30:5–6; Revelation 22:19.
Dialogue immortalized, Job 19:23.
Endless book supply, Ecclesiastes 12:12.
Book thrown into river, Jeremiah 51:63 (GNB).
Scroll of remembrance, Malachi 3:16–18.
Source of joy, Luke 10:20.
Public book burning, Acts 19:19.
Volumes of judgment, Revelation 20:12.

BOREDOM

Boring life, Ecclesiastes 2:1–11 (CEV).

BOXING

Hand-to-hand fighting, 2 Samuel 2:14.
"Fist of the mighty," Job 5:15 (CEV).
Divine pugilism, Psalm 3:7.
Avenging fist, Ezekiel 25:12–13, 16 (LB).
Boxing technique, 1 Corinthians 9:26 (NASB, NRSV).

BRAGGING

Big mouths, Judges 9:38.
Proper time for boasting, 1 Samuel 2:1–3.
Affront to the Lord, Psalm 10:3.
Nothing to brag about, Psalm 49:6–9; 1 Corinthians 1:29; 2 Corinthians 4:6, 7; Ephesians 2:8–10.
Dishonest stewardship, Proverbs 25:14.
Boast about the Lord, Jeremiah 9:23–24.
Insincere loyalty, Matthew 26:31–35, 69–75.
Evil boasting, James 4:16.

B

BRAIN
Right, left hemispheres, Ecclesiastes 10:2.
Computer capability, 1 Corinthians 2:16; Ephesians 3:18; Philippians 2:5.

BRAVERY
Brave Joshua, Numbers 14:6–9.
Bold Gideon, Judges 7:7–23.
Boy versus giant, 1 Samuel 17:1–51.
Nehemiah's boldness, Nehemiah 6:10–13.
Brave woman, Esther 4:13–16.
Imputed bravery, Proverbs 28:1; Ephesians 3:12; Hebrews 4:16.
Unwavering courage, Daniel 6:10.
Facing adversaries, Philippians 1:27–28.
Challenge to be brave, Hebrews 4:16 (GNB).

BREAKFAST
Morning feast, Ecclesiastes 10:16–17.
Seaside breakfast, John 21:11–15 (Note verse 15 Berk.).

BRIBERY
Bribery distorts truth, Exodus 23:8.
God cannot be bribed, Deuteronomy 10:17 (CEV).
Blinded by bribes, Deuteronomy 16:19.
Asking special favor, Judges 1:13–15.
Bribed to deceive, Judges 16:5.
Sons accept bribes, 1 Samuel 8:3.
International bribery, 1 Kings 15:19.
Bribing invader, 2 Kings 15:19–20.
Anti-Semitic bribery, Esther 3:8–9.
Riches, bribes, Job 36:18–19.
Bribes to be hated, Proverbs 15:27.
Thwarting justice, Proverbs 17:23; Amos 5:12.
Use of gift, Proverbs 18:16.
Pacifying bribe, Proverbs 21:14.
Bribes corrupt character, Ecclesiastes 7:7.
Refusing bribery, Isaiah 33:15–16.
God accepts no incentive, Isaiah 45:13.
Daniel's integrity, Daniel 5:17.
Skilled in evil, Micah 7:3.
Jesus betrayed, Matthew 26:14–16, 47–50; Mark 14:10–11; Luke 22:3–6; Zechariah 11:12–13.
Resurrection perjury, Matthew 28:11–15.

Bribe offered for spiritual secret, Acts 8:9–24.
Attempting to induce bribery, Acts 24:26.

BRIDE

Search for bride, Genesis 24:1–66; Esther 2:17.
Engagement, marriage, Deuteronomy 20:7
Blessing of good wife, Proverbs 18:22.
Prophetic bride, Isaiah 62:5.
Adulterous brides, Hosea 4:13 (LB).
Bride of Christ, 2 Corinthians 11:2; Revelation 19:7; 22:17.
Remarriage, Romans 7:2–3; 1 Timothy 5:14.

BRIMSTONE

Brimstone upon Sodom, Genesis 19:24; Luke 17:29.
Threatened brimstone, Job 18:15; Psalm 11:6.

BROKENHEARTED

Heartbroken from scorn, Psalm 69:20.

BRUTALITY

Slaves mistreated, Exodus 21:20–21.
Distress makes people like animals, Deuteronomy 28:53–57.
Cutting off thumbs, toes, Judges 1:7.
No mercy shown, 2 Chronicles 36:17 (CEV).

BUDGET

Advance budget estimate, Luke 14:28–30.
Unanticipated need, no funds, John 6:5–7.

BULLHEADED

Defiant sin, Numbers 15:30–31.
King who desecrated temple, 2 Chronicles 26:16–21.
Fool airs opinion, Proverbs 18:2.

BURDEN

Big load, one animal, Exodus 4:20.
Burdens lifted daily, Psalm 68:19.
Burden for wayward, Psalm 119:136.
Jeremiah's anguish, Jeremiah 4:19.
Fountain of tears, Jeremiah 9:1.
The Lord's burden, Jeremiah 23:33 (Berk.).
Specified time for bearing burden, Ezekiel 4:4–7.
Burdened people, Ezekiel 9:4.
Heart of flesh, stone, Ezekiel 11:19.

Mourning over message, Daniel 10:1–3.
Burden lightened, Matthew 11:28–30.
Burdened for city, Acts 17:16.
Sacrificial burden for Israel's salvation, Romans 9:1–4.
Burdened unto death, 2 Corinthians 1:8–9 (GNB).
Concern for followers, Colossians 1:28–29; 2:1–5;
    1 Thessalonians 3:1–5.

BUSY
Overworked, 2 Corinthians 6:5 (GNB).

BUSYBODY
Strategy of Jesus with accusers, Matthew 21:25–27.
Looking for small point to criticize, Mark 3:1–6.
Jesus, Pharisees, Luke 14:1–6.
Disciples of darkness, John 8:13–59.
Blind man, Pharisees, John 9:13–34.
Arguing doctrine, Acts 15:1–3.
Controversial teachings, 1 Timothy 1:3–4.
Pointless quarrelling over words, 2 Timothy 2:14.

C

CALL
Call to ministry, Genesis 12:1; Exodus 3:2–10; Numbers
    27:18–23; Deuteronomy 31:23; Joshua 1:1–9; 4:1–16;
    Judges 6:11–14; 1 Kings 16:19; Isaiah 6:8–10; Acts
    26:16.
Child's call, 1 Samuel 3:4–10 (AB).
God's chosen ministers, Psalm 65:4.
Rejecting God's call, Psalm 81:11; Isaiah 65:12; Jere-
    miah 7:13; Jonah 1:1–2.
Called before birth, Isaiah 49:1; Jeremiah 1:4–10 (LB).
Selecting priests, Levites, Isaiah 66:21.
Those not called, Jeremiah 23:21.
Specific call, Ezekiel 1:3.
Shepherd called to preach, Amos 7:14–15 (CEV).
Donkey chosen to serve, Matt 21:2–3.
Calling of disciples, Mark 1:16–20; 2:13–17.
Macedonian vision, Acts 16:9–10.
Jesus' kindness, Romans 1:5 (CEV).
Relation between call, ability, Romans 11:29.
Apostolic credentials, Galatians 1:1, 15–17.
"Upward call," Philippians 3:14 (NASB, NKJV).

Christ Himself ordained for service, Hebrews 5:4–6.
Chosen of the Lord, 1 Timothy 1:12 (LB).
Saved, called, 2 Timothy 1:9.
"Confirm your call," 2 Peter 1:10 (NRSV).

CALORIES

Going without dessert, Daniel 10:3 (LB).

CAMPAIGNING

Winning people's favor, 2 Samuel 15:1–6.

CAMPING

Tent meeting equipment, Numbers 4:31–32.
Camping outside residence, Nehemiah 8:13–17.
Lakeside teaching site, Mark 4:1.

CANCER

Apparent malignancy, 2 Chronicles 21:18–19; Jeremiah
    15:18.

CAPITAL PUNISHMENT

Premeditated murder, Exodus 21:14.
Death to kidnappers, Exodus 21:16.
Death to idolaters, Exodus 22:20; Deuteronomy 13:6–
    10.
Sabbath-breaker, Exodus 35:2; Numbers 15:32–36.
Divine execution, Leviticus 10:1–2.
Death to false prophets, Deuteronomy 13:1–10.
Crime deterrent, Deuteronomy 17:12; Ecclesiastes 8:11.
Death to juvenile delinquent, Deuteronomy 21:18–21.
Achan's execution, Joshua 7:25–26.
Trampled by horses, 2 Kings 9:30–33.
Death for treason, 2 Chronicles 23:12–15.
Hanged on self-constructed gallows, Esther 7:10.
Roman government option, John 18:28–32.
Ananias, Sapphira, Acts 5:1–10.

CAREER

Woodcutters, water carriers, Joshua 9:26–27.
King David's long reign, 2 Samuel 5:4.
Experiencing God's blessing, Psalms 90:17; 138:8.
Enjoyment of work, Ecclesiastes 3:22.
Abundant opportunities, Matthew 9:37–38.
Advice to unmarried women, 1 Corinthians 7:25–26.
Ultimate career—life of love, Ephesians 5:1–2.

CARELESS

Carelessness in duty, 1 Samuel 26:7–16; 2 Chronicles 24:5.
Lazy man's house, Ecclesiastes 10:18.
Lax in the Lord's work, Jeremiah 48:10.
Careless construction, Matthew 7:26.
Careless investment, Matthew 25:14–25.

CARING

Providing for strangers, poor, Leviticus 23:22.
Caring tears, Nehemiah 1:4.
Preventive care for children, Job 1:4–5.
Concern for human weakness, Psalm 41:1.
Sharing with those deserving, Proverbs 3:27–28.
Looking after one's house, Ecclesiastes 10:18.
Neither sorrow, joy, Jeremiah 16:5–9.
Jeremiah's broken heart, Jeremiah 23:9.
Heart of flesh, stone, Ezekiel 11:19.
Caring friends facilitate healing, Mark 2:1–5; Luke 5:17–20.
Sincere care for poor, Luke 11:37–41.
Sharing with others, Luke 12:48.
Pharisee attitude to Sabbath kindness, Luke 13:10–17.
False concern for safety of Jesus, Luke 13:31.
Reaching out for those in need, Luke 14:12–14.
Hospitality toward unbeliever, Luke 15:1–2.
Father's loving heart, Luke 15:20.
Reluctance expressing concern, Romans 9:1–2.
Friend's misfortune, 2 Timothy 1:16–17.

CASH

Services paid in cash, Deuteronomy 2:6.

CATERING

Food, drink provided in desert, 2 Samuel 16:1–4.

CELEBRATION

Feast on day of weaning, Genesis 21:8.
Celebrate Passover, Exodus 12:24 (CEV).
Victory song, Exodus 15:1–18.
Three festivals honoring God, Exodus 23:14–17.
Use of trumpets, Numbers 10:10.
Reviewing many years of blessing, Deuteronomy 2:7.
"Big celebration," Deuteronomy 14:26 (CEV).
Jamboree, 2 Samuel 6:5.

Temple dedication, 1 Kings 8:62–66.
Seven-day celebration, 2 Chronicles 7:8.
Time to rejoice, not weep, Nehemiah 8:9–10.
"I feel like celebrating," Psalm 13:5 (CEV).
Town, country praising the Lord, Isaiah 42:11.
Celebrate freedom, Isaiah 48:20 (CEV).
Celebrate, shout, Zephaniah 3:14 (CEV).
Banquet for Jesus, Luke 5:27–35.
Rejoicing in heaven when sinner repents, Luke 15:3–10
    (Note v. 9 CEV).
Prodigal's return, Luke 15:22–24 (NRSV).
Dinner honoring Jesus, John 12:2.
Celebrating death of two witnesses, Revelation 11:7–
    11.

CELEBRITY

No prophet like Moses, Deuteronomy 34:10–12.
Famous Joshua, Joshua 6:27.
Solomon's fame, 1 Kings 4:29–34; 10:1.
David's fame, 1 Chronicles 14:17.
Seeking audience with ruler, Proverbs 29:26.
The Lord should be celebrity, Isaiah 26:8.
Celebrity status of Jesus, Matthew 8:1; John 7:1–10;
    12:9–13.
Humility in greatness, Matthew 23:12.
Distinguished guest, Luke 14:8.
Respect of Cornelius for Peter, Acts 10:25–26.
Few big names, 1 Corinthians 1:26 (LB).

CELEBRITY

CHALLENGE

Challenge to possess land, Deuteronomy 1:21.
March on with strong soul, Judges 5:21.
Smallest, weakest, Judges 6:14–16.
Come up, fight, 1 Samuel 14:8–12.
Giant challenge, 1 Samuel 17:4–10.
Overcoming obstacles with God's help, 2 Samuel 22:30.
Confidence to face challenge, Psalm 18:29.
Challenging God, Isaiah 5:18–19.
Challenging enemy, Isaiah 8:9–10.
Life or death, Daniel 2:1–10.
Challenge to work for divine cause, Haggai 2:4.
Becoming fishers of men, Matthew 4:19.
Abundant fishing follows challenge, Luke 5:1–11.

CHAMPAGNE

Foaming wine with dregs, Psalm 75:8.

CHANCE

Death by measurement, 2 Samuel 8:2.
Death of king by random arrow, 2 Chronicles 18:33–34.
Coin toss decision, Nehemiah 10:34 (LB).
"Time and chance," Ecclesiastes 9:11.
Guidance omens, Ezekiel 21:21.
Casting lots to determine guilt, Jonah 1:7.
Chosen by lot, Luke 1:9.
Casting lots to determine God's will, Acts 1:23–26.

CHANGE

God's command to Abram, Genesis 12:1–9.
Internal, external change, Genesis 35:2.
Time for change, Deuteronomy 1:6.
Tear down, build, Ecclesiastes 3:3.
Don't imitate ancestors, Zechariah 1:1–6.
Comparing old, new, Luke 5:36–39.
Paul feared Corinthian reunion, 2 Corinthians 12:20–21.

CHARACTER

Blameless man, Genesis 6:9.
Father's actions influence son, Genesis 9:18–27.
Prenatal description, Genesis 25:21–34.
Father's predictions, Genesis 49:1–28.
Exemplary prophet, 1 Samuel 12:3.
Deeds reveal person, 1 Samuel 24:13.

Kindness to enemy, 2 Samuel 9:1–8.
Refusing water which endangered others, 2 Samuel 23:15–17.
God's commendation of Job, Job 1:8.
Pure cannot come from impure, Job 14:4.
The Lord judges integrity, Psalm 7:8.
Description of in-depth character, Psalm 51:6.
Marks of evil character, Proverbs 6:16–19.
Good, evil influence, Proverbs 11:16.
Lacking character with wealth, Proverbs 19:10.
Childhood evidence, Proverbs 20:11.
The Lord knows inmost being, Proverbs 20:27.
Face reflects inner person, Proverbs 27:19.
Sometimes better poor than rich, Proverbs 28:6.
Wife of noble character, Proverbs 31:10–31.
Youth building character, Ecclesiastes 11:9.
Eloquent description of noble person, Isaiah 32:8.
Evil deeds, motives likened to eggs, Isaiah 59:4–5.
Search for one honest person, Jeremiah 5:1.
Act of shame, Jeremiah 13:26.
Heart, mind determine character, Jeremiah 17:10.
Description of righteous man, Ezekiel 18:5–9.
Practice deceit, Hosea 7:11.
Mark of man who pleases the Lord, Micah 6:8.
Seasoned with salt, Mark 9:50.
Revealing thoughts of heart, Luke 2:34–35.
Balanced life of Jesus, Luke 2:52.
Good fruit, bad fruit, Luke 6:43–45.
Those of good character welcomed truth, Luke 8:15.
Clean outside, dirty inside, Luke 11:37–41.
Jesus knew what was in men, John 2:24–25.
Heart motivation, Acts 13:22.
Noble character of Bereans, Acts 17:11.
Character within, Romans 2:28–29.
Man's dual nature, Romans 7:21–25.
Always doing what is right, Romans 12:17.
Overcome evil with good, Romans 12:21.
Bad company, good character, 1 Corinthians 15:33.
Fruit of Spirit, Galatians 5:22–23.
Ultimate career, life of love, Ephesians 5:1–2.

CHARITY
Giving to poor, lending to the Lord, Proverbs 19:17.
Concern for poor, Proverbs 28:27.
Those who cannot help themselves, Proverbs 31:8–9.

Open arms to poor, Proverbs 31:20.
Real meaning of fasting, Isaiah 58:3–7.
Care of those in need, Acts 4:32–35.
Woman who helped poor, Acts 9:36–42.
Devout centurion, Acts 10:2.
Kindness to poor recognized by the Lord, Acts 10:4.
Reaching out to help others, Acts 11:27–30.
Looking after needs of poor, Romans 15:26–27.
Remembering the poor, Galatians 2:10.

CHATTER
Thoughtless words, Job 38:2 (Berk.).
Godless chatter, 2 Timothy 2:16.

CHAUVINISM
Two girls per man, Judges 5:30.
Avoiding woman as cause of death, Judges 9:52–55.
Honoring husband, Psalm 45:10–11.

CHEAP
People sold for next to nothing, Psalm 44:12 (NKJV).
Poor people valued at shoe price, Amos 2:6.

CHEATING
Dishonest scales, Deuteronomy 25:13; Proverbs 11:1;
    Hosea 12:7; Micah 6:11.
Divine hatred for cheating, Proverbs 11:1 (LB).
Deceptive purchasing, Proverbs 20:14.
"You enjoy cheating," Hosea 12:7 (CEV).
Children sold for illicit use, Joel 3:3.
Cheating in business, Amos 8:5–6 (See CEV).
Skin people alive, Micah 3:2 (CEV).
Wealth from cheating, Micah 6:10 (LB).
Can dishonesty be acquitted? Micah 6:11.
Marriage cheating, Malachi 3:5 (CEV).
Cheating the Lord, Malachi 3:8–9.
Expensive gain, Matthew 16:26.
Agreement to cheat, Acts 5:2 (CEV).
"We have cheated no one," 2 Corinthians 7:2 (NKJV).
Failing to pay workman's wages, James 5:4.

CHEER
Cheer that shook ground, 1 Samuel 4:5.
Singing to heavy heart, Proverbs 25:20.
Cheering convalescent, Isaiah 39:1.

CHILDHOOD

Helpless infants, Numbers 11:12.
Child's calling, 1 Samuel 3:1–10.
Wild donkey's colt, Job 11:12.
Childhood training, Deuteronomy 6:4–9; Proverbs 22:6.
Childhood memories, Proverbs 4:3–4.
Discipline in childhood, Proverbs 22:15.
Street children, Zechariah 8:5.
Childhood same as slavery, Galatians 4:1.
Childhood guardians, Galatians 4:2.
Fickle childhood, Ephesians 4:14.
Remnant childhood, Hebrews 5:12–13.

CHILDISH

Corrective discipline, Proverbs 22:15.
Senseless children, Jeremiah 4:22.
Spiritual infants, 1 Corinthians 3:1–2.
Marks of immaturity, 1 Corinthians 13:11.
Limited rights of immature, Galatians 4:1–3.
Acting like infants, Ephesians 4:14; Hebrews 5:12.

CHILDLIKE

Childlike attitude, 1 Kings 3:7.
Spirit of weaned child, Psalm 131:2.
Childlike faith, Mark 10:15; Luke 18:16.
Adults toward evil, children toward God, 1 Corinthians 14:20.
Adults like newborns, 1 Peter 2:2.

CHILDREN

Adoptions, Genesis 15:3; 48:5; Exodus 2:10; Esther 2:7.
Births predicted in advance, Genesis 16:11; 18:10; Judges 13:3; 1 Kings 13:2; 2 Kings 4:16; Isaiah 9:6; Luke 1:13.
Abraham's relationship to stepsister, Genesis 20:12, 16.
Children born in old age, Genesis 21:1–7.
Weaning of Isaac, Genesis 21:8.
Fetal competitors, Genesis 25:22.
Grieved parents, Genesis 26:34–35.
Gift from God, Genesis 48:8–9.
Children learn by asking questions, Exodus 12:26–27.
Father's sin charged to children, Exodus 20:5–6; 34:6–7; Numbers 14:18.
Sacrificed children, Leviticus 20:1–5.
Surrogate spiritual children, Numbers 3:11–13.

Teaching children, Deuteronomy 4:9; 31:13; Proverbs 22:6; Isaiah 28:9.
Divine promises to children, Deuteronomy 5:16; Psalm 27:10; Proverbs 8:32; Mark 10:14; Acts 2:39.
Threat to firstborn, Joshua 6:26.
No sons, only daughters, Joshua 17:3.
Good works performed by children, 1 Samuel 2:18; 2 Kings 5:2–3; 2 Chronicles 24:1–2; John 6:9.
Prophetic message to child, 1 Samuel 3:1–14.
Children who need conversion, 1 Samuel 3:7.
David's many children, 2 Samuel 5:13–15.
God's promise to David, 2 Samuel 7:12.
Parental influence, 1 Kings 9:4; 22:52; 2 Chronicles 17:3; 22:3; Jeremiah 9:14; Matthew 14:8; 2 Timothy 1:5.
Children offered in pagan sacrifices, 2 Kings 3:26–27; 16:1–3; Ezekiel 16:20.
Little girl's influence, 2 Kings 5:1–3.
Good children, evil fathers, 2 Kings 12:2; 18:3; 22:2; 2 Chronicles 34:3.
Twelve-year-old king, 2 Kings 21:1.
Josiah, child king, 2 Chronicles 34:1.
Children give praise to God, Psalm 8:2.
God looks after fatherless, Psalm 10:14.
Beautiful daughter, Psalm 45:10–11.
Tell next generation, Psalm 48:13.
Child given confidence in the Lord, Psalm 71:5–6, 17–18.
Lineage of faith, Psalm 78:1–8.
Future generations, Psalm 102:18.
Father's compassion for children, Psalm 103:13–14.
Barren woman becomes happy mother, Psalm 113:9.
Young man's way to purity, Psalm 119:9.
Children the Lord's special blessing, Psalm 127:3–5.
Sadistic killing of children, Psalm 137:9.
Sons wise, shameful, Proverbs 10:5.
Sparing rod, Proverbs 13:24.
Insecure children, Proverbs 14:26.
Children proud of parents, Proverbs 17:6; Zechariah 10:7.
Hurt of foolish son, Proverbs 17:25.
Children rob parents, Proverbs 19:26; 28:24.
Character begins with childhood, Proverbs 20:11.
Properly training child, Proverbs 22:6.
Folly yields to discipline, Proverbs 22:15; 23:13–14.

Children bring joy to parents, Proverbs 23:22–25.
Wise son fortifies father, Proverbs 27:11.
Discipline rewarded, Proverbs 29:17.
Those who dishonor parents, Proverbs 30:11.
Having one hundred children, Ecclesiastes 6:3.
Government in children's hands, Isaiah 3:4.
Children of evil parents, Isaiah 57:3.
Those yet unborn, Jeremiah 1:4–5; Hebrews 7:1, 10.
Better not to have had children, Jeremiah 22:30.
Protecting orphans, widows, Jeremiah 49:11.
Children dying in mothers' arms, Lamentations 2:12.
Cannibalistic mothers, Lamentations 4:10.
Children sacrificed to idols, Ezekiel 16:20; 23:37.
When to disobey parents, Ezekiel 20:18–21.
Unblemished children, Daniel 1:4.
Unable to have children, Hosea 9:11.
Children playing in streets, Zechariah 8:5.
Gospel turns children against parents, Matthew 10:32–36.
Jesus recognized childhood comprehension, Matthew 11:25.
Desiring prestigious sons, Matthew 20:20–28.
Transcending human relationships, Matthew 22:41–46.
Jesus saw greatness in children, Matthew 18:1–6; Mark 9:42.
Failing to see importance of children, Matthew 19:13–15; Mark 10:13–16; Luke 18:15–17.
Children praise the Lord, Matthew 21:16.
Jesus' compassion for sick girl, Mark 5:21–42.
Child's value, example, Mark 9:36–37.
Joy, delight to parents, Luke 1:14–15.
Obedience of child Jesus, Luke 2:41–52.
Balanced life of Jesus, Luke 2:52.
Concern for only child, Luke 9:38.
Blessing babies, Luke 18:15–17.
Parents support children, not children parents, 2 Corinthians 12:14.
Disciplining children, Ephesians 6:4; 1 Timothy 3:4.
Children's encouragement, instruction, Colossians 3:20–21.
The Lord takes His children's hands, Hebrews 8:9.
Importance of discipline, Hebrews 12:5–11.

CHOICE

Choosing the Lord, Genesis 28:21; Ruth 1:16; 1 Kings 18:39; 2 Kings 5:17; Psalms 16:2; 31:14; 63:1; 73:25; 118:28; 140:6.

Willing to contribute, Exodus 35:20–29.

Limited freedom, Numbers 36:6.

The Lord's choice, Deuteronomy 7:6; Psalm 4:3; 1 Corinthians 1:26; Ephesians 1:4; James 2:5; 1 Peter 2:10.

Blessing, curse, Deuteronomy 11:26–28 (CEV).

Choice rewarded, Deuteronomy 30:1–20.

Family's choice, serve God, Joshua 24:15.

Loving choice, Ruth 1:16.

Israel's wrong choice, 1 Samuel 12:18–19 (GNB).

Man's choice versus God's, 1 Samuel 16:1–13.

Three choices, 2 Samuel 24:11–17.

Second best, 1 Kings 2:13–25.

Given choice, 1 Kings 3:5.

Discerning choice, 1 Kings 3:9.

Choosing between two options, 1 Kings 18:21.

God's will, freedom of choice, Ezra 7:18.

Choose heart's direction, Job 11:13 (NRSV).

Choosing to follow truth, Psalm 119:30 (Berk.).

Evil by choice, Proverbs 1:29; Isaiah 65:12; 66:3.

Man's choice, God's guidance, Proverbs 16:9.

Gentle waters, flood waters, Isaiah 8:6–7.

Choice contrary to God's will, Isaiah 66:3.

Way of life, way of death, Jeremiah 21:8.

Valley of decision, Joel 3:14.

Choose good, not evil, Amos 5:15 (CEV).

Barabbas or Christ, Matthew 27:15–26; Mark 15:6–15; Luke 23:18–19, 25; John 18:38–40; Acts 3:14.

Choosing to be clean, Mark 1:41 (NRSV).

Choice to receive, believe, John 1:12.

Wind chooses, John 3:8 (NRSV).

Ultimate choice, John 3:36.

Jesus' choice of sacrifice, John 10:17–18.

Most meaningful choice, John 15:16.

Freedom of choice removed, Romans 9:14–24 (LB).

Discipline preference, 1 Corinthians 4:21.

"Hard choice to make," Philippians 1:23 (CEV).

Good deed by choice, Philemon 12 (GNB).

God's choice, 1 Thessalonians 1:4 (CEV).

Moses' choice, Hebrews 11:24–25.

CHRIST
Angelic Christ, Genesis 48:16 (AB).
Type of sin-bearing, Numbers 21:6–9.
Names of Christ, Numbers 24:17; Joshua 5:15; Psalm
2:2; Song of Songs 2:1; Isaiah 9:6; 11:1; 53:3; Haggai
2:7; Zechariah 3:8; Matthew 11:19; John 1:1; 6:48;
10:7; Acts 10:36; Romans 10:12; Hebrews 13:20;
3 John 7; Revelation 5:5–6, 8; 19:13.
Ezekiel's vision of the Lord, Ezekiel 1:26–28.
Abraham's "seed," Galatians 3:16.
"The Christ," Hebrews 6:1 (NASB).
Beginning, End, Revelation 22:13.

CHRISTIAN
Faithful people, Psalm 16:3 (GNB).
Biblical names for Christians, Matthew 5:13; John
10:27; 15:14–15; 1 Corinthians 12:18, 25; Ephesians
5:1; 2 Timothy 2:4; 1 Peter 2:11, 16; 3:7; 1 John 2:1.
First designation of Christians, Acts 11:26.
"God's loved ones," Romans 1:7 (Berk.).
"God's people," 2 Corinthians 1:1 (GNB).
"Religion" used as synonym, Titus 1:1–2 (GNB).
Suffering as a Christian, 1 Peter 4:16.
"Royal race," Revelation 1:6 (AB).

CHRISTMAS
Initial prophecy of Christ's birth, Genesis 3:15.
Bethlehem's alternate name, Genesis 35:19.
Star of Bethlehem, Numbers 24:17.
One came, saved, was forgotten, Ecclesiastes 9:14–15.
Virgin Birth prophesied, Isaiah 7:14 (NRSV).
Messiah prophesied, Isaiah 9:1–7.
Similarity to Christmas tree, Jeremiah 10:3–5.
Bethlehem prophecy, Micah 5:2.
Christmas rumors, Matthew 2:3 (LB).
Time between birth, Magi, Matthew 2:16.
Hard-hearted generosity, Matthew 7:11 (LB).
Yuletide ambience, Luke 2:9.

CIRCUMSTANCES
Childless Abram promised offspring, Genesis 15:1–6.
Circumstances test covenant of promise, Genesis 22:1–
18; 13:16; 15:5.
Accepting circumstances, Genesis 43:14.

Evil turned to good, Genesis 50:19–21.
Circumstances gave Moses doubts, Exodus 5:22–23.
Doubting God's goodness in circumstances, Judges 6:11–13.
Romance caused by famine, Ruth 1:1.
Lost donkeys, new king, 1 Samuel 9:1—10:1.
Circumstances from the Lord, Psalm 16:5.
Circumstances change way, direction, Psalm 32:9.
"No matter what happens," Psalm 34:1 (LB).
Waters up to neck, Psalm 69:1.
God has made each day for His purpose, Psalm 118:24.
The Lord does as He pleases, Psalm 135:6.
Accept good, bad, Ecclesiastes 7:14.
"Evil times," Ecclesiastes 9:12.
Prosperity, disaster in God's control, Isaiah 45:7.
Do not question Potter, Isaiah 45:9.
Success whatever circumstances, Jeremiah 17:7–8.
Obedience in all circumstances, Jeremiah 32:6–7; 42:6.
Thanking God in adverse circumstances, Jeremiah 33:10–11.
Though crops fail, trust the Lord, Habakkuk 3:17–18.
Circumstances should not hinder confidence, Luke 8:22–25.
Reversed circumstances, Luke 16:19–26.
Human, divine circumstances, John 11:21–22, 32.
Divine power supersedes circumstances, John 11:38–44.
Unpleasant circumstances glorify God, Acts 16:16–40.
Imprisonment made Rome ministry possible, Romans 1:13.
All circumstances good, Romans 8:28.
Nothing separates us from God's love, Romans 8:37–39.
New convert accepts circumstances, 1 Corinthians 7:24, 30 (LB).
Illness caused Paul to preach Gospel, Galatians 4:13–14.
Adverse circumstances bring blessing, Philippians 1:12–14.
Thankful in all circumstances, 1 Thessalonians 5:18.
Reason for circumstances, Philemon 15–16.
Circumstances not necessarily reality, Hebrews 11:11–12.

CIRCUS
Tamed animals, James 3:7.

CIVILITY
Joseph's example, Genesis 47:1–10.
Christ's teaching, Luke 14:8–10.
Example of civility, Philippians 2:19–23.
Civility practiced, 3 John 1–6.

CIVIL WAR
Civil war in Israel, 2 Chronicles 11:1 (LB).

CLASS
Poverty no excuse for mistreatment, Exodus 23:6.
Known by pedigree, Numbers 1:18.
Classless day of judgment, Isaiah 24:2.
Simple people brought to Christ, 1 Corinthians 1:26–31.
No class distinction in Christ, Ephesians 6:9.
Paul could have boasted of class status, Philippians 3:2–11.
Wrong of discrimination, James 2:1–4.

CLEVER
Protection for baby Moses, Exodus 2:4–9.
"Sharp as a tack," Psalm 52:2 (LB).
"Cleverness of the clever," 1 Corinthians 1:19 (NASB).

CLOTHING
Skin garments, Genesis 3:21.
Deceitful apparel, Genesis 27:2–29.
Durable clothing, Deuteronomy 8:4; 29:5.
Women not to wear men's clothing, Deuteronomy 22:5.
Mixed materials, Deuteronomy 22:11.
Costly clothing, 2 Samuel 1:24; 1 Peter 3:3–4.
Blue, white clothing, Esther 8:15.
Royal garments, Psalm 45:14–15.
Sackcloth, Isaiah 3:24.
Clothed with righteousness, faithfulness, Isaiah 11:5.
Seductive clothing, Ezekiel 13:17–18.
Clothes make the man, Daniel 5:29.
Nature's clothing, Matthew 6:28–29.
Proper garment repair, Matthew 9:16.

Clothing in kings' palaces, on prophet in desert, Matthew 11:7–9.

Rich man, poor man, Luke 16:19–31.

Teachers in flowing robes, Luke 20:46–47; 21:1–4.

Royal robes, Acts 12:21.

Fine clothing compared to personal qualities, 1 Peter 3:3–4.

Those wearing clean robes, Revelation 22:14.

COIN TOSS

Decision by coin toss, Nehemiah 10:34 (LB).

COLLEGE

Three-year training program, Daniel 1:3–5.

COMFORT

Noah as comforter, Genesis 5:29.

Respite from heat, Genesis 18:1.

Springs, palm trees, Exodus 15:27.

Rainy weather, Ezra 10:13.

Avoiding sun, Nehemiah 7:3.

Search for shade, Job 7:2 (CEV).

Miserable comforters, Job 16:2.

Comfort rather than criticism, Job 16:4–5.

In trouble, God ever-present, Psalm 14:4–5.

Comfort from the Lord, Psalm 86:17; Isaiah 12:1; 51:3; 66:13; 2 Corinthians 1:3.

"Cool of the day," Song of Songs 4:6 (NASB).

Gladness, joy overcome sorrow, sighing, Isaiah 35:10.

Lambs, shepherd, Isaiah 40:11.

Sure comfort, Isaiah 51:12.

Balm in Gilead, Jeremiah 8:22.

Mourning forbidden in time of judgment, Jeremiah 16:5–7.

Padding for comfort in deliverance, Jeremiah 38:11–13.

No one to comfort, Lamentations 1:2.

Faithfulness, compassion new each morning, Lamentations 3:22–23.

Shade provided for Jonah, Jonah 4:6.

Cushion for Jesus, Mark 4:38.

Comforting Savior, Luke 7:13; John 14:1; 16:33.

Sharing comfort through experience, 2 Corinthians 1:3–5.

Secret of deliverance, 2 Corinthians 4:7–18.

Death of Christians, 1 Thessalonians 4:13–18.
Eternal encouragement, 2 Thessalonians 2:16–17.
Divine comfort, 2 Thessalonians 3:16.
Christ's temptation helps those tempted, Hebrews 2:18.
Eternal comfort, Revelation 7:16.
Tears forever wiped away, Revelation 7:17.

COMMERCE

Supply cities, Exodus 1:11 (NKJV).
Need for roads, Deuteronomy 19:3.
Import, export, 1 Kings 10:28–29.
Local, national, international, 2 Chronicles 9:21; Proverbs 31:14–18; Revelation 18:10–24.
Willing to sell, Proverbs 11:26.
Nile grain brought to Tyre, Isaiah 23:3.
Waterfront prosperity, Jeremiah 51:13.
Control of trade routes, Ezekiel 26:2 (LB).
Tyre property taken away, Ezekiel 27:1–36.
Using temple for business purposes, Mark 11:15–17; Luke 19:45–46; John 2:14–17.
Converts' limited profits, Acts 19:23–28.
Luxury no longer for sale, Revelation 18:11–13.

COMMITMENT

Aroma of good sacrifice, Genesis 8:20–21; Leviticus 23:18; 2 Corinthians 2:15; Ephesians 5:1–2.
Abraham's commitment tested, Genesis 22:1–14.
Lifetime servant, Exodus 21:2–6.
Verbal commitment, Exodus 24:7.
Anointing objects, Exodus 40:9–10.
Dedicating residence to the Lord, Leviticus 27:14.
Those who do not follow wholeheartedly, Numbers 32:11.
Preparation for future blessing, Joshua 3:5.
Call for total faithfulness, Joshua 24:14.
Commitment under pressure, Judges 10:6–16.
Prenatal commitment, 1 Samuel 1:11–12.
Mother's reward for committing son, 1 Samuel 2:18–21.
Wealth given to the Lord, 2 Samuel 8:9–12.
Solomon's partial commitment, 1 Kings 3:3; 22:43.
Total commitment, 1 Kings 20:4.
Personal treasures to temple, 1 Chronicles 29:3–4.
Set apart, Psalm 4:3.

Committing to the Lord, Psalm 31:5.
Keeping vow to God, Psalm 65:1.
Fulfill vow to God, Ecclesiastes 5:4–5.
Commitment of two loves, Song of Song 6:3; 8:6.
Answering call of God, Isaiah 6:8.
Stand firm or not at all, Isaiah 7:9.
Meaningless oaths, Isaiah 48:1–2.
Vow to Queen of Heaven, Jeremiah 44:24–30.
Someone to stand in gap, Ezekiel 22:30.
Disciples left occupation to follow Jesus, Matthew 4:20–22.
Lose life, find again, Matthew 10:39.
Calling of Simon, Andrew, James, John, Mark 1:16–20.
No looking back, Luke 9:62.
Commitment at crucifixion, Luke 23:46.
Willingness to face persecution, Acts 21:10–14.
Once slaves to sin, now righteousness, Romans 6:18.
In race one wins; serving God all win, 1 Corinthians 9:24–27.
Daily death of true commitment to Christ, 1 Corinthians 15:30–31.
Holy Spirit in life commitment, 2 Corinthians 3:7–8.
Crucified with Christ, Galatians 2:20.
Loving Christ with undying love, Ephesians 6:24.
Filled with knowledge of God's will, Colossians 1:9–12.
Eternal commitment, 2 Timothy 1:12.
True disciple described, 2 Timothy 2:1–4.
Paul endured everything to help others, 2 Timothy 2:10.
Supreme commitment of Christ as Redeemer, Hebrews 10:5–7.
Commitment in suffering, 1 Peter 4:19.

COMMUNICATION

God's rainbow, Genesis 9:12–17.
Those who spoke one common language, Genesis 11:1, 5–9.
God spoke to Abram in deep sleep, Genesis 15:12–15.
Pretending not to understand, Genesis 42:23.
Faltering lips, Exodus 6:12–30.
Inscribing Law of God on stones, Deuteronomy 27:8.
Putting instructions in writing, Deuteronomy 31:9.
Identification by manner of speech, Judges 12:5–6.
Communication with the dead, 1 Samuel 28:8–20.

Making sure someone listens, 2 Samuel 20:17.
Message from thistle to cedar tree, 2 Kings 14:9.
Communication methods, 2 Chronicles 30:1–10; Esther 1:22.
Encouraging communication during crisis, 2 Chronicles 32:6–7.
The Lord's attentive ear, Nehemiah 1:11.
Petition of protest, king's response, Ezra 4:12–22.
Language barrier, Nehemiah 13:23–37.
Communication disbelieved, Job 12:4.
Testing words, Job 12:11.
Asking God to withdraw, Job 13:20–21.
Tip of tongue, Job 33:2.
Communication with God, Psalm 18:25.
God speaks through nature, His Word, Psalm 19:1–14.
Twisting words, Psalm 56:5.
Communicating with God, Psalm 99:6.
Iron sharpens iron, Proverbs 27:17.
Secret thoughts expressed, Ecclesiastes 10:20.
Finding right words, Ecclesiastes 12:10.
Earth permeated with divine knowledge, Isaiah 11:9.
Too young to understand, Isaiah 28:9.
"Senseless sound," Isaiah 28:13 (Compare CEV, NIV, NKJV).
Farmer illustrates over-communication, Isaiah 28:24.
Speaking in language understood, Isaiah 36:11.
Mouth like sharpened sword, Isaiah 49:2.
Instructed tongue, Isaiah 50:4.
Boldness of speech given by God, Jeremiah 1:6–10.
Those of strange language, Jeremiah 5:15.
Letter to exiles in Babylon, Jeremiah 29:4–23.
Divine invitation to communicate, Jeremiah 33:3.
Danger of writing truth, Jeremiah 36:4–32.
Young Hebrews taught Babylonian communication, Daniel 1:3–5.
Writing on wall, Daniel 5:5.
Message written with clarity, Habakkuk 2:2.
Gigantic flying scroll, Zechariah 5:1–2.
Celestial announcement, Matthew 2:1–2.
Communication by dreams, Matthew 2:12, 19–20.
Effect of attitudes on understanding, Matthew 13:14–15.
Mute's written communication, Luke 1:63.
Spectacular communication from heaven, Luke 2:8–14.

Jesus knew when He had been touched, Luke 8:43–48.
When great truth sounds like nonsense, Luke 24:9–11.
Slow to understand, Luke 24:15–31.
Symbolism misunderstood, John 2:19–21.
Rapport with communicator, John 8:47.
Some heard thunder, others angel's voice, John 12:28–29.
Day of Pentecost, Acts 2:1–12.
Not understanding what one reads, Acts 8:27–35.
Speaking effectively, Acts 14:1.
Gathering together for report, Acts 14:27.
Quoting poets of Athens, Acts 17:28.
Encouraged in vision, Acts 18:9–10.
Effect of speaking in people's language, Acts 22:2.
Seeing light, not understanding voice, Acts 22:9.
Use of eyes for impact, Acts 23:1.
Message communicated in nature, Romans 1:18–20.
Entrusted with conveying God's Word, Romans 3:1–2.
Truth communicated in human terms, Romans 6:19.
Words beyond normal vocabulary, Romans 8:16, 26–27.
Prayer for acceptable ministry, Romans 15:31–32.
Conversation enriched in Christ, 1 Corinthians 1:5–6.
Clear call to action, 1 Corinthians 14:8
Importance of being understood, 1 Corinthians 14:13–19; 2 Corinthians 1:13–14.
Tact with unbelievers, 2 Corinthians 2:15–16.
Earning right to be heard, 2 Corinthians 4:1–2.
Lifestyle communicated by example, 2 Corinthians 6:4–10.
Hearts opening to each other, 2 Corinthians 6:11–13.
Writing more effective than speaking, 2 Corinthians 10:10.
Profound truth briefly presented, Ephesians 3:1–3.
Paul's insistence to followers, Ephesians 4:17.
Fathers should not exasperate children, Ephesians 6:4.
Keeping in touch, Ephesians 6:21–22.
Good news between believers, Philippians 2:19.
Fullness of deity in Christ, Colossians 2:9.
Prayer supports successful communication, Colossians 4:3–4.
Wise use of names, Colossians 4:7–17.
Communication with followers, Colossians 4:8.
Onesimus introduced, Colossians 4:9; Philemon 10–11.

Gospel communicated with words, power, 1 Thessalonians 1:4–5.
Responsibility of those who hear, 1 Thessalonians 2:13.
Teaching by means of speech, writing, 2 Thessalonians 2:15; 1 Timothy 3:14–15.
Responsibility to proclaim message, Titus 1:1–3.
Make teaching attractive, Titus 2:10.
Superior communication, Hebrews 1:1–4; 3:5–8.
Faith gives credibility, Hebrews 4:2.
Scripture's penetrating impact, Hebrews 4:12.
Short letter, Hebrews 13:22.
Responsibility proclaiming God's message, 1 Peter 4:11.
Divine purpose in giving Scriptures, 2 Peter 1:20–21.
Purpose of Peter's letters to friends, 2 Peter 3:1.
World's viewpoint, 1 John 4:5.
In person rather than correspondence, 2 John 12; 3 John 13–14.
Those who take Scriptures to heart, Revelation 1:3.
God in direct fellowship with men, Revelation 21:3–5.

COMMUNISM

Believers under pagan leaders, Genesis 39:2–4, 20–23.
Godless king, nation, Daniel 11:36–39.
Christian kind of sharing, Acts 2:44.

COMPASSION

Compassion for baby Moses, Exodus 2:5–6.
Divine concern for suffering people, Exodus 3:7.
Leader's compassionate prayer, Deuteronomy 9:25–29.
Compassion to enemy, 2 Samuel 9:1–13; Proverbs 24:17–18.
Compassion to prisoners, 2 Chronicles 28:15.
Pity fallen Jerusalem, 2 Chronicles 30:14–15.
Lack of compassion, Job 12:5.
Caring for weak, Psalm 41:1.
Continuous compassion, Psalm 78:38.
God's abounding compassion, Psalms 86:15; 119:156.
Penalty for lack of compassion, Proverbs 21:13 (LB).
No compassion for evil, Isaiah 9:17.
Divine compassion never decreases, Isaiah 54:10.
Pointless compassion, Jeremiah 7:16.
Jeremiah's compassion, Jeremiah 9:1.

C

Judgment precedes compassion, Jeremiah 12:14–17; Lamentations 3:32.
Crying out to those who reject, Jeremiah 22:29.
Loved with everlasting love, Jeremiah 31:3.
The Lord shows no pity in judgment, Lamentations 2:2.
Compassion new every morning, Lamentations 3:22–26.
Ezekiel feared Israel's destruction, Ezekiel 11:13.
Heart of flesh, of stone, Ezekiel 11:19.
Divine compassion for lost, Ezekiel 18:23, 32.
New heart, new spirit, Ezekiel 36:26.
Daniel's compassion for condemned wise men, Daniel 2:10–13, 24.
Demonstrated compassion, Hosea 11:4.
Joseph's compassion for pregnant Mary, Matthew 1:19.
Compassion of Jesus, Matthew 9:36; 23:37; Luke 13:34; 19:41–44.
"Filled with pity," Mark 1:41 (GNB).
Good Samaritan, Luke 10:30–37.
Full measure of compassion, Luke 14:1–14.
Compassionate preaching, Acts 20:30–31.
Consideration shown to Paul, the prisoner, Acts 27:3.
Kind islanders, Acts 28:2.
Paul's compassion for Israel, Romans 9:1–4; 10:1.
Divine compassion to disobedient, Romans 10:21.
Strong looking after weak, Romans 15:1.
Love expressed through anguish, 2 Corinthians 2:4.
Paul's compassion for Galatians, Galatians 4:19–20.
"Gently lead," Galatians 6:1–2 (CEV).
Carrying each other's burdens, Galatians 6:2.
Concern for those ill, Philippians 2:26–27.
Tears of compassion, Philippians 3:18 (CEV).
Struggle over converts, Colossians 2:1.
Wide compassion, 1 Thessalonians 3:1–5.
Compassion for slave, Philemon 8–21.

COMPATIBILITY

Compatible brothers, Psalm 133:1.
Two walk together, Amos 3:3.
Shared suffering, comfort, 2 Corinthians 1:7.
Adapting to others, Ephesians 5:22 (AB).
Avoid disruptive conduct, Philippians 2:14–16.
"Try to get along," 1 Thessalonians 5:13 (CEV).

COMPETITION
Fetal competitors, Genesis 25:22.
Competing for father's love, Genesis 37:1-4; Luke 15:25-31.
Unable to compete, Exodus 9:11.
One on one, 1 Samuel 17:8-10.
David, Saul, 1 Samuel 18:6-16.
Evil world versus God, Psalm 2:1-4.
Joyful competition, Psalm 19:5 (Berk.).
At peace with one's enemies, Proverbs 16:7.
Gloating over enemy failure, Proverbs 24:17-18.
Keeping up with the Joneses, Ecclesiastes 4:4.
"The Lord tolerates no rivals," Nahum 1:2 (GNB).
Strong man, stronger man, Luke 11:21-22.
Jesus evaded accusation of competition, John 4:1-3.
Coming in second, Acts 1:23-26.
Competitive Christians, Romans 13:13; 15:20 (LB); Galatians 5:26.
Run to win, 1 Corinthians 9:24-27.
Competition purposely avoided, 2 Corinthians 10:16 (LB).
Ministry to Jews, to Gentiles, Galatians 2:8.
"Competing against one another," Galatians 5:26 (NRSV).

COMPLAIN
Complaining to God, Exodus 5:22-23; Numbers 11:10-15; Psalm 142:1-2.
Remembering Egypt instead of trusting God, Exodus 16:2-3.
Rejected advice of elders, 1 Kings 12:1-11.
Bitterness against God, Job 23:2.
"Quit complaining," Psalm 39:1 (LB).
Still alive, shouldn't complain, Lamentations 3:39 (CEV).
Sour grapes, Ezekiel 18:2.
Martha's discontent with Mary, Luke 10:38-42.
"Do not grumble," John 6:43 (NASB).
Talking back to God, Romans 9:20-21.
Do everything without complaint, Philippians 2:14-15.
Forgive complaints, Colossians 3:12 (NASB, NRSV).

COMPLIMENT
High compliments, 1 Samuel 29:6-9.
Public relations approach, 1 Kings 1:42.

Avoiding partiality, flattery, Job 32:21–22.
Flattering lips speak deception, Psalm 12:2.
Praise, glory belong to God, Psalm 115:1; 1 Corinthians 3:7.
Word of encouragement, Proverbs 12:25 (LB).
Timely word, Proverbs 15:23.
Honor not fitting fools, Proverbs 26:1, 8.
Folly of flattery, Proverbs 28:23.
Noble person eloquently described, Isaiah 32:8.
Jesus' evaluation of John the Baptist, Matthew 11:11–14.
Duty of true servant, Luke 17:7–10.
Complimented, encouraged followers, Acts 20:1–2; Romans 1:8; 2 Corinthians 1:13–14; Philippians 1:3–6; Colossians 2:5; 1 Thessalonians 1:3; 2 Thessalonians 1:3–4; 2 Timothy 1:3–5.
"Good things to say," Romans 16:1 (CEV).
Complimenting friends, Romans 16:3–16.
Paul's compliment to those who followed teachings, 1 Corinthians 11:2.
Expression of confidence, 2 Corinthians 7:4 (LB).
Paul's commendation of Timothy, Philippians 2:19–23.
No search for praise, 1 Thessalonians 2:6 (GNB).
Boasting about perseverance, faith of others, 2 Thessalonians 1:4.
Compliments precede request, Philemon 1–7.
Complimented for skills, Hebrews 3:3 (LB).
One author commended another, 2 Peter 3:15–16.
Strength, weakness at Ephesus, Revelation 2:1–6.
Commendation before reproof, Revelation 2:2–6, 13–16, 19–20.
One worthy of praise, Revelation 5:13–14.

COMPROMISE

Unacceptable compromise, Exodus 8:25–28.
Desire to be like unbelievers, 1 Samuel 8:1–22.
Calling disobedience compromise, 1 Samuel 15:9–15 (LB).
Abner's compromise with David, 2 Samuel 3:6–21.
Compromised commitment of King Solomon, 1 Kings 3:3.
Heathen worship for Solomon's wives, 1 Kings 11:8.
Incomplete faithfulness to God, 1 Kings 22:43.

Failing to be completely obedient, 2 Kings 14:1–4; 15:1–4, 34–35.
Secretly disobeying the Lord, 2 Kings 17:9.
Worshiping the Lord, other gods, 2 Kings 17:33.
Assisting evil, 2 Chronicles 19:2.
Doing right, not wholeheartedly, 2 Chronicles 25:2.
Day as night, night as day, Job 17:12 (LB).
Calling evil good, good evil, Isaiah 5:20.
Those who do not want to hear truth, Isaiah 30:10–11.
Hezekiah intimidated, Isaiah 36:4–10.
Desire to be like others, Ezekiel 20:32–38.
No one can serve two masters, Matthew 6:24.
Marriage between unbelievers, believers, 1 Corinthians 7:16.
Refusal to compromise, 1 Thessalonians 2:3–4.
No hospitality to false teachers, 2 John 10–11.
Jezebel's influence in Thyatira church, Revelation 2:20.

COMPUTER

Beyond digital analysis, 1 Corinthians 2:9; Ephesians 3:17–19.

CONCEIT

Goliath's macho, 1 Samuel 17:42–44.
Haughtiness despised, 2 Samuel 22:28.
Sanballat's taunts, Nehemiah 4:1–3.
Enemy's loss of self-confidence, Nehemiah 6:16.
God's attitude toward conceit, Job 37:24 (Berk.).
Conceited affluence, Psalm 49:5–6; Proverbs 25:14.
Limitless conceit, Psalm 73:7.
Wise in one's own eyes, Proverbs 3:7; 26:5–16.
Impaired by conceit, Proverbs 14:6 (GNB).
Worse than a fool, Proverbs 26:12 (LB).
Proud, conceited, put down, Isaiah 2:12 (CEV).
Conceited women, Isaiah 3:16.
Empty boasting, Isaiah 16:6.
Boast only about the Lord, Jeremiah 9:23–24.
No time for conceit, Romans 11:20 (NASB).
Avoid conceit, Romans 12:16.
Conceited false doctrine, 1 Timothy 6:3–5 (AB, CEV).
"Swollen with conceit," 2 Timothy 3:4 (NRSV).
Evil queen refused to admit sin, Revelation 18:7–8.

CONCERN

Concern for family welfare, Exodus 4:18.
How are you? Exodus 18:7 (KJV).
Father's concern for children, Job 1:4–5.
Too concerned to sleep, Psalm 132:4–5.
Who cares? Jeremiah 15:5.
Heart of flesh, of stone, Ezekiel 11:19.
Concern for human need, Mark 8:1–2.
Love expressed through anguish, 2 Corinthians 2:4.
Christians keeping in touch, Ephesians 6:21–22.
One who cares, Philippians 2:20 (CEV, NRSV).
Revived concern, Philippians 4:10 (NASB, NRSV).
Concern for others' spiritual needs, Colossians 1:9.

CONCERT

Village concert, Judges 5:11 (LB).

CONCUBINE

Preferred treatment for concubines, Esther 2:8–14.

CONDESCEND

Lower myself, honor you, 2 Corinthians 11:7 (CEV).
Prerequisite to salvation, Hebrews 2:17–18.

CONDITION

Divine ultimatum, Exodus 15:26.
Spiritual preparation for future victory, Joshua 3:5.
Conditions for God's blessing, judgment, 2 Chronicles 7:11–22.
God's blessing dependent upon obedience, Jeremiah 11:1–5.
God's great invitation, Jeremiah 33:3.
For God's return to us, we return to Him, Zechariah 1:3.
Conditions of relationship with the Lord, 2 Timothy 2:11–13.

CONFESSION

Pharaoh's insincerity, Exodus 9:27–30.
Son's confession to mother, Judges 17:1–5 (LB).
"Throwing himself down," Ezra 10:1 (NRSV).
Nehemiah's prayer, Nehemiah 1:4–7.
Confessing ancestors' sins, Nehemiah 9:2.

Immediate confession, Psalm 32:6 (LB).
Confession, restoration, Psalm 50:1–23.
Folly of concealing sin, Proverbs 28:13.
Confessing to priest, Ecclesiastes 5:6 (GNB).
Private confession, Matthew 18:15–17.
Judas' remorse, suicide, Matthew 27:3–5.
Confess to each other, James 5:16.
Our Advocate with Heavenly Father, 1 John 2:1–2.

CONFIDENCE

God's assurance to Abram, Genesis 15:1.
Trusting God against unsurmountable opposition, Exodus 14:5–14.
Confident in face of danger, Numbers 14:8–9.
Confident ability, 1 Samuel 17:32–37.
Lack of confidence facing danger, 1 Samuel 27:1.
Giving confidence during crisis, 2 Chronicles 32:6–7.
Sure of God's plan, purpose, Job 42:2.
Facing opposition with confidence, Psalm 3:6.
The Lord our sure refuge, Psalm 9:9–10.
God's unfailing love, Psalm 13:5–6.
Confidence in chariots or the Lord? Psalm 20:7.
Sure faith, Psalm 27:1.
All in God's hands, Psalm 31:15.
Confidence in midst of trouble, Psalm 34:19.
Be still, wait, Psalm 37:7.
Wrongly placed confidence, Psalms 44:6; 49:6–7; 146–3; Jeremiah 17:5; 48:7; Ezekiel 33:13.
Steadfast inner spirit, Psalms 51:10; 57:7.
God's love, strength, Psalm 62:11–12.
No fear day, night, Psalm 91:4–6.
Sure the Lord is God, Psalm 100:3.
Fear of man, Psalm 118:6–9.
Trusting God like small child, Psalm 131:2.
The God who answers prayer, Psalm 138:1–3.
Prayer for instruction, confidence, Psalm 143:10.
Certainty of God's promises, Psalm 145:13.
Gossip betrays confidence, Proverbs 20:19.
Trustworthy messenger, Proverbs 25:13.
Fear of man a snare, Proverbs 29:25.
Strength, dignity, Proverbs 31:25.
Pointless confidence in men, Isaiah 2:22.
In time of danger, Isaiah 7:4; Luke 7:1–10.

Danger of fearing wrong things, Isaiah 8:12–14.
Kept in perfect peace, Isaiah 26:3.
Tested stone in Zion, Isaiah 28:16.
Confidence in the Lord rather than men, Isaiah 36:4–10.
Do not question Potter, Isaiah 45:9.
Confident in one's own wickedness, Isaiah 47:10.
All in God's hands, Isaiah 49:4.
Walking with confidence in the dark, Isaiah 50:10.
Fear, reluctance proclaiming message, Jeremiah 1:6–10.
Confidence in difficult times, Jeremiah 1:17.
Erroneous confidence, Jeremiah 7:8.
Those who trust the Lord, Jeremiah 17:7–8.
Nothing too hard for the Lord, Jeremiah 32:17.
Confidence facing fiery furnace, Daniel 3:16–18.
Believe in Good News, Mark 1:14–15.
No need to fear in Jesus' presence, John 6:20.
Antidote for troubled hearts, John 14:1.
Going with confidence into difficult places, Acts 20:22–24.
Sure of destiny, Acts 27:23–24.
Hope when no basis for hope, Romans 4:18–22.
Nothing can separate us from God's love, Romans 8:37–39.
Confident of the Lord's blessing, Romans 15:29.
Confidence comes from God, 2 Corinthians 3:4–5.
Confidence in unseen, 2 Corinthians 4:18.
Living by faith, not by sight, 2 Corinthians 5:1–7.
Standing at end of struggle, Ephesians 6:13.
Firm whatever circumstances, Philippians 1:27–30.
Prayer brings peace, Philippians 4:6–7.
Confidence rewarded, Hebrews 10:35.
Obedience toward unknown objective, Hebrews 11:8.
Believing wisdom will be granted, James 1:5–7.
Absolute confidence of salvation, 1 John 4:13.
No fear in love, 1 John 4:18.

CONFIDENTIAL

Intimate talks, Psalm 55:14 (GNB).
Betrayed by gossip, Proverbs 11:13.
Careful with words, Ecclesiastes 12:10.
Whispers to be proclaimed, Matthew 10:27.
Evil cannot be kept confidential, Luke 12:2–3.

CONFLICT

David fought the Lord's battles, 1 Samuel 25:28.
Futility of strife among brothers, 2 Samuel 2:27–28.
Struggle between strong, weak, 2 Samuel 3:1.
At peace with enemies, Proverbs 16:7.
Provocation by fool, Proverbs 27:3.
Noise of battle, destruction, Jeremiah 50:22.
Love your enemy, Matthew 5:43–48.
Family conflict, Matthew 10:34–39.
Satan divided against himself, Matthew 12:22–32.
No peace on earth, Mark 13:6–8.
Clash of personalities, Acts 15:36–41.
Stress between evil, good, Romans 7:14–20.
Those who purposely cause trouble, Romans 16:17.
Lawsuits among believers, 1 Corinthians 6:1–8.
Purpose of conflict, 1 Corinthians 11:19 (Berk.).
Purpose of trouble, 2 Corinthians 4:17–18.
Peter, Paul face-to-face, Galatians 2:11–21.
Handling conflict with firmness, love, 1 Timothy 1:3–7.

CONFORMITY

Following wrong of others, Exodus 23:2; Deuteronomy
    12:29–30.
Desiring pagan political structure, 1 Samuel 8:1–22.
Conforming to pagan ways, 2 Kings 17:13–15.
Conformity to Christ, Romans 8:29.
Conformed, transformed, Romans 12:1–2.

CONFRONTATION

Satan's confrontation with Jesus, Luke 4:1–13.
Critics of Jesus, Luke 20:1–8.

CONFUSION

Wandering Israelites, Exodus 14:1–4.
Confusing shadows, Judges 9:34–37.
Lamp of the Lord, 2 Samuel 22:29.
Confused about God, Job 10:2–12.
"Make a tumult," Psalm 2:1 (Berk.).
Walking about in darkness, Psalm 82:5.
"At their wits' end," Psalm 107:27 (Berk.).
"Nothing makes sense," Ecclesiastes 1:2 (CEV).
A fool does not know way to town, Ecclesiastes 10:15.
Spirit of dizziness, Isaiah 19:14.
"My head spins," Isaiah 21:4 (CEV).
Sick drunk, Isaiah 28:7.

Walking in dark, Isaiah 50:10.
Blind without guidance, Isaiah 59:9–10.
Government disarray, Ezekiel 7:26–27.
Confused between monotheism, idolatry, Daniel 3:28–
  30; 4:18.
Herod's lack of perception, Luke 9:7–9.
Confused Pharisees, John 9:13–16.
"Terribly upset," Acts 15:24 (CEV).
Avoiding confusion in worship, 1 Corinthians 14:29–
  33, 40.

CON MAN

Victim of con man, Psalm 109:11 (KJV).
Speech disguises malicious heart, Proverbs 26:24–26.

CONSCIOUSNESS

Injured man half dead, Luke 10:30.

CONSIDERATION

Returning neighbor's lost property, Deuteronomy
  22:1–3.
Padding for Jeremiah's comfort, Jeremiah 38:11–13.

CON MAN

Joseph wanted to spare Mary public disgrace, Matthew 1:19.
First things first, Luke 10:38–42.
Consideration shown Paul, prisoner, Acts 27:3.
Tactful conversation with others, Colossians 4:6.
Tact in times of duress, James 1:19–20.

CONSPIRACY

Conspiracy of Joseph's brothers, Genesis 37:12–18.
Guards unwilling to follow king's evil command, 1 Samuel 22:16–17.
Conspiracy of Absalom, 2 Samuel 15:1–12.
Murderous officials, 2 Kings 12:19–21; 14:19; Daniel 6:1–5.
Plot to kill Paul, Acts 23:12–22.

CONTEMPORARY

Daily manifestation, Psalm 19:1 (Berk.).
Contemporary compassion, Lamentations 3:22–23.
Examples from daily life, Galatians 3:15.

CONTENTMENT

Tent or palace, 2 Samuel 7:1–7.
Food-induced contentment, 1 Kings 4:20 (GNB).
Everyone very happy, 1 Chronicles 12:40 (CEV).
"Restful water," Psalm 23:3 (Berk.).
Contented with little, Psalm 37:16–17.
Believer's contentment, Psalm 84:10–12.
"Wonderful to be grateful," Psalm 92:1 (CEV).
Desires satisfied, strength renewed, Psalm 103:5 (See 37:4).
Satisfaction only from the Lord, Psalm 107:8–9.
"Oh, the bliss," Psalm 112:1 (Berk.).
Rejoicing in day the Lord has made, Psalm 118:24.
No citizen complaints, Psalm 144:14 (KJV).
Contentment aids good health, Proverbs 14:30 (CEV).
Little with contentment, Proverbs 15:16.
Do not envy sinners, Proverbs 23:17; 24:19–20.
Happiness from honesty, Proverbs 30:7–9.
Joy in working, Proverbs 31:13 (NASB).
Accomplishment better than wealth, Ecclesiastes 2:10.
Special gift of God, Ecclesiastes 3:12–13.
Contented life of toil, Ecclesiastes 5:18–20.
Enjoying life, Ecclesiastes 8:15.
Live within income, Luke 3:14.

Secret of contentment, Philippians 4:11–13.
Godliness with contentment, 1 Timothy 6:6–8; Hebrews
13:5.
Do not grumble against each other, James 5:9.

CONTEST
Beauty contest, Esther 2:1–4.

CONTRACEPTION
Onan's procedure, Genesis 38:8–10.

CONTRADICTION
Saying one thing, meaning another, Exodus 14:5–8;
Psalms 55:12–23; 78:34–37; Proverbs 26:18–26; Isaiah
29:13–16.
Worship without true reverence, Amos 5:21–24.
Insincere piety, Matthew 23:1–39; Mark 12:38–40; Luke
6:46; 11:39–52.
Practice what you preach, Romans 2:21–25.
Avoid contradiction, 1 Timothy 6:20 (NRSV).
Beyond contradiction, Hebrews 7:7 (AB).

CONTROL
God in control, Jeremiah 34:1–3; 36:1–3; 44:29–30.
Controlled by Christ's love, 2 Corinthians 5:14 (GND).
Desire to be church officer, 1 Timothy 3:1.
Controlled tongue, body, James 3:2 (LB).
Man enslaved to whatever masters him, 2 Peter 2:19.
Holy Spirit's control, Revelation 21:10 (GNB).

CONTROVERSY
Discontent with leadership, Numbers 14:1–4.
Two factions, 1 Kings 16:21–22.
Strife caused by pride, hatred, Proverbs 10:12; 13:10.
Evidence turns against accuser, Proverbs 25:8.
Promoting controversy, 1 Timothy 1:4.
"Morbid craving for controversy," 1 Timothy 6:4 (NRSV).
Foolish questions, Titus 3:9.

CONVERSATION
Speaking neither good, evil, Genesis 31:24.
Spiritual matters, Deuteronomy 6:4–7.
Prophetic error, Deuteronomy 18:21–22.
Samson, Philistine woman, Judges 14:7.
Left with nothing to say, Nehemiah 5:8.

Windy conversation, Job 8:2.
Accused of not speaking sensibly, Job 18:2.
Resolving not to sin with one's mouth, Psalm 17:3.
Keeping tongue from speaking wrong, Psalm 39:1.
Words known before spoken, Psalm 139:4.
Serpent tongues, Psalm 140:3.
How to avoid gossip, Psalm 141:3.
Speech of righteous, wicked, Proverbs 10:11.
Good, evil tongue, Proverbs 10:31–32.
Fruit of lips, Proverbs 12:14.
Words aptly spoken, Proverbs 15:23; 25:11; Ecclesiastes 5:2.
Silence elevates fool, Proverbs 17:28.
Fool's opinions, Proverbs 18:2.
Gossip talks too much, Proverbs 20:19.
Guarding tongue, Proverbs 21:23.
Conduct, conversation linked together, Proverbs 22:11.
Disguising true self by false speech, Proverbs 26:24–26.
Saying yes, no, Matthew 5:37.
Words condemn, acquit, Matthew 12:37.
Not what goes into mouth, what comes out, Matthew 15:10–20.
Use of gracious words, Luke 4:22.
Talking about latest ideas, Acts 17:21.
Conversation enriched in Christ, 1 Corinthians 1:5–6.
Foolish talk, coarse joking, Ephesians 5:4.
Discussion topic, Ephesians 5:19–20.
Exemplary speech, 1 Timothy 4:12.
Speaking to varied age groups, 1 Timothy 5:1–2.
Avoid godless chatter, 2 Timothy 2:16.
Quick to listen, slow to speak, James 1:19.
Deceitful, unruly tongue, James 1:26.
Guard tongue well, James 3:3–6.
Speaking, serving to glory of God, 1 Peter 4:11.
Empty, boastful words, 2 Peter 2:18.
Pride, blasphemy, Revelation 13:5.

COOPERATION
Willing to serve, contribute, Exodus 35:10–35; 36:4–7.
Ox, donkey cannot plow together, Deuteronomy 22:10.
Cooperation for survival, Joshua 9:1–2 (LB); 10:1–5; 11:1–5.
Nation united, Joshua 10:29–42.
"No help at all," Judges 5:15 (CEV).
Cooperation refused, Ezra 4:1–3.

Hearty cooperation, Nehemiah 4:6.
Living together in unity, Psalm 133:1–3.
Iron sharpens iron, Proverbs 27:17.
Advantage in cooperation, Ecclesiastes 4:9–12.
No one to help, Isaiah 63:5.
Two in agreement, Amos 3:3.
Mutual faith required for healing, Mark 6:4–6.
The Lord's cooperation, Mark 16:20 (Berk.).
Those for, against, Luke 11:23.
Laying on hands, Acts 13:1–3.
United mind, thought, 1 Corinthians 1:10.
Total function Body of Christ, 1 Corinthians 12:14–20.
Harmonious ministry to Jews, Gentiles, Galatians 2:8.
Philippians shared ministry expense, Philippians 4:15–
    19.
"Uncontentious," Titus 3:2 (NASB).

CORRUPTION
Vanishing faithful, Psalm 12:1 (LB).
Corrupt from birth, Psalm 58:3.
Deceptive wages, Proverbs 11:18.
Moral rot in government, Proverbs 28:2 (LB).
Silver to dross, wine to water. Isaiah 1:22.
Ravages of wickedness, Isaiah 9:18.
Corruption among priests, Jeremiah 5:31; Ezekiel
    22:26; Matthew 27:20.
Defiled with blood, Lamentations 4:14.
Despising those who tell truth, Amos 5:10.
Shameless evil, Zephaniah 3:5 (CEV).
Bad corrupts good, Matthew 13:24–30.
Roman official wanted bribe, Acts 24:26.
Gaining benefit misusing others, James 5:4–5.
Surviving in evil surroundings, 2 Peter 2:4–9.
Sin committed in broad daylight, 2 Peter 2:13–23.
Suggested social disease, Jude 7–8.

COSMETICS
Aroma of romance, Ruth 3:3.
Body lotions, 2 Samuel 12:20 (NIV).
Eye makeup, 2 Kings 9:30; Ezekiel 23:40.
Extensive beauty treatment, Esther 2:9, 12.
Perfumed clothing, Psalm 45:8.
Jewelry, cosmetics snatched away, Isaiah 3:18–24.
Makeup in poor taste, Jeremiah 4:30.

Anointing Jesus, Matthew 26:6–13; Mark 14:3–9.
Expensive perfume on Jesus' feet, John 12:1–8.

COST

Cheap stewardship refused, 2 Samuel 24:21–24.
Stingy man's food, Proverbs 23:6–8.
High cost discipleship, Luke 14:26–27.
Need for counting cost, Luke 14:28–30.
Cost of spiritual blindness, Luke 19:41–44.
High cost resurrection relevance, Philippians 3:10.

COUNSEL

Family counsel, Genesis 49:1–2.
Aged father's counsel, 1 Kings 2:1–9.
Kings consulted Solomon, 1 Kings 4:34.
Little girl's influence, 2 Kings 5:1–3.
Self-advised, Nehemiah 5:7.
He who counseled others becomes discouraged, Job
    4:3–5.
Miserable comforters, Job 16:2.
God's Word undergirds good counsel, Psalm 37:30–31.
Righteous man's rebuke, Psalm 141:5.
Refusing counsel, Proverbs 1:29–31.
Wise listen to good counsel, Proverbs 9:9; 20:18.
Good, bad sources for advice, Proverbs 12:5.
Taking advice, Proverbs 13:10.
Multitude of counselors, Proverbs 15:22.
Refreshing counsel, Proverbs 18:4 (GNB).
Advice, instruction, Proverbs 19:20.
Making plans, waging war, Proverbs 20:18.
Advice from friend, Proverbs 27:9.
Those who refuse counsel, Proverbs 29:1.
Paul's counsel, sad parting, Acts 20:25–38.
Eager for proper counsel, 1 Thessalonians 3:1–5.
Gently instruct backslider, 2 Timothy 2:23–26.

COUNTERFEIT

Friends, brothers not trustworthy, Jeremiah 9:4–8.
Counterfeit Christs in later days, Matthew 24:4–5, 24.
Ego displayed by teachers of Law, Mark 12:38–40.
Ultimate identification of hypocrite, Luke 13:23–27.
Disciples disbelieved Saul's conversion, Acts 9:26–27.
Counterfeit Christian leaders, 2 Corinthians 11:13–15.
Genuine ministry not counterfeit, 2 Corinthians 13:6
    (Berk.).

False humility, Colossians 2:18.
Counterfeit intellectualism, 1 Timothy 6:20.
Deceitful claim of holy life, 1 John 1:8–10.
Feigning life when spiritually dead, Revelation 3:1.

COURAGE

Fear submits to assurance, Exodus 14:13–14.
Courage at God's command, Joshua 1:9.
Lost courage, Joshua 5:1.
Courageous old age, Joshua 14:10–12.
People risked lives, Judges 5:18.
March on with strong soul, Judges 5:21.
Facing big opposition, Judges 7:7–23; 1 Samuel 17:32,
    50.
Courageous youth, 1 Samuel 14:6–45.
Prophet's lost courage, 1 Kings 19:1–4.
Facing danger to assist David, 1 Chronicles 9:15–19.
Laughing at fear, Job 39:22.
Facing ten thousand, Psalm 3:6.
Moving ahead in spite of circumstances, Psalm 44:18.
Witness to those in authority, Psalm 119:46.
Bold stouthearted, Psalm 138:3.
Courage in troubled times, Proverbs 24:10.
Mighty lion, Proverbs 30:30.
Fearing wrong things, Isaiah 8:12–14.
Face set like flint, Isaiah 50:7.
Weary but winning, Isaiah 57:10.
Courage to face adverse circumstances, Ezekiel 2:6–7.
Witness in king's court, Daniel 3:8–18.
Faith before loyalty to king, Daniel 6:5–11.
Failed courage, Amos 2:14–16.
Attempted walk on water, Matthew 14:22–31.
Prayer augments courage, Luke 18:1.
Reward of standing firm, Luke 21:19.
Fear of authority, John 19:38.
Courageously preaching Christ, Acts 3:12–26.
Endeavoring to silence Peter, John, Acts 4:16–20.
Ministry under persecution, Acts 5:37–42; 8:1.
Confidence in difficult places, Acts 20:22–24.
Willing for suffering, death, Acts 21:13.
Paul arrested, asked witness opportunity, Acts 21:37 –
    22:21.
Strength in subdued approach, 2 Corinthians 10:1.
Prayer not to be ashamed, Philippians 1:20.

Standing firm whatever circumstances, Philippians 1:27–30.
Boldly facing opposition, 1 Thessalonians 2:1–2.
Power, love replace timidity, 2 Timothy 1:7.
Not embarrassed by Paul's chains, 2 Timothy 1:16–18.
Faithful to point of death, Revelation 2:13.
Holding on to faith, Revelation 2:25.

COURTESY
Sister in strange country, Genesis 12:10–13.
Returning neighbor's lost property, Deuteronomy 22:1–3.
Courtesy to stranger, Ruth 2:14–18.
Gentleness of Boaz to Ruth, Ruth 3:7–15.
Wasted compliments, Proverbs 23:8.
One of ten grateful for healing, Luke 17:11–19.
Courteous conversation, Colossians 4:6.
"Courtesy to everyone," Titus 3:2 (NRSV).
Respect for everyone, 1 Peter 2:17.

COURTSHIP
Noticing opposite sex, Genesis 6:1–2 (Berk.).
Arranged marriages, Genesis 21:21; 24:1–67.
Asking for guidance sign, Genesis 24:14.
Angelic assistance, Genesis 24:40.
Seven-year wait, Genesis 29:18–20.
Rape, romance, Genesis 34:1–3.
Moses, Zipporah, Exodus 2:16–22.
Samson, Philistine woman, Judges 14:1–7.
Kidnapped brides, Judges 21:23.
Women's initiative, Ruth 3:1–18.
Bargaining hearts, 1 Samuel 18:17.
Times of restraint, Ecclesiastes 3:5.
No romantic serenades, Psalm 78:63 (Berk., NIV).
Stealing heart, Song of Songs 4:9.
Males easily find wild donkey, Jeremiah 2:24.
Evil woman's courtship, Hosea 2:11–16 (LB).

COWARD
Cowardly brothers, Genesis 42:21–28.
Frightened by falling leaf, Leviticus 26:36.
Feeling small like grasshoppers, Numbers 13:33.
Infectious cowardice, Deuteronomy 20:8.
Melting because of fear, Joshua 2:24.
Thousand flee one enemy, Joshua 23:10; Isaiah 30:17.

Timid soldiers, 1 Samuel 23:1–5.
Dubious loyalty, 1 Chronicles 12:19.

CRAVING

Continual lust for more, Ephesians 4:19.

CREATIVITY

Adam's creativity, Genesis 2:19.
Creator's power, authority, Job 9:1–10.
Good talent displayed, Psalm 45:1.
Producing, enjoying, Psalm 49:3–4.
Skilled in one's work, Proverbs 22:29.
Artist is mortal, Isaiah 44:11.
Ashamed of idols he had made, Jeremiah 10:14–15.
Builder, work, Hebrews 3:3.

CREATOR

Praising Creator, Nehemiah 9:6.
Creator's power, authority, Job 9:1–10.
"Outskirts of His ways," Job 26:14 (NRSV).
Creation proclaims God's righteousness, Psalm 50:6.
Creator knows creation, Psalm 50:11.
Ruler over all nature, Psalm 89:8–13.
Eternal God predates creation, Psalm 90:1–2.
Creator's work, Psalm 95:1–5.
Difference between Creator, idols, Psalm 96:5.
Nature praises Creator, Psalm 96:11–12.
Eternal God, temporal creation, Psalm 102:25–27.
Poem to God of nature, Psalm 104:1–26.
Creator's command, Psalm 104:7–9 (LB).
Skillful Creator, Psalm 136:5 (NASB).
Creator urged not to abandon creation, Psalm 138:8.
Creator's hands, Psalm 143:5.
Each star known by name, Psalm 147:4.
Savior, Creator, Proverbs 30:4.
Remembering Creator, Isaiah 17:7–8.
Creator's wisdom, greatness, Isaiah 40:12–28.
Creator cares for His creation, Isaiah 42:5–7.
God's purpose creating earth, Isaiah 45:18.
Heavenly throne, earthly footstool, Isaiah 66:1.
Earth, sky reflect God's wisdom, Jeremiah 10:12.
Omnipresent Creator, Jeremiah 23:23–24.
Creator's ownership, Jeremiah 27:5.
Sovereign power, Jeremiah 32:17.
Earth, man, Zechariah 12:1.

Christ as Creator, John 1:1–4, 10; Colossians 1:15–17; Hebrews 1:3, 10–12.
Author of life itself, Acts 3:15.
One who fills universe, Ephesians 4:10.
Jesus Christ, Word of life, 1 John 1:1–4; John 1:1–3.
Unique name for Jesus, Revelation 3:14.

CREDIT

Loans to poor, Exodus 22:25–27.
Credit encouraged, Deuteronomy 15:8; Matthew 5:42.
No interest charge to locals, Deuteronomy 23:19–20.
Security for loan, debt, Deuteronomy 24:6; Job 24:3.
Cruel creditor's demands, 2 Kings 4:1.
Lender rules borrower, Proverbs 22:7.
Charging high interest, Proverbs 28:8.
Shrewd settlement, Luke 16:1–8.
Obligation to pay debts, Romans 13:8.

CRIME

Rising crime rate. Genesis 6:11 (LB).
Stabbing death, 2 Samuel 3:27; 4:6; 20:10.
Conspiracy against leadership, 2 Samuel 15:10; 1 Kings 16:15–20; Esther 2:21.
Roadside ambush, 2 Kings 12:21.
Criminals in pagan temple, 2 Kings 19:37.
Planning perfect crime, Psalm 64:6.
History's greatest crime, Matthew 27:35; Mark 15:20; Luke 23:33; John 19:18.
Wages of crime, Acts 1:18 (Berk.).

CRIMINAL

Habitual criminal, Psalm 69:27.
Boastful criminals, Psalm 94:4 (GNB).
Criminal motivated by hunger, Proverbs 28:21.
Habitual criminal, Ecclesiastes 8:12.
Pardon for nation's blood guilt, Joel 3:21.
Cheating, polluting, Amos 8:5–6.
Night criminals, Micah 2:1–2.
Notorious Barabbas, Matthew 27:16.

CRISIS

Power of God's name, Exodus 6:1–8.
Bad advice, Job 2:9–10.
Sure refuge, Psalm 46:1–11.
Value of crisis, Proverbs 20:30.

Crisis tests strength, Proverbs 24:10.
Go to neighbor for help, Proverbs 27:10.
Silver, gold no value when judgment falls, Zephaniah
   1:18.

C

CRITICISM

Rule to follow when criticizing, Numbers 23:8.
Father's criticism refused, 1 Samuel 2:22–25.
Open to criticism, Job 6:24–25; Proverbs 15:32.
Response to criticism, Job 16:1–5.
Job accused of not speaking sensibly, Job 18:2.
Verbal persecution, Job 19:2.
Admitting personal error, Job 19:4.
Zophar upset by criticism, Job 20:2–3.
Tantalizing critics, Job 21:3.
Thick skin, Job 34:7.
Criticizing family members, Psalm 50:20.
Razor sharp tongue, Psalm 52:2–4.
Avoiding leader's criticism, Psalm 105:15.
Tongues of serpents, Psalm 140:3.
Acceptable rebuke, Psalm 141:5.
Unable to take criticism, Proverbs 9:8.
Willing to be disciplined, Proverbs 10:17.
Silent when others err, Proverbs 11:12.
Healing tongue, deceitful tongue, Proverbs 15:4.
Word power, Proverbs 18:21.
Faithful wounds of friend, Proverbs 27:6.
Friend's valued counsel, Proverbs 27:9.
Rebuke better than flattery, Proverbs 28:23.
Refusing criticism, Proverbs 29:1.
Secret words of disdain, Ecclesiastes 7:21–22.
Dislike for strong preaching, Amos 7:16.
Satan's role as accuser, Zechariah 3:1–2.
Untruthful criticism, Matthew 5:11.
Judging, criticizing others, Matthew 7:1–5.
Slander spoken against Jesus, Matthew 11:18–19.
Jesus criticized for picking grain on Sabbath, Matthew
   12:1–8.
Jesus criticized for casting out demons, Matthew 12:22–
   32.
Response of Jesus to critics, Matthew 21:23–27; Mark
   14:53–62.
Jesus criticized on cross, Matthew 27:39–44.
Jesus criticized for healing, Mark 2:6–12.
Looking for something to criticize, Mark 3:1–6.

Jesus' family thought Him deranged, Mark 3:20–21 (Note v. 31).
Jesus confounded critics, Mark 11:29–33.
Trying to catch Jesus in His own words, Mark 12:13–17.
Rejoice when criticized for faith, Luke 6:22–23.
Wrong of criticizing others, Luke 6:37; Romans 2:1.
Speck in brother's eye, plank in your own, Luke 6:41–42.
Folly of unfounded criticism, Luke 8:49–56.
Jesus watched by Pharisees, Luke 14:1.
Critics confronted, Luke 20:1–8.
Judging mere appearances, John 7:24.
Dissension, jealousy in the church, Acts 6:1.
Criticizing others, Romans 2:1.
God the only judge, Romans 8:33.
Proper attitude to weak, Romans 14:1.
Judging others, Romans 14:13.
Help weak rather than criticize, Romans 15:1.
Criticizing another's conduct, 1 Corinthians 10:27–33.
Judging one's self, 1 Corinthians 11:28–32.
Positive, productive criticism, 2 Corinthians 7:8–13.
Trying to please others, Galatians 1:10.
Fathers should not exasperate children, Ephesians 6:4.
Paul's attitude toward opponents, Philippians 1:15–18.
Judged by food, drink, Colossians 2:16.
Conversation full of grace, Colossians 4:6.
Living above criticism, Titus 2:8.
Remember your past before criticizing others, Titus 3:1–3.
Slander no one, James 4:11–12.
Do not grumble against each other, James 5:9.
Judgment begins with God's family, 1 Peter 4:17.
Commendation before reproof, Revelation 2:2–6, 13–16, 19–20.

CROSS

A worm, not a man, Psalm 22:6 (Berk.).
Crucifixion agony, ignominy, Isaiah 53:1–12 (CEV).
Redeemer, King, Isaiah 63:1.
Prophecy of Judas, thirty pieces of silver, Zechariah 11:12–13.
Crucifixion prophecy, Zechariah 12:10–11.
Disciples could not understand, Mark 9:30–32; Luke 9:44–45.

Jesus foretold death, resurrection, Mark 10:32–34.
Vineyard parable, Mark 12:1–12.
Weight of sin, not cross, killed Jesus, Mark 15:33–37, 44.
Jesus could not die until time had come, Luke 4:28–30.
Jesus willingly lay down His life, John 10:17–18.
Prior to Cross, Jesus saw resurrected Lazarus, John 12:1–10; 11:1–44.
Jews had no right to crucify, John 18:28–32.
God's perfect timing in Christ, Romans 5:6.
Setting free from power of sin, Romans 8:1–4.
Jesus took penalty for all, Hebrews 2:9.
First covenant validated with blood, Hebrews 9:18–22.
Willing to suffer with Christ, Hebrews 13:11–14.
Vision of resurrected Christ, Revelation 1:17–18.

CROSS-CULTURAL

Earth divided, people scattered, Genesis 10:5; 11:1–9.
Abraham, Lot, Sodom, Gomorrah, Genesis 18:20–33; 19:1–29.
Clash of moral viewpoints, Genesis 39:1–23.
Joseph's relevance to Pharaoh, Genesis 41:1–40.
Solomon, Queen of Sheba, 1 Kings 10:1–13.
Bible is cross-cultural, Isaiah 55:5; Micah 4:3–4; Romans 10:12–13.
Value of heathen culture, Jeremiah 10:1–5.
Jesus and cross-cultural communication, John 4:4–26.
Philip, Ethiopian eunuch, Acts 8:26–40.
Peter's lesson in cultural prejudice, Acts 10:9–23; 11:1–14.
Paul, Athenians, Acts 17:16–27.
Cultural dissipation of revealed truth, Romans 1:21–32.

CROWDS

Very great gathering, Genesis 50:9 (NKJV).
God can single out individual, Deuteronomy 29:21.
Vast assembly, 1 Kings 8:65.
Myriads of people, Psalm 3:6 (Berk.).
Multitudes making decisions, Joel 3:14.
Crowd forced Jesus into boat, Matthew 13:1–2; Mark 4:1.
Entire town gathered, Mark 1:33.
Overflow crowd, Mark 2:1–5.
Avoiding undisciplined crowd, Mark 3:9–10 (NKJV).

Triumphal entry Jesus into Jerusalem, Mark 11:1–10.
Potential Passover mob violence, Mark 14:1–2.
Crowd stirred up against Jesus, Mark 15:11–15; 11:8–10.
Crucifixion of Jesus, Mark 15:21–32.
Entry through roof, Luke 5:17–26.
Thronging thousands, Luke 12:1.
Jesus' enemies feared public opinion, Luke 22:3–6.
Curious to see miracles performed, John 6:2, 26–27.
Drawn to main attraction, John 3:29 (LB).
Influence of many, Acts 4:21.
Entire city in uproar, Acts 19:23–41.
City aroused by troublemakers, Acts 21:30.

CRUELTY

Brotherly brutality, Genesis 37:19–24.
Male infants destroyed, Exodus 1:22.
Animal mistreatment, Numbers 22:27–28; Judges 15:4–5; 2 Samuel 8:4; 1 Chronicles 18:4.
Body mutilation, Judges 1:6; 1 Samuel 11:2; 2 Kings 25:7.
People burned to death, Judges 9:49.
Prophet's ignominy, Jeremiah 38:6.
Into fiery furnace, Daniel 3:12–27.
Mental cruelty, Matthew 5:11; Acts 9:16.
Killing prisoners to prevent escape, Acts 27:42–43.
Bodily harm, Romans 8:17; 2 Corinthians 4:11; 1 Peter 2:20.

CULT

Wayward community, Deuteronomy 13:12–18.
Detecting false prophet, Deuteronomy 18:21–22.
Wrong Scripture interpretation, Jeremiah 8:8.
Prophecy of imagination, Ezekiel 13:1–23.
Cults prevented, Micah 5:12.
Hindering others from entering kingdom, Matthew 23:13–15.
Many claiming to be Christ, Matthew 24:4–5, 11, 24; Mark 13:22–23.
Those who fast while others do not, Mark 2:18–20.
Only one gate to sheep pen, John 10:1–21.
Avoid wrong teaching, Romans 16:17.
Futility of no resurrection message, 1 Corinthians 15:13–19.
False disciples dilute Gospel, Galatians 2:4–5.

Impact of error, Galatians 2:13.
Alienated from truth, Galatians 4:17.
Danger of deceptive philosophy, Colossians 2:8.
Demon theology, 1 Timothy 4:1–4.
Proud of false doctrine, 1 Timothy 6:3–5.
Godless chatter, opposing ideas, 1 Timothy 6:20–21.
Those deceived who deceive others, 2 Timothy 3:13.
Rejecting sound doctrine, 2 Timothy 4:3–4.
Ministering for dishonest gain, Titus 1:10–16.
Careful of strange teachings, Hebrews 13:9.
Cleverly invented stories, 2 Peter 1:16.
Falling away from truth, 2 Peter 3:17.
Walking in darkness, 1 John 1:5–7.
Leading believers astray, 1 John 2:26.
Counterfeit anointing, 1 John 2:27.
Test of spirits, false prophets, 1 John 4:1.
Many deceivers, 2 John 7.
Those of another teaching unwelcome, 2 John 10–11.
Warn against false teaching, Jude 3–4 (AB).
Discerning those who are false, Revelation 2:2.
Finality of Scripture record, Revelation 22:18–19.

CULTURE
"Manner of life," Judges 18:7 (LB).
Culture affected by intermarriage, Nehemiah 13:23–26.
Influence of nation upon nation, Jeremiah 10:2.
Language, literature, Daniel 1:3–4.
Noble character of Bereans, Acts 17:11.
Ministry to all cultures, Romans 1:14–17.
Wisdom, foolishness, 1 Corinthians 1:18–21.
Adapting to culture, 1 Corinthians 9:19–23.

CURIOSITY
Father's nudity, Genesis 9:22–23.
Plight of Lot's wife, Genesis 19:17, 26.
Baby Moses, Pharaoh's daughter, Exodus 2:5–6.
Moses, burning bush, Exodus 3:1–3.
Death for looking into ark, 1 Samuel 6:19.
Endless curiosity, Ecclesiastes 1:8.
Investigate scheme of things, Ecclesiastes 7:25.
Roadside curiosity, Jeremiah 48:19.
Those who pass by, Lamentations 1:12.
"You stood there and watched," Obadiah 11 (CEV).
Waiting to see spectacle of judgment, Jonah 4:5.

Large crowds witness miracles, Matthew 4:23–25; 8:1, 18; 19:2; Luke 14:25; John 6:1–2.
Asking to see miracle, Matthew 12:38.
Things people go to see, Luke 7:24–26.
Compassionless curiosity, Luke 10:32.
Curiosity led to blessing, Luke 18:35–43.
Drawn to main attraction, John 3:29 (LB).
Needing signs, wonders to believe, John 4:48.
Motivated by curiosity, John 6:2; 12:9.
Mind your own business, John 21:21–22.
Staring at those God uses, Acts 3:12.
Intellectual curiosity, Acts 17:21 (NRSV).
Following crowd in confusion, Acts 19:32.
Curiosity of angels, 1 Peter 1:12.
Suffering as meddler, 1 Peter 4:15.

CURSE
Penalty for disobedience, Deuteronomy 28:15–68.
Mother's predicament, Judges 17:1–5.
Venereal disease, 2 Samuel 3:29 (GNB).
Punishment for curses, 1 Kings 2:8–9.
Cursing expertise, Job 3:8 (LB).
Exiles instructed to use curse, Jeremiah 29:21–23.
Blessing becomes curse, Malachi 2:2 (CEV).
Old Testament conclusion, Malachi 4:6.

——————— **D** ———————

DANCING
Tambourines, dancing, Exodus 15:19–21.
Backslidden dancers, Exodus 32:19.
Dance of death, Judges 11:30–39; Matthew 14:6–12.
Celebration dancing, 1 Samuel 18:6–7.
Dancing before the Lord, 2 Samuel 6:14–16.
Infant dancers, Job 21:11.
Sorrow gives way to dancing, Psalm 30:11.
Dance of praise, Psalms 149:3; 150:4.
Time to dance, Ecclesiastes 3:4.
Israel dancing, Jeremiah 31:4.
Dancing curtailed, Lamentations 5:15.
Music without dancing, Matthew 11:17.

DANGER
Holding hands, Genesis 19:16.
Jacob reassured, Genesis 46:1–4.

Safety in dangerous area, Numbers 24:21 (GNB).
Lives at risk, Judges 5:18.
Companions in danger, 1 Samuel 22:23.
Overlooking danger, Esther 4:9–16.
Wicked bend their bows, Psalm 11:2.
Facing danger with confidence, Psalm 27:3.
In grave danger, Psalm 73:2.
Do not fear, Isaiah 8:12–14.
Thousands flee, Isaiah 30:17.
Safely through danger, Isaiah 43:2.
Fear of public places, Jeremiah 6:25.
Snorting enemy horses, Jeremiah 8:16.
Unsuspected danger, Jeremiah 11:18–19.
Good news, bad news, Jeremiah 34:1–7.
Loud noise, Jeremiah 46:17.
Watchman's responsibility, Ezekiel 33:1–9.
Assured safety, Ezekiel 34:25.
Returning from battle, Micah 2:8 (GNB).
River gates open, Nahum 2:6.
Neighbor versus neighbor, Zechariah 8:10.
Jesus facing danger, Luke 13:31–33; John 7:1.
Avoiding unnecessary danger, John 11:53–54.
Angelic protection, Acts 27:21–25.
Risked their necks, Romans 16:4 (NASB, NKJV, NRSV).

DARKNESS
Total darkness, Genesis 1:2–4.
No travel after sunset, Genesis 28:11.
The Lord our lamp, 2 Samuel 22:29.
No God, no priest, no law, 2 Chronicles 15:3.
Time of day for evil, Job 24:14–17.
Dark, slippery path, Psalm 35:6; Jeremiah 23:12.
Walking in darkness, Psalm 82:5; Proverbs 2:13–15;
    1 John 1:6.
God sees through darkness, Psalm 139:12.
Deep darkness, Proverbs 4:19.
Deepest darkness illuminated, Isaiah 9:2.
Darkness as light, Isaiah 42:16.
Creator of darkness, light, Isaiah 45:7.
Land of darkness, Isaiah 45:19.
Light in darkness, Isaiah 50:10.
Vain search for light, Isaiah 59:9.
Covenant with day, night, Jeremiah 33:20–21.
Evil covered by darkness, Ezekiel 8:12
Eternal darkness, Matthew 8:12; 22:13; 25:30.

Fear at night, Luke 2:8–14.
Light, darkness in conflict, John 1:5; Romans 13:12–13.
Jesus, Nicodemus, John 3:2; 19:39.
Loving darkness, avoiding light, John 3:19–20.
Night walking, John 11:9–10.
Plight of Judas, John 13:27–30.
Spiritual darkness, Acts 13:8–11.
Cover of darkness, Acts 17:10.
Darkness to light, Acts 26:18.
Night navigation, Acts 27:27–29.
Deeds of darkness, Romans 13:12.
No hiding place, 1 Corinthians 4:5.
Not of the darkness, 1 Thessalonians 5:4.

DAUGHTER
Daughter's rights, Exodus 21:7–10.
Marriage to both mother, daughter forbidden, Leviticus 20:14.
Father's authority, Numbers 30:3–5.
Given in marriage, Judges 1:12–13; 1 Samuel 17:25; 18:20–21.
Daughter's request, Judges 1:13–15.
Daughter sacrificed, Judges 11:29–40.
Father decides daughter's relationship, Judges 15:1–2.
Exploiting daughter's love, 1 Samuel 18:20–29.
Beautiful daughters, Job 42:15.
Father's attitude toward daughter, 1 Corinthians 7:36–38 (NASB).

DAUGHTER-IN-LAW
Cause of parental grief, Genesis 26:34–35.
Ruth, Naomi, Ruth 1:8–18.
Valued more than seven sons, Ruth 4:13–15.

DAYDREAMING
Hard work, fantasy, Proverbs 28:19.
Daydreaming leads to senseless talk, Ecclesiastes 5:7 (CEV).
Dozing, day dreaming, Isaiah 56:10 (CEV).

DEATH
Return to earth, Genesis 3:19.
Promised pleasant death, Genesis 15:15.
Closing dead man's eyes, Genesis 46:4.
Embracing corpse, Genesis 50:1.

Life's final moment, Mark 15:37–39.
No need for tears, Luke 7:11–13.
Alive to God, Luke 20:38.
Spiritual commitment of Jesus, Luke 23:46.
Mortals resurrected, John 5:28–29.
True immortality, John 8:51.
Falling asleep, John 11:11–15; Acts 7:60.
Post-resurrection, pre-resurrection fellowship, John 12:1–10 (See 11:1–44).
Threat to kill resurrected Lazarus, John 12:10.
Better option, John 16:5–7.
Life's work concluded, John 17:4.
Aware of imminent death, John 18:1.
Sin caused Jesus' death, John 19:28–30, 33.
Vulgar death of Judas, Acts 1:18.
Messianic implications, David and Jesus, Acts 2:29–35.
Martyr's death, Acts 7:54–56.
Falling asleep, John 11:11–14; Acts 7:60.
Doomed enemy, 1 Corinthians 15:26.
Death swallowed in victory, 1 Corinthians 15:53; Isaiah 25:8 (KJV).
Eden serpent's harmless sting, 1 Corinthians 15:55.
Earthly, eternal, 2 Corinthians 5:1.
Apostle's anticipation, 2 Timothy 4:6–8.
Probate will, Hebrews 9:16–17.
His death, our life, 1 Thessalonians 5:10.
Rich man like wildflower, James 1:10–11.
Withered grass, flowers, 1 Peter 1:24–25.
Death desired in vain, Revelation 9:4–6.
Blood of dead man, Revelation 16:3.

DEBT

Refusing to become indebted, Genesis 14:22–24.
Debt to relatives, others, Deuteronomy 15:1–3.
"Paid in full," Deuteronomy 15:2 (LB).
Miraculous repayment, 2 Kings 4:1–7.
Mortgaged property, Nehemiah 5:3.
Children taken for debts, Job 24:9.
Sold to creditors, Isaiah 50:1 (LB).
Creditors seize all, Psalm 109:11.
Bed taken for debt, Proverbs 22:27.
Debt mercifully canceled, Matthew 18:23–27.
Love the only debt, Romans 13:8 (CEV).
Pay what is owed, Romans 13:7–8.
Debt owed by slave, Philemon 18–19.

DECEPTION
Satan's reasoning, Genesis 3:1-5.
Wife poses as sister, Genesis 12:10-20; 20:2; 26:7.
Sibling impersonation, Genesis 27:6-23.
Hiding father's gods, Genesis 31:31-35.
Circumcision ploy, Genesis 34:13-31.
Joseph deceiving brothers, Genesis 42-44.
Murderous deceit, Judges 3:12-21.
Samson, Delilah, Judges 16:4-20.
Pretended madness, 1 Samuel 21:10-15.
Incest by deception, 2 Samuel 13:1-14.
Attempted deception, Nehemiah 6:1-14.
Deceptive wages, Proverbs 11:18.
Hurt by deception, Proverbs 26:28.
Deliberate deception, Isaiah 5:20.
Friends, brothers untrustworthy, Jeremiah 9:4-8.
Self-deception, Jeremiah 37:9 (LB).
Believing lie, Jeremiah 43:1-7.
Truth despised, Amos 5:10.
Herod's Nativity ploy, Matthew 2:7-12.
Awkward Pharisee, Matthew 22:15-22.
Contemplated deception, Mark 14:1.
Ananias, Sapphira, Acts 5:1-9.
Accused of deception, 2 Corinthians 12:16 (LB).

DECISION
Harmed by wrong decision, Genesis 16:1-6.
Freedom of decision, Genesis 24:54-58.
Garment for decision making, Exodus 28:15, 29.
God changed His mind, Exodus 32:14.
Good, bad decisions, Deuteronomy 30:15.
Throwing dice, Joshua 14:1-2 (LB).
Time for decision, Joshua 24:15.
Two options, 1 Kings 18:19-21.
Decision conditioned by God's will, Ezra 7:18.
Coin toss, Nehemiah 10:34 (LB).
No change of mind, Psalm 110:4.
Choosing truth, Psalm 119:30.
Oath to follow Scripture, Psalm 119:106.
"Inspired decisions," Proverbs 16:10 (NRSV).
Decision without facts, Proverbs 18:13 (LB).
Flip coin, Proverbs 18:18 (LB).
Correct choice, Proverbs 21:2.
Decision requested, Isaiah 16:3.
Divine decision changed, Jeremiah 26:19.

"I won't change my mind," Amos 1:3 (CEV).
Date of decision, Haggai 2:18.
Immediate decision, Matthew 4:20–22.
Jesus, Barabbas, Matthew 27:15–26.
Urged to action, Mark 1:15 (LB).
Prayer precedes decision, Luke 6:12–16.
Prepared for persecution, Luke 21:12–15.
Decision to turn back, John 6:66–71.
Reaching out to God, Acts 17:27.
King not persuaded, Acts 26:28.
Mind made up, 2 Corinthians 2:1 (NKJV).
"Determine what is best," Philippians 1:9–10 (NRSV).
Challenge to decide, Hebrews 3:7–14.
Determined resistance, 1 Peter 5:8–9.

DEFEAT
Pharaoh's army wiped out, Exodus 14:28.
Vanquished king, 1 Samuel 31:1–6; 2 Samuel 1:1–12.
Failure into success, 1 Kings 8:33–34.
Defeat caused by sin, 2 Kings 17:7; 18:11–12.
Utter defeat, 2 Kings 13:7.
Loathing life, Job 10:1.
Hopeless future, Job 17:11.
Shamed by defeat, Psalm 25:2.
Broken hearts, spirits, Psalm 34:18 (Berk.).
No help from God, Psalm 44:9.
Enemy bones scattered, Psalm 53:5.
Food for jackals, Psalm 63:10.
Desolation of defeat, Isaiah 1:7.
Satan's defeat, Isaiah 14:12–17.
Death of mighty army, Isaiah 18:6 (LB).
No resistance to capture, Isaiah 22:3.
"Silent ruin," Isaiah 23:7 (LB).
Desolate city, Isaiah 27:10.
Defeated time after time, Jeremiah 4:20 (CEV).
Predestined defeat, Jeremiah 34:1–5.
Certain defeat, Jeremiah 37:1–10; 38:14–28.
Defeat aftermath, Jeremiah 39:1–7.
Battlefield bedlam, Jeremiah 46:12.
Augmented defeat, Jeremiah 46:15.
Hiss of fleeing serpent, Jeremiah 46:22.
Continual bad news, Jeremiah 51:31–32.
Giving up to enemy, Lamentations 1:5.
Cause of defeat, Lamentations 4:12–13.
Broken bow symbol, Hosea 1:5.

Ninety percent loss, Amos 5:3.
Irreparable ruin, Micah 2:10.
Ninevah's fate applauded, Nahum 3:19.
"Never give up," 2 Corinthians 4:16 (CEV); Ephesians
    6:18 (GNB).

DEFENSIVE
Defending personal intelligence, Job 13:2.
Upset by criticism, Job 20:2–3.
Avoid being defensive, Luke 21:14.
Jesus defensive, John 7:1.

DELINQUENCY
Juvenile delinquent executed, Deuteronomy 21:18–21.
Sons of sorceress, Isaiah 57:3.
Unfaithful sons, Jeremiah 3:19.
Father's evil influence, Jeremiah 16:10–12.
God loves delinquents, Hosea 11:1–4.
Multiple delinquency, Amos 2:1, 6 (AB).
Prodigal son, Luke 15:11–32.

DEMOCRACY
"We, the people," Nehemiah 10:28, 34 (GNB).

DEMONS
Divination forbidden, Leviticus 19:26
Protected by blessing, Numbers 22:12.
God's use of demons, 1 Samuel 16:15.
"Evil spirit from God," 1 Samuel 16:16 (NIV, NKJV).
Demon use of bodies, Matthew 8:28–33; Mark 5:1–5.
Jesus accused of demonism, Matthew 9:32–34; 12:22–
    32; John 8:48–52.
Depraved spirits, Matthew 10:1 (Berk.).
Authority over evil, Matthew 10:1–8; Romans 8:37–39;
    Colossians 2:15; Jude 9.
Shrieking demons, Mark 3:11 (LB).
Satan versus Satan, Mark 3:20–26.
Name of demon, Mark 5:8–9 (GNB).
Demon rebuked, Mark 9:25.
Demons recognized Jesus, Luke 4:33–36, 41.
Mary Magdalene's seven demons, Luke 8:2.
Multiple demon possession, Luke 8:30.
Demon confronted Jesus, Luke 9:37–43.
Mute demon, Luke 11:14.
Crippled by demon, Luke 13:10–16.

Controlled by Satan, Luke 22:3; John 13:27; 1 Timothy 5:15.

Jesus accused of demon possession, John 10:19–21.

Tormented by demons, delivered, Acts 5:16.

Contending sorcerer, Acts 13:6–8.

Reverence to demons, Acts 17:22 (AB).

Opportunist exorcists, Acts 19:11–13.

Demons cause physical harm, Acts 19:13–16.

Pagan idols, 1 Corinthians 10:20.

False angels, 2 Corinthians 11:14–15.

Enslaved by demons, Galatians 4:8–9 (NRSV).

Satanic cause of anger, Ephesians 4:26–27.

Armor of God, Ephesians 6:10–18.

Cosmic powers, Ephesians 6:12 (Berk.).

Rescue from darkness, Colossians 1:13–14.

Hindered by Satan, 1 Thessalonians 2:18.

Possessed by Satan, 1 Timothy 1:18–20.

Demon theology, 1 Timothy 4:1–4 (See CEV).

Deceived widows, 1 Timothy 5:11–15.

Satan's trap, 2 Timothy 2:25–26.

Resisting Satan, James 4:7; 1 Peter 5:8–9.

Testing false spirits, 1 John 4:1–6.

Angels versus demons, Revelation 12:7–9.

Global control, 1 John 5:19; Revelation 16:13–14.

Demon residence, Revelation 18:2.

DEN

DENIAL

Denying Christ, Matthew 10:33; Mark 8:38; 2 Timothy 2:12.
Peter's denial, Matthew 26:34, 69–70, 73–74.

D

DEPRESSION

Deep waters, 2 Samuel 22:17.
Broken hearts, spirits, Psalm 34:18; Proverbs 17:22.
Desperate times, Psalm 60:3.
Walking in darkness, Isaiah 9:2.
No joy, Jeremiah 48:33.
Hopeless hope, Romans 4:18–22.
God comforts the depressed, 2 Corinthians 7:6 (NASB).

DESIRE

Selfish desire, Numbers 11:4; Mark 10:35–37.
Divinely-implanted desires, Psalms 37:4 (CEV), 145:16; 2 Corinthians 8:16.
Desires known to Lord, Psalm 38:9.
Desired obedience, Psalm 119:1–5.
Evil desire, Proverbs 21:10; Habakkuk 2:4–5; Mark 4:19; 1 Corinthians 10:6.
Fulfilled desires, Psalm 73:25; Proverbs 13:12.
Spiritual desire, Isaiah 26:9; Luke 6:21; 1 Peter 2:2.
Jesus said, "I want to," Mark 1:41 (CEV).
Fulfilling Satan's desires, John 8:44.
Carnal gratification, Ephesians 2:3.
Impure desires, Ephesians 4:19; James 1:13–15.
Paul's supreme desire, Philippians 3:7–11.
Unfulfilled desire, James 4:2.
Love of the world, 1 John 2:15–16.

DESPERATION

Desperate times, 2 Kings 6:24–31.
Plea for mercy, Esther 7:7.
Face to wall, Isaiah 38:2.
Resorting to cannibalism, Lamentations 2:20.

DESSERT

Going without dessert, Daniel 10:3 (LB).

DESTINY

Destined for greatness, Genesis 18:16–19.
Sympathy, destiny, Exodus 2:5–6.
Children destined for war, Job 27:15.

Time for everything, Ecclesiastes 3:1–8.
Pre-planned destiny, Isaiah 25:1; 46:8–11; 49:1; Jeremiah 1:5; Ephesians 1:4; 1 Peter 2:8.
"Who controls human events?" Isaiah 41:4 (CEV).
Jerusalem's destiny, Jeremiah 31:38–40.
Savior's dual mission, Luke 2:28–32.
Destined crucifixion, John 7:30.
Jesus knew His destiny, John 13:1.
Confident of destiny, Acts 27:23–25.
Revealed destiny, Romans 8:18–23.

DESTRUCTION

Canaanite devastation, Numbers 21:3.
No survivors, Deuteronomy 2:34; 3:6; Joshua 6:21; 8:24–29.
Destructive cities, nations, 2 Chronicles 15:6.
"Rebuild ruins," Job 3:14 (NRSV).
Divine destruction, Isaiah 34:2.
Total destruction, Jeremiah 25:9.
Earth's destruction, Zephaniah 1:2–3 (GNB).
Destroyed beyond remedy, Micah 2:10.
Flaming destruction, Malachi 4:1.
Babylon destroyed, Revelation 18:21.

DETERMINATION

Relentless determination, Numbers 23:24.
Strong soul, Judges 5:21.
"Don't give up," 2 Chronicles 15:7 (CEV).
Consistent determination, Psalm 44:18.
Wholehearted determination, Psalm 119:10.
Standing firm, Isaiah 7:9.
Face like flint, Isaiah 50:7.
Divine determination, Jeremiah 23:20.
Heart, action, Jeremiah 32:38–39.
Determined to obey, Colossians 1:9–12.

DIARY

King's diary, Esther 6:1–2.
Need for diary, Job 19:23–24.
Tear-stained page, Psalm 56:8.

DICTATOR

Wandering leaders of earth, Job 12:14–15.
Weakness of one-man government, Proverbs 11:14.
Unjust government, Isaiah 10:1–2.

Oppressed people, Isaiah 26:13.
Have no fear, Romans 13:3–4 (GNB).

DIET

Meat diet, Genesis 43:16.
Bread without yeast, Exodus 12:15.
Bread, meat, Exodus 16:1–12.
Edible, inedible insects, Leviticus 11:20–23.
Grape abstinence, Numbers 6:2–4.
No more manna, Joshua 5:12.
Pregnancy diet, Judges 13:1–5.
Refreshing breakfast, Judges 19:5–8.
Forbidden to taste, 1 Samuel 14:24–28.
Simple, happy diet, Proverbs 15:17; 17:1.
Watching calories, Proverbs 23:1–2, 20–21.
Regular meal times, Ecclesiastes 10:17.
Pigs, rats, Isaiah 66:17.
Royal diet refused, Daniel 1:8–16.
Red meat, Amos 6:4.
John the Baptist's diet, Matthew 3:4.
Pigs' diet, Luke 15:16.
Special dinner guest, Luke 24:29–30.
Vegetarian, nonvegetarian, Romans 14:2; Daniel 1:12.
No better, no worse, 1 Corinthians 8:8.
Stomach god, Philippians 3:19.
Legalistic diet, 1 Timothy 4:3; Hebrews 13:9.

DIFFICULTY

"Rivers of difficulty," Isaiah 43:2 (LB).
Grateful for problems, Jeremiah 33:10–11.
Means of ministry, Acts 28:17–28.

DIGESTION

Happy meals, Deuteronomy 27:7; Acts 14:17.
Enforced indigestion, 1 Samuel 14:24.
Digestive disease, 2 Chronicles 21:15.
Love aids digestion, Proverbs 15:17.
Stingy man's food, Proverbs 23:6–8.
Regular meal regular hours, Ecclesiastes 10:17.
Undigestible food, Jonah 2:10.
Attitude and food, Acts 14:17.
Wine aids digestion, 1 Timothy 5:23.

DISAGREEMENT

Peace before battle, Deuteronomy 20:10.
Futile disagreement, 2 Samuel 2:27–28.
Disagreeing prophets, 1 Kings 22:6–25.
Preventing disagreement, Proverbs 17:14, 19.
Words of restraint, Proverbs 17:27.
Potential value of disagreement, Proverbs 27:17.
Disagreement quickly settled, Matthew 5:25.
Settled out of court, Luke 12:58.
Doctrinal disagreement, Acts 15:2, 3; 1 Corinthians 11:16; Galatians 2:11–21.
Settling disputes between Christians, 1 Corinthians 6:1–7.
Tolerant to others, 1 Corinthians 6:20 (LB).
Disagreement clarified, Philippians 3:15.
Settling disagreements, Philippians 4:3; 2 Timothy 2:23–26.
"Petty controversy," 2 Timothy 2:14 (AB).

DISAPPOINTMENT

Prepared circumstances, Deuteronomy 8:16.
Unharvested vineyard, Deuteronomy 28:39: Micah 6:15.
More victorious in death than life, Judges 16:30.
Facing disappointment without complaining, Job 1:22.
Disappointed with life, Job 10:1 (Berk.).
Hope a dying gasp, Job 11:20.
Mourning unanswered prayer, Psalm 35:13–14.
No fear of bad news, Psalm 112:7–8.
Agony of waiting, joy of fulfillment, Proverbs 13:12.
Disappointed parents, Proverbs 17:25.
Handling disappointment, Proverbs 19:23.
Lost harvest, Isaiah 17:10–11.
Awakening to find dream untrue, Isaiah 29:8.
Frustrated hopes, Jeremiah 14:19.
Jonah's Nineveh disappointment, Jonah 4:1–3.
Houses unoccupied, Zephaniah 1:13.
Expecting much, receiving little, Haggai 1:9.
"Deep groan," Mark 8:11–12 (GNB).
Purpose of suffering, Romans 5:3.
Made sad by those who should cause joy, 2 Corinthians 2:3 (LB).
Rejoicing although prayer not answered, 2 Corinthians 12:7–10.
Surprised, astonished, Galatians 1:6 (AB).

Disappointment widened influence, Philippians 1:12–14.

Sharing troubles, Philippians 4:14.

Attitude toward deserting friends, 2 Timothy 4:16.

Reason for circumstances, Philemon 15–16.

Made perfect through suffering, Hebrews 2:10.

Confident now of promises fulfilled, Hebrews 11:13.

All tears wiped away, Revelation 21:4.

DISASTER

God's promise to Noah, Genesis 9:8–16.

Small town spared large city's disaster, Genesis 19:15–22.

Death caused by shock, 1 Samuel 4:12–18.

Predicted disasters, 2 Samuel 3:29 (LB).

Disaster aid, Job 30:24 (NRSV).

Facing disaster with confidence, Psalm 57:1.

Unanticipated disaster, Ecclesiastes 9:12 (NRSV).

Gentle waters, flood waters, Isaiah 8:6–7.

One night's destruction, Isaiah 15:1.

Judgment brings righteousness, Isaiah 26:9.

Slaughter on battlefield, Isaiah 37:36.

Leaders, priests, prophets lose heart, Jeremiah 4:9.

Disobedience brings disaster, Jeremiah 4:18.

Disaster in all directions, Ezekiel 7:2–3 (LB).

Great disaster, Ezekiel 7:5.

Fourth of earth destroyed, Revelation 6:7–8.

Disaster upon all earth, Revelation 8:6–13.

Greatest all-time earthquake, Revelation 16:18–20.

Hailstones from sky, Revelation 16:21.

One-hour conflagration, Revelation 18:17–19.

DISCIPLESHIP

Servant for life, Exodus 21:2–6.

Battle-experienced soldiers given preference, Numbers 31:27–31.

Material security versus God's will, Numbers 32:14–27.

Old Testament discipleship, Deuteronomy 5:1.

Taking care of business, Deuteronomy 20:5–9.

Eagle training young to fly, Deuteronomy 32:11.

Care required in loving God, Joshua 23:11.

Disqualified to build temple, 1 Chronicles 22:7–8.

Characteristics of holy life, Psalm 15:1–5.

Key to walking with God, Psalm 18:25–26.

Weeping in determination, Psalm 126:5–6.

Those who seek find, Proverbs 8:17.
Old Testament discipleship, Isaiah 8:16.
Definition meaning of fasting, Isaiah 58:3–7.
Sincere search for God, Jeremiah 29:10–14.
Lax in doing the Lord's work, Jeremiah 48:10.
Someone to stand in gap, Ezekiel 22:30.
Those who obey the Lord, Joel 2:11.
Those who hunger, thirst for righteousness, Matthew 5:6.
Salt, light in the world, Matthew 5:13–16.
Counting cost, Matthew 8:19–20.
Following Jesus, Matthew 9:9.
Marks of disciple, Matthew 10:24–25; 16:25; Luke 14:23–26; John 8:31; 13:35; 14:15; 15:8.
Loving God above all, Matthew 10:37–39.
Jesus makes burden light, Matthew 11:28–30.
Jesus evaluated His mother, Matthew 12:46–50.
Mark of disciple, Matthew 16:24.
Forsaking all follow Christ, Matthew 19:28–30; Mark 10:28–31; Luke 18:28–30.
Attitude of servant, Matthew 23:8–12.
Calling Simon, Andrew, James, John, Mark 1:16–20.
Wishing easy discipleship, Mark 8:31–38.
First must be last, Mark 9:35.
Disciples promoted to apostles, Luke 6:12–15.
Family loyalty, cost of discipleship, Luke 14:26, 27.
True servant's duty, Luke 17:7–10.
Follow light, avoid darkness, John 8:12.
Death of wheat kernel, John 12:24–26.
Role of hardship, Acts 14:21, 22.
Itinerary of Paul, Barnabas, Acts 15:36.
Discipling new converts, Acts 18:23.
Confidence in difficult places, Acts 20:22–24.
First a servant, then a ministry, Romans 1:1.
Devotion to one another, Romans 12:10.
Testimony confirmed in convert, 1 Corinthians 1:4–6.
Depth of disciple's thought, 1 Corinthians 2:6–16.
Discipling example, 1 Corinthians 4:15–16.
Marriage, discipleship, 1 Corinthians 7:32–35.
Servant attitude in preaching Gospel, 1 Corinthians 9:19–23.
One winner per race, all win serving God, 1 Corinthians 9:24–27.
Follow Christ's example, 1 Corinthians 11:1.
Dying daily, 1 Corinthians 15:31.

Loving those who cause grief, 2 Corinthians 2:5–11.
Marks of disciple, 2 Corinthians 6:3–13.
Sharing leader's concerns, 2 Corinthians 8:16.
Pledged to truth, 2 Corinthians 13:8.
Crucified with Christ, Galatians 2:20.
Serve one another in love, Galatians 5:13.
Live for Christ, gain in death, Philippians 1:21.
Consider others better, Philippians 2:3–4.
Forgetting past, pressing forward, Philippians 3:12–16.
Filled with knowledge of God's will, Colossians 1:9–12.
Life centered in Christ, Colossians 3:1–17.
Diligent discipleship, Colossians 3:23–24.
Properly motivated, 1 Thessalonians 1:3.
True son in the faith, 1 Timothy 1:2.
Danger of financial priorities, 1 Timothy 6:10.
True disciple description, 2 Timothy 2:1–4.
Persecution inevitable, 2 Timothy 3:12.
Servant and apostle, Titus 1:1.
Toward maturity, Hebrews 6:1.
Faithfully running race, Hebrews 12:1–2.
Strangers in the world, 1 Peter 1:1–2, 17.
Spiritual building materials, 1 Peter 2:4–5.
Becoming chosen people, 1 Peter 2:9.
Walking in Christ's steps, 1 Peter 2:21–25.
Resisting Satan, 1 Peter 5:8–9.
Taking Scriptures to heart, Revelation 1:3.
Partial holiness insufficient, Revelation 2:1–6, 13–15, 18, 20.
Holding on to faith, Revelation 2:25.
Clean in society of deceit, Revelation 3:4, 10.

DISCIPLINE
Poor leadership causes laxity, Exodus 32:25.
Purpose for moral, physical cleanliness, Leviticus 20:26.
Group participation destroying blasphemer, Leviticus 24:14–16.
Lacking spiritual discipline, Deuteronomy 12:8–9.
Care required in loving God, Joshua 23:11.
Whipping with thorns, briers, Judges 8:16.
Honey refused, 1 Samuel 14:24–26.
Undisciplined son, 1 Kings 1:5–6.
Regulation of worship music, 1 Chronicles 6:31–32.
Discipline of the Lord, judgment of men, 1 Chronicles 21:13.

Degrees of punishment, Ezra 7:26.
Less punishment than deserved, Ezra 9:13.
Laws, regulations, Nehemiah 9:13.
Wild ox must be tamed, Job 39:9–12.
Evil resisted, Psalm 18:23.
Bit, bridle, Psalm 32:8–9.
Discipline does not alter God's love, Psalm 89:32–33.
Blessing of divine discipline, Psalm 94:12–13.
Discipline of good father, Proverbs 3:11–12.
Those who hate discipline, Proverbs 5:12–13.
Willingness to be disciplined, corrected, Proverbs 10:17.
Positive value, Proverbs 12:1.
Discipline of children, Proverbs 13:24; 19:18.
Folly in child's heart, Proverbs 22:15; 23:13–14; 29:15.
Eating too much honey, Proverbs 25:16.
Discipline for horse, donkey, fool, Proverbs 26:3.
Discipline rewarded, Proverbs 29:17.
Sins paid back, Isaiah 65:6.
Resisted discipline, Jeremiah 5:3.
Discipline with justice, Jeremiah 30:11.
Those who resist discipline, Jeremiah 32:33.
Rod of discipline, Ezekiel 21:13.
Torn but healed by the Lord, Hosea 6:1.
Discipline for those most loved, Amos 3:2.
Those who refuse correction, Zephaniah 3:2.
Attitude of students to teachers, Matthew 10:24.
Jesus disciplined demons, Mark 1:33–34.
Discipline for doubting angel, Luke 1:18–20.
Mother reprimanded boy Jesus, Luke 2:41–50.
Barren branches, John 15:2.
Struggle against sin, Romans 6:12–13.
Both kind, stern, Romans 11:22.
Incest not disciplined in Corinth, 1 Corinthians 5:1–2.
Satan's disciplines, 1 Corinthians 5:5.
Engaged couples, 1 Corinthians 7:36.
Exercising Christian liberty, 1 Corinthians 8:9.
Runner, prize, 1 Corinthians 9:24–27.
Painfulness of good correction, 2 Corinthians 7:8–9.
Helping someone who has sinned, Galatians 6:1.
Discipline of children, Ephesians 6:4.
Avoid antagonizing those who do wrong, 2 Thessalonians 3:14–15.
Preventing teaching of false doctrine, 1 Timothy 1:3–5.
Satan as teacher, 1 Timothy 1:18–20.

Public discipline, 1 Timothy 5:20.
Disciplined for maturity, 1 Timothy 4:13; 2 Timothy 1:7.
Disciplined good soldier, 2 Timothy 2:1–4.
Athlete's discipline, 2 Timothy 2:5.
Elder's disciplined family, Titus 1:6.
Discontinued discipline, Titus 3:10.
Jesus and discipline, Hebrews 5:8–9.

DISCOUNT
Discounting bill, Luke 16:1–8.

DISCOURAGEMENT
Disrupted communication, Exodus 6:12.
Down and out, Joshua 7:10.
Once full, now empty, Ruth 1:21.
Discouraged with righteous effort, Psalm 73:13.
Fainthearted, Psalm 143:4–7.
Poverty's debilitating effects, Proverbs 10:15.
Discouraged by illness, Isaiah 38:9–12.
Joy, gladness gone, Jeremiah 48:33.
No one to restore spirit, Lamentations 1:16.
Vision comes to nothing, Ezekiel 12:22–25.
Exercising hope without basis, Romans 4:18–22.
Certain victory in Christ, 1 Corinthians 15:57–58.
Dynamic of Cross, 2 Corinthians 13:4.

DISCRETION
"Discreet and wise," Genesis 41:39 (KJV).
Clean, unclean meat, Leviticus 11:1–47.
Discretion in physical relationships, Leviticus 18:1–30 (chapter 20).
Foolish sins, Numbers 12:11.
Search for wisdom, insight, Proverbs 2:1–6.
Lack of discretion, Proverbs 7:6–23.
Making wise choices, Proverbs 8:6–11.
Speaking what is fitting, Proverbs 10:32.
Guided by integrity, Proverbs 11:3, 6.
Judgment, understanding, Proverbs 11:12.
Conduct in king's presence, Proverbs 25:6–7.
Discretion in neighborly visits, Proverbs 25:17.
Discreet speech, thought, Ecclesiastes 5:2.
Learned discretion, Isaiah 28:26 (KJV).
Indiscreet daughters of Babylon, Isaiah 47:1–3.
Aware of false prophets, 1 John 4:1–6.

DISCRIMINATION

Man, woman as plurality, Genesis 1:26–27.
God's plan for women's rights, Genesis 3:16.
Generic name for man, woman, Genesis 5:2.
Egyptian discrimination against Hebrews, Genesis 43:32.
Same rules for all, Numbers 15:15.
Census involved men twenty or older, Numbers 26:2.
Daughters with no brother, Numbers 27:1–11.
Samson desired Philistine wife, Judges 14:1–2.
Abundant reward for kind act, 1 Samuel 30:11–18.
Daughters assist rebuilding wall, Nehemiah 3:12.
Pledge to avoid intermarriage, Nehemiah 10:30.
Wealth, prestige couldn't numb resentment, Esther 5:10–14.
Faith of Canaanite woman, Matthew 15:21–28.
Treatment given Gentiles, Matthew 20:25.
Mutual hatred Samaritans, Jews, Luke 9:51–56.
Deliverance from discrimination, Acts 10:24–28.
One in Christ, Galatians 3:28.
Slave, owner have same Master, Ephesians 6:9.
Wrong of discrimination, James 2:1–4.
Darkness of hatred, 1 John 2:9–11.

DISEASE

Wasting diseases, Leviticus 26:15, 16.
Divine immunity, Exodus 15:26; Deuteronomy 7:15.
Skin infection, Leviticus 13:9–17; Deuteronomy 28:27.
Leprosy, Exodus 4:6–7; Deuteronomy 24:8; 2 Kings 5:1–14; 2 Chronicles 26:19–21.
Affliction resulting from sin, Psalm 107:17; Isaiah 3:16–17.
Sin as disease, Romans 5:12 (LB).
"He is a weakling," 2 Corinthians 10:10 (CEV).
Suggestion of social disease, Jude 6–7; Leviticus 15; 22:4–5.

DISGRACE

Causing contempt, 2 Samuel 12:14; Nehemiah 5:9; Ezekiel 36:20; Romans 2:23, 24.
Becoming byword, Job 17:6.
Scattered enemy bones, Psalm 53:5.
Causing disgrace to others, Psalm 69:6–8.
Fall of Moab, Jeremiah 48:16–39.
Disgracing the Lord, Ezekiel 6:9 (CEV).

Evil in broad daylight, 2 Peter 2:13–23.
Disgrace of getting caught, Jeremiah 2:26.
Prophet in public disgrace, Jeremiah 20:1–2.
Disgraced disobedience, Daniel 9:7 (CEV).

D

DISGUISE

Daughter-in-law's disguise, Genesis 38:13–19.
Disguising true identity, Joshua 9:3–6.
David feigns madness, 1 Samuel 21:12–14.
Seance disguise, 1 Samuel 28:8.
Queen in disguise, 1 Kings 14:1–18.
Prophet in disguise, 1 Kings 20:38.
Royal disguise, 1 Kings 22:30; 2 Chronicles 35:20–24.
Wolves as sheep, Matthew 7:15.

DISGUST

"Don't eat disgusting animals," Deuteronomy 14:3
    (CEV).
Detesting display of emotion, 2 Samuel 6:14–16.
Thrown shoe, Psalm 108:9 (NRSV).
"Seen it all," Ecclesiastes 1:2 (CEV).
Disgusted with unbelief, Acts 18:5, 6.

DISHONESTY

Inaccurate weights, Leviticus 19:35–36; Proverbs 11:1;
    Hosea 12:7; Micah 6:11.
"Crooked deals," Psalm 101:3 (LB).
Dishonest report for personal gain, 2 Samuel 1:2–16.
Neighborhood dishonesty, Psalm 12:2.
Practicing deceit, Psalm 101:7.
Lying tongue, Proverbs 12:19–22; 13:5.
Fortune made by dishonesty, Proverbs 21:6.
Extortion, bribe, Ecclesiastes 7:7.
Stolen eggs like unjust riches, Jeremiah 17:11.
Despising those who tell truth, Amos 5:10.
Dishonest price, Amos 8:5–6.
"You crooks," Micah 2:10 (CEV).
Wealth by extortion, Habakkuk 2:6.
King Herod, Magi, Matthew 2:7–8, 13.
"You cheat people," Luke 11:42 (CEV).
"Crooked judge," Luke 18:6 (CEV).
Ananias, Sapphira, Acts 5:1–11.
Rule of integrity, Romans 12:17.
Truth, deceit, Ephesians 4:14–15.
Taking advantage of others, James 5:4–5.

DISHWASHING

DISHWASHING
Necessary ceremony, Mark 7:1–4.

DISLIKE
Dislike among family members, Genesis 4:2–9; 27:1–46;
    37:1–11; Luke 15:11–32.
Becoming stench, 2 Samuel 10:6.
Saul's dislike for David, 1 Samuel 18:8; 16:21.
Attitude toward those disliked, Matthew 5:38–47.
Quarrelsome Christians, 1 Corinthians 1:10–17; 3:3;
    2 Corinthians 12:20; Philippians 4:2.

DISLOYALTY
Disloyal to Moses, Exodus 32:23.
Broken disloyalty to God, Deuteronomy 32:51.
Proper disloyalty, 1 Samuel 22:16–17.
Servants disloyal to masters, 1 Samuel 25:10.
Philistine commander feared David's loyalty, 1 Samuel
    9:1–11.
Disloyal government officials, 2 Kings 12:19–20.
Disloyalty in battle, Jeremiah 41:11–14.
Obeying alien laws, Ezekiel 5:7–9.

DISOBEDIENCE
First act of disobedience, Genesis 3:1–11.
Plight of Lot's wife, Genesis 19:17, 26.
Foul odor of disobedience, Exodus 16:19–24.

Unauthorized fire for worship, Leviticus 10:1.
Penalty for national disobedience, Numbers 14:22–24.
Complaint about Moses' leadership, Numbers 16:12–14.
Disobeying instructions, Numbers 20:1–12.
Curse upon disobedience, Deuteronomy 11:26–28.
Obedience, disobedience, Deuteronomy 28:1–68.
Disobedience of faithful, 1 Samuel 12:15–20.
Disobeying command to do evil, 1 Samuel 12:16–17.
Better fall into God's hands than men's, 2 Samuel 24:10–14.
Incomplete faithfulness to God, 1 Kings 22:43.
Disobedience flaunting God's mercy, judgment, Psalm 8:32.
Judgment withheld against disobedience, Psalm 78:38.
Spiritual vagabonds, Jeremiah 2:31.
Sorrow of disobedience, Jeremiah 3:21.
Obedience, disobedience, Jeremiah 7:22–26.
Birds compared to people, Jeremiah 8:7.
Disobedience negates God's blessing, Jeremiah 11:14; 18:17.
Judgment upon disobedient people, Jeremiah 15:1–2; 44:1–14.
Trust in man, Jeremiah 17:5, 13.
Obedience cited as lesson, Jeremiah 35:1–16.
Disobedience negates past righteousness, Ezekiel 18:24.
When to disobey parents, Ezekiel 20:18–19.
Disobedient Israel, Ezekiel 20:21.
Civil disobedience, Daniel 3:1–30.
God's love for errant child, Hosea 11:1–4.
Disobedience causes downfall, Hosea 14:1.
Three sins, even four, Amos 1:3, 6, 9, 11, 13; 2:1, 4, 6.
Denied materialistic possessions, Amos 6:11.
Disobedience to God's call, Jonah 1:3.
Rebellious disobedience, Zephaniah 3:2.
Disobedient forefathers, Zechariah 1:4–6.
Salt loses flavor, lights are hidden, Matthew 5:13–16.
Seeming disobedience of boy Jesus, Luke 2:41–51.
Wrath of God, Ephesians 5:6.
Disobeying gospel, 2 Thessalonians 1:8.
Avoid association with disobedient, 2 Thessalonians 3:14–15.
Unable to hold true to faith, 1 Timothy 1:18–20.

Disobedience by neglect, Hebrews 2:2–3.
Sure judgment upon false teaching, 2 Peter 2:1–10.

DISPUTE

Abram's attitude toward Lot, Genesis 13:8–9.
Disputes solved by clergy, Deuteronomy 17:8–9.
Futility of strife, 2 Samuel 2:27–28.
Evidence turns against accuser, Proverbs 25:8.
Settle misunderstandings quickly, Matthew 5:25.
Theological dispute in secular courtroom, Acts 18:12–17.
Daring to dispute God, Romans 9:20.
Paul, Peter in dispute, Galatians 2:11.
Teachings which cause controversy, 1 Timothy 1:3–4.
Dispute over words, 2 Timothy 2:14, 23.
Rules for teacher handling dispute, 2 Timothy 2:23–26.

DISRESPECT

Disrespect toward judge, Deuteronomy 17:12.
Elisha's bald head, 2 Kings 2:23–24.
Disrespect for age, Job 30:1; Lamentations 5:12.
Disrespect for parents, Proverbs 30:17.
Youth disrespects age, Isaiah 3:5.
Idols replace delivering God, Jeremiah 2:5–8.
Jehoiakim burned scroll dictated by Jeremiah, Jeremiah 36:1–26.
Disrespect for temple, Ezekiel 25:3 (LB).
Jesus accused of disrespect, John 18:19–24.

DISTRACTION

Sexual distraction, Deuteronomy 17:17.
Distracted soldiers, Deuteronomy 20:5–9.
Household distractions, Luke 10:39.
"Undistracted devotion," 1 Corinthians 7:35 (NASB, NKJV).

DISTURB

Progress purposely disturbed, Ezra 4:1–5; Nehemiah 4:8.
Job's disturbing "friends," Job 2:11–13.
Disturbing the prophets, Isaiah 30:6–11; Amos 2:12.
Satanic disturbance, Zechariah 3:1–2; 1 Peter 5:8.
Blind man's disturbance, Mark 10:46–48.
Silencing disturber, Acts 13:1–13.
Unprincipled loungers, Acts 17:5 (Berk.).

Enough is enough, Acts 18:5–8.
Open door in spite of opposition, 1 Corinthians 16:5–9.
"Those who unsettle," Galatians 5:12 (NRSV).
Trouble from layman, 2 Timothy 4:14–15.

DIVERSITY
Variety in nature, Proverbs 30:18–19.
Diverse gifts, service, Romans 12:6; 1 Corinthians 12:4–11.
No two alike, 1 Corinthians 4:7.
Diversity in all creation, 1 Corinthians 15:39–46.
God intends diversity to produce unity, Ephesians 4:11–13.
The Lord invites diversity in prayer, Ephesians 6:18.

DIVINATION
Information by divination, Genesis 44:15.
Remunerated fortune tellers, Numbers 22:7.
Practice of sorcery, divination, Deuteronomy 18:14.
Seeking guidance for sacred object, 1 Samuel 6:2.
False oracles, prophets, Jeremiah 23:33–40.
False encouragement, Jeremiah 27:9; Zechariah 10:2.
Certain guidance, Ezekiel 13:22–23.
Seeking omen at road fork, Ezekiel 21:18–23.
Slave girl fortune teller, Acts 16:16–18.

DIVORCE
Earliest conditions of divorce, Exodus 21:10–11; Ezra 10:1–16.
Divorce, remarriage, Deuteronomy 24:1–4.
Rejected young wife, Isaiah 54:6 (CEV).
Exception in divorce, Jeremiah 3:1 (LB).
Wife leaves husband, Jeremiah 3:20 (KJV).
Wife returns to husband, Hosea 2:7 (CEV).
Divorce displeases God, Malachi 2:13–16 (LB).
Quiet divorce, Matthew 1:19.
Cause, procedure, Matthew 5:31–32; 19:7–8.
Jesus on divorce, Matthew 19:3–9; Mark 10:11–12.
Conditions prior to return of Christ, Matthew 24:37–38.
Conflicting views, Mark 10:2–10 (LB).
Plain talk about divorce, Romans 7:1–3; 1 Corinthians 7:10–11.
Hurt to children, 1 Corinthians 7:14 (LB).
People without love, 2 Timothy 3:3.

DONATION
Jewelry given to God, Exodus 35:22.
Ample donations, Exodus 36:5.
Varied gifts, Numbers 7:3.
Personal treasures, 1 Chronicles 29:3, 4.
Freely receive, freely give, Matthew 10:8.
More blessed to give, Acts 20:35.
Some pay, others receive, 2 Corinthians 11:7–8.

DONKEY
Role of donkey in Isaac's near sacrifice, Genesis 22:3.
Talking donkey, Numbers 22:26–34.
Incompatible ox, donkey, Deuteronomy 22:10.
Riding white donkeys, Judges 5:10.
Thirty in a row, Judges 10:3.
Lost donkeys, 1 Samuel 9:3–4.
Divine privilege, Matthew 21:1–2.

DOUBT
Doubt overcome by faith, Genesis 15:1–6.
Disobedience, doubt, Genesis 16:1–16.
God's guidance questioned, Exodus 5:22–23.
Doubting divine authority, Exodus 6:12.
Doubting in difficult times, Judges 6:11–13.
Doubting antidote, Psalm 46:10.
Effort to instill doubt, Isaiah 36:1–20.
Divine integrity questioned, Jeremiah 20:7–8.
Doubt hinders spiritual sight, Matthew 6:23.
Doubt rebuked, Matthew 14:31.
Doubters rebuked, Mark 16:14.
Angelic announcements doubted, Luke 1:18, 34.
Doubt augmented by hearing truth, John 8:45–47.
Continuing to doubt sure evidence, John 12:37–38.
Doubt does not alter truth, Romans 3:3.
Implications of doubting resurrection, 1 Corinthians 15:12–19.
Message death smell, 2 Corinthians 2:16.
Sinful, unbelieving hearts, Hebrews 3:12.
Faith sure antidote for doubt, Hebrews 11:1–3.
Helping those who doubt, Jude 22–23.

DOVE
Messenger dove, Genesis 8:8–11.
Sacrificial doves, Genesis 15:9.

Doves used in purification, Leviticus 12:6, 8; 14:22; Numbers 6:10.
Mourning dove, Isaiah 38:14.
Slave girls moan like doves, Nahum 2:7.
Doves as symbols, Matthew 3:16; Luke 3:22; John 1:32.

D

DREAMS

Thick, dreadful darkness, Genesis 15:12.
Seeking God's will, Genesis 28:11–22.
Revealing future, Genesis 37:5–10.
Divine utilization of visions, dreams, Numbers 12:4–6.
Dreams as vehicles of evil, Deuteronomy 13:1–5; Zechariah 10:2.
Perilous bread loaf, Judges 7:13.
Symbol of unreality, Job 20:8.
Warning in dreams, Job 33:14–17.
Cause of dreams, Ecclesiastes 5:3.
Dreaming of food, awakening hungry, Isaiah 29:8.
Prophetic dreams of delusion, Jeremiah 23:25–29.
Pleasant sleep, Jeremiah 31:26.
Interpreting visions, dreams, Daniel 1:17 (Chapters 2, 3, 4).
Dreamless sleep, Micah 3:6.
Instructional dream, Matthew 1:20–21.
Macedonian vision, Acts 16:9–10.
Assured in a vision, Acts 18:9–11.

DRUNKENNESS

Godly woman thought drunk, 1 Samuel 1:9–17.
Royal drinking party, 1 Kings 20:16.
Unlimited consumption, Esther 1:8.
"Drinking spree," Esther 3:15 (LB).
Drunkard's song, Psalm 69:12 (Berk.).
Led astray by alcohol, Proverbs 20:1.
Bloodshot eyes, Proverbs 23:29–31.
Drunken spree, Isaiah 5:11; Romans 13:13.
Sick drunk, Isaiah 28:1–8; Jeremiah 25:27.
"Can't walk straight," Isaiah 51:17 (CEV).
Pseudo drunkenness, Isaiah 29:9–10.
Drunken watchmen, Isaiah 56:10–12.
Drunkenness fostered by the Lord, Jeremiah 13:12–14.
Dead drunk, Jeremiah 51:57.
"Wine flowed freely," Daniel 5:1 (LB).
Drunkard's foolishness, Hosea 7:5 (LB).
Sobering drunkard, Joel 1:5 (CEV).

Too much wine, Nahum 1:10.
Drunken nudity, Habakkuk 2:15.
Drunk wedding guests, John 2:10 (NRSV).
Morning sobriety, Acts 2:15 (AB).
Spiritual drunken stupor, 1 Corinthians 15:34 (AB).

DUTY

Collecting daily manna, Exodus 16:4.
Carelessness in duty, 1 Samuel 26:7–16.
Half stand guard, other half work, Nehemiah 4:21.
Daily vows, Psalm 61:8.
Entrusted with secret things of God, 1 Corinthians 4:1–2.
Aim for perfection, 2 Corinthians 13:11.

E

EAGERNESS

David's eagerness to confront Goliath, 1 Samuel 17:48.
Full of words, about to burst, Job 32:17–22.
Eager horses straining for action, Zechariah 6:7.
Young man eager for truth, Mark 10:17.
Early to temple, Luke 21:38.
Eager for ministry, John 4:40.
Disciple who outran Peter, John 20:4.
Eagerness to be baptized, Acts 8:36–37.
Open, receptive, Acts 10:33; 17:19.

EARNINGS

Prostitute's unacceptable offering, Deuteronomy 23:18.
Debtor's earning power, Deuteronomy 24:6.
Giving fee rather than receiving, Ezekiel 16:32–34.
No wages, no business, Zechariah 8:10.
Woman who helped support Jesus, Luke 8:3.
Wages an obligation, not gift, Romans 4:4.

EASTER

Prophecy of Christ riding on donkey, Zechariah 9:9.
Judas and thirty pieces of silver, Zechariah 11:12–13.
Prophecy of the cross, Zechariah 12:10–11.
First recorded Easter observance, Acts 12:3.
Easter experienced personally, Ephesians 1:15–21.

ECLIPSE

Daytime darkness, Job 5:14; Amos 8:9.
One cannot look at sun, Job 37:21.
Sun, moon darkened, Isaiah 13:10; Joel 2:10; Matthew 24:29.
Covered heavens, Ezekiel 32:7.

ECONOMY

Good time and bad, Genesis 41:35, 36; Ecclesiastes 7:14.
Failure of money, Genesis 47:15 (KJV).
Mortgaging to buy food, Nehemiah 5:3-5.
First things first, Proverbs 24:27.
Woman with economic skills, Proverbs 31:10-31.
God's great bargain, Isaiah 55:1, 2.
No wages, no opportunities, Zechariah 8:10.
Treasures on earth or in heaven, Matthew 6:19-21.
Human equations and divine power, John 6:1-13.
Spiritual economics, Acts 3:6.

EDUCATION

Forbidden knowledge, Genesis 2:16-17.
Learning about creation, Deuteronomy 4:32.
Wisdom exceeds material gain, 1 Kings 3:5-15; 4:29-34.
Nationwide education for all, 2 Chronicles 17:7-9.
Teaching with parables, Psalm 78:1-8.
Stated learning objectives, Proverbs 1:1-6.
Wisdom, understanding greater than money, Proverbs 16:16.
Properly training child, Proverbs 22:6.
Knowledge gives strength, Proverbs 24:5-6.
Finding wisdom like eating honey, Proverbs 24:13-14.
Education causing grief, Ecclesiastes 1:18.
Knowledge better than wealth, Ecclesiastes 7:12.
Wearisome study, Ecclesiastes 12:12.
Ultimate knowledge, Ecclesiastes 12:13.
Sealed scroll, Isaiah 29:11-12.
Greatest treasure, Isaiah 33:6.
Misled by incorrect knowledge, Isaiah 47:10.
Three-year training program, Daniel 1:3-5.
Worldwide education, Habakkuk 2:14.
Teaching truth, Malachi 2:6.
Attitude of students to teachers, Matthew 10:24.

Perception of adults compared to children, Matthew 11:25.
Hearing, not understanding, Matthew 13:14–15.
Student, teacher, Luke 6:40.
Mouth speaks what heart contains, Luke 6:43–45.
Truth understood by children, Luke 10:21.
Knowledge beyond classroom, John 7:14–16.
Holy Spirit as teacher, John 14:26.
Simple men confound scholars, Acts 4:13.
Egyptian wisdom, Acts 7:22.
Interest of intelligent man, Acts 13:6–7.
Intellectual pride, Acts 17:16–34.
Erudite man, Acts 22:3.
Wisdom, foolishness, 1 Corinthians 1:18–21.
Message of wisdom to mature Christians, 1 Corinthians 2:6.
Folly of intellectual pride, 1 Corinthians 3:18–20; 8:1–3.
Faith is ultimate intelligence, 1 Corinthians 3:18–23.
"Knowledge causes arrogance," 1 Corinthians 8:1 (NASB).
Information without eloquence, 2 Corinthians 11:6.

EDIBLE SCROLL
Ezekiel 3:1–3 (L.B.)

HIGH FIBER DIET

Spirit of wisdom, revelation, Ephesians 1:17.
Learn what pleases the Lord, Ephesians 5:10.
Home school, Ephesians 6:4.
Both knowledge, insight, Philippians 1:9.
Godless chatter, false knowledge, 1 Timothy 6:20–21.
Unable to acknowledge truth, 2 Timothy 3:7.
Sure antidote for doubt, Hebrews 11:1–3.
Lacking wisdom, ask God, James 1:5–6.

EFFORT

Effort required in loving God, Joshua 23:11.
"Grasping for the wind," Ecclesiastes 2:17 (NKJV).
Sow wheat, reap thorns, Jeremiah 12:13.
Be not slothful, Romans 12:11 (KJV).
Lifeblood extended, Philippians 2:17 (LB).
Effort for the Lord, Colossians 3:23–24.

EGO

God only rightful ego display, Genesis 1:1; Isaiah 42:8.
"Make name for ourselves," Genesis 11:4 (AB).
Captured city named after captor, Numbers 32:42.
Fame, honor decreed by God, Deuteronomy 26:19.
Appealing to king's ego, Ezra 4:14.
Evaluating faithfulness, Nehemiah 5:19.
Ego flaunts wealth, prestige, Esther 5:11.
Contempt for unfortunate, Job 12:5.
Glory belongs only to the Lord, Psalm 115:1.
Sluggard's ego, Proverbs 26:16.
Proud of ability, Isaiah 5:21.
Artist only mortal, Isaiah 44:11.
Pharaoh a loud noise, Jeremiah 46:17.
Self-deification of self, Ezekiel 16:23–25.
Ego versus faith, Daniel 3:8–20.
Religion of sham, Matthew 23:5–7.
Asking for prestige, not earning it, Mark 10:11–40.
Ego displayed by teachers of law, Mark 12:38–40.
"Claiming to be somebody," Acts 5:36.
Sorcerer's ego, Acts 8:9–10.
Price paid for flagrant ego, Acts 12:19–23.
Falsely evaluating one's self, 2 Corinthians 10:12.
Exalting self, 2 Corinthians 11:17.
Egotistical preaching, Philippians 1:15 (LB).
Paul's wise use names of followers, Colossians 4:7–17.
One worthy of praise, Revelation 5:13–14.
Evil queen refused to admit sin, Revelation 18:7–8.

ELECTION
Selection of leader, Numbers 27:16.
Elect of the Lord, Deuteronomy 7:6; John 15:16; Ephesians 1:4; 1 Peter 1:2.
Divinely elected king, Deuteronomy 33:5 (LB).
Selection by lot, Nehemiah 11:1.
Choosing best leader, Deuteronomy 17:14–15; Hosea 8:4.
Trees seek a king, Judges 9:7–15.
Put out of office, Isaiah 22:19.

EMBARRASSMENT
Fear of being killed by woman, Judges 9:54.
Embarrassing sons, 1 Samuel 8:1–3.
Simpleton's taunt, Psalm 39:8 (Berk.).
God embarrassed, Malachi 1:7 (CEV).
Joseph avoided embarrassing Mary, Matthew 1:19–25 (CEV).
Made to look foolish, Matthew 22:34 (CEV).
Embarrassed disciples, Mark 9:34–35.
Jesus embarrassed opponents, Luke 13:10–17.
Coming to Jesus at night, John 3:1–2.
Paul prayed not to be ashamed, Philippians 1:20.
Gazingstock, Hebrews 10:33 (AB).

EMERGENCY
"Hurry up," Genesis 19:14 (GNB).
Reaction to emergency, Genesis 19:14–17.
Neighbor's assistance, Proverbs 27:10.

EMOTION
Hagar's love for Ishmael, Genesis 21:14–16.
Isaac meeting Rebekah, Genesis 24:62–67.
Bitter emotion, Genesis 27:34; Joshua 7:6.
Fears of Joseph, Genesis 42:24; 43:29–30.
Estranged brothers, Genesis 45:1–15.
Joseph's eagerness to meet father, Genesis 46:29.Clever wiles of Samson's wife, Judges 14:11–19.
Joshua's lament, Joshua 7:6.
Citywide outcry, 1 Samuel 4:13–14.
Profuse tears of gratitude, 1 Samuel 20:41.
Emotional confession, 1 Samuel 24:16–17.
Emotionally exhausted, 1 Samuel 30:1–4.
Loss of friends, 2 Samuel 1:11–12, 26; 3:33–37; 18:19–33.

Returning ark to Jerusalem, 2 Samuel 6:5.
Weeping, mourning, 2 Samuel 19:1–4.
Divine grief, 1 Chronicles 21:14–15.
Emotional joy building temple, Ezra 3:10–13.
Physical act of disdain, Ezra 9:3.
Tears of contrition, Ezra 10:1.
Emotional response to Scriptures, Nehemiah 8:9.
Emotion for others not remembered, Job 30:25.
Emotional worship, Job 37:1.
Creation of emotions, Job 38:36.
Broken heart, spirit, Psalm 34:18.
Sweetness of God's promises, Psalm 119:103.
Songs of Zion silenced, Psalm 137:1–4.
Uplifting emotions, Proverbs 4:23.
Hotheaded fool, Proverbs 14:16–17.
Zeal without knowledge, Proverbs 19:2; Romans 10:1–2.
Beware hot-tempered man, Proverbs 22:24–25.
Lacking self-control, Proverbs 25:28.
Angry man causes dissension, Proverbs 29:22.
Weeping, laughter, Ecclesiastes 3:4.
Showing restraint, Ecclesiastes 3:5.
Death silences emotion, Ecclesiastes 9:5–6.
Unquenched love, Song of Songs 8:7.
Moon, sun emote, Isaiah 24:23.
Drunk but not from wine, Isaiah 29:9; 51:21.
Anguish of guilt, Jeremiah 4:18–19.
"Fountain of tears," Jeremiah 9:1.
Skilled in wailing, Jeremiah 9:17–20.
Jeremiah tried to suppress feelings, Jeremiah 20:9.
Power of holy words, Jeremiah 23:9.
Weeping, wailing as judgment comes, Jeremiah 25:34.
Tears of joy, Jeremiah 31:9.
Joy, gladness gone, Jeremiah 48:33.
Tears of repentance, Jeremiah 50:4.
No one to comfort, Lamentations 1:16.
Ezekiel overwhelmed, Ezekiel 3:15.
Knocking knees of frightened king, Daniel 5:6.
Emotional overload, Daniel 8:27.
Daniel overwhelmed by vision, Daniel 10:7–8.
Preaching with compassion, Joel 2:17.
Weeping wailing, Micah 1:8.
Loss of children under Herod, Matthew 2:18.
Weeping, misunderstanding, Matthew 17:22–23.
Evil emotions, Matthew 26:65.

Mixed emotions, Matthew 28:8.
Gethsemane emotion, Mark 14:33.
Crowd stirred up against Jesus, Mark 15:11–15; 11:8–10.
Frightened shepherds, Luke 2:8–10.
Mary's emotions compared to shepherds', Luke 2:19, 20.
Effect of music upon emotions, Luke 7:31–32.
Joy of Jesus, Luke 10:21.
Concern of Jesus for Jerusalem, Luke 13:34; 19:41–44.
Heaven's emotion when sinner repents, Luke 15:3–10.
Clouded reality, Luke 24:41.
Sustaining joy of disciples, Luke 24:50–53.
Emotion from within, John 7:38–39.
Tears of Jesus, John 11:35.
Too excited to open door, Acts 12:12–16.
Sorrow of parting, Acts 20:36–38.
Empathy in sorrow, Acts 21:13.
Keep your spiritual fervor, Romans 12:11.
Characteristic of God, 2 Corinthians 1:3–4.
Spiritual sorrow, 2 Corinthians 7:10–11.
Anger without sin, Ephesians 4:26.
Drunk on wine, filled with Spirit, Ephesians 5:18.
Affection Jesus gives, Philippians 1:8.
Paul's tears, Philippians 3:18.
Rejoice in the Lord, Philippians 4:4.
Convicting power of Holy Spirit, 1 Thessalonians 1:4–5.
Remembering tears, anticipating joy, 2 Timothy 1:3–4.
Cries of Jesus to His Father, Hebrews 5:7.
Call to repentant emotions, James 4:9.
Happy singing, James 5:13.
Lamenting lost wealth, Revelation 18:11–19.

EMPATHY

Remembering from experience, Exodus 23:9.
Shared misery, Job 2:13.
Male pangs as of childbirth, Jeremiah 30:6.
Faith of friends, a man's healing, Mark 2:1–5.
Empathy for others, 2 Corinthians 1:3–4; 11:29 (GNB).
Sharing another's difficulty, Philippians 4:14.
Paul's concern for followers, Colossians 2:1–5.
High priest's weaknesses, Hebrews 5:2.
Remembered tears of others, 2 Timothy 1:3–4.
Experiencing what is taught to others, 2 Timothy 2:6.
Empathy with prisoners, Hebrews 13:3.

EMPLOYEE

Faithful employee, Proverbs 25:13 (LB).
Employees diligent for Christian employer, 1 Timothy 6:2.
Trustworthy employees, Titus 2:9–10.
Wages withheld, James 5:4.

EMPLOYMENT

Women employed, Genesis 29:9.
Fair wages commanded, Leviticus 19:13.
Hiring those who need employment, Deuteronomy 24:14–15.
Room, board, clothes, spending money, Judges 17:7–13.
Sabbath duty shifts, 2 Kings 11:4–8.
Thousands working on government project, 2 Chronicles 2:2.
Amos, the shepherd, Amos 1:1.
Concern of centurion for servant, Matthew 8:5–13.
Workers earn their pay, Matthew 10:10; Luke 10:7; 1 Timothy 5:18.
Women with means helped support Jesus, Luke 8:3.
Association of tent makers, Acts 18:1–3.
Evangelist supporting himself, 1 Corinthians 9:6–7.
Slaves, masters, Ephesians 6:5–9.
Consistent worker, Ephesians 6:6–7 (LB).
Relationship of slaves to masters, Colossians 3:22–25; 4:1.
Paul as model in daily conduct, employment, 2 Thessalonians 3:6–10.
Employees diligent for Christian employer, 1 Timothy 6:2.
Trustworthy employees, Titus 2:9–10.
Withheld wages, James 5:4.

ENCOURAGEMENT

No need to fear, Genesis 26:24; 2 Kings 6:16; Isaiah 41:10; 43:1.
Encouraging leadership, Exodus 14:13.
Strength of rising sun, Judges 5:31.
Miserable encouragement, Job 16:2–3.
Encourage rather than criticize, Job 16:4–5.
Encourage those who deserve, Proverbs 3:27.
Nourishment of kind words, Proverbs 10:21; 12:25 (LB); 15:23; 16:24.
Hope deferred, longing fulfilled, Proverbs 13:12.

Good news, cheerful looks, Proverbs 15:30.
Encouragement refused, Proverbs 25:20.
Mutual encouragement, Isaiah 41:7.
Divine encouragement, Isaiah 41:13; Matthew 9:2;
    14:27; 17:7; Acts 23:11.
Gift of encouragement, Isaiah 50:4.
Challenge to work for divine cause, Haggai 2:4.
Surest therapy for anxious hearts, John 16:33.
Paul took time to encourage, Acts 20:1–2.
Encouragement in time of storm, Acts 27:22.
Strong help weak, Romans 15:1.
Skill of giving compliments, Romans 16:3–16; 1 Corin-
    thians 11:2; 2 Corinthians 7:4–7.
Encouraging others, 1 Corinthians 16:18.
"God, the Encourager," 2 Corinthians 7:6 (Berk.).
Truthful hyperbole, 2 Corinthians 7:14.
Encouraged by new convert, Galatians 1:23–24.
Mutual encouragement, Philippians 2:1–2 (LB).
Wise use of names of followers, Colossians 4:7–17.
Encouraging believers, 1 Thessalonians 2:11–12.
Paul encouraged by conduct of Thessalonians, 1 Thes-
    salonians 3:6–10.
Boasting about perseverance, faith of others, 2 Thessa-
    lonians 1:4.
Strengthened by the Lord, 2 Thessalonians 2:16–17.
Not embarrassed by friend's misfortune, 2 Timothy
    1:16–17.
Encouraging one another daily, Hebrews 3:13.
Encouraging others, Hebrews 10:24.
Remember those in prison, Hebrews 13:3.

ENEMY

Protected from superior enemy, Exodus 14:15–31.
Kindness to enemy, Exodus 23:4–5; 2 Samuel 9:1–8 (See
    Proverbs 25:21–22).
Harass, attack, Numbers 25:17 (NKJV).
Exaggerating size of enemy, Deuteronomy 1:28.
No fear of great enemy, Deuteronomy 9:1–3; Psalm 27:3.
Enemies in all directions, 1 Samuel 12:11.
Prayer for guidance confronting enemy, 2 Samuel 5:17–
    19.
David, defeated Moabites, 2 Samuel 8:2.
Enemy conquered through blindness, 2 Kings 6:8–23.
Arm of flesh, 2 Chronicles 32:8.
Enemies, bandits, Ezra 8:31.

Enemy's loss of self-confidence, Nehemiah 6:16.
Rejoicing in trouble of others, Job 31:29.
Facing opposition with confidence, Psalm 3:6; 4:8.
Anguished assault, Psalm 7:1–2.
David became leader to strangers, Psalm 18:43–45.
Let the Lord face your enemy, Psalm 35:1–7.
Enemy falls into pit he designed, Psalm 57:6.
Those who hate peace, Psalm 120:6–7.
Do not rejoice in enemy's failure, Proverbs 24:17–18.
Turning back battle at gate, Isaiah 28:6.
Thousand fear one adversary, Isaiah 30:17.
Egyptians were but men, Isaiah 31:3.
Dependence upon God's promises, Isaiah 37:1–38.
Angel destroys enemy soldiers, Isaiah 37:36.
Persecutors put to shame, Jeremiah 17:18.
Only loud noise, Jeremiah 46:17.
Babylon's defeat, Jeremiah 50:46.
Giving up to enemy, Lamentations 1:5.
Plundering with glee, Ezekiel 36:5.
Nine out of ten lost in battle, Amos 5:3.
Gates wide open to enemy, Nahum 3:13.
Love your enemy, Matthew 5:43–48.
Enemy can kill body, not soul, Matthew 10:28.
Silence of Jesus before accusers, Matthew 26:57 67.
Basics of Golden Rule, Luke 6:27–36.
Jesus avoided enemies, John 7:1.
Hated by the world, John 15:18–21.
Forgiving spirit of martyr, Acts 7:60.
Mob incited against Paul, Silas, Acts 17:5–7.
Christian attitude to enemies, Romans 5:10; 12:14, 20.
Revenge in God's hands, 2 Thessalonians 1:6–7

ENERGY

Creator's need for rest, Genesis 2:2.
Old man's spirit, Genesis 45:27.
"Gird up his loins," 1 Kings 18:46 (KJV).
Energizing food, 1 Kings 19:7–8.
Weeping until exhausted, 1 Samuel 30:4.
Too exhausted to cross ravine, 1 Samuel 30:10, 21.
Wasted energy, Job 39:13 (NRSV).
Exerting strength for the Lord, Psalm 29:1 (KJV).
Worn out, Ecclesiastes 3:9 (Berk.).
Energy in full use, Ecclesiastes 9:10.
Working with dull axe, Ecclesiastes 10:10.
Feet of deer, Habakkuk 3:19.

Creator's energy, John 5:17.
Holy Spirit, resurrection, Romans 8:11; Ephesians 1:18–21.
Vigor, strength, Colossians 1:11 (AB).
Energy for spiritual labor, Colossians 1:29.
Working hard for the Lord, Colossians 3:23–24.
Energizing faith, 1 Thessalonians 1:3 (AB).

ENGAGEMENT

Bride for Isaac, Genesis 24:1–58; 25:19–20.
Bridal consent to marriage, Genesis 24:58.
Engagement for marriage, Deuteronomy 20:7.
Fate of virgin, Deuteronomy 22:23–27.
Ruth proposed to Boaz, Ruth 3:9 (GNB).
Commitment of two loves, Song of Songs 6:3.
Death of fiance, Joel 1:8 (GNB).
Like the Lord's signet ring, Haggai 2:23.
Decision to marry, 1 Corinthians 7:36.

ENTERTAINMENT

Heterosexual activity for homosexual, Judges 19:22–25.
Fighting to death for entertainment, 2 Samuel 2:12–16.
Joy of victory, Psalm 126:2.
Hired musicians, Ecclesiastes 2:8.
Nonspiritual entertainment, Isaiah 5:12.
Forgotten prostitute, Isaiah 23:16.
Wild parties, Romans 13:13 (LB).
Lovers of pleasure, 2 Timothy 3:4.

ENVIRONMENT

Choice of environment, Genesis 13:10–13.
Parental environment, Proverbs 6:20–23.
Sons of sorceress, Isaiah 57:3.
"No place to raise a family," Jeremiah 16:2 (CEV).
Evil influence of fathers, Jeremiah 16:10–12.
Mouths speak what hearts contain, Luke 6:43–45.
Marred creation liberated, Romans 8:20–21.
Earth under judgment, Romans 9:28.
Childhood environment, 2 Timothy 3:14–15.
Surviving in evil surroundings, 2 Peter 2:4–9.

ENVY

Examples of envy, Genesis 4:5; 37:5, 11; Numbers 11:28, 29; 12:2; 1 Samuel 18:6–9; Esther 5:13; Psalm 73:3; Mark 15:10; Acts 13:45.

Envy caused by wealth, Genesis 26:12–14.
Sibling envy, Genesis 37:11.
Never envy evil, Psalm 37:1 (LB); Proverbs 24:19–20.
Someone enviable, Psalm 41:1 (AB).
Envying evil affluence, Psalm 73:2–28.
Physical result of envy, Proverbs 14:30.
Neighborhood envy, Ecclesiastes 4:4.
Envying another's success, Daniel 6:4.
Proper envy, Luke 10:23 (AB).
Religious envy, Acts 13:45.
Israel's envy of Gentiles, Romans 11:13–14.
Purification of love, 1 Corinthians 13:4.
Avoid being cause of envy, Galatians 5:26.
Envy as cause of murder, 1 John 3:12.

EQUALITY

Apparel worn by opposite sex, Deuteronomy 22:5.
Jealous wife, 1 Samuel 1:3–7.
Prosperity of wicked, Jeremiah 12:1.

EROTIC

Mixing religion with immorality, Numbers 25:1–2.
Continual lust for more, Ephesians 4:19.

ESTEEM

Respect for those older, Job 32:4.
Loving esteem, Song of Songs 5:10–16.
Esteemed for strength, Isaiah 25:3.
Cornelius' esteem for Peter, Acts 10:25–26.

ETERNAL LIFE

Life forever, Psalms 21:4; 121:8.
Old Testament concept, Daniel 12:2.
Impossible to earn, Matthew 19:16–21; John 14:6.
All this and heaven, too, Luke 18:29–30.
Key to eternal life, John 3:16; 5:24–25; 12:25.
Bread of Heaven, John 6:50–58.
Eternal purpose of Scripture, John 20:30–31.

EVICTION

Thrown out of the land, Leviticus 20:22 (LB).
Jesus evicted, Luke 4:28–30.

EVIL
Evil made attractive, Genesis 3:6.
Pre-deluge depravity, Genesis 6:5.
No curse on those blessed, Numbers 22:12.
Evil aids God's plans, Judges 14:1–4; Jeremiah 25:11–
   14; Revelation 17:17.
Source of demons, 1 Samuel 16:15; 18:10.
Death of infamous hero, 1 Samuel 17:51.
Evil sanctioned, 1 Kings 22:23.
God's command to destroy, 2 Kings 9:6–7.
Ultimate result of evil, Job 20:4–11.
The old path, Job 22:15.
Peril to evil doers, Psalms 5:10 (Berk.); 7:15–16 (Berk.).
Sinful nature inherited, Psalm 51:5.
Wicked as wax, Psalm 68:2.
Man's wrath praises God, Psalm 76:10 (KJV).
Evil versus evil, Psalm 140:11 (NRSV).
Evil categorized, Proverbs 6:16–19 (LB).
When evil prospers, Ecclesiastes 8:12.

EXECUTION

"Hatred of evil," Proverbs 8:13 (NKJV, NRSV).
Kingdom of idols, Isaiah 10:10.
Those who trust in wickedness, Isaiah 47:10–11.
Source of evil, Isaiah 54:16–17.
Wicked prosperity, Jeremiah 12:1–3.
Evil outweighs good, Ezekiel 33:12 (CEV).
Hosea commanded to marry evil woman, Hosea 1:2–3.
Evil influence over good, Matthew 13:24–30.
Evil effort avoided by Jesus, Luke 4:28–30.
Satan entered Judas, Luke 22:3.
Approving wrong done by others, Acts 8:1.
Those handed over to Satan, 1 Timothy 1:18–20.
Love good, hate evil, Hebrews 1:9.
God tempts no one, James 1:13–14.
Work of devil, 1 John 3:7–8.
Inevitable defeat of Satan, Revelation 12:1–9.
Demons powerless against angel Michael, Revelation 12:7–9.
Mark of beast, Revelation 13:16–18; 14:9–10.
Sins piled up to heaven, Revelation 18:4–5.
One angel binds Satan, Revelation 20:1–3.

EVOLUTION

Distinction of species, Genesis 1:24–25; 1 Corinthians 15:39.
Human, animal similarity, Ecclesiastes 3:18–19 (NRSV).
Creator's statement, Isaiah 45:11–12 (LB).
Need for designer, Hebrews 3:4.
Alternative to evolution, Hebrews 11:1–3.
Earth formed out of water, 2 Peter 3:5 (NRSV).

EXCUSES

Blaming another, Genesis 3:12.
Claim of inadequacy, Exodus 3:11; 4:10; Judges 6:15; Jeremiah 1:7.
Excused idolatry, Exodus 32:24.
Blaming employer, Matthew 25:24–25.
First things first, Luke 9:59–62.
Excuses for not attending banquet, Luke 14:16–24.

EXERCISE

Running to bring bad news, 2 Samuel 18:24–33.
Impetus for keeping in shape, 1 Corinthians 6:19–20.
Foot racing, Jeremiah 12:5; 1 Corinthians 9:24–26.
Physical training and godliness, 1 Timothy 4:8.

EXHAUSTION
Long hours, hard work, Exodus 18:14–18 (LB).
Exhausted beyond tears, 1 Samuel 30:4.
Exhausted soldiers, 1 Samuel 30:9–10.
"Completely worn out," Psalm 31:9 (GNB).

EXORCISM
Musical exorcism, 1 Samuel 16:23.
Saul expelled mediums, spiritualists, 1 Samuel 28:3.
Demons forced out, Mark 1:34 (CEV).
Jesus rebuked demon, Luke 4:33–36, 41.
Submissive demons, Luke 10:17–20.
Cured by casting out of demon, Luke 13:10–13.
Miracles in ministry of Paul, Acts 19:11–12.
Modified use of name of Jesus, Acts 19:13.
Vain effort to cast out evil spirits, Acts 19:13–16.

EYES
Closing eyes of corpse, Genesis 46:4.
Eyes have seen, Deuteronomy 29:2–3.
Possible cataracts, 1 Samuel 4:14–15.
Flashing eyes, Job 15:12.
"Ogle at a girl," Job 31:1 (Berk.).
"Make my eyes sparkle," Psalm 13:3 (CEV).
Winking eyes, Proverbs 6:13 (Berk.).
Unable to weep, Lamentations 2:11 (LB).
Bodies full of eyes, Ezekiel 10:12.
Abominations of eyes, Ezekiel 20:7 (KJV).
Blessing implements, Luke 10:23.
Eye-to-eye with sorcerer, Acts 13:9–11.
Paul possibly poor eyesight, Galatians 6:11.

F

FACTS
Facts before decisions, Proverbs 18:13 (LB).
"Present your case," Isaiah 41:21.
Knowledge of Old Testament facts, Acts 7:1–60.
Unable to get facts, Acts 21:34 (Berk.).
Always get the facts, Romans 14:1.

FAILURE
When God terminates a project, Genesis 11:1–9.
Vineyards with little harvest, Deuteronomy 28:38–42.

Turning failure into success, 1 Kings 8:33–34.
Contempt for unfortunate, Job 12:5.
Admitted failure, Job 17:11.
Success doomed to failure, Job 24:22 (CEV).
Debilitating effects of poverty, Proverbs 10:15.
Gloating over enemy's failure, Proverbs 24:17–18.
"Keep me from failure," Jeremiah 17:18 (CEV).
Enemies rejoice, Lamentations 1:21.
Ridicule of once-exalted city, Lamentations 2:15.
Failed visions, Ezekiel 12:22–25.
Failure of Nebuchadnezzar's wise men, Daniel 2:1–11.
Architectural failure, Matthew 7:27.
Failure at healing, Matthew 17:16.
Fishermen's failure, Luke 5:1–11.
Death to failing guards, Acts 12:18–19.
Faith versus failure, Romans 4:18–22.
Failed life, 1 Corinthians 3:15; Hebrews 4:6.
Fear of failure, Galatians 2:1–2.
Successful failure, 1 Thessalonians 2:1–2.

FAINT

Fainting wounded, Lamentations 2:12.
Total weakness, Ezekiel 7:17.
Exhausted, ill, Daniel 8:27.

FAME

Heroes of old, Genesis 6:4.
"Make ourselves famous," Genesis 11:4 (Berk.).
Bestowed fame, Genesis 12:2 (LB); 1 Samuel 2:7.
Men of renown, Numbers 16:2 (NKJV).
Greatness of Moses, Deuteronomy 34:10–12.
Famous Joshua, Joshua 6:27.
Legitimate fame, Ruth 4:14.
Little known royal family, 1 Samuel 14:49.
Famous David, 2 Samuel 7:9; 8:13.
Worldwide acclaim, 1 Kings 4:31; 10:1.
Local celebrities, 1 Chronicles 12:30.
David's fame, 1 Chronicles 14:17.
Given great name by the Lord, 1 Chronicles 17:21.
Byword to all, Job 17:6.
Divine fame, Psalm 111:4 (CEV).
Dreaded armies, Jeremiah 6:24 (See LB).
Vanished fame, Lamentations 4:7–8.
Worldwide fame, Zephaniah 3:20 (See CEV).
Fame of Jesus, Matthew 4:24; 9:31; Luke 5:15.

Fame of Jesus because of miracles, Mark 1:35–45.
First last, last first, Mark 10:31.
Predicted future fame, Luke 1:15 (AB).
Avoiding limelight, John 7:4 (Berk.).
Respect of Cornelius for Peter, Acts 10:25–26.
Famed ministry, 2 Corinthians 8:18 (NASB, NRSV).

FAMILIARITY

The Lord knew Moses face-to-face, Deuteronomy 34:10.
Familiarity breeds contempt, Mark 6:4; John 4:44.
Becoming too familiar, 1 Timothy 6:2.

FASHION

When silver was out of style, 1 Kings 10:21.
Discussing latest intellectual subjects, Acts 17:21.
Head covering and hair style, 1 Corinthians 11:13–16.

FAST FOOD

Abraham's fast food, Genesis 18:6–8.

FAN

FATE

Death by random arrow, 2 Chronicles 18:33, 34.
If I perish, I perish, Esther 4:16.
All days pre-ordained, Psalm 139:16.
Time for everything, Ecclesiastes 3:1–8.
Things planned long ago, Isaiah 25:1.
Individual fate, Jeremiah 15:2.
Filled with knowledge of God's will, Colossians 1:9–12.

F

FATHER

Musical father, Genesis 4:21.
Forefathers of all mankind, Genesis 9:18–19.
Exemplary fathers, Genesis 17:18; 35:1–5; 2 Samuel
   12:15–16; 1 Chronicles 29:19.
Father's love to God and son, Genesis 22:1–14.
Father's finances, Genesis 31:1.
Father's sorrow and joy, Genesis 45:25–28.
Children suffer father's sin, Exodus 20:5–7; 34:6–7;
   Numbers 14:18.
No male survivors, Numbers 27:1–11.
Father's authority over daughter, Numbers 30:3–5.
Father prays for guidance, Judges 13:8.
Attitude toward affections of daughters, Judges 15:1–2.
Salaried father, Judges 17:7–13.
Father's famous son, 1 Samuel 1:1–20.
Father's immoral sons, 1 Samuel 2:22–23.
Eli's grief for ark and sons, 1 Samuel 4:16–18.
Son's influence over father, 1 Samuel 19:1–6.
Father, son together in death, 2 Samuel 1:23.
Rivalry between father, son, 2 Samuel 15:1–37.
David's rebellious son, 2 Samuel 18:5.
Father would have died for son, 2 Samuel 18:32–33.
Famous father's more famous son, 1 Kings 1:47–48.
Aged father's counsel to son, 1 Kings 2:1–9.
Son succeeded Solomon, 1 Kings 11:41–43.
Like father, like son, 2 Kings 15:34.
Sacrifice of son, 2 Kings 16:3.
Idolatrous father sacrificed sons, 2 Chronicles 28:3.
Killed by his own sons, 2 Chronicles 32:21.
Repentance of unrepentant son, 2 Chronicles 33:1–13.
Attention to Scriptures, Nehemiah 8:13.
Fate of father, fate of sons, Esther 9:12–14.
Job's concern over family festivity, Job 1:4–5.
Discipline of good father, Proverbs 3:11–12; 4:1–10.
Leaving inheritance to children, Proverbs 13:22.

Like father, like children, Jeremiah 16:10–13.
Fathers unable to help children, Jeremiah 47:3.
Refusal to learn from father's experience, Daniel 5:18–24.
Father, son to share prostitute, Amos 2:7.
God's total approval of His Son, Matthew 3:17.
Concern for only child, Luke 9:38.
Compassion for lost son, Luke 15:11–32.
Both kind, stern, Romans 11:22.
Father inspires children, 1 Thessalonians 2:11–12.
Timothy, spiritual son, 1 Timothy 1:2, 18; 2 Timothy 1:2; 2:1.

FAVOR
"A big favor," 1 Samuel 23:21 (CEV).
Royal favor, Proverbs 16:15; 19:12.

FAVORITISM
Preference one person for another, Genesis 27:6–17; 29:30, 34; 37:3, 4; 43:34; Deuteronomy 21:15–17; 1 Samuel 1:4–5.
Jealousy of younger brother, Genesis 37:1–36.
Israel's love for Joseph, Genesis 37:3.
Favored son, Deuteronomy 33:24.
Favored daughter, only child, Judges 11:29–39.
Favoritism in romance, Ruth 2:14–15.
Favoritism to no one, Job 32:21–22; 34:18–19.
"God has no favorites," Job 33:6 (CEV).
God's favorite, Isaiah 44:2 (CEV).
Evil seemingly favored, Jeremiah 12:1.
Israel loved best of all, Jeremiah 31:20 (CEV).
Good favor used to glorify God, Daniel 1:9–10.
Jerusalem, apple of God's eye, Zechariah 2:8.
Sun rises on all men, Matthew 5:43–48.
No racial boundaries, Acts 10:34–35; Romans 10:12.
Favoring one against another, 1 Corinthians 4:6.
No favoritism with God, Ephesians 6:9; Colossians 3:25.
Avoid partiality, 1 Timothy 5:21.

FEARLESS
No fear of enemy on all sides, Psalms 3:6; 27:3.
Fearless day, night, Psalm 91:5.
No fear of man, Psalm 118:6.
Peaceful sleep, Proverbs 3:24.

Confidence in the Lord, Isaiah 12:2.
Not one moment's fear, Philippians 1:28 (AB).

FEMINIST

Generic name for both sexes, Genesis 5:2.
Women at historic events, Matthew 28:8; Mark 15:47;
   Luke 2:36–38; John 20:1; Acts 16:13–14.

FERTILITY *(Human)*

Creator's command, Genesis 1:28; 9:7.
Pregnancy at advanced age, Genesis 16:16; 17:1–21;
   21:1 5.
Wombs closed, opened, Genesis 20:17–18.
Pregnancy in answer to prayer, Genesis 25:21.
Old Testament morality, Genesis 30:1–24.
Beyond age of childbearing, Ruth 1:11.
Prayer for fertility, Ruth 4:11–12 (LB).
Fruitful, barren wives, 1 Samuel 1:2 8, 20; 2:21.
Childless Hannah, 1 Samuel 1:5, 20; 2:21.
Blessing of producing children, Psalm 127:5.
Fertility gods, Jeremiah 2:20 (GNB).

FICKLE

Love like morning mist, Hosea 6:4.
Pretended weddings, funerals, Luke 7:32 (LB).
Fickle Galatians, Galatians 1:6–9.
"Wanting to have ears tickled," 2 Timothy 4:3 (CEV).

FINANCE

Monetary values, Leviticus 27:25
Temple collection box, 2 Kings 12:9–14 (GNB).
Interest-bearing loan, Psalm 15:5 (AB).
Avoid unwise financial ties, Proverbs 6:1–5 (LB).
Neither debtor nor creditor, Jeremiah 15:10 (LB).
Treasures on earth or in heaven, Matthew 6:19–21.
Advance cost estimation, Luke 14:28–30.
Human equations, divine power, John 6:1–13.
Importance of paying debts, Romans 13:8.
Sharing ministry expense, Philippians 4:15–19.
Paul worked to provide income, 1 Thessalonians 2:9;
   2 Thessalonians 3:6–10.
Endured poverty glorifies God, Hebrews 11:37–38.
Avoid pagan financing, 3 John 7.

FITNESS
Hindrance to worship, Leviticus 21:16–23.
Death of healthy person, Job 5:26.
Candidates for government service, Daniel 1:3–5.
Qualifications for following Jesus, Luke 9:23–26.

FLATTERY
Sincere sibling flattery, Genesis 33:10.
King likened to angel, 2 Samuel 14:17.
Flattering lips, Psalm 12:2–3.
Evil flattery, Psalms 36:1–4; 78:36; Proverbs 2:16; Romans 16:18.
Self-flattery, Psalm 36:2.
Adulteress' lips drip honey, Proverbs 5:3.
False flattery, Proverbs 24:24.
Rebuke better than flattery, Proverbs 28:23.
Flattering one's neighbor, Proverbs 29:5.
Dishonest flattery, Matthew 22:16; Luke 20:21.
Empty sincerity of Pharisees, Mark 12:15–17.
Glory belongs to God alone, 1 Corinthians 3:7.
Complimenting those previously rebuked, 2 Corinthians 7:14.
Flattery avoided in fund raising, 1 Thessalonians 2:5–6.

FLIRTATION
Noticing opposite sex, Genesis 6:1–2 (Berk.).
Ogled eyes, Genesis 39:7 (Berk.).
Lustful look, Job 31:1 (See Berk.).
Haughty women of Zion, Isaiah 3:16–17.
Learned flirtation, Jeremiah 2:33.
Adulterous look, Hosea 2:2.

FLOOD
Noah's escape, Genesis 7:1–24.
"Roaring floods," Genesis 7:17 (LB).
Evil men destroyed, Job 22:16.
Flood waters restrained, Job 28:11 (KJV, Note NKJV).
Never another flood, Psalm 104:9.
Divine promise, Isaiah 54:9.
Rising waters, Jeremiah 47:2.
Flood authenticated by Jesus, Matthew 24:36–39.
Apostolic validation, 1 Peter 3:18–22; 2 Peter 2:4–5.
Water spewed from serpent's mouth, Revelation 12:15–16.

FOOD

Let land produce, Genesis 1:11–12.
Vegetarian man, animals, Genesis 1:29–30.
Meat as food, Genesis 9:3.
Stolen supply, Genesis 14:11.
Food and hospitality, Genesis 18:1–8.
Food eaten by angels, Genesis 19:1–4; Judges 13:16.
Last request, Genesis 27:1–4.
Tasty food, Genesis 27:7.
Basic food, Exodus 3:17.
Forbidden food, Leviticus 11:13–40.
Craving for meat, Deuteronomy 12:20.
Vitality of bread, Judges 7:13–15.
Sampling food offered for sacrifice, 1 Samuel 2:13–14.
Soldiers denied nourishment, 1 Samuel 14:24–30.
Food containing blood, 1 Samuel 14:31–33.
Unpalatable food, 2 Kings 4:40.
Eating unplanted crop, 2 Kings 19:29.
Salt improves flavor, Job 6:6.
Blessing better than food, Psalm 63:5.
Manna, bread of angels, Psalm 78:25.
Hunger inspires hard work, Proverbs 16:26.
Avoid over-eating, Proverbs 23:1–3.
Wisdom like eating honey, Proverbs 24:13–14.
Nutritious food, Ecclesiastes 10:17.
Curds, honey, Isaiah 7:15.
Lion eating straw, Isaiah 11:7.
Abominable food, Isaiah 66:17.

FLOOD

THEY ALL LAUGHED AT NOAH'S FLOOD ROBE.

Bread secured at risk of death, Lamentations 5:9.
Food defiled by unclean fuel, Ezekiel 4:12–15.
Priests given best food, Ezekiel 44:28–31.
Failure of harvest, Hosea 9:2.
Forbidden food denied, Zechariah 9:7.
Cooking pots in the Lord's house, Zechariah 14:20–21.
Food of John the Baptist, Matthew 3:4.
Food supplied to those who trust, Matthew 6:31.
Sabbath corn picking, Matthew 12:1–8; Mark 2:23–27.
Feeding five thousand, Matthew 14:13–21; Mark 6:30–
    44; 8:1–9.
Mealtime prayer, Mark 14:22.
Jesus needed food, Luke 4:1–2.
Banquet celebrating commitment, Luke 5:27–32.
Food for dead girl, Luke 8:55.
Too concerned for food, Luke 12:29.
Spiritual food, John 4:34.
Food desired above spiritual results, John 6:26–40.
Dinner honoring Jesus, John 12:2.
Love feast, John 13:1–2.
Bread implicated Judas, John 13:21–27.
Trance caused by hunger, Acts 10:10.
No food unclean, Romans 14:14.
Eating an act of faith, Romans 14:23.
Limited spiritual diet, 1 Corinthians 3:1–2.
Unmuzzled ox, 1 Corinthians 9:9–14.
Physical hunger, spiritual sustenance, 1 Corinthians
    11:34.
Stomach as god, Philippians 3:19.
Sweet in mouth, sour to stomach, Revelation 10:9–10.
Wedding supper in heaven, Revelation 19:9.

FOOLISH

Foolishly blaming God, Job 1:22 (KJV).
Wild donkey's colt, Job 11:12.
No wise man, Job 17:10.
Foolish woman, Proverbs 9:13–16.
Careless about danger, Proverbs 22:3.
Parables to a fool, Proverbs 26:1–12.
Foolish drunkard, Hosea 7:5 (LB).
Tolerate another's foolishness, 2 Corinthians 11:1
    (GNB).
Our own foolish past, Titus 3:3.

FORECLOSURE
"Merciful creditor," Ezekiel 18:7 (LB).
Charge no interest, Exodus 22:25.
Protecting debtor's earning power, Deuteronomy 24:6.

FORGERY
Forged signature, 1 Kings 21:1–16.
Alleged letters, 2 Thessalonians 2:2 (AB).

F

FORGIVENESS
Filial forgiveness, Genesis 45:14–15.
Evil act forgiven, Genesis 50:15–21.
Forgiving spirit, Exodus 23:4–5; Proverbs 24:17; 25:21–22.
Parable convinces need to forgive, 2 Samuel 14:1–21.
Forgiving prayer, Job 42:7–10.
Forgiven sins honor God, Psalm 25:11.
God's forgiveness and punishment, Psalm 99:8.
Forgiven, forgotten, Psalm 103:12.
None deserves forgiveness, Psalm 130:3–4 (NRSV).
Depth of mercy and grace, Psalm 145:8–9.
Love's power, Proverbs 10:12.
Controlled anger, Proverbs 19:11.
God's reason for forgiving, Isaiah 43:25 (CEV).
Forgiveness like cloud swept away, Isaiah 44:22–23.
God's love to faithless Israel, Jeremiah 3:12–13.
God's total forgiveness, Jeremiah 50:20.
Anger forever gone, Hosea 14:4 (CEV, LB).
Forgiving Lord, Joel 2:12–13.
Given a second chance, Jonah 1:1–3; 3:1–3.
Forgiving grace, mercy of God, Micah 7:18.
Stewardship, forgiveness, Matthew 5:23–24.
Forgiving, forgiven, Matthew 6:14–15.
Principles of forgiveness, Matthew 18:21–22; Mark 11:25; Luke 6:37; 17:3–4; 2 Corinthians 2:7–10; James 5:15–16.
Forgiven, not forgiving, Matthew 18:23–35.
Judging, being judged, Luke 6:37.
Gratitude for great forgiveness, Luke 7:39–50.
Full measure of forgiveness, Luke 17:3–4.
Martyr's forgiving spirit, Acts 7:60.
Truly forgiven, Romans 4:8.
God's forgiven enemies, Romans 5:10.
Forgiving member of congregation, 2 Corinthians 2:5–11.

Forgive complaints, Colossians 3:12 (NASB, NRSV).
Forgiveness, patience, Colossians 3:13.
Sins of ignorance, 1 Timothy 1:12–14.
Paul's attitude toward deserters, 2 Timothy 4:16.
Record cleared, Hebrews 1:3 (LB).
Mercy of salvation, Hebrews 10:17.
Love and forgiveness, 1 Peter 4:8.
Our advocate with Heavenly Father, 1 John 2:1, 2.

FORTUNE-TELLING

Follow God, not dreamers, Deuteronomy 13:1–5 (CEV).
"Silly lies," Zechariah 10:2 (LB).
Pretended belief in divination, Genesis 44:5.
Divination outlawed, Deuteronomy 18:9–13.
Future cannot be known, Ecclesiastes 7:14.
"Chirp and mutter," Isaiah 8:19–20 (GNB).
Fortune-tellers made fools, Isaiah 44:25 (GNB).
Tools of fortune-teller, Isaiah 65:11.
Royal fortune-tellers, Daniel 2:1–4.
King's dream interpreted, Daniel 2:24–49.
Fortune teller's conversion, Acts 16:16–19.

FRAUD

Do not defraud neighbor, Leviticus 19:13.
Despising the truthful, Amos 5:10.
No acquittal of fraud, Micah 6:11.
Conversion considered a fraud, Acts 9:26–27.
Believers in litigation, 1 Corinthians 6:3–8.
Fraudulent gain, James 5:4–5.
False teachers, 2 Peter 2:1.

FREEDOM

Freedom of choice, Genesis 13:10–13.
"Rid of bondage," Exodus 6:6 (KJV).
Slavery preferred, Deuteronomy 15:16–17.
Freed slaves, Job 3:19.
Wild donkey set free, Job 39:5–6.
Youthful freedom, Ecclesiastes 11:9.
Yoke removed, Isaiah 9:4; 10:27; 14:25.
Proclaiming freedom, Isaiah 61:1.
Slaves rule free men, Lamentations 5:8.
Truth sets free, John 8:31–32, 36.
Freedom from legalism, Acts 10:24–28; Romans 7:1–6.
Clean, unclean, Acts 11:4–10.
No license to sin, Romans 6:1.

Freedom from sin's mastery, Romans 6:14.
Deliverance through Christ alone, Romans 7:24–25.
No longer slaves, Romans 8:15 (LB).
Unmuzzled ox, 1 Corinthians 9:9–14.
Freedom in the Spirit, 2 Corinthians 3:17.
Childhood a time of "slavery," Galatians 4:1.
"Christ has set us free," Galatians 5:1 (CEV).
Called to be free, Galatians 5:13 (CEV).
Filled with knowledge of God's will, Colossians 1:9–12.
Rescued from darkness, Colossians 1:13–14.
Freedom under authority, 1 Peter 2:13–17.
Christian liberty, 1 Peter 2:16.

FRIEND
David, Jonathan, 1 Samuel 18:1–4; 19:1–6; 20:17, 41;
    23:18; 2 Samuel 1:26.
False friends, 2 Samuel 16:16–23.
Adversarial friends, Job 2:11–13.
Friend in need, Job 6:14.
Evil friends, Psalm 50:18.
Loss of close friends, Psalms 55:12–14; 88:8.
Closer than nearest kin, Proverbs 18:24 (NRSV).
Wounds of friend, Proverbs 27:6.
Friend's counsel, Proverbs 27:10.
God's friend, Isaiah 41:8 (CEV).
Slandering friends, Jeremiah 9:4–5.
Anticipating friend's failure, Jeremiah 20:10.
Betrayed by friends, Lamentations 1:2, 19.
Best friend untrustworthy, Micah 7:5 (CEV).
Friends of paralytic man, Mark 2:1–12; Luke 5:17–26.
Letter to friend, Luke 1:1 (LB).
Definition of friend, John 15:12–17.
"My friend," Romans 2:1–3 (GNB).
Friendly to many, Romans 16:1–2.
Conduct of true friend, 2 Timothy 1:16–18.

FRUSTRATION
Frustrated with life, Job 6:11.
"Months of emptiness," Job 7:3 (NRSV).
Plans torn apart, Job 17:11 (CEV).
Two-handed frustration, Ecclesiastes 4:6 (KJV).

FUGITIVE
Fugitive of Moses, Exodus 2:11–15.
Sheltering a slave, Deuteronomy 23:15–16.

David's flight from Saul, 1 Samuel 21:10–11.
Flight from revenge murder, 2 Samuel 13:30–38.
Fugitive slaves, 1 Kings 2:39–40.
Holy family's escape to Egypt, Matthew 2:13–15.
Return of fugitive, Philemon 1–25.

FUN

Living for fun, James 5:5 (LB).
"Wild parties," 2 Peter 2:13 (CEV).

FUTURE

Promise to Abraham, Genesis 13:14–17; 15:1–21. (Note: some "dust of the earth" as Jewish or earthly family, "the stars" as the future church or heavenly family.)
God's promise to David, 2 Samuel 7:12.
Invincible plan, Job 42:2.
Future assured, Psalms 2:7–9; 25:14.
All in God's hands, Psalm 31:15.
Future hope, Psalm 37:37.
Hope for the future, Psalm 42:5.
Fear of future, Psalm 55:4–5.
Children not yet born, Psalms 78:6; 102:18; Isaiah 49:1.
Future of evil, Psalm 92:6–7.
Bright path of righteous, Proverbs 4:18.
Future in God's hands, Proverbs 20:24.
Boast about future, Proverbs 27:1.
Enjoy present, accept future, Ecclesiastes 3:22.
God plans future, Isaiah 14:24; Jeremiah 29:11–13.
New future assured, Isaiah 43:19; Habakkuk 2:3.
Future in God's hands, Isaiah 46:8–11; 1 Corinthians 2:9–10.
Tools of fortune-teller, Isaiah 65:11.
Good news, bad news, Jeremiah 34:1–7.
Book of future, Daniel 10:20 (LB).
Prophecy hidden from prophet, Daniel 12:8–9, 13.
Future growth assured, Micah 7:11.
Death, resurrection foretold, Matthew 16:21; 20:17–19.
Angel prophesied John the Baptist's future, Luke 1:11–17.
Confidence in unseen future, 2 Corinthians 4:18.
Foreseen future, Galatians 3:8.
Fulfillment of future, Ephesians 1:9–10.
Citizenship in Heaven, Philippians 3:20–21.
Son in body of ancestor, Hebrews 7:9–10.

Uncertain future, James 4:13–16.
Imperishable future inheritance, 1 Peter 1:3–4.
Unlimited future blessing, 1 John 3:1–3.
Sure word of prophecy, Revelation 22:10.

G

GAMBLING
"Throwing dice before the Lord," Joshua 14:1–2 (LB).
Make a bet, Judges 14:12 (CEV).
Gambling for Christ's robe, John 19:23–24.

GANGS
Street gangs, Proverbs 1:10–16 (LB).
Prostitute son's gang, Judges 11:1–3 (RSV).

GARDENER
Adam as Eden's gardener, Genesis 2:15 (LB).
Consecrated gardeners encounter impurity, Isaiah 66:17.
Gardens to be planted, Jeremiah 29:5.
God as gardener, John 15:1 (CEV, NIV).
Jesus mistaken as gardener, John 20:15.

GENEROSITY
Generous giving with willing heart, Exodus 25:2.
Consistent generosity, Psalm 37:26.

GARDENER

Deserved generosity, Proverbs 3:27–28.
Giving to poor is lending to the Lord, Proverbs 19:17.
Blessing for generous man, Proverbs 22:9.
Generous to all, Matthew 5:42.
Secret acts of charity, Matthew 6:1–4.
Generous payment in vineyard, Matthew 20:1–16.
"Generous hearts," Acts 2:46 (NRSV).
Extreme poverty induces generosity, 2 Corinthians 8:2 (NRSV).
Generosity of poor, 2 Corinthians 8:2–5 (GNB).
Grace of giving, 2 Corinthians 8:7.
Generosity rewarded, 2 Corinthians 9:6–11.
Holy Spirit's fruit, Galatians 5:22 (NRSV).
God's generous grace, Ephesians 1:7–8.

GENETICS

Like father, like son, Genesis 5:1–3.
Genetic animal experiment, Genesis 30:37–39.
Seeds, animals, Leviticus 19:19.
Productive cattle, Job 21:10 (KJV).

GENUINE

Genuine and false foundations, Matthew 7:24–27.
Authentic Messiah, Matthew 11:1–5.
Genuine wisdom, Acts 5:33–39.
Genuine friendship, Acts 9:26–27.
Seal of genuineness, 2 Corinthians 1:21–22.
Marks of Jesus, Galatians 6:17 (See Berk.).
Validity of faith, 1 Thessalonians 1:8–10.
True son in faith, 1 Timothy 1:2.
Nongenuine profession, 1 John 2:4–6.

GESTURE

Shake out lap, Nehemiah 5:13 (KJV, NIV).
Eyes, feet, fingers, Proverbs 6:13.
Prophet's hand clap, Ezekiel 21:14.
Clap hands, stomp feet, Ezekiel 25:6.
Dipping into dish, Matthew 26:23 (GNB).
Use of hand gestures, Acts 13:16.

GIFT

Betrothal gifts, Genesis 24:53.
Gifts for Joseph in Egypt, Genesis 43:11–15.
Gifts for estranged brothers, Genesis 45:21–23.
Gift of spring water, Judges 1:13–15.

Town given as gift, 1 Samuel 27:5-6.
Gift from plunder, 1 Samuel 30:26.
Royal gift, 1 Kings 10:10; 2 Chronicles 9:12.
Gifts celebrate prosperity, Job 42:10-11.
Seeking favor with gifts, Psalm 45:12 (Berk.).
Divine promise, Psalm 84:11.
Secret gift, Proverbs 21:14.
Gift for departing visitor, Jeremiah 40:5.
Parting gifts, Micah 1:14 (CEV).
Gifts of Magi, Matthew 2:11.
Gift of rest, Matthew 11:28.
Water given as gift, Revelation 21:6 (NRSV).

GIVING

Giving from the heart, Exodus 25:2; 35:5.
Generosity provides abundance, Deuteronomy 15:1-6 (LB).
Freewill offering, Deuteronomy 16:10.
Wholehearted giving, 1 Chronicles 29:9.
According to ability, Ezra 2:69.
Challenge to tithe, Malachi 3:10.
Giving to glorify God, Matthew 6:1-4.
Widow's mite, Mark 12:42; Luke 21:2.
First day giving, 1 Corinthians 16:2.
Giving in sparse times, 2 Corinthians 8:2-7.
Sowing and reaping, 2 Corinthians 9:6-7.

GLUTTONY

Manna, maggots, Exodus 16:18-27.
Enforced gluttony, Numbers 11:18-20, 31-34.
Craving for meat, Deuteronomy 12:20.
Knife to throat, Proverbs 23:1-3.
Sure road to poverty, Proverbs 23:21.
Too much honey, Proverbs 25:16.
Overstuffed fool, Proverbs 30:21-22.
Full stomach hinders sleep, Ecclesiastes 5:12 (NASB).
Best meats, finest wine, Isaiah 25:6.
Stuffed with food, Isaiah 28:1 (CEV).
Canine gluttony, Isaiah 56:11.
Symbolic gluttony, Jeremiah 51:34.
Affluent gluttony, Amos 6:4-7.
Eat, drink, be merry, Luke 12:19-20.
Sacrilegious eating, 1 Corinthians 11:20-22.
Physical hunger, spiritual supply, 1 Corinthians 11:34.

Immoral gluttony, Ephesians 4:19.
Stomach as god, Philippians 3:19.

GOAL

Desire for full obedience, Psalm 119:1–5.
Eyes on goal, Proverbs 4:25–27.
Man's plans, God's purposes, Proverbs 19:21.
Goal oriented, Isaiah 32:8; Jeremiah 32:38–39.
Enlarged goals, Isaiah 54:2–3.
Self-centered goals, Jeremiah 45:4–5.
"Aim in life," 2 Timothy 3:10 (NRSV).

GOD

God seen by humans, Genesis 12:7; 16:13–14; 17:1; 18:1;
    26:2; 35:9; Exodus 3:16; 1 Kings 3:5; 9:2; 2 Chronicles
    1:7; 3:1; Isaiah 6:1–9.
God defined, Exodus 3:13–14.
Two of God's names, Exodus 6:3 (KJV).
Angel mistaken for God, Judges 13:21–23.
God destroys enemies, 1 Samuel 15:1–10.
Limiting God, 1 Kings 20:28.
God's attributes, actions, Nehemiah 9:6–37.
God accused of wrong, Job 7:2–3 (CEV).
Questioning God, Job 9:24 (AB).
Unfathomable God, Job 11:7.
Enmity with God, Job 22:21 (GNB).
God thought ignoring wrong, Job 24:12 (AB).
Declaring God's greatness, Job 36:22–26.
Age of God, Job 36:26.
God of creation, Job 38 – 39.
Presuming "God is dead," Psalm 10:4 (LB).
God's anger, love, Psalm 30:5.
Awesome God, Psalm 47:2.
"Friend of mine," Psalm 54:4 (LB).
God's name, Psalm 68:4 (NKJV).
The Lord awakens, Psalm 78:65.
Divine love, happiness, Psalm 80:3 (LB).
"God of gods," Psalm 84:7 (NRSV).
Hidden God, Psalm 89:46.
Creator greater than creation, Psalm 108:4–5.
God consciousness in human hearts, Ecclesiastes 3:11.
Omniscient God, Isaiah 40:13–14.
First, last, only, Isaiah 44:6.
Incomparable God, Isaiah 46:5.

God never forgets, Isaiah 49:15.
God's thoughts above man's thoughts, Isaiah 55:8–9.
Unprecedented God, Isaiah 64:4.
Accusing God, Jeremiah 4:10.
Near, far, Jeremiah 23:23.
God's visible glory, Ezekiel 43:1–5.
God identified among "holy gods," Daniel 5:11.
God visualized, Daniel 7:9.
God's thoughts, Amos 4:13 (CEV).
Forgiving God, Micah 7:18–19.
Misconception about God, Zephaniah 1:12.
"Abba, Father," Mark 14:36; Romans 8:15; Galatians
    4:6 (Note: Spanish Bible translates word **Pepito** as
    "Daddy.")
God incarnate in Christ, John 10:30; 14:9–14.
See God through Jesus, John 12:44–46.
All-encompassing goodness, Romans 4:16.
Kind and stern, Romans 11:22.
Mediator between God and men, 1 Timothy 2:5.
Majestic God, Hebrews 8:1.
God's great love, 1 John 3:1–3.

GODS AND GODDESSES
"All of you are gods," Psalm 82:6 (CEV).
God of gods, Psalm 136:2.
Queen of Heaven, Jeremiah 7:18.
God identified among "holy gods," Daniel 5:11.
Goddess Artemis, Acts 19:24, 28, 35.
Nonexistent gods, Galatians 4:8 (AB).

GOLDEN RULE
First statement of Golden Rule, Leviticus 19:18.
Negative reciprocation, Leviticus 24:19–20.
Memories of Egypt, Deuteronomy 10:19; 24:17–18.
Returning lost property, Deuteronomy 22:1–3.
Bad example of others, Deuteronomy 25:17–18.
Golden rule exemplified, 2 Kings 6:8–23.
Evil for good, Psalm 35:12.
Golden Rule reversed, Psalm 109:5; Proverbs 21:13;
    24:29; Matthew 18:21–35; Galatians 5:15.
Old Testament negative, Proverbs 24:29.
Golden Rule Old Testament version, Obadiah 15.
Mercy to those who show mercy, Matthew 5:7.

Criticizing, criticized, Matthew 7:1–2 (CEV, LB).
Golden Rule defined, Matthew 7:12 (See CEV).
Seeking mercy, mistreating another, Matthew 18:23–35.
Golden Rule basics, Luke 6:27–36.
Golden Rule in action, Luke 6:38 (CEV); 2 Corinthians 2:5–11; 1 Thessalonians 5:15.
Altruistic motives, 1 Corinthians 10:24.
Returning good for evil, 1 Thessalonians 2:14–16.
Inverted Golden Rule, 2 Thessalonians 1:6 (AB).
Golden Rule stated negatively, Revelation 18:6.

GOOD WORKS

Trying to do right, Psalm 26:9–11 (LB).
Good works insufficient for salvation, Matthew 19:16–26; Romans 10:5 (LB).
Scope of good works, Matthew 25:35–36.
Good works rewarded, Matthew 26:6–13.
Conduct toward enemies, Luke 6:35.
Roman built synagogue, Luke 7:1–4 (See LB).
Patriotic, religious good works, Luke 7:4–5.
"Lovely fruit," John 15:16 (LB).
Rewarded good works, Romans 2:5–11.
Faith in action, 1 Thessalonians 1:3; James 2:17–18.
Rich in good deeds, 1 Timothy 6:18.
Sin of not doing good, James 4:17.

GOSSIP

Speak neither good nor evil, Genesis 31:24.
Gossip condemned, Leviticus 19:16.
Basic rule for gossips, Numbers 23:8.
Giving false testimony, Deuteronomy 19:16–21.
Intimidation for pay, Nehemiah 6:12–13.
Secret report, Job 4:12.
Avoid private gossip, Job 19:4.
Scorn consumed like water, Job 34:7.
Pray for those who hurt you, Job 42:10.
Only God knows how many foes, Psalm 3:1–2.
Dishonest words, Psalm 5:9.
Neighborhood lies, Psalm 12:2.
Divine vindication, Psalm 17:2.
Committed not to gossip, Psalm 17:3; Proverbs 4:24.
Gossip hinders happiness, Psalm 34:12–13.
Gossip against brother, Psalm 50:20.

Gossip as sin, Psalm 59:12.
Lying mouths silenced, Psalm 63:11.
Hatred without reason, Psalm 69:4.
Neighborhood gossip, Psalm 101:5; Proverbs 11:9; 1 Timothy 5:13.
Lying tongues, Psalm 109:1–3.
Target for gossip, Psalm 109:25, 29, 31.
Scriptural protection against gossip, Psalm 119:69–70, 78.
Prayer when hurt by gossip, Psalms 120:1–2; 123:3–4, Lamentations 3:55–66.
Gossip like snake's fangs, Psalm 140:3.
Avoiding gossip, Psalm 141:3; Luke 6:37; Ephesians 4:29.
Corrupt mouth, Proverbs 6:12–14; Micah 6:12.
Pride, behavior, gossip, Proverbs 8:13.
Speech of righteous, of wicked, Proverbs 10:11.
Fool's gossip, Proverbs 10:18.
Gossip betrays confidence, Proverbs 11:13; 20:19; 25:9.
Healing tongue, deceitful tongue, Proverbs 15:4.
Sin of listening to gossip, Proverbs 17:4.
"Choice morsels" for gossip, Proverbs 18:8 (LB); 26:22.
Gossip's potential harm, Proverbs 25:18 (LB); Galatians 5:15.
Silence combats gossip, Proverbs 26:20; Amos 5:13.
Hatred-motivated gossip, Proverbs 26:28.
Power of words, Isaiah 29:20–21.
Confidence overcomes gossip, Isaiah 51:7.
Deceitful tongue, Jeremiah 9:3.
Bloody tales, Ezekiel 22:9.
Gossip set to music, Micah 2:4.
Punishment for those who mock, Zephaniah 2:9–10.
Satan the accuser, Zechariah 3:1–2.
Joseph wanted to protect Mary from gossip, Matthew 1:19.
Rejoice when victimized by gossip, Matthew 5:11–12.
Judging, criticizing, Matthew 7:1–5; Romans 14:13; 1 Corinthians 10:27–29.
Gossip attacks against Jesus, Matthew 9:10–12; 11:18–19; Mark 14:53–59; John 7:12.
Words condemn or acquit, Matthew 12:37.
Gossip denotes unclean heart, Matthew 15:10–20.
Avoid going public, Matthew 18:15–17.
Silence of Jesus, Matthew 27:12–14.

Rejoice when criticized for faith, Luke 6:22–23.
Inaccurate gossip, John 7:24; 8:3–11.
Deceitful tongues, Romans 3:13.
Response to hurtful gossip, Romans 12:14.
Attitude toward weakness, Romans 14:1.
Love prevents gossip, 1 Corinthians 13:6.
Spiritual solution to gossip, Galatians 6:1–5.
Conversation full of grace, Colossians 4:6.
Positive "gossip," Colossians 4:7; 1 Thessalonians 3:6.
Minding one's own business, 1 Thessalonians 4:11.
Godless chatter, 1 Timothy 6:20; 2 Timothy 2:16.
Slander no one, Titus 3:2; James 4:11–12 (CEV).
Fear of man, Hebrews 13:6.
Guard tongue well, James 3:3–6.
Decline retribution, 1 Peter 3:9.
Shaming those who gossip, 1 Peter 3:16.
Insulted because of name of Christ, 1 Peter 4:14.
Pride leads to gossip, 3 John 9–10.
Those who do not lie, Revelation 14:5.

GOVERNMENT

Government for the people, Genesis 41:25–57.
Scriptural attitude toward government, Matthew 22:18–21; Acts 5:29; Romans 13:1–7; 1 Timothy 2:1–3.
Fairness in time of famine, Genesis 47:13–26.
Civil disobedience, Exodus 1:15–21.
Change of leadership, Exodus 2:23–25.
Respecting church, state, Deuteronomy 17:12.
Senseless nation, Deuteronomy 32:28.
Monarchy replaces theocracy, 1 Samuel 8:1–22.
God's preference, man's choice, 1 Samuel 10:17–19.
Good government procedure, 1 Samuel 12:13–25.
Respect for disliked leader, 1 Samuel 24:1–11; 26:9–10.
Immorality in politics, 2 Samuel 3:6–11.
Government departments, 2 Samuel 8:15–18; 20:23–26; 1 Kings 4:1–7.
Fairness to all, 2 Samuel 8:15.
Solomon's cabinet, 1 Kings 4:1–7.
Solomon's good, large reign, 1 Kings 4:20–21.
Servant leader, people serving, 1 Kings 12:7.
David's good leadership, 1 Chronicles 18:14.
Good government, corrupt citizens, 2 Chronicles 27:2.
Obey God and government, Ezra 7:26.
Government travel authorization, Nehemiah 2:1–8.

Government for the people, Esther 10:3.
Fate of world governments, Psalm 2:7–9.
God over nations, Psalm 9:7–8.
Nations dig pit, fall in, Psalm 9:15.
Righteous government and citizens, Proverbs 14:34.
Government secured by love, Proverbs 20:28.
Detestable prayers of lawbreakers, Proverbs 28:9.
Hiding from evil government, Proverbs 28:28.
Good, bad government, Proverbs 29:2.
Sobriety, good government, Proverbs 31:4–7.
City government, Proverbs 31:23.
Discontent with government, Ecclesiastes 4:13–16.
Government controlled by children, Isaiah 3:4.
Unjust laws, oppressive decrees, Isaiah 10:1–4.
Community in turmoil, Isaiah 22:2.
Exemplary government, Isaiah 32:1–4.
All governments displease God, Isaiah 34:2.
Lost confidence in government, Jeremiah 4:9.
Government for good of people, Jeremiah 29:4–7.
Local government, Jeremiah 30:20.
King, priest forsaken, Lamentations 2:6.
Misguided by evil government, Ezekiel 11:1–4.
Wicked government officials, Ezekiel 22:27.
High position in pagan government, Daniel 2:48–49.
Distinguished government position, Daniel 6:3.
God's guidance refused, Hosea 8:4.
King given, taken away, Hosea 13:11.
Continued sinning, certain judgment, Amos 1:3, 6, 9,
    11, 13.
Leaderless people, Habakkuk 1:14.
Evil government leadership, Malachi 3:5.
Government taxes, Matthew 22:15–22; Luke 20:21–25.
Census at time of Jesus' birth, Luke 2:1–5.
Government action refused, Acts 18:12–17.
Pagan official rebuked religious dispute, Acts 19:35–
    41.
Government leaders serve divine purposes, Romans
    9:17–18.
Submission to authorities, Romans 13:1–7; Titus 3:1;
    Hebrews 13:17; 1 Peter 2:13–17.
City director of public works, Romans 16:23.
Privileged citizenship, Ephesians 2:19–20.
Spiritual citizenship, Philippians 3:20.

Praying for government, 1 Timothy 2:1–4.
World government, Revelation 13:7.
One-hour reign of ten kings, Revelation 17:12.

GRAVE

Desecrated graves, Jeremiah 9:5, 8.
Not to be touched, Numbers 19:16–18.
Preferred to earthly home, Job 17:13.
Wishing burial near parents' grave, 2 Samuel 19:37.
Respect for dead bodies, 2 Samuel 21:13–14.
Zero activity in grave, Ecclesiastes 9:10.
Rock-hewn graves, Isaiah 22:16.
Ignominious burial, Jeremiah 22:19.
Grave robbed of victory, 1 Corinthians 15:55.

GRAVITY

Earth forces, Psalm 104:5 (LB).
Law of gravity, Proverbs 26:27.

GREED

Greed for land, Genesis 13:5–7; Deuteronomy 2:5.
Dispute over water rights, Genesis 26:19–22.
Manna supply forbids greed, Exodus 16:16–18.
"They grew fat on plunder," Judges 5:7 (NRSV).
Interested only in money, 1 Samuel 8:3 (GNB).
Payment sought for master's ministry, 2 Kings 5:20–27.
Greed causing harm of others, Psalm 52:7.
Greedy prayer, Psalm 106:14–15.
No thought of kindness, Psalm 109:16.
Greed hurts family, Proverbs 15:27.
Three things never satisfied, Proverbs 30:15–16.
Money never satisfies, Ecclesiastes 5:10.
"Greedy dogs," Isaiah 56:11 (Berk.).
Dishonest gain, Jeremiah 17:11; 22:17.
Prospering from another's failure, Ezekiel 26:1–3.
Selfish shepherds, Ezekiel 34:2.
Greed for plunder, Amos 3:10.
Grape pickers leave a few grapes, Obadiah 5.
Wealth by extortion, Habakkuk 2:6, 9 (CEV).
Greedy as wolves, Zephaniah 3:3.
"What will we get?" Matthew 19:27 (CEV).
Thirty silver coins, Matthew 26:14–16, 47–50.
Folly of material greed, Luke 12:13–21.
Christianity for personal advantage, Romans 16:17–18.

Greedy lust, Ephesians 4:19.
Greed for money, 1 Timothy 6:9–10.
Unsatisfied greed, James 4:1–2.
Corrosion of gold and silver, James 5:1–3.

GRIEF

Father's grief, Genesis 37:33–35.
Time of mourning concluded, Genesis 50:4.
Shaving head of mourner, Deuteronomy 14:1–2.
Grief for ark greater than for sons, 1 Samuel 4:16–18.
Death of grieving widow, 1 Samuel 4:19–20.
Personal grief put aside, 2 Samuel 19:1–8.
Unmanly grief, Job 6:2 (AB).
Eyes grown dim, Job 17:7.
Eyes weakened by sorrow, Psalm 6:7.
No song for heavy heart, Proverbs 25:20.
Grieving the Holy Spirit, Isaiah 63:10; Ephesians 4:30.
Professional grief, Jeremiah 9:17–20.
Grief-stricken city, Lamentations 1:4.
Grief of Jesus, Luke 19:41–44.
Grief of others remembered, 2 Timothy 1:3–4.
Refusal to repent, Revelation 16:10–11.

GROCERIES

Grocery shopping, John 4:8.
Meat market products, 1 Corinthians 10:25 (NASB, NKJV, NRSV).

GRUDGE

Do not seek revenge, Leviticus 19:18; Proverbs 20:22; 24:29.
Golden Rule exempted, Proverbs 24:29.
Repaying evil for evil, Romans 12:17; 1 Peter 3:9.
Avoid grudges, Colossians 3:13 (LB).

GUARANTEE

God's promise to Noah, Genesis 9:8–16.
Son's guarantee to father, Genesis 42:37.
Guarantee well-being, Psalm 119:122 (NRSV).
Eternal life guaranteed, 1 John 5:11–12.

GUILT

Passing blame to others, Genesis 3:8–13, 17–19.
Cain's denial of guilt, Genesis 4:8–10.

Guilt less than murder, Genesis 37:19–27.
Circumstantial evidence, Genesis 39:6–20.
False accusation, Genesis 39:11–20.
Fabricated guilt, Genesis 44:1–34.
Murder exposed, Exodus 2:11–14.
Old Testament scapegoat, Leviticus 16:20–22.
One brings guilt upon all, Numbers 16:22.
Clergy responsibility, Numbers 18:1.
Guilt of leadership, Numbers 20:12.
Insufficient murder witness, Numbers 35:30; Deuteronomy 17:6; 19:15.
False witness, Deuteronomy 19:16–19.
Sacrifice for unsolved guilt, Deuteronomy 21:1–9.
Guilty before God, man, 1 Samuel 2:22–25.
Plea for evidence of guilt, 1 Samuel 20:1.
Accused of murder for abetting suicide, 2 Samuel 1:1–16.
Parable of guilt, 2 Samuel 12:1–7.
Claim of righteousness, innocence, 2 Samuel 22:21–25.
Executing fathers, sparing sons, 2 Kings 14:5–6.
"Do not cover their guilt," Nehemiah 4:5 (NRSV).
Agonizing guilt, Psalm 38:4; Proverbs 28:17.
Awareness of sin, guilt, Psalm 51:3.
Guilt added to guilt, Psalm 69:27 (NRSV).
God's forgiveness, Psalm 130:3–4.
Evil attitude toward guilt, Proverbs 17:15.
Those who accuse guilty, Proverbs 24:24–25.
Abundant guilt, Isaiah 1:4.
Guilt atoned by fire, Isaiah 6:6–7.
Past guilt, Isaiah 43:18.
Indelible guilt stain, Jeremiah 2:22.
Disgrace of getting caught, Jeremiah 2:26.
Innocence proclaimed, guilt obvious, Jeremiah 2:34–35.
Sincere disgrace realizing sinfulness, Jeremiah 3:24–25.
Total forgiveness, Jeremiah 50:20.
Ezekiel bearing sin of people, Ezekiel 4:4–6.
Degrees of sin in God's sight, Ezekiel 16:48–52.
Parents and children responsible for sin, Ezekiel 18:4–20.
Innocent congregation, guilty priests, Hosea 4:4 (CEV).
Blamed for prostitution, Hosea 4:13–14 (See CEV).
Casting lots to determine guilt, Jonah 1:7.
Admitting guilt, Jonah 1:10–12.
Guilt cannot be overlooked, Micah 6:11.

Guilt must be punished, Nahum 1:3.
Unpardonable sin, Matthew 12:31–32.
Hypocrisy akin to murder, Matthew 23:29–32.
Accomplice to murder, Matthew 26:14–16; 27:3.
Delayed realization, Mark 14:66–72.
Guilty of much, of less, Luke 7:36–50.
Indictment of Pharisees, Luke 11:45–54.
Hidden guilt, John 3:20.
Universal guilt, John 8:6–11.
Morsel of bread to implicate guilt, John 13:21–27.
"Not guilty," John 19:6 (LB).
Sin of ignorance, Acts 3:17; 1 Timothy 1:12–14.
Approving wrong done by others, Acts 8:1.
Guilt by snake bite, Acts 28:1–6.
Guilt of self-righteousness, Romans 2:1–16.
No accounting of past sins, Romans 4:8 (GNB).
Blame for evil placed on women, 1 Timothy 2:14.
Deserved punishment for wilful sin, Hebrews 10:28–31.
Those who turn backs, 2 Peter 2:20–22.
Guilty of all, 1 Samuel 15:23; James 2:10.

G

GUITAR

Heaven's guitars, Revelation 5:8 (AB).

GUITAR

H

HABIT
Serving God habitually, Genesis 24:40 (AB).
Habitual sin, Psalm 92:9 (Berk.).
Cursing habitually, Psalm 109:17–19.
Habitual disobedience, Jeremiah 2:5 (AB).
Habitual evil, Jeremiah 13:23; 22:21; Micah 2:1; Ephesians 2:2 (AB).
Habitual idolatry, Hosea 4:12 (AB).
Habitual joy, confidence, Romans 5:4–5 (AB).
Habitual hospitality, Romans 12:13 (LB).
Habitually spiritual, Galatians 5:16 (AB); 2 Peter 1:5–8.
Enslaved by what masters you, 2 Peter 2:19.
Habitual sin, 1 John 3:9 (AB).

HANDS
Holding hands in time of danger, Genesis 19:16.
Prestigious right hand, Genesis 48:14.

HAIR

SAMSON HAS A BAD HAIR DAY.

Conquering right hand, Exodus 15:6.
Hands of Moses supported in battle, Exodus 17:11–12.
Sacramental hand, Leviticus 1:4.
Laying on of hands, Numbers 27:18; Deuteronomy 34:9;
	Matthew 19:15; Acts 6:6; 1 Timothy 4:14; 2 Timothy
	1:6.
Left-handed, Judges 3:15.
Right-handed murder, Judges 5:26.
Seven hundred left-handed soldiers, Judges 20:16.
Helping hand, 2 Kings 10:15.
Right-hand source, Psalm 16:8.
Uplifted hands, Psalms 28:2; 63:4.
The Lord's right hand, Psalms 48:10; 118:16.
Hands gesture praise, Psalms 134:2; 141:2.
Prayer posture, Psalm 143:6; Lamentations 2:19; 1 Ti-
	mothy 2:8.
Shake hands, Proverbs 6:1 (NKJV).
Right hand in oath, Isaiah 62:8.
Hand of judgment, Daniel 5:5–6.
Secrets between hands, Matthew 6:3.
Healing hands, Matthew 9:25; Mark 6:5; 7:32; Luke
	4:40; 13:13; Acts 3:7; 9:41; 28:8.
Hands washed of guilt, Deuteronomy 21:6; Psalm
	26:6–7; Matthew 27:24.
Speaking with signing, Luke 1:62.
Too hasty with hands, 1 Timothy 5:22.

HANDSOME

Handsome young man, 1 Samuel 9:2 (NKJV).
Boy David, 1 Samuel 16:12.
Handsome Absalom, 2 Samuel 14:25 (GNB).
Most handsome man, Psalm 45:2 (NRSV).
Outstanding among ten thousand, Song of Songs 5:10.
Handsome princes, Lamentations 4:7.
Attractive young men, Zechariah 9:17.

HAPPINESS

Happy eating, Deuteronomy 27:7.
Everyone very happy, 1 Chronicles 12:40 (CEV).
Strength in happiness, Nehemiah 8.10.
Reading Scriptures daily, Nehemiah 8:17–18.
Heart's desire, Psalm 37:4.
Oil of joy, Psalm 45:7; Hebrews 1:9.
Promised happiness, Psalm 97:11.
Key to happiness, Psalm 100:3 (LB).

Desires satisfied, strength renewed, Psalm 103:5.
Delight in Bible study, Psalm 119:24.
Enjoying fruit of labor, Psalm 128:2.
Evasive happiness, Ecclesiastes 1:16–18; 6:8 (AB).
Crown of happiness, Isaiah 35:10 (CEV); 51:11 (CEV).
Forgotten happiness, Lamentations 3:17 (RSV, GNB).
"Make everyone happy," Luke 2:10 (CEV).
Banquet for Jesus, Luke 5:27–35.
Living water from within, John 7:37–39.
Joy complete, John 15:11.
Sharing comfort through experience, 2 Corinthians 1:3–5.
Theology should bring happiness, 2 Corinthians 1:24 (GNB).
Rejoice in the Lord, Philippians 4:4.
"Oil of gladness," Hebrews 1:9 (NASB, NRSV).
Joy of problems, testing, James 1:2–4.
Inexpressible happiness, 1 Peter 1:8–9.
Joy of good reputation, 3 John 3–4.
Source of happiness, Jude 24–25.

HATRED
Avoid hatred, Leviticus 19:17; Proverbs 15:17.
Mistaking love for hatred, Deuteronomy 1:27.
Hated prophet, 1 Kings 22:8.
Royal hatred, Esther 5:10–14.
Hatred without reason, Psalm 69:4.
"Perfect hatred," Psalm 139:22 (NKJV, NRSV).
Cure for hatred, Proverbs 10:12.
Love for enemies, Matthew 5:43–44.
Hating heavenly light, John 3:20 (LB).
Hatred's basic cause, John 15:18–24.
Darkness of hatred, 1 John 2:9–11.
Hatred same as murder, 1 John 3:15.
Cannot love God, hate brother, 1 John 4:20–21.

HEALING
Depending on physicians, 2 Chronicles 16:12.
Healed of leprosy, Leviticus 14:1–57 (NKJV).
The Great Healer, Psalm 103:3.
Healing blind, deaf, dumb, lame, Isaiah 35:5–6.
No balm in Gilead, Jeremiah 8:22.
Decisive healing, Jeremiah 17:14.
Useless remedies, Jeremiah 46:11.

Isaiah's prophecy of healing, Matthew 8:16–17; Isaiah 53:4.
Relationship of illness to sin, Matthew 9:1–7.
Double healing, Matthew 9:18–25.
Authority over illness, Matthew 10:1; Acts 3:11–16.
Arms, legs replaced, Matthew 15:31 (LB).
Epilepsy caused by demon, Matthew 17:14–20.
Healing increased popularity of Jesus, Mark 3:7–10.
Faith lacked for healing, Mark 6:4–6.
Fever rebuked, Luke 4:38–39.
Healing power emerged from Jesus, Luke 6:19.
Emphasizing healing above Healer, Luke 7:21–23.
Illness caused by spirit, Luke 13:10–16.
Long wait for healing, John 5:1–8.
Purpose for sickness, John 11:4.
Misunderstood healing of lame man, Acts 14:8–18.
Miracles in Paul's ministry, Acts 19:11–12.
Church sleeper restored, Acts 20:9–10.
Healing omitted among gifts, Romans 12:4–6 (See Romans 15:17–19).
Priority of healing ministry, 1 Corinthians 12:28–31.
Prayer for healing, no answer, 2 Corinthians 12:7–10.
Praying for sick, James 5:13–15.

HEALTH

Disease, sin, Leviticus 26:14–16.
Lifelong virility, Deuteronomy 34:7.
Evil spirits, poor health, 1 Samuel 16:16.
Hearty, healthful greeting, 1 Samuel 25:6.
Satan challenged God for Job's health, Job 2:3–6.
Death of healthy person, Job 5:26.
Worthless physicians, Job 13:4.
Bad breath, Job 19:17.
Wicked live to old age, Job 21:7.
Health restored, feel young again, Job 33:25 (CEV); Psalm 23:3 (LB).
Long life in answer to prayer, Psalm 21:4.
In great pain, Psalm 38:1–22.
Bodies sound, sleek, Psalm 73:4 (NRSV).
Pessimism over ill health, Psalm 116:10–11 (LB).
Healthy children, Psalm 128:3 (LB).
Fearfully, wonderfully made, Psalm 139:14.
Good news, good health, Proverbs 15:30.
Good sight, hearing, Proverbs 20:12 (LB).
Illness likened to poverty, Proverbs 22:22–23 (LB).

Dying before one's time, Ecclesiastes 7:17.
Nation of healthy citizens, Isaiah 33:24.
Fifteen years added to life, Isaiah 38:1–6.
"Please make me healthy," Isaiah 38:16 (CEV).
Forgotten health, Lamentations 3:17 (GNB).
Healthy youth for royal service, Daniel 1:3–6.
Refusing unhealthful food, Daniel 1:8–20.
Years of medical expense, Mark 5:25–26.
Impaired physically, not spiritually, Mark 9:43–48.
Crippled body caused by demon, Luke 13:10–13.
Sin as cause of ill health, John 5:14.
Responsibility for health of child, John 9:1–12.
Illness prompts Gospel ministry, Galatians 4:13–14.
Possibly poor eyesight, Galatians 6:11.
Physical training and godliness, 1 Timothy 4:8–9 (See CEV).
Keeping soul in good health, 3 John 2 (See CEV).
Health, wealth, spiritual vitality, 3 John 2–4.

HEART

Hardened hearts, Zechariah 7:12 (LB).
God knows inner heart, 1 Samuel 16:7; 1 Chronicles 28:9; Matthew 9:4.
Softened heart, Job 23:16.
Center of emotion, Psalm 26:2–3; Proverbs 4:23; Ezekiel 11:19; 36:26; Colossians 3:15–17.
Throbbing heart, Psalm 38:10 (NRSV).
Prayer for pure heart, Psalm 51:10.
Heart attitudes, Proverbs 15:13–15; Matthew 15:18–20.
Eternity in the heart, Ecclesiastes 3:11.

HEAVEN

"Firmament," Genesis 1:6–7 (KJV).
Holy dwelling place, Deuteronomy 26:15; 1 Kings 8:30; John 14:2.
Joy in heaven and earth, 1 Chronicles 16:31.
God's dwelling place, 2 Chronicles 6:33, 39.
Confused about eternal future, Job 10:19–22.
Alleged remoteness of God, Job 22:12–14 (LB).
Heaven's potential northern sky location, Job 26:7 (NKJV); Psalm 48:2 (NKJV).
More desirable than earth, Psalm 73:25.
Homesick for heaven, Psalm 84:2 (AB, Berk.).
"Holy height," Psalm 102:19 (NRSV).
Heaven as up, Ecclesiastes 3:21 (AB).

Seeing the King, Isaiah 33:17, 21.
Everlasting light, Isaiah 60:19–20.
Heaven throne, earth footstool, Isaiah 66:1.
Ministering in heaven, Zechariah 3:1–10.
Treasure site, Matthew 6:19–20.
"Highest heaven," Mark 11:10 (NRSV).
View at death, Acts 7:55–56.
Anticipating heaven, 1 Corinthians 2:9–10; 2 Corinthians 5:2 (CEV).
Heaven cleansing, Revelation 12:7–9 (AB).

HELL

Confused about eternal future, Job 10:19–22.
"Down to the pit," Job 33:24.
Depth of the earth, Psalm 63:9.
Enlarged capacity, Isaiah 5:14 (KJV).
Agreement with hell, Isaiah 28:18 (KJV).
Fires of Topheth, Isaiah 30:33.
"The world below," Ezekiel 32:19 (CEV).
Broad road to hell, Matthew 7:13 (See GNB).
Fiery furnace, Matthew 13:37–42, 49–50.
Excluded from God's presence, 2 Thessalonians 1:9.
Lake of fire, Revelation 19:19–21.
Those not in Book of Life, Revelation 20:7–15.

HELP

Divine helper, Deuteronomy 33:29; 2 Chronicles 25:8; Psalm 27:9.
Strength, shield, Psalm 28:7.
Deliverer, Psalm 40:17.
Vainly crying for help, Psalm 69:3.
Antidote to fear, Isaiah 41:10; Hebrews 13:6.
Vain cry for help, Habakkuk 1:2 (LB).
Holy Spirit as helper, John 14:16–17 (GNB).
Helping others, Romans 12:13 (LB).

HEROES

No prophet like Moses, Deuteronomy 34:10–12.
How David became famous, 2 Samuel 8:13.
Anonymous heroes, Hebrews 11:35–39.
Heroic suffering, 1 Peter 2:19.

HIGHWAY

Public thoroughfare, Numbers 20:19.
Need for highways, Deuteronomy 19:1–3.

Highways abandoned for paths, Judges 5:6.
Fortified highway, 2 Chronicles 16:1 (LB).
Intercontinental highway, Isaiah 19:23.
Holiness highway, Isaiah 35:8.
Way through desert, Isaiah 40:3–4; 43:19.
Signs, guideposts, Jeremiah 31:21.
Broad and narrow way, Matthew 7:13–14.
Dangerous highway, Luke 10:30–33.

HIKING

Long hike, no blisters, Deuteronomy 8:4 (Berk.).
Too exhausted to continue, 1 Samuel 30:10, 21.
Held to your paths, Psalm 17:5.

HISTORY

Days of old, Deuteronomy 32:7.
Extensive genealogy, 1 Chronicles 1:1–5 — 5:38.
Joseph, the unknown, Exodus 1:8.
Recorded stages of journey, Numbers 33:1–49.
Asking about former days, Deuteronomy 4:32–35.
Reading history book to induce sleep, Esther 6:1.
Future history in God's hands, Job 12:23; 34:29–30;
    Psalms 2:1–6; 113:4.
Apostasy of nations, Psalm 2:1–3.
Inevitable fate of world governments, Psalm 2:7–9.
God will have last word in history, Psalm 9:5.
Evil brings about its own retribution, Psalm 9:15.
Promise of God to Israel, Psalm 45:16.
Time when peace will cover earth, Psalm 46:8–10.
Learning from history, Psalm 77:5, 11–12.
History in song, Psalm 78:1–72; 106:1–48.
Ponder the Lord's hand in history, Psalm 111:2–4.
History repeats itself, Ecclesiastes 1:9; 3:15.
World history capsule, Ecclesiastes 9:14–15.
Evil deeds recorded, Isaiah 30:8.
Divine evaluation of nations, Isaiah 40:15–17.
God knows end from beginning, Isaiah 46:10–11.
Ruins rebuilt, Isaiah 58:12.
A nation takes time to develop, Isaiah 66:8.
Ark of Covenant forgotten, Jeremiah 3:16.
The Lord of history revealed, Ezekiel 20:42.
Date recorded for future, Ezekiel 24:2.
Image depicting world history, Daniel 2:29–45.
Divine goodness in Israel's history, Micah 6:3–5.
Words of Jesus concerning end times, Mark 13:1–37.

Many recorded New Testament events, Luke 1:1–2.
Orderly account of happenings, Luke 1:3–4.
Jesus identified with history, John 8:57–58.
Purpose of sacred history, John 20:30–31.
Inexhaustible history of Jesus, John 21:25.
History cited as defense, Acts 7:1–60.
Resume of Old Testament, gospel proclamation, Acts 13:16–41.
God's plan through history, Romans 1:1–6.
History's ultimate purpose, Romans 8:18–23.
Certain future judgment, Romans 9:28.
Lessons from history, 1 Corinthians 10:1–12.
Fulfillment of history, Ephesians 1:9–10.
Succinct history of Christ, 1 Timothy 3:16.
Demonic influence in history, Revelation 16:13–14.
When evil serves God's purpose, Revelation 17:17.

HOMELESS

Restless wanderer, Genesis 4:14.
Woman in desert, Genesis 21:14.
Israelites homeless forty years, Numbers 32:13; Acts 7:35–36; Hebrews 3:1–11.
Lack of shelter, Job 24:8.
Unable to find residence, Psalm 107:4.
Street people, Lamentations 4:5.
Wandering Jews, Hosea 9:17.
Homeless Savior, Luke 9:58.
"Festival of Shelters," John 7:2 (GNB).
Hungry, homeless, 1 Corinthians 4:11.

HOMOSEXUAL

Sodom's angelic visitors, Genesis 19:5.
Forbidden relationship, Leviticus 18:22–23; 20:13.
Male prostitutes, Deuteronomy 23:17.
Example of homosexual conduct, Judges 19:22–24.
Approved masculine love, 1 Samuel 18:1–4; 20:17–41; 2 Samuel 1:26; 19:1–6.
Eradication of deviates, 1 Kings 15:12 (See 14:24).
Male prostitutes enshrined, Job 36:14.
Boy prostitutes, Joel 3:3.
Unnatural passion and desire, Romans 1:24–27.
Homosexual activity condemned, 1 Corinthians 6:9–10.
Sexual perversion, 1 Timothy 1:10 (See AB).
Mother of perversion, Revelation 17:5 (GNB).

HONESTY

Leadership integrity, Numbers 16:15; 1 Samuel 12:1–5.
Bribe refused, 2 Samuel 18:12; 1 Kings 13:8.
Expense vouchers not needed, 2 Kings 12:15.
Honest workers, 2 Chronicles 34:12 (CEV).
Claim of honesty, Job 33:1–5.
Honesty before the Lord, Psalm 24:3–4.
Protected by integrity, Psalm 25:21.
No deceit in God's house, Psalm 101:7.
Defended by honesty, Proverbs 12:13 (LB).
Honest life-style, Proverbs 20:7.
Weights and measures, Proverbs 20:10; Ezekiel 45:9–10.
Honest answer like a kiss, Proverbs 24:26.
Honest rebuke, Proverbs 27:5.
Integrity despised, Proverbs 29:10; Amos 5:10.
Honest character desired, Proverbs 30:7–9.
Search for one honest person, Jeremiah 5:1.
"Refuse to tell lies," Zephaniah 3:13 (CEV).
Advice to tax collectors, Luke 3:12–13.
Utter honesty, 2 Corinthians 1:12 (LB).
Deceit, honesty, Ephesians 4:14–15.
Testimony of man, testimony of God, 1 John 5:9.

HONOR

Sister's disgrace avenged, 2 Samuel 13:23–29.
Honor, respect, Job 29:7–10.
Honoring God, Psalm 23:3 (LB).
Nature, people praise the Lord, Psalm 148:1–14.
Humility before honor, Proverbs 18:12.
Usurped honor, Proverbs 25:6–7.
Noble man, Isaiah 32:8.
Honor among thieves, Jeremiah 49:9.
Honored prophet, Zechariah 3:1–9.
Humility begets honor, Matthew 23:12.
Place of honor, Luke 14:8–11.
Respect of Cornelius for Peter, Acts 10:25–26.
Success must glorify God, 1 Corinthians 3:7.
Double honor, 1 Timothy 5:17.

HOPE

Keep hoping, Job 13:15 (Berk.).
Eloquent declaration of hope, Job 19:25–26.
Hope for poor, needy, Psalm 9:18.
Hope in the Lord, Psalm 31:24.

Antidote for despair, Psalm 42:5; Jeremiah 31:15–17.
Continuity of hope, Psalm 71:5.
Deferred hope, Proverbs 13:12.
Hope in death, Proverbs 14:32.
Light shining in darkness, Isaiah 60:1–2.
False promises, Jeremiah 28:1–11.
Safety in times of trouble, persecution, Jeremiah 42:1–22.
Optimism in time of pessimism, Jeremiah 48:47.
"One ray of hope," Lamentations 3:21 (LB).
Behind devastation, ahead anticipation, Joel 2:3.
Hope against all hope, Romans 4:18.
Eternal encouragement, 2 Thessalonians 2:16–17.
Blessed hope, Titus 2:11–14.
Steadfast anchor, Hebrews 6:19 (See AB).
Living hope, 1 Peter 1:3.
Resurrection hope, 2 Peter 1:13–14.
No safety in horses, Psalm 33:17; Proverbs 21:31.
Horses swifter than eagles, Jeremiah 4:13.

HUMAN RELATIONS

Handling people, Exodus 18:14–27.
Courtesy to foreigners, Exodus 23:9.
Neighborhood relationship, Leviticus 6:2.
Witness opportunities, Deuteronomy 6:4–7.
Debt canceled every seven years, Deuteronomy 15:1.
Attitude toward poor, Deuteronomy 15:7–11.
Protection of escaped slave, Deuteronomy 23:15–16.
Manner of speech, Judges 12:5–6.
Praising subject above king, 1 Samuel 21:11.
Warm salutation, 1 Samuel 25:6.
Showing favor for personal interest, 1 Samuel 27:12.
Commendation of king, 1 Samuel 29:6–7.
Share and share alike, 1 Samuel 30:24.
Misunderstood kindness, 2 Samuel 10:1–4.
Wisdom of Solomon, 1 Kings 4:29–34.
Exemplary human relations, 2 Kings 7:3–9.
Inequity among citizens, Nehemiah 5:1–5.
Wisdom in appealing to king, Esther 7:3–4.
Abandoned by friends, Job 6:14–17.
Caring for those in need, Proverbs 3:27–28.
Equity toward poor, Proverbs 29:14.
Revelation in human relations, Proverbs 29:18.
Human inequity, Proverbs 30:21–23.
Beauty for ashes, Isaiah 61:1–3.

Daily administration of justice, Jeremiah 21:12.
Justice, mercy, compassion, Zechariah 7:8–10.
Cords of human love, Hosea 11:4.
Complaining about another's generosity, Matthew 20:1–16.
Prophet without honor, Mark 6:4–6.
Greatest in kingdom, Luke 9:46–48.
Relationship between strangers, Luke 10:5–12.
Frankness of Jesus to Pharisees, Luke 11:37–54.
Desire for recognition in congregation, Luke 11:43.
Sharing with others, Luke 12:48.
Settling disputes out of court, Luke 12:58–59.
Honor for some above another, Luke 14:7–11.
Hospitality toward unbelievers, Luke 15:1–2.
Attitude of father, resentful brother, Luke 15:11–31.
Wealth in human relations, Luke 16:9.
Wrongly influencing others, Luke 17:1.
Ingratitude to foreigner, Luke 17:11–19.
Kindness to Paul, the prisoner, Acts 24:23.
Joy, gentleness, Philippians 4:4–5.
Interest in other people, Colossians 4:7.
Relating mother's gentleness, 1 Thessalonians 2:7–8.
Mind your own business, 1 Thessalonians 4:11.
Paying poor wages, James 5:4.

HUMILIATION

Imposed guilt of Joseph's brothers, Genesis 44:1–34.
Locals humiliated by aliens, Deuteronomy 28:43–44.
Cutting off thumbs and big toes, Judges 1:7.
Humiliation over another's success, 1 Samuel 18:7 (See 21:11; 29:5).
Act of kindness misinterpreted, 2 Samuel 10:1–4.
Stripped of one's honor, Job 19:9.
"Scorn of fools," Psalm 39:8.
Fortified city humiliated, Isaiah 27:10.
Into silence, darkness, Isaiah 47:5.
Fall of Moab, Jeremiah 48:16–39.
Jerusalem humiliated, Lamentations 1:1.
Humiliation of Satan as king of Tyre, Ezekiel 28:11–19.
Added humility of the cross, Matthew 27:39–44.
Pilate's question to King of kings, Mark 15:2.
Pre-Crucifixion humiliation, John 19:1–3.
Gazingstock, Hebrews 10:33 (AB).

HUMOR *(Light touches, Whimsy)*
Sorrowful laughter, Genesis 18:10–15.
No laughing matter, Genesis 19:14.
Talking donkey, Numbers 22:21–34.
Incompatible ox, donkey, Deuteronomy 22:10.
Tent flattened by bread loaf, Judges 7:13.
Reckless adventurers, Judges 9:4.
Trees seek king, Judges 9:7–15.
Big mouths, Judges 9:38.
Earth-shaking cheer, 1 Samuel 4:5.
Brave boy meets blustering giant, 1 Samuel 17:42–47.
Hearty, healthful greeting, 1 Samuel 25:6.
Grasped by the beard, 2 Samuel 20:9.
Public relations approach, 1 Kings 1:42.
Imported apes, baboons, 1 Kings 10:22; 2 Chronicles 9:21.
Laughter and tears, Ezra 3:12–13.
Divine sarcasm, Job 38:35.
Short on smarts, Job 39:13–17.
Resourceful elephant, Job 40:15–24.
Bad-natured leviathan (crocodile), Job 41:5.

H

HUMOR

Causing God to laugh, Psalm 2:4 (LB).
God as pugilist, Psalm 3:7.
Mouths filled with laughter, Psalm 126:2.
Good news, cheerful looks, Proverbs 15:30.
Hunger makes man work harder, Proverbs 16:26.
Wisdom of silence elevates fool, Proverbs 17:28.
Stingy man's hospitality, Proverbs 23:6–8.
Drunkard's confusion, Proverbs 23:30–35.
Honest answer is like kiss, Proverbs 24:26.
Honor does not fit fool, Proverbs 26:1.
Herod the fox, Luke 13:31–32.

HUNGER

Severe famine, Genesis 12:10.
Remembering past hunger, forgetting God, Exodus 16:2–3.
Craving meat, Deuteronomy 12:20.
Hungry soldiers, 1 Samuel 14:24–30.
Motivated by appetite, Proverbs 16:26.
Dreaming of food, awakening to reality, Isaiah 29:8.
Hard work causes hunger, Isaiah 44:12.
Desperation hunger, Lamentations 1:11.
Hungry children, Lamentations 4:4.
Death from famine, Lamentations 4:9.
Feverish hunger, Lamentations 5:10.
Spiritual hunger, Amos 8:11–12; Matthew 5:6; 1 Peter 2:2.
Picking corn on Sabbath, Matthew 12:1–8.
Hunger hinders worship, 1 Corinthians 11:34.

HURT

Partial blindness as disgrace, 1 Samuel 11:2–11.
"I am hurting," Psalm 31:9 (CEV).
Comfort when hurting, Psalm 119:50 (CEV).
Hurting others, Psalm 139:24 (NASB).
Deep wounds, Lamentations 2:13.
Response when hurt by others, Luke 17:3, 4.

HUSBAND

Wife from husband's rib, Genesis 2:21–24.
Supernatural husbands, Genesis 6:4 (CEV).
Husband's involvement in wife's contracts, Numbers 30:10–15.
Husband rules household, Esther 1:22; 1 Corinthians 11:3.

Young marrieds, Proverbs 5:15–19 (See CEV).
Fury of betrayed husband, Proverbs 6:27–35.
Husband enjoying life, Ecclesiastes 9:9.
Husband's duty, Ephesians 5:25; 1 Corinthians 7:3;
   1 Peter 3:7.
Winning unsaved husband, 1 Peter 3:1–2.

HYPOCRISY

Insincere repentance, Exodus 9:27.
Feigned rapport in time of need, Judges 11:1–10.
Doing right with limitations, 2 Chronicles 25:2.
Accused of hypocrisy, Job 4:1–3; 11:4–6.
Undependable friends, Job 6:15–17.
Unable to fool God, Job 13:9.
Condemned by one's own words, Job 15:6.
Hypocritical cordiality, Psalm 28:3.
Motives different from speech, Psalms 55:21; 62:4.
Hypocritical prayers incite God's anger, Psalm 80:4.
Double-minded men, Psalm 119:113.
Disguising true self by false speech, Proverbs 26:24–26.
Sincere, insincere rapport, Proverbs 27:6.
Early morning religiosity, Proverbs 27:14.
Detestable prayers of lawbreakers, Proverbs 28:9.
Meaningless oaths, Isaiah 48:1–2.
Mockery fasting, Isaiah 58:4–5.
Flagrant hypocrisy, Jeremiah 7:9–11.
Hypocritical rapport, Jeremiah 12:6.
Threat to hypocrisy, Ezekiel 14:4.
Scorned for hypocrisy, Ezekiel 16:56–57.
Listening, not practicing, Ezekiel 33:31.
Boasting hypocrite, Hosea 12:8.
God's blessing misused, Hosea 13:6.
Boasting of hypocrisy, Amos 4:4–5.
Witnessing hypocrite, Jonah 1:9.
Hypocrite leaders, priests, Micah 3:11.
Worshiping the Lord, Molech, Zephaniah 1:5.
Defiled offerings from defiled people, Haggai 2:13–14.
Hypocritical fasting, repentance, Zechariah 7:1–6.
Repenting hypocrites, Malachi 2:13.
King Herod and the Magi, Matthew 2:7–8, 13.
Satan's use of Scripture, Matthew 4:1–11.
Righteousness of the Pharisees, Matthew 5:20.
Performing righteousness in public, Matthew 6:1.
Avoid hyper-piety, Matthew 6:16–18.

Hypocrisy of Pharisees, Matthew 15:7–9; 21:31–32; 23:1–3; Luke 11:45–54.
Seeking mercy while mistreating another, Matthew 18:23–35.
Man without wedding clothes, Matthew 22:11–13.
Clean outside, filthy inside, Matthew 23:25–28.
Hypocrisy akin to murder, Matthew 23:29–32.
Faithful, unfaithful service, Matthew 24:45–51.
Lip service, Mark 7:6.
Hypocrite miracles, Mark 9:38–41.
Practice what you preach, Luke 3:7–8.
Identification of hypocrite, Luke 13:23–27.
Hypocritical honesty, Luke 20:20.
Hypocrite's praise, John 5:41–42.
Devious search for salvation, John 10:1.
Hypocrite's judging others, Romans 2:1.
Saying one thing, doing another, Romans 2:21–24.
Those who cause divisions, Romans 16:17–18.
Social hypocrisy, Galatians 2:11–13.
Insincere attention, Galatians 4:17.
Hypocritical pretense, Galatians 6:12–15.
False humility, Colossians 2:18.
Hypocritical godliness, 2 Timothy 3:5.
Unbridled tongue, James 1:26.
Profession versus possession, Titus 1:16; 1 John 2:4–6; Jude 12–13.
Walking in darkness, 1 John 1:5–7.
Disruptive hypocrite, 3 John 9–10.
Misuse of Christian liberty, Jude 4.
Feigning life when spiritually dead, Revelation 3:1.

——————————— I ———————————

IDOLATRY
Make no idols, Exodus 20:4.
Speak no idol's name, Exodus 23:13.
Food for idols, Exodus 34:15; Acts 21:25; 1 Corinthians 8:1–6.
Death to idolaters, Numbers 25:5.
God never appears as image, Deuteronomy 4:15–16.
Secret idols, Deuteronomy 27:15.
Making idol to please the Lord, Judges 17:3.
Toppled idol, 1 Samuel 5:1–5.
Strange use of idol, 1 Samuel 19:13–16.

Abandoned idols, 2 Samuel 5:21.
Idolatrous king, 2 Chronicles 28:1–4.
Repentant idolater, 2 Chronicles 33:1–17.
Idolatry put away, 2 Chronicles 34:1–7.
Worthless idols, Psalm 31:6.
Creator versus idols, Psalm 96:5.
Graphic description of idols, Psalm 115:2–8.
Idols made by hands, Psalm 135:15–18; Jeremiah 16:20.
Israel's superstitions, Isaiah 2:6–8.
Idolatry described, Isaiah 44:9–20.
Shamed idol makers, Isaiah 45:16.
Ignorance of idol worship, Isaiah 45:20.
Burdensome images, Isaiah 46:1.
Impotent idols, Isaiah 46:6–7.
As many gods as towns, Jeremiah 2:28; 11:15.
Queen of Heaven, Jeremiah 7:18.
Worthless, silly idols, Jeremiah 10:15 (LB); Jonah 2:8.
Futility of idols, Ezekiel 6:13.
Idols in the heart, Ezekiel 14:1–11.
Children sacrificed to idols, Ezekiel 23:37.
Decorative images in temple, Ezekiel 41:17–20.
Image built by Nebuchadnezzar, Daniel 3:1–6.
Misuse of God's provisions, Hosea 2:8.
Worship of what hands have made, Hosea 14:3.
False security of man-made idols, Habakkuk 2:18–19.
Worship of men, Acts 14:8–18.
Athenian idolatry, Acts 17:16–34.
Gospel hindered idol makers, Acts 19:20–41.
Worshiping created, not Creator, Romans 1:25.
"No such thing as an idol," 1 Corinthians 8:4 (NASB).
Pagan idols actually demons, 1 Corinthians 10:20.
Led astray to dumb idols, 1 Corinthians 12:2.
Keep yourself from idols, 1 John 5:21.
Idols into lake of fire, Revelation 21:8; 22:15.

IDLENESS

WORKER ANT

NON-WORKER ANT

IGNORANCE

Sins of ignorance, Leviticus 22:14; Numbers 15:22–26; Hosea 4:5–6; Luke 23:34; John 16:2; 1 Timothy 1:13.
Innate ignorance, Job 11:7–8; 28:12–13; Psalm 139:6.
Ignorance covered by lies, Job 13:4 (GNB).
Foolish ignorance, Psalm 73:22 (NKJV).
Ignorance of future, Proverbs 27:1; Jeremiah 10:23.
Illiteracy, Isaiah 29:11–12.
Closed eyes, Isaiah 44:18.
Senseless skill, Jeremiah 10:14.
Pretended ignorance, Luke 22:57–60.
Altar to unknown god, Acts 17:23.
Ignorance overlooked, Acts 17:30.
Inexcusable guilt, Romans 1:19–25.
Spiritual ignorance, 1 Corinthians 2:7–10.
Partial ignorance, 1 Corinthians 13:12.
Willful ignorance, 1 Corinthians 15:34 (AB).
Uninformed opinions, 1 Timothy 1:7.
Ignorant, misguided, Hebrews 5:2 (NASB).
Ignorance with confidence, Hebrews 11:8.
That which is not understood, Jude 10.

ILLNESS

Illness caused by sin, Leviticus 26:14–16; Matthew 9:1–7; John 5:14.
Hezekiah's illness, recovery, 2 Chronicles 32:24–26.
Satanic illness, Job 2:6–7.
Instructive illness, Job 33:14, 19–21.
Afflicted since youth, Psalm 88:15.
Will to live, Proverbs 18:14 (GNB).
Extensive medical expense, Mark 5:25–26.
Illness rebuked, Luke 4:38–39.
Illness caused by spirit, Luke 13:10–16.
Invalid for thirty-eight years, John 5:1–9.
Present suffering, coming glory, Romans 8:18; 2 Corinthians 4:17–18.
Illness causes concern, Philippians 2:26–27.
Made perfect through suffering, Hebrews 2:10.
Value of testing, trials, problems, James 1:2–4, 12; 1 Peter 1:6–7; 4:1–2.
Praying for sick, James 5:13–15.

IMITATION

Imitating heathen, 1 Samuel 8:19–20; 2 Kings 17:15.
Faulty original cisterns, Jeremiah 2:13.

Conversion suspected as imitation, Acts 9:26–27.
Imitators invited, 1 Corinthians 4:16; Philippians 4:9.
Model to imitate, 2 Thessalonians 3:9.

IMMATURITY
"Lay aside immaturity," Proverbs 9:6 (NRSV).
Easily deceived, Hosea 7:11.
Immaturity of new convert, Acts 8:13–24.
New convert's instruction, Acts 18:24–26.
Immature believers, Acts 19:1–7.
Milk, solid food, 1 Corinthians 3:1–2.
Worldly immaturity, 1 Corinthians 3:3.
Thinking like children, 1 Corinthians 14:20 (CEV).
No longer infants, Ephesians 4:14 (See CEV).
Immature prophecies, 2 Thessalonians 2:1–2.
Unable to teach, Hebrews 5:12–13 (LB).
Spiritual immaturity, Revelation 3:8.

IMMORTALITY
Deliverance from sinful immortality, Genesis 3:22.
Enoch's walk with God, Genesis 5:24.
Angel refused temporal food, Judges 13:16.
Rejoining lost loved ones, 2 Samuel 12:23.
Chariot ascent to heaven, 2 Kings 2:11.
No desire to live forever, Job 7:16.
Confusion about immortality, Job 10:19–22; 14:7–14.
Classic statement of faith, Job 19:25–26.
Eternal inheritance, Psalm 37:18.
Confidence of immortality, Psalm 49:15.
"Surely there is a hereafter," Proverbs 23:18 (NKJV).
Eternity in hearts of men, Ecclesiastes 3:11.
Spirits of mortals, beasts, Ecclesiastes 3:21.
Resurrection of all mankind, Daniel 12:2–3.
Eternal life, John 3:14–16.
True immortality, John 8:51.
Jesus could not die before God's time, John 19:11.
Death of martyr, Acts 7:54–56.
Spiritual body, earthly body, 1 Corinthians 15:42–55.
Mortality and immortality, 2 Corinthians 5:1.
One who never changes, Hebrews 1:10–12.
Melchizedek, the immortal, Hebrews 7:1–3.
Perpetual life, Hebrews 7:8 (AB).
Blessed after life, James 5:10–11 (LB).
Born of immortal seed, 1 Peter 1:23.
Mortal body put aside, 2 Peter 1:13–14.

Divine sperm, 1 John 3:9 (AB).
Mortals unable to die, Revelation 9:6.
Immunity to second death, Revelation 20:4–6.

IMPATIENCE

Lacking patience, Genesis 16:1–4.
Impatient community, Exodus 16:2.
Divine impatience, Deuteronomy 3:26.
Too impatient, Job 6:2 (AB).
Giving vent to anger, Proverbs 29:11.
Impatience with God, Isaiah 5:18–19; 45:9.
Jonah's impatience, Jonah 4:8–9.
Impatience of Jesus, Mark 9:19; Luke 12:50.
Impatient disciples, Luke 9:51–56.
Impatient housekeeper, Luke 10:40.
Exhausted patience, Acts 18:4–6.

IMPOTENCE

Advanced in years, 1 Kings 1:1–4.
Lost desire, Ecclesiastes 12:5.
Impotent city, Ezekiel 26:2 (CEV).

INCOME

Income from prostitution unacceptable, Deuteronomy 23:18.
Protecting debtor's income, Deuteronomy 24:6.
Giving on first day of week, 1 Corinthians 16:2.
Providing income for personal ministry, 1 Thessalonians 2:9.

INDEPENDENCE

Defiant sin, Numbers 15:30–31.
Greatest independence, Psalm 119:45.
Independent of God's way, Jeremiah 11:7–8.
Truth sets free, John 8:31–32, 36.
Body as unit, 1 Corinthians 12:12–30.

INDIFFERENCE

Angels' warning taken as joke, Genesis 19:14.
Indifferent to wonders, Psalm 106:7, 13.
Indifferent women, Isaiah 32:9.
Who cares? Jeremiah 12:11.
Those who pass by, Lamentations 1:12.
Indifferent to future judgment, Ezekiel 12:25–28.
Slumbering indifference, Jonah 1:5–6.

Spiritual indifference, Zephaniah 1:6.
Fate of carefree city, Zephaniah 2:15.
Indifferent priests, Malachi 1:6–14.
Rejected wedding invitation, Matthew 22:1–14.
Indifferent disciples, Mark 14:32–41.

INDULGENCE

Too much food and drink, Proverbs 23:20.
From one sin to another, Jeremiah 9:3.
Jesus accused of indulgence, Matthew 26:6–13.
Continual indulgence, Ephesians 4:19.

INFATUATION

Samson's infatuation for Delilah, Judges 14:1–3.
True love mistaken as infatuation, 1 Samuel 18:20–29.
David, Bathsheba, 2 Samuel 11:2–5.
Love like morning mist, Hosea 6:4.

INFERTILITY

Infertility in God's timing, Genesis 16:1–4.
Closed wombs, Genesis 20:17.
Husband, wife tension, Genesis 30:1–2, 22.
Beloved but barren, 1 Samuel 1:2–7.
Infertile land made productive, 2 Kings 2:19–22.
Land that produces sparingly, Isaiah 5:10.
Plight of eunuch, Isaiah 56:3–5.
Scatter salt on condemned land, Jeremiah 48:9.
Wombs that miscarry, Hosea 9:14.
Place of saltpits, Zephaniah 2:9.

INFIDELITY

Other men's wives, 1 Corinthians 10:8 (LB).

INFLATION

Inflation caused by famine, 2 Kings 6:24–25.
Declining value, James 5:3 (LB).

INFLUENCE

Like father, like son, Genesis 5:1–3.
Following wrong crowd, Exodus 23:2.
Righteous conduct, Deuteronomy 4:5–6.
Wrong family influence, Deuteronomy 13:6–10.
Influence of good women, Ruth 4:11.
Son's influence over father, 1 Samuel 19:1–6.

Bad influence of children, grandchildren, 2 Kings 17:41.

Victim of bad influence, 2 Chronicles 13:7.

Evil woman's influence, 2 Chronicles 21:6.

Challenged to use influence with king, Esther 4:12–14; 9:12–13.

Influence used for good of others, Esther 10:3.

Parental influence, Proverbs 6:20–23.

Good and bad influence, Proverbs 13:20.

Best influence of no avail, Jeremiah 15:1.

Like father, like children, Hosea 4:14.

Father's immoral influence over son, Amos 2:7.

Influencing neighbors to alcoholism, Habakkuk 2:15.

Let your light shine, Matthew 5:14–16; Philippians 2:15.

Evil influence over good, Matthew 13:24–30.

Wrong influence over children, Matthew 18:6; Mark 9:42.

Mother's desire for favors for sons, Matthew 20:20–24.

Like teacher, like student, Luke 6:40.

Influencing others to sin, Luke 17:1–3.

Plot to kill Lazarus because of influence, John 12:9–11.

Satanic influence, John 13:2.

Influence used against Paul, Barnabas, Acts 13:50.

Influential women follow Christ, Acts 17:4.

Influence of Roman Christians, Romans 1:8.

Differing influences of Christians, 2 Corinthians 2:15–16.

Convert's influence encouraged others, Galatians 1:23–24.

Persecution widened sphere of influence, Philippians 1:12–14.

Channel of much blessing, Philippians 1:25–26.

Model to other believers, 1 Thessalonians 1:7–8.

How father should deal with children, 1 Thessalonians 2:11–12.

Avoid idle brothers, 2 Thessalonians 3:6.

Desire to be influential, 1 Timothy 3:1.

Do not share sins of others, 1 Timothy 5:22.

Grandmother's faith passed on, 2 Timothy 1:5.

Influence of Scriptures since childhood, 2 Timothy 3:14–15.

Avoid favoritism, James 2:1.

Strategic control of speech, James 3:2–6.

Influence unto salvation, 1 Peter 3:1–2.

Surviving in evil surroundings, 2 Peter 2:4–9.
Children of good parents, 2 John 4.
Wrong kind of congregational authority, 3 John 9–10.

INJURY
Perilous activities, Ecclesiastes 10:9.

IN-LAWS
In-laws as source of grief, Genesis 26:34–35 (See NKJV).
Taking father-in-law's advice, Exodus 28:1–27.
Wealthy in-law, Ruth 2:1 (LB).

INNOCENCE
Innocent accused, Genesis 39:11–20.
Innocents protected, Exodus 23:7.
Sacrifice with unsolved murder, Deuteronomy 21:1–9.
Accusation against innocence, 1 Samuel 22:11–15.
David's innocence in murder of Abner, 2 Samuel 3:22–37.
Claim of righteousness, innocence, 2 Samuel 22:21–25.
No one innocent in God's sight, Job 9:2 (CEV).
Cleansed for worship, Psalm 26:6.
Suffering in innocence, Psalms 59:3–4; 119:86.
Beauty with innocence, Song of Songs 4:7.
Innocent congregation, guilty priests, Hosea 4:4 (CEV).
Guilty Jonah seen as innocent, Jonah 1:14.
Dishonest innocence, Micah 6:11.
Pilate's claim of innocence, Matthew 27:24.
Suffering, innocence of Jesus, Luke 23:15–16; John 19:1–6.
Redemptive cleansing, Ephesians 5:26–27; 1 Thessalonians 3:13.
From guilt to innocence, Philippians 2:15 (See GNB).
Legalistic innocence, Philippians 3:6.
Innocent of accusation, Colossians 1:22; Titus 1:6.
Life-style of innocence, 1 Timothy 3:2–4.
Unpolluted innocence, James 1:27.
Attained innocence, 2 Peter 3:14.
Blameless before the Lord, Revelation 14:5.

INSENSITIVE
People like animals in distress, Deuteronomy 28:53–57.
As one under anesthesia, Proverbs 23:34–35.
Burning truth not understood, Isaiah 42:25.
Wealth numbs conscience, Hosea 12:8.

Insensitive to miracles, Matthew 11:20.
Caring neither for God or man, Luke 18:1–5.
Insensitive hearts, closed ears, eyes, Acts 28:27.
Seared conscience, 1 Timothy 4:1–2.

INSOMNIA

Reading at night, Esther 6:1.
Restless night, Job 7:3–4 (See KJV).
"Night racks my bones," Job 30:17 (NRSV).
Companion of night creatures, Job 30:29.
Tossing, turning, Psalm 56:8 (LB).
Stressful insomnia, Psalm 77:2–6 (RSV).
Frogs in bedrooms, Psalm 105:30.
Purposeful insomnia, Psalm 119:148.
"Restless minds," Ecclesiastes 2:23 (NASB, NRSV).
Rich man's gluttony, Ecclesiastes 5:12 (NASB).
Pondering world problems (Ecclesiastes 8:16 (CEV).
Wandering streets at night, Song of Songs 3:1, 2.
Cardiac insomnia, Song of Songs 5:2.
Time remaining until morning, Isaiah 21:11–12.
Short bed, narrow blanket, Isaiah 28:20.
Troubled dreams, Daniel 2:1.
Conscience-agitated insomnia, Daniel 6:16–23.
"Many a sleepless night," 2 Corinthians 11:27 (NRSV).

INSULT

Deviates' insult to angelic guests, Genesis 19:5.
Silent response to insult, 1 Samuel 10:27.
Wife's insult, 2 Samuel 6:20 (LB).
Bald head insulted, 2 Kings 2:23–24.
Upset by criticism, Job 20:2–3.
Heart-breaking insults, Psalm 69:20 (NRSV).
Hometown insulted, John 1:46.
Cheap wine offered to Jesus, John 19:29 (CEV, NRSV).
"Know-it-all," Acts 17:18 (CEV).
Cretians insulted, Titus 1:12.
Insulting language, 1 Peter 2:1 (GNB).
Insulted for Christ, 1 Peter 4:14.

INTEGRATION

Ways of the heathen, Deuteronomy 18:9.
Dark, lovely, Song of Songs 1:5–6.
Jews and centurion, Acts 10:22, 28, 34–35.

INTELLECTUAL

Intellectual humility, Psalm 131:1.
Religion without reality, Proverbs 14:12.
Intellectuals destroyed, Obadiah 8.
Grecian Jews, Acts 9:29.
Demeaned by intellectuals, Acts 17:18 (See Berk.).
Profuse discussion of ideas, Acts 17:21.
Intellectuals, message of Cross, 1 Corinthians 1:18–24.
Spiritual wisdom, 1 Corinthians 2:6.
World's wisdom, 1 Corinthians 3:18–23.
Eyes of heart, Ephesians 1:18–19.
So-called intellectualism, Colossians 2:8 (See AB, LB);
    1 Timothy 6:20–21.
God cannot lie, Titus 1:2.
Lacking wisdom, ask God, James 1:5–6.

INTIMACY

First human conception, Genesis 4:1.
Meet the Lord three times annually, Deuteronomy
    16:16.
"Deep calls to deep," Psalm 42:7.
God as friend, Psalm 54:4 (LB).
Intimate love, Song of Songs 4:16.
God's favorite, Isaiah 44:2 (CEV).
Marital intimacy, Ephesians 5:31–32.
Reach most holy place, Hebrews 6:19 (CEV).

INTIMIDATION

Intimidating presence, Numbers 22:3–4.
David intimidated Saul, 1 Samuel 18:29.

INSECTS

Fear tactics, Ezra 4:4.
Hired intimidator, Nehemiah 6:13.
Song of ruthless made silent, Isaiah 25:5.
Many intimidated, Jeremiah 22:1–3 (CEV).
Needlessness of worry, Matthew 6:25–27.
Attempt to intimidate apostles, Acts 4:16–20.
Saul's intimidation of the church, Acts 8:3.
Resisting intimidation, Philippians 1:28 (AB).
No need for intimidation, 1 Peter 3:14 (RSV).

INTOXICATION

Hilarious drinking, Genesis 43:34 (Berk.).
"Good spirits," Ruth 3:7.

INVESTMENT

Owning share of king, 2 Samuel 19:43.
Giving as spiritual investment, Proverbs 19:17.
Risky investment, Ecclesiastes 5:13–14 (LB).
Foreign and diversified investments, Ecclesiastes 11:1–2 (GNB).
Treasures on earth, treasures in heaven, Matthew 6:19–21.
Purchase of sure investment, Matthew 13:44.
False economy of materialism, Mark 8:36.
Gain world, lose self, Luke 9:25.
Wise and unwise use of money, Luke 19:11–27.
Safe eternal investment, 1 Timothy 6:17–19 (LB).

IRONY

A wife's biting tongue, 2 Samuel 6:20.
Elijah's irony concerning Baal, 1 Kings 18:27.
Job and his accusers, Job 12:2.
Ironical declaration of "freedom," Jeremiah 34:17.
Taunted by Roman soldiers, Matthew 27:27–29.
Ironical evaluation of weak Christians, 1 Corinthians 4:8–18.

IRRESPONSIBLE

Oath taken irresponsibly, Leviticus 5:4.
Irresponsible house maintenance, Ecclesiastes 10:18.
Deliberately writing falsehoods, Jeremiah 8:8.
False prophets, Jeremiah 23:16–18.
Prophets who see nothing, Ezekiel 13:1–3.
Forgetting necessities, Mark 8:14.

JAIL

House arrest, Jeremiah 37:15.
Adventure in Philippian jail, Acts 16:23–34.
Jail ministry, Philemon 9 (See AB, GNB).

JEALOUSY

Negative attitude of Cain, Genesis 4:3–7.
Attitude of Ishmael toward Isaac, Genesis 21:8–10.
Envy caused by wealth, Genesis 26:12–14.
Sibling jealousy, Genesis 37:3–4.

JANITOR J

Divine jealousy, Exodus 20:5; Deuteronomy 32:16, 21; Psalm 78:58; Isaiah 30:1–2.
God's name is "Jealous," Exodus 34:14.
Legal specifications for jealous husband, Numbers 5:12–31.
Jealousy of Miriam, Aaron, Numbers 12:1–9.
Facing competition, 1 Samuel 17:55–58.
Jealous citizens, 2 Samuel 19:43.
Marital jealousy, 1 Chronicles 15:29.
Poison to soul, Job 5:2.
Envy of prosperity, Psalm 73:3–12.
Jealous husband, Proverbs 6:34.
Cancerous jealousy, Proverbs 14:30 (GNB).
Do not envy sinners, Proverbs 23:17.
Jealousy more cruel than anger, Proverbs 27:4.
Neighborhood envy, Ecclesiastes 4:4.
Jealous love, Song of Songs 8:6.
Idol of jealousy, Ezekiel 8:5.
Divine jealousy subsided, Ezekiel 16:42.
Burning with jealousy, Zechariah 8:2.
Parable of vineyard workers, Matthew 20:1–16.
Jealousy within family, Luke 15:11–32.
Dissension, jealousy in church, Acts 6:1.
Religious jealousy, Acts 13:45.
Opposition caused by jealousy, Acts 17:5.
Spiritual envy, Romans 10:19.
Do not compare yourself with others, Galatians 6:4–5.
Envy among those who preach Christ, Philippians 1:15.
Jealousy cause of murder, 1 John 3:12.

JESUS
Conceived by Holy Spirit, Matthew 1:20.
Led by Holy Spirit, Luke 4:1.
Bread of life, John 6:35.
Light of the world, John 8:12.
The Door, John 10:9.
Way, truth and life, John 14:6.
True vine, John 15:1–7.
Melchizedek, Jesus, Hebrews 7:3 (AB).
Jesus Christ Himself, the Word of life, 1 John 1:1–4 (See John 1:1–3).
Advocate with Heavenly Father, 1 John 2:1–2.
Unique name for Jesus, Revelation 3:14.
Rider on white horse, Revelation 19:11–16.
Totality of the Son of God, Revelation 22:13.

JEWELRY

Nose ring, Genesis 24:47.
Betrothal gifts, Genesis 24:52–53.
Hindrance to righteousness, Genesis 35:2–4.
Rings on fingers, Genesis 41:42; Esther 8:8; Luke 15:22.
Items of plunder, Exodus 3:22; 11:2; 12:35; 33:4–6; Isaiah 3:18–23.
Jewelry removed during mourning, Exodus 33:4.
Given to the Lord, Exodus 35:22; Numbers 31:50–52.
Jewelry and cosmetics snatched away, Isaiah 3:18–24.
Maiden and bride, Jeremiah 2:32.
Dull gold, strewn jewels, Lamentations 4:1.
Silver, gold, jewelry lose value, Ezekiel 7:19, 20.
Adulterous charms, Hosea 2:2 (Berk.).
Becoming like the Lord's signet ring, Haggai 2:23.
Pearl of great value, Matthew 13:45, 46.
Hairstyles and jewelry, 1 Timothy 2:9–10.
Inner beauty, 1 Peter 3:3–4.
Jewels adorning evil woman, Revelations 17:4.

JOKE

Impractical joking, Proverbs 26:18–19.
Coarse joking, Ephesians 5:4.

JURY

Protect the innocent, Exodus 23:7.
Priests assist judge, Deuteronomy 17:8–12.
Ten-man jury, Ruth 4:1–4.
Infamous "trial" of Jesus, Matthew 27:11–26; Mark 15:1–15; Luke 23:1–25; John 18:28–40.

JUSTICE

Mood of Old Testament justice, 2 Samuel 1:1–16.
David guilty, not followers, 2 Samuel 24:12–17.
Justice to murderer's sons, 2 Kings 14:5–6.
Justice to unjust Haman, Esther 7:1–10.
"Perfectly fair" judge, Psalm 7:11 (LB).
Unjust judges, Psalm 58:1–2.
Future divine justice, Psalm 98:8–9.
The Lord defends the poor, Proverbs 22:22–23.
Those who convict the guilty, Proverbs 24:24–25.
Justice, injustice, Proverbs 28:8 (LB).
Fate of good, evil, Isaiah 65:13–14.
Disputing God's justice, Ezekiel 33:10–20.
"Judges are wolves," Zephaniah 3:3 (CEV).

Savior, Judge, John 5:22–27.
Justice for Judas, Acts 1:18–20.
Case against Paul, Acts 23:23–30.
Impartial justice, 1 Peter 1:17.
God's justice, Revelation 16:5–7.

--------------------- **K** ---------------------

KEY

Key with authority, Isaiah 22:22.
Kingdom keys, Matthew 16:19.
Keys of death and hades, Revelation 1:18.
David's key, Revelation 3:7.
Key to the abyss, Revelation 9:1; 20:1.

KINDNESS

Enemy subdued by kindness, 2 Kings 6:18–23.
"Plumage of kindness," Job 39:13 (Berk.).
Returning good for evil, Genesis 50:15–21.
Kindness to man, daughters, Exodus 2:16–21.
Kindness to strangers, Leviticus 19:34.
Kindness rewarded, 1 Samuel 30:11–18.
Enemy shown kindness, 2 Kings 6:8–23.
Kindness of pagan king, 2 Kings 25:27–30.
Divine loving-kindness, Psalm 23:6 (NASB).
Outreach to others, Proverbs 14:21.
Mother's kindness, Proverbs 31:20.
Evil name, deeds of kindness, Jeremiah 52:31–34.
Joseph's kindness to Mary, Matthew 1:19.
Kindness as spiritual service, Matthew 25:34–36; Luke
    6:34–35.
"Jesus was kind," Romans 1:5 (CEV). (Note use of *kind,
    kindness* CEV throughout translation.)
Kindness in action, Romans 12:10–15.
Love is kind, 1 Corinthians 13:4.
Christian life-style, Ephesians 4:32; Colossians 3:12.
Experienced kindness, 1 Peter 2:3.
Faith plus kindness, 2 Peter 1:5–7.

KISS

First recorded kiss involved deceit, Genesis 27:22–27.
Men kissing, Genesis 27:27; 33:4; 45:15; 48:10; Exodus
    4:27; 18:7; 1 Samuel 20:41; Luke 15:20; Acts 20:37.
Emotional kiss, Genesis 29:11; 45:15.

Parting kiss, Ruth 1:14.
Kiss of death, 2 Samuel 20:9–10; Luke 22:47–48.
Throw a kiss, Job 31:27 (NASB).
Departure from parents, 1 Kings 19:20.
Taste of bridal lips, Song of Songs 4:11.
Kiss an idol, Hosea 13:2 (NASB).
Betraying kiss, Matthew 26:48; Luke 22:48.
Kiss of contrition, Luke 7:38.
Worshipful kiss, Acts 20:37–38.
Holy kiss, Romans 16:16.

KNOWLEDGE

Inception of secular knowledge, Genesis 3:5–6, 22–23.
Solomon's knowledge, 1 Kings 4:29–34; 10:1–3.
Secret things belong to God, Deuteronomy 29:29.
Source of knowledge and wisdom, Proverbs 2:1–5.
Divine performance, Proverbs 3:19–20.
Prudent knowledge, Proverbs 14:8.
Quest for knowledge, Proverbs 15:14.
Knowledge brings sorrow, Ecclesiastes 1:18.
Seduced by knowledge, Isaiah 47:10.
Gift from God, Daniel 1:17.
Knowledge increased, Daniel 12:4.
Common knowledge, Luke 1:1 (AB).

K

KEY

Unable to comprehend, Luke 9:44–45.
Putting knowledge into action, John 13:17.
Coming fullness, 1 Corinthians 13:9–12.
Knowing the Lord, Philippians 3:8.

KOSHER
Restricted meat, Genesis 32:32.
Kosher food, Judges 13:4 (LB).
Non-kosher food, Ezekiel 44:6–7.
Demonic pork, Mark 5:11–13.
All foods kosher, Mark 7:19 (LB).

———————— **L** ————————

LABOR
Task of producing food, Genesis 3:17–19.
Value of laborers, Genesis 14:21.
Female labor, Genesis 29:9.
Management and labor, Exodus 5:2–5.
Day of rest, Exodus 20:9–11.
Foreign laborers, Deuteronomy 29:11.
Prayer for laborer's skills, Deuteronomy 33:11.
Forced labor, Exodus 6:5; 1 Kings 9:15.
Foreign labor, 1 Chronicles 22:2.
Hired man, Job 7:1.
Labor, manager, Psalm 123:2.
Blessing of hard labor, Proverbs 14:23.
Hard work induces sound sleep, Ecclesiastes 5:12.
Laboring with all your might, Ecclesiastes 9:10.
Labor unrest incited, Ezra 4:1–6.
Defrauding laborers, Malachi 3:5.
Concern for servant, Matthew 8:5–13.
Labor shortage, Matthew 9:37–38.
Only a carpenter's son, Matthew 13:55; Mark 6:1–3.
Continually working, John 5:17.
Labor, ministry, Acts 18:3; 2 Thessalonians 3:6–10.
Wages an obligation, not gift, Romans 4:4.
Wearying labor, 1 Corinthians 4:12 (AB).
Payment for labor, 1 Corinthians 9:7.
Manual labor, Ephesians 4:28.
Doing good work as unto the Lord, Ephesians 6:5–8.
Slave, masters, Ephesians 6:9; Colossians 3:22–25; 4:1;
    1 Timothy 6:1–2; Titus 2:9–10.
Working overtime, 1 Thessalonians 2:9.

Dignity of labor, Titus 3:14.
Slave who became brother, Philemon 8–21.
Work before rest, Hebrews 4:11.
Failing to pay laborer's wages, James 5:4.

LAMB

Lamb of God, Isaiah 53:7; John 1:29; 1 Corinthians 5:7;
  1 Peter 1:19; Revelation 5:6; 6:1; 15:3; 17:14; 19:9;
  21:22.

LAUGHTER

Laughter out of place, Genesis 18:10–15.
Divine laughter, Psalm 2:4.
Laughter with aching heart, Proverbs 14:13.
Meaningless laughter, Ecclesiastes 2:2.
Sorrow better than laughter, Ecclesiastes 7:3.
Laughter of fools, Ecclesiastes 7:6.
Scornful laughter, Ezekiel 25:1–4.
Laughter today, tears tomorrow, Luke 6:25; James 4:9.

LAWYER

Legal cases decided, Exodus 18:13 (CEV).
Cheating in court, Job 31:21 (GNB).
Avoid hasty litigation, Proverbs 25:8.
"Lord, you are my lawyer," Lamentations 3:58 (LB).
Settle out of court, Matthew 5:25.
Lawyer pharisee, Matthew 22:35 (NKJV).
Mosaic lawyer, Luke 7:30 (AB).
Carnal lawyers, Luke 10:25; 11:46.
Defending oneself, Acts 26:1.
Christian versus Christian, 1 Corinthians 6:1.
Zenas, the lawyer, Titus 3:13.

LAZY

Too much sleep, Proverbs 6:10–11; 20:13; 24:33.
Blessing of hard work, Proverbs 14:23.
Similarity of slackness, destruction, Proverbs 18:9.
Lazy man like swinging door, Proverbs 26:14 (GNB).
Too lazy to eat, Proverbs 26:15.
Those who do nothing, Isaiah 30:7.
Dozing, daydreaming, Isaiah 56:10 (CEV).
Lax in the Lord's work, Jeremiah 48:10.
Disciples sleeping while Jesus prayed, Mark 14:32–41.
"Do not be lazy," Romans 12:11 (GNB).
"Loaf around," 2 Thessalonians 3:6–7, 10 (CEV).

Living lazy lives, 2 Thessalonians 3:11 (GNB).
Busybodies, 2 Thessalonians 3:11–12.
"Never be lazy," Hebrews 6:12 (CEV).

LEADERSHIP

Man's authority over creation, Genesis 1:26.
Resentment toward youth in leadership, Genesis 37:5–11.
Youth in government service, Genesis 41:46.
Humbly facing leadership responsibility, Exodus 3:11.
Decline caused by absence of good leader, Exodus 32:1–6.
Respect for leader, Exodus 33:8.
Revolt against leaders, Numbers 14:1–30; 20:1–5.
Debilitating guilt of leadership, Numbers 20:12.
Training for future leadership, Numbers 27:18–23.
Impartial leadership, Deuteronomy 1:17.
God-given leadership, Deuteronomy 2:25.
Faithful leadership, Deuteronomy 8:2, 15.
Choosing right leader, Deuteronomy 17:14–15.
Transfer of leadership, Deuteronomy 34:9.
Honoring former leader, Joshua 22:1–5.
Good leader's influence, Joshua 24:31.
Rapport between leaders and people, Judges 5:2.
Leader's assessment of constituency, Judges 6:15; 1 Samuel 9:21.
Example for leadership success, Judges 7:17–18.
Evil conduct following death of good leader, Judges 8:33–34.
Too talented to lead only one family, Judges 18:19.
From divine leadership to mortal, 1 Samuel 8:1–9.
Compromising leadership, 1 Samuel 15:24.
Respect for disliked leader, 1 Samuel 24:1–11; 26:9–10.
David's respect for King Saul, 1 Samuel 24:1–7; 26:7–11.
Leader blamed for disaster, 1 Samuel 30:1–6.
David replaced Saul, 2 Samuel 2:1–7.
First words of new leader, 2 Samuel 2:5–7.
Leadership struggle, 2 Samuel 3:1.
Success through divine guidance, 2 Samuel 22:44–45.
David made Solomon king, 1 Kings 1:28–53.
Joyful transfer of leadership, 1 Kings 1:47–48.
Delegating responsibility, 1 Kings 4:7.
Organization for building temple, 1 Kings 5:12–18.

King Solomon's admonition to people, 1 Kings 8:55–61.

Rehoboam succeeded father, Solomon, 1 Kings 11:41–42.

Transfer of leadership, 2 Kings 2:1–18.

Young kings of Judah, 2 Kings 23:31, 36; 24:8, 18.

Good leadership, 1 Chronicles 18:14.

Exemplary stewardship by leaders, 1 Chronicles 29:9.

King's righteous example ignored, 2 Chronicles 27:2.

Delegated responsibility, Nehemiah 3:1–32.

Disgruntled people distress leader, Nehemiah 5:1–12.

Leader consults others, Esther 1:13.

Scorned leader, Job 19:15.

Great men not always wise, Job 32:9–13.

Leader to strangers, Psalm 18:43–45.

Spiritual leader, Psalm 21:7.

Leadership by small tribe, Psalm 68:27.

Divine use of human leaders, Psalm 77:20.

Leaders come and go, Psalm 109:8.

Death terminates leadership, Psalm 146:3–4.

Kings search out concealed matters, Proverbs 25:2.

King and teacher, Ecclesiastes 1:12.

Respect for king, Ecclesiastes 8:4.

Prejudiced leaders, Ecclesiastes 10:5–7.

Inexperienced leadership, Isaiah 3:4.

Carnal leaders, Isaiah 1:23.

Guiding people astray, Isaiah 9:16.

Fools, deceived leaders, Isaiah 19:13.

Leaders captured without fight, Isaiah 22:3.

Example of faithful leadership, Isaiah 37:1–38.

Leaders, priests, prophets lose heart, Jeremiah 4:9.

Leaders, people turn against the Lord, Jeremiah 5:3–5.

Lax leaders delight people, Jeremiah 5:31.

Leaders rendered powerless, Jeremiah 15:1.

Leader from within ranks of those to be led, Jeremiah 30:21.

Both king and priest forsaken, Lamentations 2:6.

Misguided by evil government, Ezekiel 11:1–4.

Leader's recognition of sovereign God, Daniel 4:34–37.

King at age of sixty-two, Daniel 5:30–31.

Ignoring God's guidance in choice of leadership, Hosea 8:4.

Prophet and leader, Hosea 12:13.

Prophet given revelation of the Lord, Amos 3:7.

Complacency among national leaders, Amos 6:1.

Ineffective leadership, Habakkuk 1:4.
Leaderless people, Habakkuk 1:14.
Murderous leadership of King Herod, Matthew 2:13–18.
Jesus taught with authority, Matthew 7:28–29.
Centurion unworthy to have Jesus in his home, Matthew 8:5–10.
Instructions to twelve apostles, Matthew 10:5–42 (See 11:1).
Respect without obedience, Luke 6:46.
Management evaluated, Luke 16:2.
Jesus demonstrated servant leadership, John 13:3–9.
Delegating distribution of welfare to widows, Acts 6:1–4.
False leadership of Herod, Acts 12:21–23.
Giving encouragement, Acts 20:1.
Diligent leadership, Romans 12:8.
Respect, honor to all, Romans 13:7–8.
Humility in leadership, 2 Corinthians 1:24.
Rapport with those being led, 2 Corinthians 7:2–4.
Sharing concerns of leader, 2 Corinthians 8:16.
Avoiding harsh use of authority, 2 Corinthians 13:10.
Leaders as pillars, Galatians 2:9.
Penalty for misleading others, Galatians 5:10.
For the good of all, Ephesians 4:11–13.
Submissive leadership, Ephesians 5:21.
Leadership in the home, Ephesians 5:22–33.
Paul's great love for followers, Philippians 1:3–11.
Leader's imprisonment caused others to witness, Philippians 1:12–14.
Leadership in absentia, Philippians 2:12, 14.
Exemplary leadership, Philippians 4:9.
Qualifications of Christ, Colossians 1:15–20.
Relentless effort on behalf of followers, Colossians 1:28–29.
Christ head over all, Colossians 2:9–10.
Paul's use of names, Colossians 4:7–17.
Leadership model, 1 Thessalonians 2:1–16.
Desire to be overseer, 1 Timothy 3:1.
Recent convert unqualified, 1 Timothy 3:6.
Communication in person, by writing, 1 Timothy 3:14–15.
Servant, apostle, Titus 1:1.
Second level leadership, Titus 1:5.
Elder's credentials, Titus 1:5–9.

Leadership with authority, Titus 2:15.
Request instead of command, Philemon 8–10.
High priest selected from among people, Hebrews 5:1.
Gentle mark of good leadership, Hebrews 5:2–3.
Leaders who are examples, Hebrews 13:7.
Respect for leaders, Hebrews 13:17.
If you lack wisdom, ask God, James 1:5–6.
Exercising Heaven's wisdom, James 3:17–18.
Joy of good report about followers, 3 John 3–4.
Wrong kind of authority in congregation, 3 John 9, 10.
Delegation of satanic authority, Revelation 13:2.
Temporary authority of beast, Revelation 13:5.
Demons influence leaders, Revelation 16:13–14.
One-hour reign of ten kings, Revelation 17:12.

LIBERTY

King imprisoned and set free, 2 Kings 24:15; 25:27–29.
Greatest freedom, Psalm 119:45.
Proclaim freedom, Isaiah 61:1.
Conditional freedom, Jeremiah 34:8–11.
Feasting not fasting, Luke 5:33 (LB).
Truth sets us free, John 8:31, 32, 36.
Peter's vision of clean and unclean, Acts 10:9–16; 11:4–
    10.
Deeper meaning of deliverance from legalism, Acts
    10:24–28.
Visitation privilege for prisoner, Acts 27:3.
Liberty no excuse for sin, Romans 6:1, 2.
Freedom from mastery of sin, Romans 6:14.
Once slaves to sin, now slaves to righteousness, Romans
    6:18.
Atonement assures freedom free from legality, Romans
    7:1–6.
Restricted liberty, 1 Corinthians 6:12 (GNB).
Liberty without license, 1 Corinthians 6:12 (See CEV).
Exercise of liberty eating, drinking, 1 Corinthians 8:7–
    13.
Restricted freedom, 1 Corinthians 8:9 (CEV).
Unmuzzled ox, 1 Corinthians 9:9–14.
Freedom in believer's conduct, 1 Corinthians 10:23–33.
Freedom in the Spirit, 2 Corinthians 3:17.
Human standards, 2 Corinthians 10:2 (NRSV).
From law to grace, Galatians 4:1–7 (Also previous
    chapter).
Called to be free, Galatians 5:13.

Filled with knowledge of God's will, Colossians 1:9–12.
Rescued from dominion of darkness, Colossians 1:13–14.
Word of God not chained, 2 Timothy 2:8–9 (See CEV).
Legalism of old, liberty of new, Hebrews 12:18–24.
Timothy released from prison, Hebrews 13:23.
The law that gives freedom, James 2:12–13.
Liberty misused, 1 Peter 2:16; Jude 4.

LIE

Purge lying, Deuteronomy 19:16–19.
Lying to protect life, 1 Samuel 20:5–7.
Divinely approved discrepancy, 2 Chronicles 18:18–22.
Condemned by one's own words, Job 15:6.
"God's breath," Job 27:3–4 (Berk.).
Totally untrue, Psalm 5:9 (LB).
Punishment for false witness, Proverbs 19:5.
Prophets proclaimed lies, Jeremiah 27:14–15.
Initially positive response to false prophecy, Jeremiah 28:1–17 (Note verses 5–9).
Prophet commanded by king to lie, Jeremiah 38:24–27.
Believing lie, Jeremiah 43:1–7.
Two kings lie to each other, Daniel 11:27.
Tongues that speak deceitfully, Micah 6:12.
Contradictory reports, Matthew 26:60–61 (LB).
Jesus called a liar, Matthew 27:63 (CEV).
False witness against Jesus, Mark 14:53–59.
Worst kind of lie, James 3:14 (LB).

LIFESTYLE

Domestic lifestyle, Deuteronomy 6:7–9.
Lifestyles of believers, unbelievers, Psalm 1:1–6.
Not the way of righteous, Psalm 15:1–3.
Blameless lifestyle, Psalms 84:11; 101:2.
Kindness ignored, Psalm 109:16.
Exemplary lifestyle, Psalm 119:1–5; Micah 6:8.
Divinely taught lifestyle, Psalm 143:8.
Lifestyle procedure, Proverbs 4:25–27.
Recommended lifestyle, Ecclesiastes 8:15.
Fool's lifestyle, Ecclesiastes 10:3.
Testing lifestyles, Jeremiah 6:27.
Lifestyle of righteous man, Ezekiel 18:5–9.
Practice what is preached, Ezekiel 33:31.
Walking in ways of the Lord, Hosea 14:9.
Shining light of witness, Matthew 5:16.

Truth put into practice, Matthew 7:24.
Deathly lifestyle, Romans 6:21.
Altered lifestyle, Romans 8:3–4.
Contrasting lifestyles, Romans 8:5.
Christian lifestyle, Romans 12:3–21; 13:12–14; Ephesians 4:1–3; 1 Thessalonians 4:9–12.
Loving lifestyle, 1 Corinthians 13:1–13.
Christians with worldly lifestyle, 2 Corinthians 10:2.
Fruit of the Spirit, Galatians 5:22 (Spanish Bible translates "gentleness" *manseumbree,* "tameness" as with tamed animal).
First priority in conduct, Galatians 6:15.
Lifestyle worthy of calling, Ephesians 4:1–2.
New lifestyle in Christ, Ephesians 4:22–24.
Imitators of God expressing love, Ephesians 5:1–2.
Ultimate career, life of love, Ephesians 5:1–2.
Enemies of the cross, Philippians 3:18–21.
Joy and gentleness, Philippians 4:4–5.
Attitude of mind dictates lifestyle, Philippians 4:8–9.
Filled with knowledge of God's will, Colossians 1:9–12.
Those who died with Christ, Colossians 2:20–23.
Resurrection lifestyle, Colossians 3:1–17.
Prepared for return of Christ, 1 Thessalonians 3:13.
Motivated to Christian lifestyle, 1 Thessalonians 4:11–12.
Faith plus good conscience, 1 Timothy 1:19.
Young Christians' lifestyle, 1 Timothy 4:12.
"Rich in good deeds," 1 Timothy 6:18.
Lifestyles in last days, 2 Timothy 3:1–5.
Marks of Christian lifestyle, Titus 3:1–2.
Enoch pleased God, Hebrews 11:5.
Instructions for Christian life-style, Hebrews 13:1–9.
Living by Scriptures, James 2:8–10.
True faith demonstrated, James 3:13.
Mature Christian life, 2 Peter 1:5–9.
Live for the eternal, 2 Peter 3:11–14.
Lifestyle producing spiritual growth, 2 Peter 3:18.
Living by truth, 1 John 1:9, 10.
Doing what is right, 1 John 2:29.
Love results from obedience to Scripture, 2 John 6.
Evil conduct as negative witness, Jude 7.

LIQUOR
Drink stronger than wine, Leviticus 10:9.
Other fermented drink, Deuteronomy 29:6.

Alcohol and pregnancy, Judges 13:4–5.
Wine and beer, Proverbs 20:1; 31:4–6.
Beer with bad taste, Isaiah 24:9.
Drunken priests and prophets, Isaiah 28:7.
No strong drink for John the Baptist, Luke 1:15.

LONELINESS

Deep sense of loneliness, Job 19:13–14.
Companion of night creatures, Job 30:29.
Joyfully alone, Psalm 4:8 (LB).
Fair-weather friends, Psalms 31:11; 38:11; 2 Timothy
   4:16.
Loss of closest friends, Psalm 88:8.
Insomnia induced by loneliness, Psalm 102:7.
No one cares, Psalm 142:4.
Neither son nor brother, Ecclesiastes 4:8.
Silently alone, Lamentations 3:28 (CEV).
Utter loneliness of Calvary, Mark 15:34.
Prodigal's loneliness, Luke 15:14–17.
Alone in time of need, John 5:7.
"Yearning to see you," Romans 1:11 (Berk.).
Spiritual loneliness, Philippians 2:25–30; 1 Thessalon-
   ians 2:17–20; 3:1–5.
Tears of loneliness, 2 Timothy 1:4.
Lonely for face-to-face fellowship, 3 John 14.

LORD'S DAY

Setting aside day for rest, Genesis 2:2–3; Jeremiah
   17:21–27.
No business on Sabbath, Nehemiah 10:31.
Merchandising on Sabbath, Nehemiah 13:15–18.
Avoid Sabbath desecration, Isaiah 56:2.
Sabbath fun, Isaiah 58:13 (LB).
The Lord's Sabbaths, Ezekiel 20:12.
Jesus criticized for Sabbath conduct, Mark 2:23–27;
   Luke 6:1–5.

LOSS

Fall asleep rich, awaken poor, Job 27:19 (CEV).
Loss of material possessions, Hebrews 10:34 (GNB).

LOVE

Mistaking love for hatred, Deuteronomy 1:27 (LB).
Love between two men, 2 Samuel 1:26.
Determining identity of true mother, 1 Kings 3:16–28.

Steadfast love, Job 10:12 (NRSV); Psalm 90:14 (NRSV).
Unfailing love, Psalm 23:6 (Berk.).
"Steady love," Psalm 33:18 (LB).
God's love better than life, Psalm 63:3 (KJV).
Loving those who hate, Psalm 109:4 (LB).
Our Lord's enduring love, Psalm 136:1–26.
Lovesick, Song of Songs 2:5 (Berk.).
True love cannot be quenched, Song of Songs 8:7.
"Kingdom of love," Isaiah 16:5 (CEV).
God's love never lessens, Isaiah 54:10.
Sex spoken of as "love," Ezekiel 16:8.
Lust called love, Ezekiel 23:17.
How God loves, Malachi 1:2.
Marriage on earth, relationship in heaven, Mark 12:18–27.
Greatest act of love, John 3:16.
Love's highest degree, John 13:1 (AB).
Implanted love, John 17:26.
Forgiving spirit of martyr, Acts 7:60.
Love fulfills law, Romans 13:8–10.
Others' good above self, 1 Corinthians 10:24.
Guided by love, 1 Corithians 13:1 (CEV).
Apt definition, 1 Corinthians 13:4–7 (GNB).
"Pursue love," 1 Corinthians 14:1 (NASB, NKJV, NRSV).
Loving heartcry, 2 Corinthians 6:11–12 (LB).

LOUD

Covered with His love, Ephesians 1:4 (LB).
Imitators of God expressing love, Ephesians 5:1–2.
Christians keeping in touch, Ephesians 6: 21–22.
Undying love, Ephesians 6:24.
Affection Jesus gives, Philippians 1:8.
Ministry of love, Colossians 3:12–14. (Japanese: "Love binds everything together in perfect harmony.")
Increasing love, 1 Thessalonians 3:12; 4:9–10.
Realizing, sharing, 2 Thessalonians 3:5 (AB).
Spiritual love's basis, 1 Timothy 1:5.
"Mutual love," Hebrews 13:1 (NRSV); 1 Peter 1:22 (NRSV).
Love's forgiving power, 1 Peter 4:8 (See NASB).
"Affection with love," 2 Peter 1:7 (NRSV).
God's perfect love, 1 John 2:5 (NRSV).
God's great love, 1 John 3:1–3 (See AB).
Mark of Christian, 1 John 3:11–14.
Actions speak louder than words, 1 John 3:18 (See AB).
Truth, love united, 2 John 3, 5–6.
Love in the truth, 3 John 1.
Love dearly, tenderly, Revelation 3:19 (AB).

LOYALTY

Tested love to God, son, Genesis 22:1–14.
Lacking wholehearted loyalty, Numbers 32:11.
Turning from wrong family influence, Deuteronomy 13:6–10.
Continuing loyalty, Joshua 1:16–17.
Turning to rejected brother in time of need, Judges 11:1–10.
Loyal assistant, 1 Samuel 14:7.
Transferred loyalty, 1 Samuel 14:21–23.
Loyalty torn between father, close friend, 1 Samuel 19:1–2.
Friendship, loyalty at cutting edge, 1 Samuel 20:1–4.
Pagan feared David's loyalty, 1 Samuel 29:1–11.
Angelic loyalty, 1 Samuel 29:9 (GNB).
Loyalty of servant to king, 2 Samuel 15:19–21.
King David's loyalty doubted, 2 Samuel 19:1–8.
Protection for future king, 2 Kings 11:1–3.
Divided loyalty, Psalm 119:113 (CEV).
Talk is cheap, Proverbs 20:6 (GNB).
Loyalty to gods, Jeremiah 2:11.
Loving God above all, Matthew 10:37–39.
You cannot serve two masters, Luke 16:13.

Loyal to Christ's commands, John 14:21–24.
Hypocritical loyalty to Caesar, John 19:15.
Tested loyalty, John 21:15–17.
Daily death of true loyalty, 1 Corinthians 15:30–31.

LUST

Lot's offer of virgin daughters, Genesis 19:4–8.
Mixing immorality with worship, Numbers 25:1–2.
David and Bathsheba, 2 Samuel 11:1–27.
Immorality used for vengeance, 2 Samuel 16:20–23.
Weakness of King Solomon, 1 Kings 11:1–13.
Avoiding lust requires discipline, Job 31:1.
"Ogle at a girl," Job 31:1 (Berk.).
Lust as a crime, Job 31:11 (LB).
Take away lust, Psalm 141:4 (LB).
Lost value through lust, Proverbs 6:25–26.
Playing with fire, Proverbs 6:27.
Preventive wisdom, Proverbs 7:4–17 (LB).
Thinking only of sex, Isaiah 57:5 (CEV).
Searching for sex, Jeremiah 2:24 (LB).
Shameless lust, Jeremiah 3:3 (See CEV).
Adultery with stone and wood, Jeremiah 3:9.
Description of profligate men, Jeremiah 5:8.
Adultery, lust in heart, mind, Ezekiel 6:9.
Merchandising feminine beauty, Ezekiel 16:15.
Visual abomination, Ezekiel 20:7 (KJV).
Violation of family members, Ezekiel 22:11.
Two adulterous sisters, Ezekiel 23:1–49.
Lustful caressing, Ezekiel 23:2–3.
Lust induced by pornography, Ezekiel 23:14–17 (LB).
Lust called love, Ezekiel 23:17.
Father, son to same prostitute, Amos 2:7.
Adultery in heart, mind, Matthew 5:27–28.
Sexual impurity, Romans 1:24–26.
Slaves to lust, Romans 7:5.
Overcoming lust, Romans 13:14; Galatians 5:16, 24.
Engaged couples, 1 Corinthians 7:36–38.
Inward burning, 2 Corinthians 11:29.
Continual lust for more, Ephesians 4:19.
"Lusts of deceit," Ephesians 4:22 (NASB).
Death to lust, Colossians 3:5.
Heathen lust, 1 Thessalonians 4:5.
Evil desires of youth, 2 Timothy 2:22.
Expanding lust, James 1:15.
Sensual pleasures, James 4:3 (AB).

Abstain from lust, 1 Peter 2:11.
"Depraved lust," 2 Peter 2:10 (NRSV).
Overt lust, 2 Peter 2:14 (AB, GNB).
"Lust of the eye," 1 John 2:16.
Those who keep themselves pure, Revelation 14:4.

LUXURY

Palace diet, 1 Kings 4:22–23.
Solid gold table setting, 1 Kings 10:21–22.
A tent or a palace, 1 Chronicles 15:1 (LB).
Week-long banquet, Esther 1:5–6.
Going without dessert, Daniel 10:3 (LB).
Sumptuous bed and board, Amos 6:3–4.
People in fine homes, temple in ruins, Haggai 1:1–4.
Jesus accused of luxury, Matthew 26:6–13.
Expensive perfume prepared Jesus for Cross, Mark 14:3–9.
Hairstyles and jewelry, 1 Timothy 2:9–10.

M

MAGIC

Seeking God's will by divination, Genesis 30:27.
Unwise men of Egypt, Genesis 41:1–24.
Pretending to believe in divination, Genesis 44:5.
Professional magicians, Exodus 7:8–12; 8:1–19.
Israel superstitions, Isaiah 2:6–8.
False oracles, prophets, Jeremiah 23:33–40.
Baffled magicians, Daniel 1:20; 2:1–13; 4:4–7.
Sorcerer's vanity, Acts 8:9–11.
Satan's evil tricks, Ephesians 6:11 (GNB).
Counterfeit miracles, 2 Thessalonians 2:9–10.
Magicians into lake of fire, Revelation 21:8; 22:15.

MANAGEMENT

Slave drivers, Exodus 1:11 (GNB).
Relative assisted management, Exodus 4:18.
Government attitude toward management, Exodus 5:2–5.
Young kings of Israel, 2 Kings 23:31, 36; 24:8, 18.
Delegated responsibility, Nehemiah 3:1–32.
Job assignments, Nehemiah 13:30.
Lazy employee, Proverbs 10:26 (NRSV).
Management by objective, Proverbs 6:6–8 (LB).

Unjust management, Jeremiah 22:13; Malachi 3:5; Luke
  12:42–46; James 5:4.
Labor relations, Matthew 20:6–16; 21:33–41.
Faithful, prudent manager, Luke 12:42 (NRSV).
Trade unions, Acts 19:23–27.
Payment to laborers, Romans 4:4.
"Guardians and managers," Galatians 4:2 (NRSV).
Concern for servant, Matthew 8:5–13; Luke 7:3.
Avoiding harsh management, 2 Corinthians 13:10.

MARRIAGE
First arranged marriage, Genesis 2:18–24.
Deceitful marital status, Genesis 12:10–20; 20:1–18;
  26:7–11.
Search for Isaac's bride, Genesis 24:1–58; 25:19–20.
Marriage after wife's death, Genesis 25:1–2.
Bride's consent to marriage, Genesis 24:58; 1 Samuel
  25:19–43.
Marriage between relatives, Genesis 29:23–30.
Premarital sex, Genesis 34:1–31.
Responsibility after illicit relationship, Exodus 22:16.
Husband's involvement in wife's business, Numbers
  30:10–15.
Limited choice for women, Numbers 36:6.
Divorce, remarriage, Deuteronomy 24:1–5.
Daughter given as reward, Joshua 15:16.
Father's intervention, Judges 15:1–2.
Kidnapped wives, Judges 21:20–23.
David's many wives, 2 Samuel 5:13.
Marital strife, hatred, 2 Samuel 6:16–23.
Famous child of bad marriage, 2 Samuel 12:24–25.
Terminated relationships, 2 Samuel 20:3.
Marriage alliance, 1 Kings 3:1.
Marriage to unbelievers, 1 Kings 11:1–8.
King and queen, Nehemiah 2:6.
Beautiful queen refused display, Esther 1:9–21.
Marital conflict, Job 2:9–10.
Strategic verse for marriage, Psalm 34:3.
Key to happy marriage, Proverbs 5:18–20.
Fury of betrayed husband, Proverbs 6:27–35.
Blessing of good wife, Proverbs 12:4.
Favor of the Lord, Proverbs 18:22.
Two better than one, Ecclesiastes 4:9–12.
Enjoy life together, Ecclesiastes 9:9.
Sister, bride, Song of Songs 4:9 (Also see 8:1).

Taste of bridal lips, Song of Songs 4:11.
Marital intimacy, Song of Songs 4:16.
True love cannot be quenched, Song of Songs 8:7.
Israel as God's bride, Jeremiah 2:1–3.
Culminated joy, Jeremiah 7:34.
Marriage in distressing times, Jeremiah 33:10–11.
Husbands, wives rebel against God, Jeremiah 44:16–19.
Wife preferred strangers to husband, Ezekiel 16:32.
Restrictions on marriage for priests, Ezekiel 44:22.
Hosea commanded to marry evil woman, Hosea 1:2–3.
Restored marriage, Hosea 2:16–20.
Love for adulterous wife, Hosea 3:1.
Unable to have children, Hosea 9:11.
Agreement necessary for walking together, Amos 3:3.
Marriage to daughter of god, Malachi 2:11.
Vows of youth, Malachi 2:15.
Cause for divorce, Matthew 5:31–32.
Jesus and divorce, Matthew 19:3–9.
Advice of Pilate's wife, Matthew 27:19.
Heaven, marriage and remarriage, Mark 12:18–25; 1 Corinthians 7:39–40.
Brief marriage of prophetess, Luke 2:36–37.
One woman, many husbands, John 4:17–18.
Relationship of husband and wife, 1 Corinthians 7:1–7.
Bachelor's advice on marriage, 1 Corinthians 7:1–7.
Marriage between unbelievers and believers, 1 Corinthians 7:10–16.
Paul described role of women, 1 Corinthians 11:2–16.
Role of husband and wife, Ephesians 5:21–33.
Rapport between wives and husbands, Colossians 3:18, 19; 1 Peter 3:1–2, 7.
Absence of love, 2 Timothy 3:3.
Elder permitted one wife, Titus 1:6.
Honorable, pure, Hebrews 13:4.
Wife loves husband's enemies, James 4:4 (LB).
Avoiding problems in marriage, 1 Peter 3:1–7.
No fear in love, 1 John 4:18.
No bride, bridegroom in Babylon, Revelation 18:23.
Garments of bride, Revelation 19:7–8; 21:2.

MARTYR
Martyred priests, 1 Samuel 22:17–18.
Predicted martyrs, Matthew 10:21.
Death of John the Baptist, Matthew 14:1–12.

Those who only destroy body, Luke 12:4–5.
Stoning of Stephen, Acts 6:8–15; 7:1–60.
James slain with sword, Acts 12:2.
Prepared for martyrdom, Acts 21:13.
Living martyrdom, Romans 8:36.
Measure of love, 1 Corinthians 13:3.
Willing to lay down one's life for others, 1 John 3:16.
Faithful in persecution, Revelation 2:13.
Put to death for witness, Revelation 6:9.
Drunk with blood of saints, Revelation 17:6.
Beheaded for faithfulness and testimony, Revelation 20:4.

MEDIATOR

People in need of mediator, Exodus 20:19; Deuteronomy 5:27.
Burdened leadership, Deuteronomy 9:18.
Standing between living and dead, Numbers 16:48.
Job's cry for mediator between him and God, Job 9:33–35.
Ineffective mediators, Jeremiah 15:1.
People's dependence upon mediator, Jeremiah 42:1–4.
Message came through prophet, Haggai 1:1.
Faith of friends caused man's healing, Mark 2:1–5.
God only known through Christ, Luke 10:22; 1 Timothy 2:5; Hebrews 8:6; 9:15, 24; 12:24; 1 John 2:1.
Go between, Galatians 3:20 (AB).

MEAT

HEY NOW, STOP LOOKING AT ME THAT WAY!

Jesus between, 1 Timothy 2:4–5 (LB).
Jesus our guarantee, Hebrews 7:22.

MEDICARE
Medical bills, Mark 5:25–34.

MEDITATION
Daily meditation, Joshua 1:8.
Constant meditation, Psalm 1:2 (See Berk.).
"Silently search your heart," Psalm 4:4 (CEV, NKJV).
Time for reflection, Psalm 16:7.
Heart meditation, Psalm 19:14.
Thirst for living God, Psalm 42:1–2.
Deep calling unto deep, Psalm 42:7–8.
Meditation in temple, Psalm 48:9.
Silently seeking God, Psalm 62:1 (NKJV, NRSV).
Nightlong meditation, Psalm 63:6.
Grateful reflections, Psalms 77:10–12; 143:5.
Bible insight, Psalm 119:18 (Berk.).
Daylong experience, Psalm 119:97.
Wisdom from Scriptures, Psalm 119:98–100.
Prayer for inner peace, righteousness, Psalm 139:23–24.
Glory of kings, Proverbs 25:2.
"Think what God has done," Ecclesiastes 7:13 (CEV).
Spiritual delicacy, Jeremiah 15:16.
Communing outdoors, Ezekiel 3:22–23.
Silent before the Lord, Zephaniah 1:7; Zechariah 2:13.
Prayer closet, Matthew 6:5–6.
Pondering profound event, Luke 2:19 (See AB).
Daybreak solitude, Luke 4:42.
Jesus withdrew to pray, Luke 5:16.
Ultimate "Holy of Holies," 1 Corinthians 3:16.
Alone in Athens, 1 Thessalonians 3:1.
Reward of careful reflection, 2 Timothy 2:7.
Fix thoughts on Jesus, Hebrews 3:1.
Meditate about message, 1 John 2:24 (CEV).
Those who take Scriptures to heart, Revelation 1:3.

MERCHANDISE
Prostitute who paid, Ezekiel 16:33–34.
Accurate scales, Ezekiel 45:9–10.
Merchandise aborted in storm, Jonah 1:5.
No merchandise sales, Revelation 18:11.

METAPHOR
Rising like the sun, Judges 5:31.
Lord and shepherd, Psalm 23:1.
Sun and shield, Psalm 84:11.
Shield and rampart, Psalms 84:11; 91:4.
Sow and reap, Hosea 10:12.
Wickedness in the flesh, Zechariah 5:7, 8.
Salt of earth, Matthew 5:13.
Seed and soil, Matthew 13:19–23, 37–43.
Bread and body, Matthew 26:26.
Lamp of witness, John 5:35.
Bread of life, John 6:35.
Light of world, John 8:12.
Jesus as the gate, John 10:9.
True vine, John 15:5.
Sorrow turned to joy, John 16:20.
Speaking plainly, John 16:25.
Lampstands and stars, Revelation 1:20.
Incense and prayers, Revelation 5:8.

MIDDLE AGE
Prime of life, Job 29:4.
Death at middle age, Psalm 102:24.
"Noontide of my days," Isaiah 38:10 (Berk.).

MIDNIGHT
Midnight peril, Exodus 11:4.
Midnight prayer, Psalm 119:62.
Ten virgins, Matthew 25:6.
Midnight song, prayer, Acts 16:25.
Preaching until midnight, Acts 20:7.

MILITARY
Clergy exemption, Numbers 1:47–49 (GNB).
Threat of iron chariots, Judges 1:19.
God as militarist, Judges 3:1–2.
Seeking divine strategy, 1 Samuel 14:8–15.
Sexual restraint before combat, 1 Samuel 21:4–5.
Military concern above promises, 2 Samuel 24:10.
Complete devastation, 2 Kings 3:19.
Men trained for service, 1 Chronicles 5:18.
Battle lines, 1 Chronicles 19:17.
Strength of God's army, Psalm 68:17.
"King among his troops," Job 29:25 (NRSV).
Fallible military, Isaiah 31:1–3.

Angel in military, Isaiah 37:36.
Call to arms for Israel invasion, Ezekiel 38:8.
Women in military, Nahum 3:13.
Nonmilitant resistance, John 18:36.
Centurion's devout family, Acts 10:1–2, 22.
Good Christian soldiers, 2 Timothy 2:1–4.
Fellow soldier, Philemon 2.
War in heaven, Revelation 12:7.

MIND

The Lord knows our thoughts, Psalms 94:11; 139:1–4.
Anxiety control, Ecclesiastes 11:10.
Evil thoughts, Jeremiah 4:14.
Revealing thoughts of heart, Luke 2:34–35; 6:8.
Depraved minds, Romans 1:28.
Conflict between mind, body, Romans 7:21–25.
Natural mind, Spirit-controlled mind, Romans 8:6–9.
Futility thinking, Ephesians 4:17.
Attitude of mind dictates conduct, Philippians 4:8–9.
Egotistical mind, Colossians 2:18.
Corrupt mind, conscience, Titus 1:15.
Thoughts fixed on Jesus, Hebrews 3:1.
Minds prepared for action, 1 Peter 1:13.

MIRACLES

False prophet's miracles, Deuteronomy 13:1–5.
Purity prior to miracles, Joshua 3:5 (GNB).
Many, many miracles, Psalm 40:5 (LB).
Selfish prayer rewarded, Psalm 106:14–15.
Not testing God, Isaiah 7:11–12.
Blind see, deaf hear, Isaiah 35:5.
Hezekiah's miracle, Isaiah 38:1–6.
Sun's shadow reversed, Isaiah 38:7–8.
Fiery furnace, Daniel 3:22–27.
Tell no one, Matthew 8:4.
Miracles could have saved Sodom, Matthew 11:23.
Loaves, fishes feed thousands, Matthew 16:7–10; Mark 8:1–21.
Attempt to prevent miracle, Matthew 27:62–66 (See 28:11–15).
Emphasizing healing above Healer, Luke 7:21–23.
Appointed time for miracles, John 2:4 (LB).
Purpose of miracles, John 2:11 (See AB).
Those who must see miracles to believe, John 4:48.
Miracles as publicity, John 7:1–5.

Messianic miracles, John 7:31.
Purpose of miracles, John 10:22–39; 20:30–31.
Sorcerer confounded by miracle, Acts 13:6–12.
Miracles in Paul's ministry, Acts 19:11–12.
Holy Spirit's miraculous resurrection power, Romans 8:11; Ephesians 1:18–21.
Pretended miracles, 2 Thessalonians 2:9 (CEV).
Functioning gifts of Spirit, Hebrews 2:4.

MISUNDERSTANDING
Making wrong right, Numbers 5:6–7.
When others speak evil of you, Psalm 109:20.
Twisting of words, Psalm 56:5.
Better spoken than written, 2 John 12; 3 John 13–14.

MODESTY
Innocent nudity, Genesis 2:25.
First awareness of nudity, Genesis 3:7 (See 2:25).
Noah's nakedness, Genesis 9:20–27.
Modest maiden, Genesis 24:61–65.
Touching private parts, Deuteronomy 25:11.
Secret parts, Isaiah 3:17 (NKJV).
Immodest threat, Jeremiah 13:26.
Shocking conduct, Ezekiel 16:27.
Lessons from lewdness, Ezekiel 23:48 (NKJV).
Miracles to be kept private, Matthew 9:29–31.
Modest thinking, Romans 12:3 (GNB).
Special modesty for body organs, 1 Corinthians 12:22–25.
Modest dress, 1 Timothy 2:9–10.

MONEY
Currency by weight, Genesis 23:16; Ezra 8:24–27; Jeremiah 32:9.
Animals, land, people replace money, Genesis 47:16–21.
Monetary value of human being, Leviticus 27:1–8.
Value of silver in stewardship, Numbers 7:13–85; 10:2.
Services paid in cash, Deuteronomy 2:6.
Money carefully used, Ezra 7:17 (CEV).
Lending money without interest, Psalm 15:5.
Easy money, Proverbs 20:21 (GNB).
Money never satisfies, Ecclesiastes 5:10.
Distorted view of money, Ecclesiastes 10:19.
"Cheat and shortchange," Isaiah 59:6 (LB).
Valueless money, Ezekiel 7:19 (LB).

Prostitute giving rather than receiving fee, Ezekiel 16:32–34.
Currency value, designation, Ezekiel 45:12.
Silver, gold belong to God, Haggai 2:8.
Reward of good stewardship, Malachi 3:8–10.
Cannot serve God, money, Matthew 6:24.
Tainted money for betraying Jesus, Matthew 27:3–10; Luke 22:3–6.
No need for expense money, Mark 6:8–11.
Fraction of cent, Luke 12:59 (AB).
Estimating cost before construction, Luke 14:28–30.
Two coppers, Luke 21:2 (Berk.).
Human equations, Divine power, John 6:1–13.
Spiritual economics, Acts 3:6.
Power of God not for sale, Acts 8:18–24.
Angered by loss of income, Acts 16:16–24.
Profit limited by new life of converts, Acts 19:23–28.
Evangelist seeking employment, 1 Corinthians 9:6–7.
Unmuzzled ox, 1 Corinthians 9:9–14.
Root of evil, 1 Timothy 6:10.
"Not for sordid gain," 1 Peter 5:2 (NRSV).

MORALE

Taking care of business, Deuteronomy 20:5–9.
Leadership for those in trouble, 1 Samuel 22:2.
Ineptness of king's viewpoint, 1 Kings 12:1–15.
People working diligently together, Nehemiah 4:6.
Inequity among citizens, Nehemiah 5:1–5.
Security in the Lord, Psalm 127:1, 2.
Persecuted for destroying morale of soldiers, Jeremiah 38:1–6.
Joy, gladness gone, Jeremiah 48:33.
Demoralizing influence of hunger, Luke 15:13–20.
Morale, firm faith, Colossians 2:5 (NRSV).

MORALITY

Abram, Sarai, Egyptians, Genesis 12:10–20.
Divine guidance in moral conduct, Genesis 20:1–18.
Remarriage of divorced persons, Deuteronomy 24:1–4.
Moral conduct of Boaz, Ruth 3:1–14.
Military morality, 1 Samuel 21:1–5.
Parable rebuking David, 2 Samuel 12:1–4.
David's respect for concubines, 2 Samuel 20:3.
Senile morality, 1 Kings 1:1–4.
Eunuchs looked after queen, Esther 1:10–11; 2:3.

Avoiding lust requires discipline, Job 31:1.
Morality vital part of spirituality, Jeremiah 3:1–5.
Dramatic puberty, Ezekiel 16:5–9.
Stern principle, Matthew 1:19 (LB).
Morality does not bring salvation, Matthew 19:16–26.
Those who need Great Physician, Mark 2:17; 10:17–20.
As in the days of Noah, Luke 17:26–30.
Loose marriage standards, John 4:16–18.
Frightening Felix, Acts 24:24–25 (Berk.).
Function of conscience, Romans 2:14–15.
Morality stems from youth training, Romans 2:17–18 (LB).
Overcoming immoral conduct, Romans 13:14.
Result of new birth, 2 Corinthians 5:17.
Special modesty toward body organs, 1 Corinthians 12:22–25.
"Bad company corrupts good morals," 1 Corinthians 15:33 (NASB).
Prompted by Holy Spirit, Galatians 5:22–23.
"Troublesome moral faults," Galatians 6:2 (AB).
Fruit of the heart, Hebrews 8:10.
"Moral excellence," 2 Peter 1:5 (NASB).
Those who keep themselves pure, Revelation 14:4.

M

MORTALITY

Death marks deliverance from sinful nature, Genesis 3:22.
Desire for immortality, 1 Kings 1:31.
Way of all earth, 1 Kings 2:2.
"Fragile as moths," Job 4:19 (CEV).
Lacking strength of stone, Job 6:12.
Life, breath in God's hands, Job 12:10.
Length of life determined, Job 14:5.
Pessimistic view of mortality, Job 14:7–11.
We are but men, Psalm 9:20.
Mortality in useless time of trouble, Psalm 60:11–12 (NKJV).
Life's mere breath, Psalms 62:9; 144:3–4.
Experiencing divine wonders before death, Psalm 88:10–12.
Created as mortals, Psalm 89:47 (GNB).
Imperfection for mortals, perfection for God, Psalm 119:96.
Wise man and fool soon forgotten, Ecclesiastes 2:16.
No power over day of death, Ecclesiastes 8:8.

Egyptians mere mortals, Isaiah 31:3.
Death in early years, Isaiah 38:10.
Wide contrast between temporal, spiritual, Isaiah 40:7–8.
Those who should live die, should die live, Ezekiel 13:19.
"Son of dust," Ezekiel 40:4 (LB).
Dual nature of man, Romans 7:21–25.
Constant threat of death, Romans 8:36 (see also GNB).
God's preparation exceeds human perception, 1 Corinthians 2:9–10.
Mortal body "perishable container," 2 Corinthians 4:7 (LB).
Human body's rapid deterioration, 2 Corinthians 4:16–18.
Human body as a tent, 2 Corinthians 5:4.
Paul experienced anxiety, Philippians 2:28.
Our body but a tent, 2 Peter 1:13.
Mortality of Jesus, 1 John 5:6.
Limited authority of the beast, Revelation 13:1–18.

MORTGAGE

Machinery not to be mortgaged, Deuteronomy 24:6.
Mortgaging property to buy food, Nehemiah 5:3.
Borrower, lender, Proverbs 22:7.

MOUNTAINS

Ark rested on Ararat, Genesis 8:4.
Abraham offered Isaac on Moriah, Genesis 22:2.
Law given on Sinai, Exodus 19:20.
Moving mountains, Job 9:5; Ezekiel 38:20.
Many mountain peaks, Psalm 68:15 (GNB).
Pre-historic landscape, Psalm 90:1–2.
God's mountains, Psalm 95:4.
Melting mountains, Psalm 97:5.
Temple mountain, Isaiah 2:2.
Astonishment mountain, Ezekiel 35:7 (AB).
Object of divine affection, Ezekiel 36:1–12.
Oceanic mountains, Jonah 2:6 (AB, LB).
Renowned Mount Zion, Micah 4:1 (LB).
Ascension from Olivet, Acts 1:9–11.

MURDER

First murder, Genesis 4:1–16.
Institution of capital punishment, Genesis 9:6.

Premeditated murder, Genesis 27:41–45; 2 Samuel 13:28–29.
Murder averted, Genesis 37:21–24.
Murder forbidden, Exodus 20:13; Matthew 19:18; Romans 13:9; 1 Peter 4:15; 1 John 3:15.
Hired murderer, Deuteronomy 27:25.
Sisera's plight, Judges 4:14–21; 5:24–31.
Thwarted murder, 1 Samuel 19:9–17.
Accused of aiding suicide, 2 Samuel 1:1–16.
Killing in self-defense, 2 Samuel 2:22–23.
David's plot against Uriah, 2 Samuel 11:14–17.
Smothered king, 2 Kings 18:14–15.
Murderer digs own grave, Proverbs 28:17 (GNB).
Unsuspecting victim, Jeremiah 11:18–19.
Total depravity throughout land, Micah 7:2.
Herod's slaughter of male babies, Matthew 2:13–18.
Death of John the Baptist, Matthew 14:1–12.
Judas murderers' accomplice, Matthew 26:14–16.
Seeking to murder, Mark 14:1.
Murder thwarted by Jesus, Luke 4:28–30.
Plan to murder Paul, Acts 23:12–22.
Jealousy the cause of murder, 1 John 3:12.
Incited to kill, Revelation 6:4.

M

MUSIC

First musical instruments, Genesis 4:21.
Musical send-off, Genesis 31:27.
Song of Moses, Exodus 15:1–18, 21.
Hand-wrought trumpets, Numbers 10:2.

MOUNTAIN TOP

Trumpet fanfare, Numbers 10:10.
Wide area trumpet sound, 1 Samuel 13:3.
Music therapy, 1 Samuel 16:14–23.
Prophecy set to music, 2 Kings 3:15–16.
Music ministry, 1 Chronicles 6:32.
Music with all their might, 1 Chronicles 13:8.
Praise with harp accompaniment, 1 Chronicles 25:3.
Payment to choir members, Nehemiah 12:47.
Unpaid musicians, Nehemiah 13:10–11.
Mournful music, Job 30:31; Matthew 9:23–24.
"Songs in the night," Job 35:10.
Harp an instrument of praise, Psalms 33:2–3; 43:4.
Singing with steadfast heart, Psalm 57:7.
Pleasant music, Psalm 81:2.
Marching music, Psalm 68:24–25; Isaiah 23:16.
Musical resume of history, Psalms 78:1–72; 106:1–48.
Strike up the band, Psalm 81:2.
Praising with voice and instrument, Psalm 98:4–6.
Making Scripture the theme of song, Psalm 119:54.
Laughter and music go together, Psalm 126:2.

MYRRH

Dire music, Proverbs 25:20.
"Song of fools," Ecclesiastes 7:5.
Evil woman's music, Isaiah 23:16.
Ruthless song silenced, Isaiah 25:5.
A new song, Isaiah 42:10.
Meaningless lyrics, beautiful voice, Ezekiel 33:32.
Variety of instruments, Daniel 3:5.
Divine deaf ear to praise, Amos 5:23.
Brief song, Micah 2:4.
Instrument instructions, Habakkuk 3:19.
Funeral song, Luke 7:31–32.
Angels praising God, Luke 2:13–14 (Notice, however, that the Bible uses "saying" and not "singing." Some believe angels will not sing until the work of redemption has been completed. Also, Mary's "song" is recorded in Scripture as "Mary said," Luke 1:46).
Prison hymns, Acts 16:25.
Payment for spiritual service, 1 Corinthians 9:1–14.
Distinct rendition, 1 Corinthians 14:7.
Hymns, spiritual songs, Colossians 3:16.
Congregational singing, Hebrews 2:12.
Angel choir, Revelation 5:11–12.
Song for exclusive congregation, Revelation 14:1–3.
Harps in heaven, Revelation 15:2–4.
Music forever silenced, Revelation 18:22.

MYSTERY
Exceedingly mysterious past, Ecclesiastes 7:24 (NASB).
Mysterious sight, Revelation 12:1, 3 (GNB).

MYTH
Myths, old wives' tales, 1 Timothy 1:3–4; 4:7.

N

NAKEDNESS
Initial awareness of nudity, Genesis 3:7 (See 2:25).
Noah's nakedness, Genesis 9:20–25.
Act of shame, Jeremiah 13:26.
Gethsemane nude, Mark 14:51–52.

NATIONS
Nations destroyed, Genesis 7:21.
Native-born, Numbers 15:13.

Earth divided into nations, Deuteronomy 32:8.
Powerful government at God's mercy, 1 Samuel 12:25.
Nations rise and fall, Job 12:23.
Wealth and idolatry, Isaiah 2:7–8.
Divine list of judged nations, Jeremiah 25:15–29.
Land of luxury brought down, Ezekiel 27:1–36 (See 28:1–19).
For continued sinning, certain judgment, Amos 1:3, 6, 9, 11, 13; 2:1, 4, 6 (Note the nature of sins).
All nations important to God, Amos 9:7 (CEV).

NATIVITY

Star of Bethlehem prophesied, Numbers 24:17.
Birth of Jesus prophesied, Isaiah 7:10–14.
Bethlehem prophecy, Micah 5:2.
The Christmas story, Matthew 1:18–25; Luke 2:1–20.
Birth of Christ reviewed, Revelation 12:1–5.

NEED

Exact need provided, Exodus 16:17–20.
Help from God alone, 2 Kings 6:26–27.
Turning to rejected brother, Judges 11:1–10.
Wealth numbs sense of need, Hosea 12:8.
Ignoring need, Amos 4:6.
Meeting need for cold water, Matthew 10:42.
Involvement in need of others, Mark 6:35–43.
Touch of need, Luke 8:43–48.
Reaching out to help others, Acts 11:27–30.

NAVY

Macedonian call, Acts 16:9.
Christ met our greatest need, Romans 5:6–8.
Diversity in prayer, Ephesians 6:18.
Need fully supplied, Philippians 4:19 (AB).
Family members in need, 1 Timothy 5:3–8.
Minimum needs, 1 Timothy 6:8.

NEIGHBOR
Responsibility toward neighbor, Genesis 9:5.
Meeting neighbors, Genesis 34:1 (Berk.).
Integrity between neighbors, Exodus 20:16; Leviticus 19:13–18.
Liability for treacherous animal, Exodus 21:28–32.
Animal injury to neighbor's property, Exodus 22:5.
Criminal hatred to neighbor, Deuteronomy 19:11–13 (See Proverbs 14:12).
Demonstrated neighborliness, Deuteronomy 22:1–4.
Loving neighbor as yourself, 1 Samuel 18:1.
Help of good neighbors, Ezra 1:6.
Equity toward neighbor, Psalm 15:3.
Insincere neighbors, Psalm 28:3.
Insulted by neighbors, Psalm 31:11 (CEV).
A reproach to neighbors, Psalm 44:13.
Doing good to others, Proverbs 3:27–28.
Settle disputes privately, Proverbs 25:9–10.
Seldom visit neighbor, Proverbs 25:17.
Neighborhood integrity, Proverbs 26:18–19.
Nearby neighbor better than distant relative, Proverbs 27:10.
Loudly blessing neighbor, Proverbs 27:14.
Keeping ahead of Joneses, Ecclesiastes 4:4.
Lust among neighbors, Jeremiah 5:8.
Speaking cordially with deceitful heart, Jeremiah 9:8.
Sharing shade, Zechariah 3:10.
Neighbors unaware of Christ's greatness, Matthew 13:53–58; Luke 4:22–24.
Love your neighbor, Matthew 22:34–40; Luke 4:22–24; Romans 13:9–10; James 2:8.
Familiarity breeds contempt, Mark 6:1–6.
Good news shared among neighbors, Luke 1:57–58.
Effective witness to neighbor, John 4:39.
Speak truthfully to neighbors, Ephesians 4:25.
Conduct toward unbelievers, Colossians 4:5.
Royal law of Scripture, James 2:8.

NEW

Nothing new, Ecclesiastes 1:10.

New song, Psalms 33:3; 40:3; 149:1; Isaiah 42:10; Revelation 14:3.

Given new name, Isaiah 56:4–5; 62:2; Acts 11:26; Revelation 3:12.

New things, Isaiah 42:9; 43:19; 48:6; Revelation 21:5.

Made new by faith, Ezekiel 11:19; 36:26; John 3:3; 2 Corinthians 5:17; Galatians 6:15; Ephesians 2:14–15; 1 Peter 1:23.

NEW AGE

Becoming like God, Genesis 3:5.

Human exaltation, Genesis 11:4 (LB).

Men as gods, Isaiah 41:23; Ezekiel 28:2–3 (See LB).

Fallible new age creed, Isaiah 47:10.

Distorted truth, Jeremiah 8:8–9.

Thinking to be God, Ezekiel 28:2–3 (LB).

"Wise as the gods themselves," Daniel 5:11 (CEV).

"Worship their own strength," Habakkuk 1:11 (CEV).

Those who mishandle truth, Matthew 7:21–23.

Sorcerer's claim of divinity, Acts 8:10.

Unknown god, Acts 17:23.

Warning against error, Acts 20:28–31.

Human incapacity to generate truth, Romans 3:10–20 (Note 3:4).

Limitless source of truth, Romans 11:33–36.

Contrary teaching, Romans 16:17–18.

Holistic knowledge of truth, Romans 12:1–2 (See LB).

Earth's wisdom, 1 Corinthians 1:18–21; 3:19; Colossians 2:8–9.

Primary truth, 1 Corinthians 15:3–4.

Mortal limitations, 1 Corinthians 15:50.

Truth obscured, 2 Corinthians 4:1–6.

Source of power, 2 Corinthians 4:7.

Contaminated body, spirit, 2 Corinthians 7:1.

Careful self-evaluation, 2 Corinthians 13:5.

Perverted truth, Galatians 1:6–9.

Inner reality, Galatians 2:20.

Misguided believers, Galatians 5:7.

Prayer for insight, Ephesians 1:18–23; 3:14–21.

Darkness, light, Ephesians 5:8–14.

Universal declaration of truth, Philippians 2:9–11.

Valid inner diety, Colossians 1:27.

Lifestyle correction, Colossians 3:1–5.

Key to truth, 1 Timothy 3:16–17.
Last days conduct, 1 Timothy 4:1; 2 Timothy 3:1–7; 4:1–5.
Pseudo-knowledge, 1 Timothy 6:20 (GNB).
Lovers of self, 2 Timothy 3:2.
Resistance to truth, 2 Timothy 4:3.
Error rebuked, Titus 1:2–16.
Reincarnation refuted, Hebrews 9:27.
Eye witness to truth, 2 Peter 1:16.
Love of the world, 1 John 2:15–17.
Denying Christ's divinity, 1 John 2:22; 4:1–3.
Discerning spirits, 1 John 4:1–3.

NEWS

Good for some, bad for others, Joshua 5:1 (LB).
Causing ears to tingle, 1 Samuel 3:11.
Death of king, 2 Samuel 1:1–12.
Good news from distant land, Proverbs 25:25.
Concurrent messages, Jeremiah 51:31–32.
"Only bad news," Ezekiel 7:26 (CEV).
Bearer of bad news, Ezekiel 33:21.
News of ministry, Colossians 4:7.
Good news of faith, love, 1 Thessalonians 3:6.

N

NIGHTMARE

Thick, dreadful darkness, Genesis 15:12 (See NKJV).
Troubled dream of future, Genesis 41:1–8.
Foreboding bread loaf, Judges 7:13–14.
Disturbing dreams, Job 4:13 (CEV).
Frightening dreams, Job 7:13–15; Daniel 2:1; 4:5.
Many cares cause dreams, Ecclesiastes 5:3.
Horrible nightmares, Daniel 2:1 (CEV).

NON-PROFIT

Priests tax free, Ezra 7:24.
Paying taxes to government, Matthew 22:15–22.

NONSENSE

Talking nonsense, Job 6:25 (GNB).
Wisdom nonsense, 1 Corinthians 3:19 (GNB).
"Bombastic nonsense," 2 Peter 2:18 (NRSV).

NONVERBAL COMMUNICATION

Dove's communication, Genesis 8:10–11.
Removed sandal, Ruth 4:8 (See Joshua 5:15).

"Shook out my lap," Nehemiah 5:13 (KJV).
Putting foot to neck, Joshua 10:24.
Shake hands, Proverbs 6:1 (NKJV).
"I hurl my shoe," Psalm 108:9 (NRSV).
Wink, shuffle, point, Proverbs 6:13.
Visible evidence of sorrow, Isaiah 15:2–3.
Shake dust off feet, Luke 9:5.
Gesture for silence, Acts 21:40.

NONVIOLENCE

Trusting God for deliverance, 2 Chronicles 32:1–21.
Evaluating military logistics, Luke 14:31–32.
Jesus nonviolent, John 18:36.

NOSTALGIA

Looking back on better days, Exodus 16:2–3.
Those who remembered glory of temple, Haggai 2:3.
Prodigal son, Luke 15:17.
Rich man in torment, Luke 16:25–27.

NOSTALGIA

NOW
Psalm 118:24.
Living for today in God's favor, Ecclesiastes 9:7.
Delay ended, Ezekiel 12:28 (LB).
Best time for salvation, 2 Corinthians 6:2.

NUCLEAR
Sky, earth destroyed by fire, 2 Peter 3:7, 10–12.

NUTRITION
Food in wilderness, Exodus 16:2–35.
Egyptian delicacies, Numbers 11:5.
Abagail's balanced diet, 1 Samuel 25:18.
Bread, fruit, 2 Samuel 16:1, 2.
Wine, oil, bread, Psalm 104:15.
Nutritious honey, Proverbs 24:13.
Nutritious raisins, Song of Songs 2:5.
Mother's milk, Isaiah 66:11.
Polluting wheat, Amos 8:6.
Salt that loses saltiness, Luke 14:34–35.
Desiring food of pigs, Luke 15:13–16.

——————————— **O** ———————————

O

OBEDIENCE
Abraham's obedience of Abram, Genesis 12:1–4.
Predicted result of obedience, Genesis 18:19.
Obedience brings blessing, Genesis 22:15–18.
Exercising complete obedience, Exodus 7:6.
Promised reward for obedience, Exodus 19:5.
Reward for father's obedience, Numbers 14:24.
Rationalized obedience, 1 Samuel 15:7–31.
Materialism versus obedience, 1 Kings 13:7–10.
Great things, small things, 2 Kings 5:13.
Obedience brings security, 2 Kings 21:8.
Scripture meaningful by obedience, Psalm 25:10; 103:17–21.
Obedient angels, Psalm 103:20.
Desire for full obedience, Psalm 119:1–5.
Once astray, now obedient, Psalm 119:67.
Guidance of Scripture for all of life, Psalm 119:111–112.
Obedience by Divine instruction, Psalm 143:10.
Man's plans, God's will, Isaiah 30:1.

Obedience under threat of death, Jeremiah 26:1–16.
Obedience to parents and grandparents, Jeremiah 35:1–16.
Mighty are those who obey the Lord, Joel 2:11.
Do what God wants, Matthew 3:15 (CEV).
Desire to obey, Matthew 5:6, 10 (CEV, GNB).
Cannot obey two masters, Matthew 6:24.
Cost of following Jesus, Matthew 9:9.
Divine kinship, Mark 3:35.
Fulfilling requirements of the law, Luke 2:39.
Wisdom from doing God's will, John 7:17.
Obedience of Jesus, John 12:50; Romans 5:19; Hebrews 5:8–9.
Doing what Christ commands, John 14:15.
Obeying God rather than men, Acts 4:18–20; 5:29.
Obedience resulting from faith, Romans 1:5.
Obedience brings righteousness, Romans 2:13.
Reputation for obedience, Romans 16:19.
Obedience in absentia, Philippians 2:12–13.
Athletes compete according to rules, 2 Timothy 2:5.
Turn away from wickedness, 2 Timothy 2:19.
Slaves' obedience, Titus 2:9–10.
By faith Noah and Abraham obeyed God, Hebrews 11:7–12.
Profession without obedience, 1 John 2:4–6.

OBSCENITY

Obscenity committed in anger, Deuteronomy 25:11–12.
Covenant to avoid lust, Job 31:1.
Obscenity avoided, Psalm 101:3 (LB).
Obscenity of two sisters, Ezekiel 23:1–49.
"Vulgar signs," Zephaniah 2:15 (CEV).
Language purified, Zephaniah 3:9.
Avoid obscenity, Ephesians 5:4 (LB).

OCCUPATION

Holiness by virtue of occupation, Leviticus 21:8.
Role of priest, Deuteronomy 18:1–2.
Occupation forces in place, Isaiah 22:7.
"What business are you in?" Jonah 1:8 (CEV).
Tentmakers, Acts 18:1–3.
Zenas, the lawyer, Titus 3:13.

OFFEND

By nothing offended, Psalm 119:165 (KJV, NRSV).
Offended by criticism, Job 20:2–3.
Offended brother, Proverbs 18:19 (NASB, NKJV).
Offensive Christian personality, 2 Corinthians 2:15–16.

OPPONENT

Facing formidable opponent, Numbers 21:21–26.
Future accomplishment assured, Numbers 21:34.
Son sought to impress father, 1 Samuel 14:1–14.
Revenge left to God's timing, 1 Samuel 26:1–11.
Trying to intimidate, Ezra 4:4.
Stirring up trouble, Nehemiah 4:8.
Facing enemy eye-to-eye, Jeremiah 34:3.
Total conquest of enemy, Jeremiah 50:35–40.
Satan, foremost opponent, Zechariah 3:1–2.
"Correcting opponents with gentleness," 2 Timothy 2:15 (NRSV).

OPPORTUNITY

Challenge, opportunity, Deuteronomy 8:1–3 (See CEV).
Given second chance, Jonah 1:1–3; 3:1–3.
Opportunity withdrawn, Proverbs 1:24–33; Hosea 5:6.
Opened doors will not be shut, Isaiah 45:1.
Seek the Lord while He may be found, Isaiah 55:6, 7.
Give glory to God before darkness comes, Jeremiah 13:16; John 12:35, 36.
Privilege of hearing Christ's message, Matthew 13:17.
Closed door of opportunity for repentence, Luke 13:25–28.
Excuses for not attending a banquet, Luke 14:16–24.
Greatest opportunity of all time, John 3:16–17.
Seizing the opportunity, John 9:4; Acts 21:40.
Turning to light before darkness comes, John 12:35–36.
Those scattered by persecution, Acts 11:19–21.
Jewish rejection, Gentile choice, Acts 13:46.
Arrested, requested witness opportunity, Acts 21:37.
Open door for gospel, 1 Corinthians 16:8, 9.
"Don't give the devil a chance," Ephesians 4:27 (CEV, NASB).
Opportunity still stands, Hebrews 4:1.
Divinely opened door, 2 Corinthians 2:12; Revelation 3:8.

OPTIMISM

Determined, confident, Joshua 1:6, 9, 18 (GNB).
Optimism brings defeat, Joshua 7:3–4.
Boy brings hope to army of Israel, 1 Samuel 17:32.
Good news expected from good man, 2 Samuel 18:27.
Laughter, joy can return, Job 8:21.
Darkness like morning, Job 11:17.
"Cheer up!" Psalm 31:24 (LB).
Certainty of deliverance, Psalm 34:19.
"Happy ending," Psalm 37:37 (LB).
Hope in time of despair, Psalm 42:5.
Pessimism turns to optimism, Psalm 73:12–28.
Light dawns in darkness, Psalm 112:4.
No fear of bad news, Psalm 112:7–8.
The day the Lord has made, Psalm 118:24.
Lifting one's eyes to hills, Psalm 121:1.
Cheerful heart like medicine, Proverbs 17:22.
Light shining in darkness, Isaiah 60:1–2 (See CEV).
God's plans for you, Jeremiah 29:10–11.
False optimism, Ezekiel 13:10 (GNB).
Behind devastation, ahead anticipation, Joel 2:3.
"Things will be better," Haggai 2:15 (CEV).
Old age optimism, Romans 4:18–22.
Always cheerful, 2 Corinthians 5:6 (CEV).
Optimistic prayer, Philippians 1:3–6.
Motivated by joy, 1 Thessalonians 1:6.
Always joyful, 1 Thessalonians 5:16.
Eternal encouragement, 2 Thessalonians 2:16–17.

ORGANIZATION

Army of chosen men, 2 Samuel 6:1; 23:8–39.
Organization for building temple, 1 Kings 5:12–18.
Foremen, laborers, 2 Chronicles 2:2.
Well organized, Proverbs 15:22.
Organized priests, Ezekiel 40:44–46.
Appointing twelve apostles, Mark 3:13–19.
Organizing for miracle, Luke 9:14–15.
Welfare to widows organized, Acts 6:1–4.
Need for proper credentials, Acts 15:22–31.
Serving the Lord in unity, Romans 15:5–6; 1 Corinthians 1:10.
Church organization, 1 Corinthians 12:28–31.

Good organization, 1 Corinthians 14:33-40.
Building fitted together, Ephesians 2:21.
Diversity to produce unity, Ephesians 4:11-13.
Orderliness commended, Colossians 2:5.
Appointing elders, organizing details, Titus 1:1-5.
Operating through proper channels, Philemon 12-14.
Regulated universe, Hebrews 1:3 (LB).
Submit to authority, Hebrews 13:17.

ORPHAN

Divine love for orphans, Exodus 22:22-24.
Tithe given to fatherless, Deuteronomy 26:12.
Background of Queen Esther, Esther 2:7.
Mistreated orphan, Job 24:9.
God looks after fatherless, Psalm 10:14; 68:5.
Orphaned by judgment, Psalm 109:9.
Protect orphan property, Proverbs 23:10; Isaiah 1:17.
Unwanted child, Ezekiel 16:2-5.
Spiritual orphan, John 14:18.

OVERCONFIDENCE

Thinking it easy to face an enemy, Deuteronomy 1:41,
42.
Overconfidence causes defeat, Joshua 7:3-4.
Putting confidence in numerical strength, Judges 7:2,
12.

O

OLD AGE

METHUSELAH'S BIRTHDAY.

PACIFISM

Unworthy to build house of God, 1 Chronicles 28:2–3.
Seek for peace, Psalm 34:14.
Warmongers, man of peace, Psalm 120:6–7.
Wisdom versus weapons, Ecclesiastes 9:18.
Coming world peace, Isaiah 2:4; Hosea 2:18.

PAGAN

Impudent gods, Exodus 18:11 (Berk.).
Strange "reverence" of pagan idol, 1 Samuel 5:1–5.
Sacrifice of son, 2 Kings 16:3.
Pagan king speaks of Israel's "god," Isaiah 37:10.
One true God, many gods, Daniel 3:28–30; 4:18.
Pagans certain of erroneous belief, Acts 19:35–36.
Instinctive truth, Romans 1:19–20 (LB).
Gathered from all tribes, nations, Revelation 7:9–10.

PAIN

"Unrelenting pain," Job 6:10 (NRSV).
Personal pain, Job 14:22.
Incessant pain, Job 30:17; 33:19; Isaiah 21:3; Jeremiah 15:18.
Painful laughter, Proverbs 14:13 (NASB).
Men suffering childbirth pains, Jeremiah 30:6.
Wounds wide as sea, Lamentations 2:13.
Response of Jesus to intense pain, Matthew 8:5–7.
Jesus faced terrible suffering, Matthew 16:21 (CEV).
Sedative at crucifixion, Mark 15:23–24, 36.
Flogging Jesus, John 19:1 (See LB).
All creation in pain, Romans 8:22.
Bite the tongue, Revelation 16:10 (GNB).
No more pain, Revelation 21:4.

PARENTS

Relationship between Adam, Eve, Genesis 4:1–2.
Like father, like son, Genesis 5:1–3.
Age of Old Testament fathers, Genesis 11:10–26.
Bearing children at advanced age, Genesis 16:16; 17:1–21; 21:1–5 (See Romans 4:18–21).
Father head of house, Genesis 18:19.
Witness to offspring, Exodus 10:2.
Teaching children, Exodus 12:26–27; Deuteronomy 6:20–24.
Reward for honoring parents, Exodus 20:12.

Remembering and following divine teaching, Deuteronomy 4:9.

Spiritual duty of parents to children, Deuteronomy 11:1-7.

Loyalty torn between father, friend, 1 Samuel 19:1-2.

Son's concern for parents, 1 Samuel 22:3.

Father, son together in death, 2 Samuel 1:23.

Rivalry between father, son, 2 Samuel 15:1-37.

Confessing ancestors' sins, Nehemiah 9:2.

When forsaken by parents, God may be trusted, Psalm 27:10.

Blessing from generation to generation, Psalms 44:1-3; 78:1-7.

Children special blessing from the Lord, Psalm 127:3-5.

Advice of King Solomon to son, Proverbs 1:8-19.

Discipline of good father, Proverbs 3:11-12; 4:1-10.

Parental influence, Proverbs 6:20-23.

Wise, foolish sons, Proverbs 10:1.

Proper discipline of children, Proverbs 13:24; Hebrews 12:5-11.

Grief caused by foolish son, Proverbs 17:25.

Children who rob parents, Proverbs 19:26; 28:24.

Properly training child, Proverbs 22:6.

Child's heart yields to discipline, Proverbs 22:15.

Father conveying God's truth to children, Isaiah 38:18-19.

Abraham and Sarah, Isaiah 51:2.

When it is better not to have had children, Jeremiah 22:30.

Fathers unable to help children, Jeremiah 47:3.

Children sacrificed to idols, Ezekiel 16:20.

Message conveyed to children's children, Joel 1:3.

Joseph and Mary into and out of Egypt, Matthew 2:13-21.

Gospel can turn children against parents, Matthew 10:32-36.

Causing child to go astray, Mark 9:42.

Mary and Joseph did not realize Son's significance, Luke 2:25-35.

Parents surprised by answer to their prayers, Luke 8:56.

Concern for only child, Luke 9:38.

Parents support children, not children parents, 2 Corinthians 12:14.

How father should deal with children, 1 Thessalonians
 2:11–12.
Influence of Scriptures since childhood, 2 Timothy
 3:14–15.
Family of elder must be exemplary, Titus 1:6.
Children of good parents, 2 John 4.
Joy of believer's children, 3 John 4.

PASSION

Quiet romance Boaz, Ruth, Ruth 3:7–18.
Pounding heartbeat, Song of Songs 5:4 (NIV).
Unrequited sexual desire, Ezekiel 16:23–30.
Intense passion, Hosea 7:6.
Marriage relationship in heaven, Mark 12:18–27.
Continual lust for more, Ephesians 4:19 (NIV).
"Passions of youth," 2 Timothy 2:22 (GNB).

PEACE

Nation at peace, Joshua 14:15; 23:1.
Three-year peace, 1 Kings 22:1–5.
Desire for peace, security, 2 Kings 20:19.
Divine ability to bring peace, Psalm 46:9.
Oceans and nations, Psalm 65:7.
Living under shadow of the Almighty, Psalm 91:1–2.
An honor to avoid strife, Proverbs 20:3.
The Peacemaker, Isaiah 53:5.
Proclaiming peace when there is no peace, Jeremiah
 6:14.
Break the bow, Jeremiah 49:35.
Israel, land of unwalled villages, Ezekiel 38:10–12.
Swords beaten into plowshares, Micah 4:3.
Blessed are the peacemakers, Matthew 5:9.
World peace impossible without Christ, Matthew
 24:6–8.
Jesus predicted no peace on earth, Mark 13:6–8.
Peace Jesus gives, Luke 24:36 (AB).
Heart peace, 1 Corinthians 1:3 (AB); 1 Thessalonians
 1:1 (AB); 2 Thessalonians 1:2 (AB).
Soul peace, Galatians 1:3 (AB).
Peace defined, Philippians 4:7 (AB).

PERFECTION

Blameless conduct, Genesis 17:1.
Divine perfection, faithfulness, Deuteronomy 32:4.
Made pure through testing, Job 23:10.

Perfect in God's eyes, Psalm 4:1 (LB).
A perfect way, Psalm 18:32.
Limited perfection, Psalm 119:96.
Impossibility of perfection, Ecclesiastes 7:20.
High cost of perfection, Matthew 19:21.
Evaluation of Nathanael by Jesus, John 1:47.
Aim for perfection, 2 Corinthians 13:11.
Progress toward perfection, Philippians 3:12 (LB).
Perfect, perfection, maturity, Philippians 3:15 (Compare NASB, NIV, NRSV).
Perfect High Priest, Hebrews 4:15; 7:26.
Suffering perfected Jesus, Hebrews 5:9 (CEV).
Those who claim perfection, 1 John 1:8–10.
Sinless Savior, 1 Peter 1:18–19; 2:22.

PERFUME

Fragrant incense, Exodus 30:7.
Temple fragrance not for personal enjoyment, Exodus 30:34–38.
Purposeful use of perfume, Ruth 3:3.
Fragrant clothing, Psalm 45:8.
Many fragrances, Song of Songs 4:10–14.
Anointing of Jesus, Matthew 26:6–13.
Aromatics, Mark 16:1 (Berk.).

P

PETS

PERMISSION

Entering God's presence, Psalm 24:3–4 (See Ephesians 2:18).
Gates open, Isaiah 26:2. (See John 10:9.)
Opportunity for anyone, Isaiah 55:1–3.
Come, Matthew 11:28, 29.
Bold admittance, Hebrews 4:14–16.
Full right to enter, 2 Peter 1:11 (GNB).

PERSONALITY

Personality of unborn child, Genesis 16:11–12.
Twins' contrasting personalities, Genesis 25:27.
Blighted personality, Deuteronomy 32:32–33.
Quarrelsome personality, Proverbs 27:15–16.
Faces reflect hearts, Proverbs 27:19.
Clash of apostolic personalities, Acts 15:36–41; Galatians 2:11.
Struggle between flesh, spirit, Romans 7:15–18, 21–25.
Reactions to Christian personality, 2 Corinthians 2:15–16.
Fruit of Spirit, Galatians 5:22.
Joy, gentleness, Philippians 4:4–5.
Personality given by Holy Spirit, 1 Thessalonians 1:6.
Inner beauty, 1 Peter 3:3–4.
Additions to faith, 2 Peter 1:5–9.

PHILOSOPHY

Human viewpoint, Ecclesiastes 1:2.
Fragile human wisdom, Isaiah 29:14.
Philosophers belittled Christian message, Acts 17:18.
Not wise but fools, Romans 1:22.
Human wisdom versus God's, 1 Corinthians 1:19–20; 2:6; 3:19–20.
Deceptive philosophy, Colossians 2:8.

PHONY

"Fake surprise," Malachi 2:17 (LB).
Hyper-piety, Matthew 6:16–18.
Phony exhibitionists, Matthew 23:5–7.
Clean outside, phony inside, Matthew 23:25–28.
Ego displayed by teachers of law, Mark 12:38–40.
Conversion believed to be phony, Acts 9:26–27.
False humility, Colossians 2:18.

PHYSICIAN
Physician morticians, Genesis 50:2.
Seeking only medical help, 2 Chronicles 16:12.
Ignorant, "quack" doctors, Job 13:4 (LB, Berk.).
Careless attention to wound, Jeremiah 8:11.
Doctor needed in Gilead, Jeremiah 8:22.
Only sick people need doctor, Matthew 9:12; Luke 5:31.
Ineffective physicians, Mark 5:25–26.
Greetings from Doctor Luke, Colossians 4:14.

PITY
Pharaoh's daughter and baby Moses, Exodus 2:5–6.
Destruction without pity, Deuteronomy 7:16.
No pity in judgment, Lamentations 2:2.
"I will show no pity," Ezekiel 7:4 (CEV).
Joseph's unfounded pity for Mary, Matthew 1:19.
Jesus refused pity, Luke 23:27–28.

PKs
Evil sons, 1 Samuel 2:12–17, 22–25; 3:10–14.

PLAN
Journey with the Lord's approval, Judges 18:6.
Hiding true intentions, 1 Samuel 16:1–5.
"Impossible scheme," Psalm 131:1 (CEV).
Planning ahead, Proverbs 13:16 (LB).
Man's plans, God's purpose, Proverbs 19:21.
Patience needed to persuade, Proverbs 25:15.
Do not hide plans from God, Isaiah 29:15 (CEV).
Drawing plan for battle, Ezekiel 4:1–3.
Design, measurement and arrangements, Ezekiel 43:10–12.
Estimate cost before construction, Luke 14:28–30.
Master planner at work, Romans 12:12 (LB).
Planning journey, 2 Corinthians 1:15–17.
No certainty of tomorrow, James 4:13–16.
Redemption planned before creation, 1 Peter 1:18–20.

PLEASURE
Time to rejoice, not weep, Nehemiah 8:9–10.
Nauseating pleasure, Job 20:12–16; Proverbs 21:17.
Giving God pleasure, Job 22:2–3.
Joy beyond levity of wine, Psalm 4:7.
True joy only from the Lord, Psalm 84:11.
Whale at play, Psalm 104:26 (LB).

Covert pleasures, Proverbs 9:17.
Love of pleasure, Proverbs 21:17.
Meaningless activity, Ecclesiastes 2:1–11.
"I commend enjoyment," Ecclesiastes 8:15 (NRSV).
Alcoholism, Isaiah 5:11–12.
Wages of sin, Lamentations 1:14; Romans 6:23.
Unable to remember enjoyment, Lamentations 3:17 (LB).
Peril of ease, Amos 6:1.
Fisherman burns incense to net, Habakkuk 1:16.
Deathly conduct, 1 Timothy 5:6.
Lovers of pleasure, 2 Timothy 3:4.
Refusing pleasures of Egypt, Hebrews 11:24–25.
Joy of problems, testing, James 1:2–4.
Sensual pleasures, James 4:3 (AB).
Those who carouse, 2 Peter 2:13–16.
Joy of good reputation, 3 John 3–4.

POISE

Poise in every circumstance, Proverbs 1:2 (LB).
Cool spirit, Proverbs 17:27 (NASB, NRSV).
"Quiet words," Ecclesiastes 9:17 (NRSV).
"Calmness will undo great offenses," Ecclesiastes 10:4 (NASB).
Silent poise, Mark 15:3–5.
Happy, unruffled, Acts 2:46–47 (Berk.).
Keep cool, 2 Timothy 4:4–5 (AB).
Inadequate poise, 2 Peter 3:17 (NASB, NKJV).

POISON

Deliverance from snakebite, Numbers 21:4–9.
Venom of vipers, Deuteronomy 32:24.
Fangs of an adder, Job 20:16.
Deaf cobra, Psalm 58:4.
Broken fangs, Psalm 58:4–6 (LB).
Poisonous speech, Psalm 140:3; James 3:8.
Pestilence of locusts, Revelation 9:7–11.

POOR

Harvest gleaning for poor, Leviticus 19:9–10.
Poor, rich, 1 Samuel 2:7.
Benevolent spirit, Job 29:11–15; 30:25; 31:15–22.
Sense of true value, Psalm 37:16; Proverbs 13:7; 28:6.
Call to altruism, Psalm 82:3–4.

Divine opportunity, Proverbs 19:17; Matthew 25:42–45.
Penalty for selfishness, Proverbs 21:13.

POPULARITY

King's lack of popularity, 1 Samuel 10:26–27.
Pleased subjects, 2 Samuel 3:36.
Winning favor of people, 2 Samuel 15:1–6.
David's fear of Absalom's popularity, 2 Samuel 15:13–14.
Many sought Job's favor, Job 11:19.
The wide, the narrow, Matthew 7:13–14.
Pharisees fear of crowd, Matthew 21:45–46.
Seeking praise of men, John 12:42–43.
Healing increased Jesus' popularity, Mark 3:7–10.
Cornelius respect for Peter, Acts 10:25–26.
Royal murder to gain popularity, Acts 12:1–4.
Unknown yet well-known, 2 Corinthians 6:9.
Popularity and effective service, Galatians 1:10 (GNB).
Favor resulting from dependability, Colossians 3:22.

POWER

Flaunting power, 1 Kings 12:1–11.
Power from wealth, Ruth 2:1 (KJV).
Raw spiritual power, Isaiah 19:1.
Power in God's name, Jeremiah 10:6 (LB).
Nothing too hard for God, Jeremiah 32:27.
No longer powerful, Ezekiel 26:2 (CEV).
Power of Divine message, Luke 4:32.
Divine power relinquished, Luke 14:41 (GNB).
"Royal power," Luke 19:12 (NRSV).
Witnessing power, Acts 1:8.
Resurrection power, Romans 8:11; Ephesians 1:18–20.
Strength from weakness, 2 Corinthians 12:9.
Divine breath will overthrow man of sin, 2 Thessalonians 2:8.
Scripture's power, Hebrews 4:12 (See AB).
Protected by God's power, 1 Peter 1:5 (NRSV).

PRAISE

Song of Moses, Exodus 15:1, 2.
"Stand up and praise the Lord," Nehemiah 9:5.
Praise for past blessings, Nehemiah 9:7–38.
Harp as instrument of praise, Psalm 43:4.
Sing praise with understanding, Psalm 47:7 (KJV).
Giving praise to God's Word, Psalm 56:10.

Singing with steadfast heart, Psalm 57:7.
"Silent praise," Psalm 65:1 (LB).
"Let God be magnified," Psalm 70:4 (NASB, NKJV).
Man's wrath praises God, Psalm 76:10 (KJV).
Cry of praise to the Lord, Psalm 89:8.
Giving the Lord glory due Him, Psalm 96:8.
David's song of praise, Psalm 103:1–22.
Motivation for praise, Psalm 107:8, 15, 21, 31.
"God of my praise," Psalm 109:1 (NKJV, NRSV).
Praise, glory belong only to God, Psalm 115:1; Acts 12:21–23; 1 Corinthians 3:7.
Nature, people praise the Lord, Psalm 148:1–14.
Let another praise you, Proverbs 27:2.
Praise, test of humility, Proverbs 27:21.
Talented people encouraging each other, Isaiah 41:7.
Joy, gladness, Jeremiah 33:11.
Daniel's gratitude to God for needed wisdom, Daniel 2:19–23.
When God turns deaf ear to praise, Amos 5:22; 8:3, 10.
Jesus' evaluation of John the Baptist, Matthew 11:11–14.
Crowd praised Jesus prior to crying out, "Crucify Him!" Matthew 21:6–11 (Note 27:20–23).
Children's praise, Matthew 21:15–16.
Receive praise from God, 1 Corinthians 4:5.
Let the Lord commend, 2 Corinthians 10:17–18.
Trying to please others, Galatians 1:10.
Motivation preaching, teaching, 1 Thessalonians 2:1–6.
Praise God for ministry success, 1 Thessalonians 3:8–10.
Good deeds made known, 1 Timothy 5:25.
Praise to Redeemer and Creator, Revelation 5:13–14.
Outcry of praise to God, Revelation 7:11–12.
Concluding proclamation of faith in God, Revelation 15:3–4.

PREGNANCY

"Pregnancy-troubles," Genesis 3:16 (Berk.).
Pregnant with divine help, Genesis 4:1.
Children born in old age, Genesis 21:1–7.
Rebekah's pregnancy answered prayer, Genesis 25:21.
Rights of pregnant woman, Exodus 21:22.
Sterile woman conceived Samson, Judges 13:1–8.
Avoiding alcohol during pregnancy, Judges 13:2–4.
Beyond age of childbearing, Ruth 1:11.

Miscarriage from bad water, 2 Kings 2:19–21 (GNB).
Embryo development, Psalm 139:13–15.
Wonder of body being formed, Ecclesiastes 11:5 (See
    CEV).
Time of birth, Isaiah 26:17; 66:9.
Fetus in God's care, Isaiah 44:2 (CEV).
God's prenatal plan for Jeremiah, Jeremiah 1:4–5.
Nursing, pregnancy, Hosea 1:8.
Pregnant virgin, Matthew 1:25 (LB).
Given son in declining years, Luke 1:5–25.
Five month seclusion, Luke 1:24.
Baby leaped in mother's womb, Luke 1:39–44.
Pain, joy in pregnancy, John 16:21.
Rejoicing although barren, Galatians 4:27.
Natural, miraculous pregnancies, Galatians 4:28 (AB).
Needed physical delivery power, Hebrews 11:11 (AB).

PREJUDICE
Prejudice without reason, Psalm 69:4.
Eyes closed to facts, Proverbs 1:29 (LB).
Fool's prejudice, Proverbs 18:2.
Prejudiced listeners, Matthew 13:14–15.
Racist tradition overlooked, Matthew 15:21–28.
Family prejudice, Luke 12:49–53.
Refusing to believe revealed truth, John 9:39–41.
Prejudiced toward truth, John 18:37.
Prejudice against new convert, Acts 9:26.
No racial prejudice in God's heart, Acts 10:34–35;
    15:5–9.
Poisoning the mind, Acts 14:2.
Acceptance of others, 2 Corinthians 7:2.
Class prejudice in church, James 2:1–8, 16 (See AB).
Viewpoint of world, 1 John 4:5.

PRESSURE
Delegating work to others, Exodus 18:17–27.
Waters up to neck, Psalm 69:1.
King Herod yielded to pressure, Matthew 14:6–11.
Divine pressure to fulfill destiny, Luke 12:50.
Night coming, work to do, John 9:4.
Paul's pressure to reach Jerusalem, Acts 20:16.
Compelled to work for living, 1 Corinthians 9:6.
Keep your head in all situations, 2 Timothy 4:5.

PRIDE

Danger of material possessions, Deuteronomy 8:11–20; Psalm 52:7; Proverbs 18:11–12; Jeremiah 48:7.

Divine attitude toward humility, pride, 2 Samuel 22:28; Psalm 138:6.

Accused of self-righteousness, Job 34:1–9; 36:4.

Pride numbs spirituality, goodness, Psalm 10:2–11.

Flattering lips, boastful tongue, Psalm 12:4.

Boast in the Lord, Psalm 34:2, 44:8.

Possessive pride, Psalm 49:11.

The Lord hates pride, Proverbs 8:13.

Pride brings destruction, Proverbs 16:18.

Patience preferred to pride, Ecclesiastes 7:8.

Example of humble tools, Isaiah 10:15.

Satanic origination of pride, Isaiah 14:13–15.

God does not yield glory to another, Isaiah 42:8; 48:11.

Spiritual pride, Isaiah 65:5.

Pride, arrogance, Jeremiah 48:29.

Vain ambition, Daniel 5:20–23.

Fate of carefree people, Zephaniah 2:15.

Desiring kingdom greatness, Matthew 18:1–10.

Vanity denounced by Jesus, Matthew 23:6–12; Mark 12:38–39.

Desire to be greatest in kingdom, Luke 9:46–48.

Pride concerning wrong things, Luke 10:17–20.

Vain man, humble man at worship, Luke 18:9–14.

Proud sorcerer, Acts 8:9–10.

Price paid for Herod's pride, Acts 12:19–23.

Intellectual pride in Athens, Acts 17:16–34.

No place for Christian pride, Romans 3:27; 4:2.

People of low position, Romans 12:16.

Simple people brought to Christ, 1 Corinthians 1:26–31.

Arrogance regarding spiritual success, 1 Corinthians 4:1–21.

Proud of immorality, 1 Corinthians 5:1–2.

Intellectual pride, 1 Corinthians 8:1–3; 2 Timothy 3:7.

Pride about authority from the Lord, 2 Corinthians 9:15; 10:8.

Falsely evaluating one's self, 2 Corinthians 10:12.

Danger of conceit, Galatians 5:26.

False estimation of greatness, Galatians 6:3.

Do nothing in vanity, Philippians 2:3.

Boasting about others, 2 Thessalonians 1:4.

Take pride in humble circumstances, James 1:9.

God resists proud people, James 4:6.
God gives grace to the humble, 1 Peter 5:5–6.
Refusing to admit sin, Revelation 18:7–8.

PRIORITY
God as first priority, Genesis 1:1.
Comparing sun, moon with stars, Genesis 1:16.
God supreme above idols, Leviticus 26:1.
The Lord's portion first priority, Numbers 18:29.
Material security versus God's will, Numbers 32:14–27.
Grief for ark greater than death of sons, 1 Samuel 4:16–18.
Palace 13 years, temple 7 years, 1 Kings 6:37–38; 7:1.
First things first, 2 Chronicles 1:7–12; Proverbs 24:27; Haggai 1:3–4; Matthew 6:33; Luke 9:59–62; 10:38–42.
Priority investing of time, Psalm 84:10.
Time for everything, Ecclesiastes 3:1–8.
Priorities change with progress, Isaiah 28:28.
Missionary, evangelistic priority, Isaiah 52:7.
Witness priority, Ezekiel 3:18–19.
Treasures on earth or in heaven, Matthew 6:19–21.
Purchasing pearl of great value, Matthew 13:45–46.
Forsaking all, Matthew 19:28–30.
First last, last first, Matthew 19:30; 20:16; Mark 10:31.
Last act of Jesus before crucifixion, Matthew 20:29–34.
Morality, materialism, Mark 10:17–25.
Priority commandments, Mark 12:28–34.
Post-resurrection priority, Mark 16:15.
Sinful woman's worship, Luke 7:36–38.
Excited about wrong phenomena, Luke 10:17–20.
Temporal and spiritual, Luke 11:27–28.
Greed over possessions, Luke 12:14–15.
Greatest priority, Luke 12:29–31.
Most highly valued, Luke 16:14–15.
Rich young ruler's priorities, Luke 18:18–23.
Earthly priority, spiritual opportunity, Acts 1:6–7.
Priority in obedience, Acts 5:29.
"Of first importance," 1 Corinthians 15:3 (NASB, NRSV).
Giving priority to stewardship, 2 Corinthians 8:10.
Faith expressed through love, Galatians 5:6.
What matters most, Galatians 6:15.
Most important priorities, 1 Timothy 6:21 (LB); 2 Timothy 1:3 (LB).
Danger of putting money first, 1 Timothy 6:10.
Priority delivery of God's message, Hebrews 1:1–2.

Disgrace for Christ preferred to earthly treasures, Hebrews 11:26.

PROCRASTINATION
Do not delay offering, Exodus 22:29.
Delayed departure, Judges 19:1–10.
Regal procrastination, Esther 5:8.
Do not wait another day, Proverbs 27:1.
Putting family first, 1 Kings 19:20–21.
No hurry to obey, 2 Chronicles 24:5 (CEV).
Ignoring Word of the Lord, Jeremiah 7:13.
Days not prolonged, Ezekiel 12:22–28.
No delay in the Lord's timing, Habakkuk 2:3; Matthew
24:48–51.
Procrastinators and temple rebuilding, Haggai 1:3–4.
Attempting to delay God's call, Matthew 8:21–22; Luke
9:59–62.
Five procrastinating virgins, Matthew 25:2–13.
Making excuses, Luke 14:16–21.
Rich man, Lazarus, Luke 16:19–31.
No time like present, Acts 24:25.
Now is the day of salvation, 2 Corinthians 6:2.
No more delay, Revelation 10:6.

PROFANITY
Misusing God's name, Exodus 20:7 (AB, GNB); Deuter-
onomy 5:11 (GNB).
"Damned woman," 2 Kings 9:34 (GNB).
Speaking against the Lord, 2 Chronicles 32:16.
Love to curse, Psalm 109:17 (See Berk.).
Challenging God, Isaiah 5:18–19.
Speech of vile person, Isaiah 32:6 (KJV).
Profaned name sanctified, Ezekiel 36:23 (See KJV).
Purified language, Zephaniah 3:9.
Satan as instructor, 1 Timothy 1:20.
Slandering the Lord's name, James 2:7.
Do not swear by heaven or earth, James 5:12.

PROMISCUITY
Discretion in relationships, Leviticus 18:30.
Defiant sin, Numbers 15:30–31.
Blatant immorality, Numbers 25:6–9.
Illicit relationships among clergy, 1 Samuel 2:22.
Promiscuous judgment, 2 Samuel 12:1–12.
Royal promiscuity, 1 Kings 11:1–3.

Apparent promiscuity, Isaiah 8:3.
Unrequited sexual desire, Ezekiel 16:23–30.
Sibling promiscuity, Ezekiel 23:1–49.
Sexual looseness, 1 Corinthians 6:18 (AB).

PROSPERITY
Joseph prospered in Egypt, Genesis 39:2.
God's provision, blessing, Deuteronomy 8:7–20.
Fortunes restored, Deuteronomy 30:1–3 (NIV).
Wicked often prosper, Job 21:7.
Prosperity terminated, Job 24:24 (See GNB).
Reward for obeying God, Job 36:11.
Prosperity of Job's remaining years, Job 42:12.
Foolish evaluations, Psalm 30:6–7 (LB).
"Pastures clothed with flocks," Psalm 65:13 (NKJV).
Prisoners find prosperity, Psalm 68:6 (NRSV).
Prosperous hands, Psalm 90:17 (NRSV).
Stealing from poor, giving to rich, Proverbs 22:16.
Prosperous idolaters, Isaiah 2:7–8.
Land "flowing with milk and honey," Jeremiah 11:5.
Prosperous wicked, Jeremiah 12:1–3.
National prosperity, Ezekiel 16:13–14.
Tree of prosperity, Ezekiel 17:22–24.
Rural prosperity, Ezekiel 36:11 (See KJV).
Prosperity linked to conduct, Daniel 4:27.
Fragile prosperity, Hosea 13:15 (CEV).
Lost prosperity returned, Joel 3:1 (CEV).
Spiritual prosperity, 2 Peter 1:2 (AB).
Health, wealth, spiritual vitality, 3 John 2–4.
Stewardship based on personal income, 1 Corinthians
    16:2.

P

PYRAMID

PSYCHIATRY
Renewed by Scripture, Psalm 119:93.
Mental renewing, Romans 12:1–2.

PSYCHOLOGY
Careful speech, Genesis 31:24, 29.
Public relations approach, 1 Kings 1:42.
Appealing to ego in protesting, Ezra 4:14.
Mob psychology at trial of Jesus, Matthew 27:15–26;
　　Mark 15:11–15 (See Matthew 21:1–11; Mark 11:8–10).
Crowd psychology, John 6:1, 2.

PUBLISH
"Publish the name of the Lord," Deuteronomy 32:3
　　(KJV).
"Published peace," Nahum 1:15 (KJV).

PUNISHMENT
Death penalty, Genesis 9:5–6; Numbers 35:16–21.
Punishment by fire, Numbers 11:1.
Swallowed by earth, Numbers 16:31–33.
Whipping with thorns and briers, Judges 8:16.
Punishment for disgracing sister, 2 Samuel 13:23–29.
Better God's punishment than men's, 2 Samuel 24:13–
　　14.
Israel uprooted, 2 Chronicles 7:20.
Less punishment than deserved, Ezra 9:13.
Fair punishment, Nehemiah 9:33 (CEV).
God has right to judge, Psalm 51:4.
Merciful punishment, Psalm 89:30–34.
Divine forgiveness and punishment, Psalm 99:8.
Punishment short of death, Psalm 118:18.
God's arm coming down in punishment, Isaiah 30:30.
Sins paid back, Isaiah 65:6.
God uses dictators, brings them into judgment, Jere-
　　miah 25:11–14.
Sword that cannot rest, Jeremiah 47:6–7.
Cost for doubting an angel, Luke 1:18–20.
Ananias and Sapphira, Acts 5:1–11.
Guards who failed to hold Peter in prison, Acts 12:18–
　　19.

PURPOSE
Hiding purpose of actions, 1 Samuel 16:1–5.
Nehemiah's avowed purpose to rebuild wall, Nehemiah
　　5:14–16.

Eloquent description of purpose, Isaiah 32:8.
Divine purpose in creating, Isaiah 45:18.
God never acts without cause, Ezekiel 14:23.
Salt, light in world, Matthew 5:13–16.
"Kind intention," Ephesians 1:5 (NASB).
Filled with knowledge of God's will, Colossians 1:9–12.
Properly motivated, 1 Thessalonians 1:3.

Q

QUACK
Worthless physicians, Job 13:4.

QUALITY
High quality gold, Genesis 2:12 (Berk.).
Clear oil used in tabernacle, Exodus 27:20.
Durable clothing, Deuteronomy 8:4.
Vineyard's gleaning exceeds another's harvest, Judges 8:2.
Quality talent, Psalm 45:1.
Purposeful activity, Ecclesiastes 4:6.
Tested for quality, Jeremiah 6:27; 1 Corinthians 3:13
   (NASB).
New every day, Lamentations 3:22–24.
Salt loses saltiness, Luke 14:34–35.
Needed qualities, 2 Peter 1:5–8.
Divine love's incredible quality, 1 John 3:1 (AB).

QUESTION
Satan's tantalizing questions, Genesis 3:1 (LB).
Question mark food, Exodus 16:31 (LB).
Questions for spies to Canaan, Numbers 13:18–20.
God asks questions, Numbers 14:11.
Questions for subversion, Judges 16:6–18.
Mother-in-law's inquiry, Ruth 3:16–17.
All questions answered, 1 Kings 10:1–3.
Divine actions questioned, 2 Kings 6:33.
Most ignorant of men, Proverbs 30:2–4.
Answers to unasked questions, Isaiah 65:1 (CEV).
Wise put to shame, Jeremiah 8:9.
Jeremiah questioned God's way, Jeremiah 12:1.
Search for answer, Jonah 1:7–8.
Inquiring about Divine love, Malachi 1:2.
Unable to understand angels, Luke 1:18, 34.
Paul accused of being terrorist, Acts 21:38.

QUICKSAND

WELL, ACCORDING TO THE MAP WE'RE ALMOST THERE.

QUICKSAND
Sinking in mire, Psalm 69:2.

QUIET TIME
Pre-dawn prayer in time of trouble, Psalm 119:147.
Strength every morning, Isaiah 33:2.
Outdoor retreat, Ezekiel 3:22–23.
Closet prayer, Matthew 6:5–6.
Jesus retired to hills, Matthew 14:23; 15:29.
Example of Jesus in early morning, Mark 1:35.
Finding quiet place, Mark 6:31; 7:24.
Jesus sought solitude, Luke 4:42; 5:16.
Spending night in prayer, Luke 6:12.
Gethsemane prayer, Luke 22:41.
Roof prayer, Acts 10:9 (CEV).

QUOTA
Daily quota, Exodus 5:13 (NKJV).

R

RACISM
Tension between Arabs, Israel, Genesis 21:8–10.
Racial intermarriage forbidden, Genesis 28:1.
Egyptians and Hebrews, Genesis 43:32.
Moses' foreign wife, Numbers 12:1.
Request to marry heathen, 1 Kings 2:13–25.
Those not assisting Israelites, Nehemiah 13:1–3.

Anti-Semitic bribery, Esther 3:8–9.
Continual racial resentment, Esther 5:10–14.
Skin color by Creator's choice, Jeremiah 13:23.
Jesus overlooked racist tradition, Matthew 15:21–28.
Treatment given gentiles, Matthew 20:25.
Black man helped Jesus carry cross, Mark 15:21; 15:21.
   (Note: Cyrene a city in North Africa).
Deliverance from racism, Acts 10:24–28.
No racial prejudice with the Lord, Acts 10:34–35;
   15:5–8.
Avoid preferences, prejudices, 1 Corinthians 4:6 (GNB);
   James 2:1–4.
All one in Christ, Galatians 3:28.

RAIN
First rainfall, Genesis 7:11–12 (See 2:4–6).
Plague of hail, Exodus 9:22–34.
Rainless sky, parched earth, Leviticus 26:19–20.
Rain denied, Deuteronomy 11:17; 28:24.
Nature's abundant blessings, Deuteronomy 33:13–16.
Thunder and rain, 1 Samuel 12:18.
Heavy rain, 1 Kings 18:41.
Hindered by rain, Ezra 10:9.
Rainy season, Ezra 10:13.
Evaporation, rain, Job 36:27–28; 37:11.
"Waterskins of the heavens," Job 38:37 (NRSV).
Heavy rain no value, Proverbs 28:3.
Storage for rain, Ecclesiastes 1:7.
Accurate meterological information, Ecclesiastes 11:3.
Rain like Scripture, Isaiah 55:10–11.
"Idols can't send rain," Jeremiah 14:22 (CEV).
Autumn and spring rains, Joel 2:23; Acts 14:17.
Ocean evaporation, rain, Amos 5:8.
Dew from heavens, Zechariah 8:12.
Prayer for rain, Zechariah 10:1 (LB).
Predicting rain, Luke 12:54.
Patient farmer awaiting rain, James 5:7.

RAPTURE
Time of Christ's return kept secret, Mark 13:32.
Watching for the Lord to come, Luke 12:35–40.
Those dead, those alive, John 11:25.
Promise of Christ's return, John 14:3.
Mistaken information about rapture, John 21:20–23.
Resurrection at rapture, 1 Corinthians 15:51–55.

"May the Lord come soon," 1 Corinthians 16:22 (CEV).
Waiting for Christ's return, 1 Thessalonians 1:10.
Those prepared for rapture, 1 Thessalonians 3:13.
Folly of date setting, 2 Thessalonians 2:1–3.
Purified by blessed hope, Titus 2:11–14.
Coming Lord and King, Hebrews 9:24–28.
Living hope, 1 Peter 1:3–5.
Scoffers in last days, 2 Peter 3:3–4.

READING

Message to read, Deuteronomy 6:9.
Literacy program, Deuteronomy 11:19–21.
Reading with clarity, Nehemiah 8:8.
Many books cause weariness, Ecclesiastes 12:12.
Consumed scroll sweet as honey, Ezekiel 3:1–3.
Posted sign, John 19:19–20.
Purposeful reading, John 20:31–32.
Reading without understanding, Acts 8:26–39.
Important reading, Colossians 4:16.
Public reading of Scripture, 1 Timothy 4:13.
Scrolls, parchments, 2 Timothy 4:13.

REALITY

Scripture blessings and curses, Joshua 8:34.
Witnessing to personal experience, Psalm 51:10–13.
Like a dream, Psalm 126:1 (NRSV).
Awakening to find dream untrue, Isaiah 29:8.
Reality precludes fasting, Mark 2:18–20.
Experiencing kingdom reality, Luke 17:20–21.
Reality of life in Christ, 2 Timothy 1:1.
Faith without works, James 2:14–18.
Reality of unseen, 1 Peter 1:8, 9.
Experiencing reality of Christ, 1 John 1:1–4.

REASON

Satanic reasoning, Genesis 3:1–5.
Reasoning with God, Exodus 32:11–14.
Refusing to listen to reason, 1 Samuel 8:4–21.
Lost reason, Job 12:24.
Questioning why wicked prosper, Jeremiah 12:1–3.
Disputing mercy and justice, Ezekiel 33:10–20.
Wisdom of Gamaliel, Acts 5:30–40.
Use of reasoning in teaching, Acts 17:1–3.
Reason versus revelation, 1 Corinthians 1:20–31.

Powerful delusion distorts reason, 2 Thessalonians 2:11–12.

RECKLESS
Driving like madman, 2 Kings 9:20.
Careless about danger, Proverbs 22:3.

RECREATION
Mighty hunter, Genesis 10:9.
Enjoying bow, arrow, Genesis 21:20.
Early morning play, Exodus 32:6.
Eating with rejoicing, Deuteronomy 27:7.
No place to rest, Deuteronomy 28:65.
Telling riddles, Judges 14:12–18.
Sadistic recreation, Judges 16:25.
Gross indecency, Judges 19:22–26.
Boxing, wrestling, 2 Samuel 2:14.
Camping out on rooftop, Nehemiah 8:13–17.
Dancing children, Job 21:11.
Whales at play, Psalm 104:26 (LB).
Meaningless pleasures, Ecclesiastes 2:1–3; 2:1–3.
Renewal of strength, Isaiah 40:30–31.
Sabbath fun, Isaiah 58:3–14 (LB).
Instrumental jam session, Amos 6:5.
Children play in streets, Zechariah 8:5.
Adults in childish recreation, Matthew 11:16–17.

R

REFEREE

Relaxed eating, Mark 14:3.
Gossip as recreation, 1 Timothy 5:13.

REGRET

Creator's regret, Genesis 6:6.
Foolish sins, Numbers 12:11.
Sacrifice of daughter, Judges 11:30–40.
Poor student's regret, Proverbs 5:12–13.
Chasing wind, Ecclesiastes 1:17–18.
Ashamed, silent before the Lord, Ezekiel 16:63.
Royal regret, Daniel 6:13–18.
Remembering glory of better days, Haggai 2:3.
Judas' regret, Matthew 27:3.
Second coming will cause regret, Revelation 1:7.

RELATIONSHIP

Three forefathers of mankind, Genesis 9:18–19.
Forbidding marriage to foreigners, Genesis 24:2–3.
Bond between relatives, Genesis 29:1–14.
Change in relationship, Genesis 31:2.
Broken circle among twelve tribes, Judges 21:1–6.
Marriage confirms alliance, 1 Kings 3:1.
Love for mother-in-law, Ruth 1:8–18.
Apple of God's eye, Psalm 17:8.
Sister, bride, Song of Songs 4:9.
Golden Rule, Matthew 7:12.
Jesus' evaluation of His mother, Matthew 12:46–50.
Attitude of Jesus toward relationships, Mark 3:31–35.
Answered prayer and good relationships, Mark 11:25.
Marriage on earth, relationship in heaven, Mark 12:18–27.
Relationship to God, neighbors, Mark 12:28–34.
Presumed relationship to the Lord, Luke 13:22–30.
Christ first above family, Luke 14:26.
Love the supreme relationship, John 13:34.
True meaning of a friend, John 15:12–17.
New relationships in Christ, John 19:26–27.
Reactions to truly Christian personality, 2 Corinthians 2:15–16.
Identified in Christ, Ephesians 1:11–12.
Relationship through Holy Spirit, Ephesians 2:22.
Husband, wife, Ephesians 5:21–33.
Slave, owner, same Master, Ephesians 6:9.
Concern for followers' development, Colossians 2:1–5.
Spiritual son, 1 Timothy 1:2, 18; 2 Timothy 1:2; 2:1.

Relationship with Christ, 2 Timothy 2:11–13; Hebrews 2:11–16.
God's friend, James 2:21–23.
Confessing sins one to another, James 5:16.
Children of God, 1 John 3:1–3.

RELAXATION

Sure rest, divine protection, Deuteronomy 33:12.
David frequently played harp, 1 Samuel 18:10.
Steadfast heart, Psalm 57:7.
Quietness, rejoicing, Zephaniah 3:17.
Importance of relaxation, Mark 6:31.
Perilous relaxation, Luke 12:19 (NRSV).

RELIABLE

Standing at end of struggle, Ephesians 6:13.
Steadfast whatever circumstances, Philippians 1:27–30.
No lie comes from truth, 1 John 2:20–21.

REMARRIAGE

Second wife, Genesis 25:1.
Remarriage of divorced persons, Deuteronomy 24:1–4.
Ruth and Boaz, Ruth 3:1; 4:10.
Return to first husband, Hosea 2:7 (GNB).
Remarriage instruction, Romans 7:1–3.
Remarriage for widows, 1 Corinthians 7:8–9; 1 Timothy 5:11.

RENEWAL

Tear down old, build new, Judges 6:25–26.
Renewed by Scripture, Psalm 119:93.
Streams on dry ground, Isaiah 44:3.
Ask for ancient paths, Jeremiah 6:16.
Introspection and renewal, Lamentations 3:40.
New heart, new spirit, Ezekiel 36:26.
"Renew you in His love," Zephaniah 3:17 (NRSV).
Flame of renewal, 2 Timothy 1:6.

REPUTATION

Righteous man blameless, Genesis 6:9.
Abraham's reputation, Genesis 21:22.
Impeccable reputation, 1 Samuel 2:1–5.
Name well known, 1 Samuel 18:30.
Found faultless, 1 Samuel 29:3.

Glorious reputation, Psalm 87:3.
Reputation as man of prayer, Psalm 109:4.
Value of good name, Proverbs 22:1; Ecclesiastes 7:1.
Building one's own reputation, Proverbs 25:27.
Parent's reputation, Proverbs 27:11.
Fragrant name, Song of Songs 1:3.
Looking for one honest person, Jeremiah 5:1.
Least, greatest, Jeremiah 42:1–3.
Daniel's reputation known to queen, Daniel 5:10–12.
Integrity in government affairs, Daniel 6:1–3.
Jealousy incited, Daniel 6:4–8.
Reputation as the Lord's messenger, Haggai 1:13.
People seek for those who know the Lord, Zechariah 8:23.
Reputation of Virgin Mary protected, Matthew 1:19.
Worthy person, Matthew 10:11.
John the Baptist's greatness, Matthew 11:11.
Role of humility in greatness, Matthew 23:12.
Neighbors did not expect divinity in Jesus, Luke 4:22–24.
Lasting reputation for wrong doing, Luke 17:32.
Nazareth's low reputation, John 1:46.
Jesus' conflicting reputation, John 7:12.
Loving reputation, John 13:35.
Spiritual reputations, Acts 6:3–6.
Mistrust by co-workers, Acts 9:26.
Righteous, God-fearing man, Acts 10:22.
Good motivation of David, Acts 13:22.
Marred reputation, Acts 15:37–38.
Spoken well of, Acts 16:2.
Highly respected, Acts 22:12.
Always doing what is right, Romans 12:17.
Reputation for obedience, Romans 16:19.
Mark of integrity, 2 Corinthians 8:18–24.
Convert's reputation encouraged others, Galatians 1:23–24.
Living life worthy of calling, Ephesians 4:1.
Exemplary reputation, Philippians 2:20–21.
Reputation as Christians, Colossians 1:3–6.
Reputation prerequisite to witness, 1 Thessalonians 4:11–12.
Conduct, doctrine, 1 Timothy 4:16.
Prostitute's faith and obedience, Hebrews 11:31.
Joy of good reputation, 3 John 3–6.

Good reputation, 3 John 12.
Positive and negative reputation, Revelation 2:1–6.

RESPECT

Respect parents, Exodus 20:12; Leviticus 19:3; Prov-
  erbs 1:8; 6:20; Ephesians 6:1–2; Colossians 3:20.
Show respect for elderly, Leviticus 19:32; 1 Timothy
  5:1–2.
Scripture respected, Nehemiah 8:5.
Respect for government leaders, Acts 23:5; Romans
  13:1.
Spiritual leaders given respect, 1 Thessalonians 5:13.
Respect for clergy, 1 Timothy 5:17.
Mutual respect, 1 Peter 2:17.

RESCUE

Kidnapping and rescue of Lot, Genesis 14:12–16.
Queen advocate for her people, Esther 8:3–11.
Mercy to suffering prophet, Jeremiah 38:6 13.
Jonah and great fish, Jonah 1:17.

RESPECT

Harm to parents forbidden, Exodus 21:15.
Stand when older person appears, Leviticus 19:32.
Mutual respect between enemies, Deuteronomy 2:4–5.
Show respect to church and court, Deuteronomy 17:12.
Do not respect prophet who proclaims error, Deuteron-
  omy 18:21–22.
Honoring former leader, Joshua 22:1–5.
Unwasted words, 1 Samuel 3:19.
Stone god's respect for ark of God, 1 Samuel 5:1–5.
Respect for position, 1 Samuel 24:1–7; 26:7–11.
Respect at city gate, Job 29:7–10.
Earned respect, Job 29:21.
Attitude toward aged parents, Proverbs 23:22.
Respect for mother, Proverbs 31:31 (See GNB).
Promise of peaceful and honorable death, Jeremiah
  34:4–5.
Respecting the Lord's name, Malachi 2:4–5.
Respect, obedience, Luke 6:46.
Jesus accused of disrespect, John 18:19–24.
Respect of Cornelius for Peter, Acts 10:25–26.
Recognition of apostle, 1 Corinthians 9:1–6.
Respect toward seniors, 1 Timothy 5:1–2.
Accused yet admired, 1 Peter 2:12.

Consideration for everyone, 1 Peter 2:17.
Respect for those older, 1 Peter 5:5.
Take Scriptures to heart, Revelation 1:3.

RESPONSE

Agreement voiced by congregation, Deuteronomy 27:14–26.
Response of poor student, Proverbs 5:12–13.
Refraining from response to one who affronted the Lord's name, Isaiah 36:18–22 (See 37:1–7).
Ignoring Word of the Lord, Jeremiah 7:13.
Those who ought to respond eagerly, Ezekiel 3:4–9.
Nineveh more responsive than Jerusalem, Matthew 12:41–42.
Do not harden heart, Hebrews 3:7–8, 15.
Opening to Him who knocks, Revelation 3:20.

REST

Creative rest, Genesis 2:2.
Time set aside for rest, Exodus 23:12; 34:21.
Comforting bed, Job 7:13.
Lie down without fear, Job 11:19.
Assurance in rest, Psalm 3:5.
Sweet sleep, Proverbs 3:24.
Uncomfortable accommodations, Isaiah 28:20.
Avoiding work on Sabbath, Jeremiah 17:21–27.
Pleasant sleep, Jeremiah 31:26.
No rest for weary, Lamentations 5:5.
Soul rest, Matthew 11:28–30.
Quiet place for rest, Mark 6:31–32.
Travel weary, John 4:6.
Sabbath rest, Hebrews 4:9 (NASB, NIV, NRSV).
Repose of death, Revelation 14:13.

RESUME

Resume of Israel's history, Psalms 78:1–72; 105:1–45; 106:1–48.
Wise man's summation, Ecclesiastes 12:13–14.
Stephen's resume of strategic history, Acts 7:1–53.
Paul's resume of Old Testament, Acts 13:16–41.
Resume of God's plan through the ages, Romans 1:1–6.
Resume of Christ's earth tenure, 1 Timothy 3:16 (See Luke 24:27).

RETALIATION

Eye for an eye, Exodus 21:23–25; Deuteronomy 19:19; Matthew 5:38–44.

Do not retaliate, Leviticus 19:18.

Reversal of fortunes, Esther 5:9; 7:10.

Jews liquidated their enemies, Esther 9:1–17.

Stark picture of vengeance, Psalms 58:10; 68:23.

Do not pay back wrong, Proverbs 20:22; 24:29.

Leave works of enemy in God's hands, Lamentations 3:55–66.

Turn other cheek, go extra mile, Matthew 5:38–41.

Basics of Golden Rule, Luke 6:27–36.

Exemplary response to evil, Romans 12:17; 1 Peter 2:12–17; 3:9.

Love those who cause grief, 2 Corinthians 2:5–11.

Leave revenge in God's hands, 2 Thessalonians 1:6–7; 2 Timothy 3:14.

RETIREMENT

Aaron's retirement, Numbers 20:26 (See Berk.).

Virility retained until death, Deuteronomy 34:7.

Work unfinished, Joshua 13:1.

Going strong at eighty-five, Joshua 14:10–11.

Joshua's farewell, Joshua 23:1–8.

Looking back across exemplary life, 1 Samuel 12:3.

Denied fruit of life's labor, Ecclesiastes 6:1, 2.

King at age sixty-two, Daniel 5:30–31.

Old age sitting in streets, Zechariah 8:4.

Consistent worship during advanced age, Luke 2:36–38.

Families should care for those in need, 1 Timothy 5:3–8.

REUNION

Reunion between Jacob, Esau, Genesis 33:1–20.

Reunion between Joseph, brothers, Genesis 45:1–15.

Eagerness to meet father, Genesis 46:29.

Absalom's return to King David, 2 Samuel 14:1–35.

Prodigal son, Luke 15:11–31.

Long absence, Romans 15:22 (GNB).

Paul fearful of reunion with Corinthians, 2 Corinthians 12:20–21.

Reunion of all believers, 1 Thessalonians 4:13–18.

Friends reunited, 2 Timothy 1:17.

REVENGE
First murder, Genesis 4:1–16.
Servant attitude to unfair employer, Genesis 16:1–10.
Revenge forbidden, Leviticus 19:18.
Threatened revenge, Judges 8:4–9.
Not taking revenge, 1 Samuel 24:1–13.
Gratitude for no revenge, 1 Samuel 25:32–34.
Murder in revenge, 2 Samuel 3:22–34.
David's attitude toward murder of Saul's son, 2 Samuel 4:1–12.
Reward of evil, 1 Kings 2:5–6.
Overt revenge, 2 Kings 11:1.
Revenge against those who did not assist, Nehemiah 13:1–3.
Proper revenge, Psalm 6:10.
Evil brings its own revenge, Psalm 9:15.
Stark picture of vengeance, Psalms 58:10; 68:22–23.
Revenge against gossip, Psalm 64:8.
Let the Lord vindicate, Psalm 135:14; Ezekiel 25:12–17; 2 Thessalonians 1:6–7; 5:15.
Avoid revenge, Proverbs 24:29.
Time for Divine vengeance, Jeremiah 51:6, 56.
Leave works of enemy in God's hands, Lamentations 3:55–66.
Revenge first in the heart, Ezekiel 25:15–17.
Vengeful spirit punished, Amos 1:11–12.
Those who mock God's people, Zephaniah 2:9–10.
Turn opposite cheek, go extra mile, Matthew 5:38–42.
Basics of Golden Rule, Luke 6:27–38.
Calling down fire from Heaven, Luke 9:54–55.
Forgiving spirit of martyr, Acts 7:60.
Do not return evil for evil, Romans 12:17.
Showing love to those who cause grief, 2 Corinthians 2:5–11.
No need to avenge wrong, Galatians 5:10.
Kindness in place of vengeance, 1 Thessalonians 5:15.
Leave revenge to God, 2 Timothy 4:14 (AB).
Do not retaliate against those who do wrong, 1 Peter 2:12–17, 23.
Walking in steps of Christ, 1 Peter 2:21–25.
Do not repay evil with evil, insult with insult, 1 Peter 3:9.
Harm received for harm done, 2 Peter 2:13.

Those who crucified witness Christ's return, Revelation 1:7.
Martyrs call out for revenge, Revelation 6:9–11.
Judgment of God upon evil, Revelation 16:5–7.
Golden Rule stated negatively, Revelation 18:6.

REWARD
Obedience rewarded, Genesis 22:15–18; Leviticus 25:18–19; Deuteronomy 4:40; 6:3.
Reward for honoring parents, Exodus 20:12; Ephesians 6:1–3.
Reward of accomplishment, Judges 8:22–23.
Delilah bribed to deliver Samson, Judges 16:1–5.
Rewarded for faithfulness to mother-in-law, Ruth 2:7–12.
Reward for act of kindness, 1 Samuel 30:11–18.
Ironical reward, Esther 5:14; 6:13.
Worthlessness rewarded, Job 15:31 (See GNB).
Bread cast upon waters, Ecclesiastes 11:1.
Good, bad deeds rewarded, Isaiah 3:10–11.
All in God's hands, Isaiah 49:4.
God sees all, rewards good, Jeremiah 32:19.
Rewarded for kindness to prophet, Jeremiah 38:7–13.
Heavenly reward following resurrection, Daniel 12:13.
Receiving what one deserves, Zechariah 1:6.
Reward for self-denial, Matthew 16:24–28.
Good works rewarded, Matthew 25:34–46; Romans 2:7, 10.
Leaving all to follow Jesus, Mark 10:28–31.
Persecution rewarded, Luke 6:22–23.
Runner trains to win crown, 1 Corinthians 9:24–27.
Followers are ministry reward, 1 Thessalonians 2:17–19.
Prayer that friend would be rewarded, 2 Timothy 1:16–18.
Sure reward for obedience, disobedience, 2 Timothy 2:11–13.
Crown rewards faithful ministry, 2 Timothy 4:6–8.
Those who forfeited reward, Hebrews 3:16–19.
God does not forget good works, Hebrews 6:10.
Confidence will be rewarded, Hebrews 10:35.
Crown of life for those who persevere, James 1:12.
Danger of losing one's full reward, 2 John 8.
Seated one day on the throne, Revelation 3:21.
Reward for what one has done, Revelation 22:12.

R

RIDDLE
Abraham laughed at God, Genesis 17:17; 18:10–15.
Riddles learned from dreams, Genesis 37:5–11; 40:9–22; 41:15–31; Daniel 2:29–45; 4:4–33.
Rhyming riddle, Judges 14:14 (NRSV).
"Dark saying," Psalm 49:4 (See NIV and KJV).
Two eagles and vine, Ezekiel 17:1–21.
Jesus accused of obscure speech, John 16:29 (GNB).

RING
Nose ring, Genesis 24:47.
Signet ring of government status, Genesis 41:42; Esther 3:10.
Rings for temple use, Exodus 35:22.
Signet ring for document seal, Esther 8:8.
Item of finery, Isaiah 3:18–23.
Relationship symbol, Luke 15:22.

RIVAL
Jealous wife, 1 Samuel 1:2–7.
Frustrated Saul, 1 Samuel 18:8.
David's opportunity to kill Saul, 1 Samuel 26:1–25.
Brother spared, 1 Kings 1:49–53.
At peace with enemies, Proverbs 16:7.
Labor, skill, rivalry, Ecclesiastes 4:4 (NASB).
"God tolerates no rivals," Nahum 1:2 (GNB).
Bickering among laborers, Matthew 20:12.
Evaluating military logistics, Luke 14:31–32.
Prodigal, brother, Luke 15:25–32.

ROBBERY
Responsibility for killing thief, Exodus 22:2–3.
Forbidden by law, Leviticus 19:13; Isaiah 61:8.

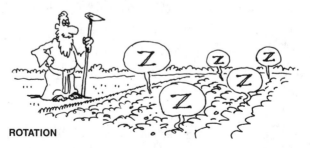

ROTATION

Need for two or three witnesses, Deuteronomy 19:15.
Lurking in ambush, Judges 9:25.
Protection against enemies of the road, Ezra 8:21–23.
Breaking and entering, Job 24:16.
Career robbers, Proverbs 1:11–16.
Bandit's prey, Proverbs 6:11 (Berk.).
Treasures surveyed for subsequent thievery, Isaiah 39:1–6.
Robbers den, Jeremiah 7:11.
Death penalty, Ezekiel 18:10–13.
Robbery and extortion, Ezekiel 22:29.
Robber bands, Hosea 6:9; 7:1.
Thievery of tax collectors and soldiers, Luke 3:12–14.
Danger on Jericho road, Luke 10:25–37.
Christian reaction to plundering, Hebrews 10:34 (AB).

ROCK AND ROLL
"Song of fools," Ecclesiastes 7:5 (NIV).
End to noisy songs, Ezekiel 26:13.
Earth's music silenced, Revelation 18:22.

ROMANCE
A mate "at last," Genesis 2:23 (Berk.).
Bride for Isaac, Genesis 24:1–58; 25:19–20.
Captive women, Deuteronomy 21:10–14.
Men outnumbered women, Judges 21:1–23.
Woman proposed to man, Ruth 3:9.
Love, infatuation, 1 Samuel 18:20–29.
Demanding another man's wife, 2 Samuel 3:12–16.
Lovesick, 2 Samuel 13:1–4.
Man and maid, Proverbs 30:18–19.
Time of restraint, Ecclesiastes 3:5.
Expressing affection, Song of Songs 1:15; 2:14; 4:1–16; 6:4–12; 7:1–8.
Romantic garden song, Song of Songs 5:1–8.

RUMOR
Fear of rumor to enemy, Numbers 14:13–16.
Evil rumor discerned, Nehemiah 6:10–13.
Wisdom a rumor, Job 28:20–22 (GNB, NRSV).
Spread no rumors, Psalm 15:1–3 (GNB).
Disbelieving threat of murder, Jeremiah 40:13–16; 41:1–2.
First one rumor, then another, Jeremiah 51:46.
Rumor from the Lord, Obadiah 1 (KJV).
Misunderstood statement, John 21:22–23 (NIV).

S

SACRED
Sacred location for altar, Deuteronomy 12:5–6.
Sacred courtroom, Deuteronomy 17:8.
Grave of Moses, Deuteronomy 34:6.
Purpose of temple, 2 Chronicles 2:5–6.
Articles from Jerusalem put into pagan temple, Daniel 1:1–2.
Truly sacred, Matthew 23:16–17.
Sacred mountain not to be touched, Hebrews 12:18–21.

SAFETY
No safe place to dock ark, Genesis 8:8–9 (See verse 12).
Safe towns, Deuteronomy 19:1–4 (CEV).
Built-in safety device, Deuteronomy 22:8.
Safety for woman in fields, Ruth 2:4–22.
Safe travel, Isaiah 35:8–9.
Crossing deep rivers, Isaiah 43:2 (CEV).
City gates open, Isaiah 60:11.
Enemies lurk along roads, fields, Jeremiah 6:25.
Wise dove, Jeremiah 48:28.
Safety in lions' den, Daniel 6:13–24; Nahum 2:11.
No safety after battle, Micah 2:8 (GNB).
Children playing in streets, Zechariah 8:5.
Safety of darkness, Acts 17:10.
Protected in storm and shipwreck, Acts 27:13–44.
Kept safe, 1 Timothy 2:15 (NIV).
"Run to God for safety," Hebrews 6:18 (CEV).
Shielded by God's power, 1 Peter 1:5 (NIV).

SALARY
Priests eat food offerings, Numbers 18:11–13.
Prostitute's unacceptable stewardship, Deuteronomy 23:18; Ezekiel 16:32–34.
Salary paid with food, 2 Chronicles 2:10.
Some money, some provisions, Ezra 3:7.
Priests, singers support themselves, Nehemiah 13:10–11.
Income for twelve apostles, Matthew 10:9–10.
Parable of workers in vineyard, Matthew 20:1–16.
Content with earnings, Luke 3:14.
Sending out of Twelve, Luke 9:1–6.
Spiritual wages, John 4:36.

Tents during week, ministry on Sabbath, Acts 18:1–5;
  20:33–35; 1 Thessalonians 2:9; 2 Thessalonians 3:6–
  10.
Volunteer ministry, Acts 28:30 (AB).
Inequity in self-support, 1 Corinthians 9:6–14.
Concern for pastor, Philippians 4:10–19.
"Paid in full," Philippians 4:18 (NRSV).
Payment for those in ministry, 1 Timothy 5:17–18.
Dignity of labor, Titus 3:14.
Withholding payment from those who labor, James 5:4.
Danger of greed in ministry, 1 Peter 5:2–3.
Grain for a day's wages, Revelation 6:6.

SARCASM
Stimulant to action, Joshua 17:14–18.
Parable of trees, Judges 9:7–15.
Challenging pagan gods, Judges 10:14.
What ails you? Judges 18:23 (NKJV).
Neglected duty, 1 Samuel 26:15.
Wife's rebuke, 2 Samuel 6:20.
Sarcastic prophet, 1 Kings 18:27 (See GNB).
Taunting pride, 1 Kings 20:10–11.
Botanical communication, 2 Kings 14:9.
Military sarcasm, 2 Kings 18:23–24.
Quip from Job, Job 12:2; 26:2 (LB).
Job's "friend," Job 18:5 (LB).
Mocking builders of wall, Nehemiah 4:1–3.
Sarcasm against intellectual pride, Job 12:2–3 (AB).
Sarcastic rebuttal, Job 38:19–21.
Scarecrow in melon patch, Jeremiah 10:5 (NIV).
Speaking truth in sarcasm, Matthew 27:28–29; Luke
  23:35–39; John 19:19.
Disciples sarcastic to Jesus, Mark 8:4 (LB).
Jesus mocked on cross, John 19:1–3.
"Super apostles," 2 Corinthians 11:5.
Deft use of words, 2 Corinthians 11:16–19.
Instructive example, 2 Corinthians 12:13 (LB).
Cut off those who cut off, Galatians 5:12 (LB).

SATAN
Brief history of fall from heaven, Isaiah 14:12–15.
Typology in king of Tyre, Ezekiel 28:11–19.
Satan's role as accuser, Job 1:12 (AB); Zechariah 3:1–2.
Satanic adversary, Job 16:9 (AB).

S

Holy Spirit led Jesus to confrontation, Matthew 4:1
(See CEV).
Satan confronted with Scripture, Matthew 4:1–11;
Luke 4:1–13.
Jesus accused of satanic power, Matthew 9:32–34.
Satan's destiny, Romans 16:20.
Satanic schemes, 2 Corinthians 2:1–11 (See LB).
Deny Satan opportunity, Ephesians 4:27 (GNB).
The tempter, 1 Thessalonians 3:5.
Lawless one's ignominious defeat, 2 Thessalonians 2:8.
Satan as teacher, 1 Timothy 1:18–20.
Satan rendered powerless, Hebrews 2:14 (CEV).
Battleground in which Satan attacks, 1 John 2:15–17.
Work of the devil, 1 John 3:7–8.
Unharmed by Satan, 1 John 5:18.
Only authority over evil, Jude 9.
Star fallen from sky, Revelation 9:1–2 (See Isaiah
14:12).
Birth of Christ reviewed, Revelation 12:1–5.
Conquered and yet conqueror, Revelation 12:7–10.
Angel overpowering, binding Satan, Revelation 20:1–3.

SATISFACTION
"Satisfied with life," Genesis 35:29 (Berk.); Psalm 103:5
(NASB, NRSV).
Pleased populace, 2 Samuel 3:36.
Satisfied to see the Lord's likeness, Psalm 17:15.
Desires satisfied, strength renewed, Psalm 103:5.
Righteous desires, Proverbs 10:24.
Voicing simple need, Proverbs 30:7–8.
Money never satisfies, Ecclesiastes 5:10.
Reward for obedience, Isaiah 48:17–18.
Needs satisfied, Isaiah 58:11; Philippians 4:19.
Wrong search for satisfaction, James 4:1–3.
Joy of good reputation, 3 John 3–4.

SCANDAL
Joseph falsely accused, Genesis 39:11–20.
Giving false testimony, Deuteronomy 19:16, 21.
Hatred without reason, Psalm 69:4.
Lying lips and deceitful tongues, Psalm 120:2.
Choice morsels to those who wish to hear, Proverbs
26:22.
Do not fear reproach of men, Isaiah 51:7.
Impeccable witness, Daniel 6:3–5.

SCOFF

Rejoice when people speak falsely of you, Matthew 5:11–12.

Avoiding scandal, Matthew 18:15–17.

SCHOOL

Home school, Deuteronomy 4:9–10; 6:7–9; 11:19–21; Psalm 78:5–6.

Specialized Bible training, Deuteronomy 31:10–13.

Small classroom, 2 Kings 6:1.

Scholarly prophet, Ezra 7:6–11 (GNB).

Babylonian training, Daniel 1:3–21.

Tutor, teacher, Acts 22:3.

SCIENCE

Science of astronomy, Job 9:9; 38:31; Amos 5:8.

Oceanography, Psalm 8:8.

Definitive statement, John 8:32

False science, 1 Timothy 6:20 (KJV).

SCOFF

Scoffing at pagans with unanswered prayers, 1 Kings 18:22–38.

Mocking God's messengers, 2 Chronicles 36:16.

Put out the scornful, Proverbs 22:10.

Daring to scoff at the Lord's name, Isaiah 36:18–21; 37:6.
Scoffing at alleged unfairness, Ezekiel 33:20.
Those who mock, Isaiah 57:3–4; Zephaniah 2:10.
Mocking Jesus, Mark 15:16–20.
Demon who laughed at Jesus, Luke 4:33–35.
Demeaning Jesus, Luke 22:63–65.
Scoffing incited by envy, Acts 13:45.
Scoffers in last days, 2 Peter 3:3–4.

SÉANCE

Sorcery forbidden, Exodus 22:18.
Sorcery abandoned, Numbers 24:1.
Prophet of God called seer, 1 Samuel 9:8–9.
Endor séance, 1 Samuel 28:5–25.
Dead cannot return, 2 Samuel 12:22–23.
Putting end to mediums, spiritists, 2 Kings 23:24.
Inquire of God rather than spiritists, Isaiah 8:19.
Spirits of the departed, Isaiah 14:9–10.
Making fools of diviners, Isaiah 44:25.
Fortune, destiny, Isaiah 65:11.
Deceitful diviners, mediums, Jeremiah 27:9–15.

SECRET

God knows deepest secret, Deuteronomy 29:29; Job 12:22; 34:21–22; Ecclesiastes 12:14; Isaiah 29:15–16; Hebrews 4:13.
Animals born in secret, Job 39:1.
"My secret heart," Psalm 51:6 (NRSV).
The Lord knows our thoughts, Psalm 94:11.
Secret slander, Psalm 101:5.
Thoughts and motives, Psalm 139:1–4.
Keeping or telling secrets, Proverbs 11:13.
Birds tell secrets, Ecclesiastes 10:20.
Deeds of darkness, Ezekiel 8:12–13.
Secrets made known, Matthew 13:35.
Time of Christ's coming a secret, Matthew 24:36; Mark 13:32.
Nothing hidden that will not be known, Luke 8:17; 12:2–3.
God's secret made known, Ephesians 1:9–10.
Not to be kept secret, Revelation 22:10 (GNB).

SECULAR

Need for building roads, Deuteronomy 19:1–3.
No time to pray, 1 Samuel 14:19 (GNB).
Seeing, hearing, not understanding, Mark 4:11–12.
Secularizing the temple, John 2:13–16.
Theological dispute in secular courtroom, Acts 18:12–17.
City director of public works, Romans 16:23.
"People of this world," 1 Corinthians 3:3 (CEV).
Earth minded, 1 Corinthians 15:47–48 (Berk.).
Praying for those in authority, 1 Timothy 2:1–4.
Christian's secular reputation, 1 Timothy 3:7 (AB).
Secular viewpoint, 1 John 4:5.

SELF-CONTROL

Tongue control, Psalm 39:1–2.
Controlling one's temper, Proverbs 16:32 (GNB).
Keeping oneself under control, Proverbs 29:11.
Refusal to drink wine, Jeremiah 35:6.
Act in times of duress, James 1:19–20.
No one is perfect, James 3:2 (NKJV).
Mature, gracious Christianity, 2 Peter 1:6.

SELF-IMAGE

Pride, arrogance, 1 Samuel 2:3.
Low evaluation of man, Job 25:6.
Wrong, right boasting, Jeremiah 9:23–24.
More than wealth makes a king, Jeremiah 22:14–15.
Religious performance, Matthew 6:1–4.
Drawing attention to alleged piety, Matthew 6:16–18.
Self-image of Jesus, Matthew 12:41.
Determining who is greatest, Mark 9:33–37.
Love of neighbor, oneself, Mark 12:31.
Loyalty exaggerated, Mark 14:31.
Prodigal's opinion of himself, Luke 15:21.
Justified in eyes of men, Luke 16:15 (NIV).
Folly distorted self-image, Acts 12:21–23.
Danger of false self-image, 2 Corinthians 10:12.
Self-image in ministry, 2 Corinthians 11:5–6; 12:11.
Productively aware of weakness, 2 Corinthians 11:30.
Mirror of truth, James 1:23–25.

SELFISHNESS

Attitude of management toward labor, Exodus 5:2–5.
Cursed for hoarding, Proverbs 11:26.

Selfish stupidity, Proverbs 18:1 (CEV).
Selfish possessiveness, Isaiah 5:8.
Selfish shepherds, Ezekiel 34:2, 18.
Religiosity, selfishness, Hosea 10:1.
Cheap value on human beings, Amos 2:6.
Dishonestly selfish, Habakkuk 2:6.
Selfish feasting, Zechariah 7:6.
People in fine homes, temple in ruins, Haggai 1:1–4.
Give to those who ask, Matthew 5:42.
Ignoring need of others, Matthew 25:43–44.
Seeking best for themselves, Mark 10:37.
Greed over one's possessions, Luke 12:14–15.
Choosing place of honor, Luke 14:7–11.
Preaching hindered business, Acts 19:20–41.
Ruled by personal desire, Romans 8:5–8 (CEV).
Self-seeking, Philippians 2:21.
Unwilling to share ministry financing, Philippians 4:15–19.
Good deeds made known, 1 Timothy 5:25.
Love of self, 2 Timothy 3:2.
Unsatisfied inner desires, James 4:1–2.

SELF-RIGHTEOUS

Self-righteousness affronted, Deuteronomy 3:3–11.
Job's attitude, Job 9:20.
Accused of being self-righteous, Job 33:8–13; 34:1–9; 36:4.
Those pure in their own eyes, Proverbs 30:12.
No need for God, Isaiah 50:11 (LB).
Righteousness as filthy rags, Isaiah 64:6.
Scorning those who have done wrong, Ezekiel 16:56–57.
Vain self-righteousness, Hosea 12:8.
Claiming piety superior to ancestors, Matthew 23:30.
Seeking self justification, Luke 10:29; 16:15.
Holier than thou, Luke 18:9.
Self-righteous accusers, John 8:3–11.
Boasting before men not valid before God, Romans 4:2.
Those who commend themselves, 2 Corinthians 10:12.
Self-delusion, Galatians 6:3.
Personal example, Philippians 3:3–11.

SEXUAL

Relationship between Adam, Eve, Genesis 4:1–2, 25.
Connubial enjoyment, Genesis 18:12 (Berk.).

SERVICE

Rape, Genesis 34:1–31.
Masculine sex appeal, Genesis 39:6–7.
Abstinence before worship, Exodus 19:14–15.
Code for sexual relations, Leviticus 18:6–23.
Sexually damaged animals unfit, Leviticus 22:24–25.
Abstinence and vows, Numbers 30:3–12 (Berk.).
Injury to sexual organs, Deuteronomy 23:1.
Chastity in conduct, Deuteronomy 25:11–12.
Restraint of soldiers, 1 Samuel 21:4–5 (GNB).
Pounding heart, Song of Songs 5:4 (NIV).
Thinking only of sex, Isaiah 57:5 (CEV).
"Making love," Jeremiah 2:33 (Berk.).
Morality vital to spirituality, Jeremiah 3:1–5.
"Age for love," Ezekiel 16:8.
Earth marriage, Heaven's relationship, Mark 12:18–27.
Sexual restraint in marriage, 1 Corinthians 7:5.
Modesty concerning body organs, 1 Cornthians 12:22–25.
Young widows' desires, 1 Timothy 5:11.
Marriage bed, Hebrews 13:4.

SHAME

First display of shame, Genesis 3:10.
Creator's regret, Genesis 6:6.
Attitude toward father's privacy, Genesis 9:20–27.
Shame for immoral sons, 1 Samuel 2:22–25; 8:1–3.
Shameful royal death, 1 Samuel 31:8–10.
Inundated by guilt, shame, Ezra 9:5–9.

Those put to shame, those not, Psalm 25:2–3.
Deep sense of disgrace, Psalm 44:15.
Put to shame, Psalm 119:78.
Asleep during harvest, Proverbs 10:5 (NKJV).
Mother's shame, Proverbs 29:15.
Moon disgraced, sun ashamed, Isaiah 24:23.
Shamed by others, Isaiah 26:11.
Mountain wilts with shame, Isaiah 33:9 (CEV).
Idol makers ashamed, Isaiah 45:16.
Shame of getting caught, Jeremiah 2:26.
Refusing to be ashamed, Jeremiah 3:3 (NKJV).
Unable to blush, Jeremiah 6:15.
Too ashamed to talk, Ezekiel 16:63.
Fallen princes, Ezekiel 32:30.
Preferring shame to honor, Hosea 4:18 (LB).
Shameless evil, Zephaniah 3:5 (See CEV).
Shamed by nudity, Revelation 16:15.

SHORT

Shortest short story, Ecclesiastes 9:14–15 (Note AB, verse 15).
Short chapter, urgent message, Jeremiah 45:1–5.
One chapter books, Obadiah 1–21; Philemon 1–25; 2 John 1–13; 3 John 1–14; Jude 1–25.
Man of short stature, Luke 19:1–6.
Shortest verse in Bible, John 11:35.

SICKNESS

Infirm eyesight, 1 Samuel 4:14–15.
Restored failing health, Psalm 23:3 (LB).
Ill and in great pain, Psalm 38:1–22.
The Lord sustains on sick bed, Psalm 41:3.
God the great healer, Psalm 103:3.
Value of affliction, Psalm 119:71.
Sickness-free Israel, Isaiah 33:24.
Royal sick call, Isaiah 39:1–2.
Furnace of affliction, Isaiah 48:10.
Do not despise rod of testing, Ezekiel 21:13.
Epilepsy caused by demon, Matthew 17:14–20.
Sick, in pain, Luke 7:21 (CEV).
Demon afflicted posture, Luke 13:11 (AB).
Purpose of sickness, John 11:4 (See LB).
Purpose of suffering, Romans 5:3.
Blessed through illness, Galatians 4:13–14.
Made perfect through suffering, Hebrews 2:10.

SIGHT

Eli may have suffered from cataracts, 1 Samuel 4:14–15.
Opening eyes to see God's provision, 2 Kings 6:16–17.
Eagle eyes, Job 39:27–29.
Sorrow weakens eyes, Psalm 6:7.
"Can't even see straight," Lamentations 5:17 (CEV).
Bodies full of eyes, Ezekiel 10:12.
Abominations before his eyes, Ezekiel 20:7 (KJV).
Visible desires removed, Ezekiel 24:16 (See KJV, LB).
Using eyes for good or evil, Matthew 6:22–23.
Partial, then full vision, Mark 8:22–25 (See LB).
Joyful gift of sight, Luke 7:21 (AB).
Eyes of heart, Ephesians 1:18–19 (NIV).

SIN

Image of God, image of man, Genesis 5:1–3.
Accidental sin, Genesis 9:22–27.
Sin against man, sin against God, 1 Samuel 2:25.
Disobedience of faithful, 1 Samuel 12:20.
One sin as great as another, 1 Samuel 15:23; James 2:10.
Sin considered trivial, 1 Kings 16:31.
Lesser degree of sin, 2 Kings 17:1–2.
Purpose for avoiding evil, Job 2:3 (AB).
Sins forgiven, discarded, Job 14:16–17 (CEV).
Cherished becomes like venom, Job 20:12–14.
Nothing hidden from God, Job 34:21–22.
Unconscious faults, Psalm 19:12 (AB).
Forgiven sins honor God, Psalm 25:11.
Strength sapped by sin, Psalm 31:10 (LB).
Lost conscience, Psalms 36:1–2.
Healing for sin, Psalm 41:4.
Sinful nature inherited at birth, Psalm 51:5; 58:3–5.
Corrupted by sin, Psalm 53:1.
Prayer unanswered when sin is cherished, Psalm 66:18–19.
Key to victory over sin, Psalm 119:11, 128.
Forgiveness of sin like cloud removed, Isaiah 44:22–23.
Need for repentance, Isaiah 64:5.
Utterly sinful heart, Jeremiah 17:9 (See AB).
Wages of sin, Lamentations 1:14; Romans 6:23.
Each individual's sins, Ezekiel 18:14 (LB).
Degrees of sin in God's sight, Ezekiel 16:48–52.
Certain wages of sin, Ezekiel 33:13.
Sins written down, stored, Hosea 13:12 (CEV).

Three sins, even four, Amos 1:3, 6, 9, 11, 13; 2:1, 4, 6.
Cleansing fountain, Zechariah 13:1 (CEV).
Old Testament ends with curse, Malachi 4:6.
Sin, not Cross, took life of Jesus, Mark 15:33–37, 44.
Much guilt, less guilt, Luke 7:36–50.
Nothing hidden but will be made known, Luke 12:2–3.
Darkness preferred to light, John 3:19–21.
Sin done in ignorance, Acts 3:17; 1 Timothy 1:12–14.
Claiming sins serve good purpose, Romans 3:5 (LB).
No one righteous, Romans 3:10–18.
Sin not accounted by God, Romans 4:8 (GNB).
Sin's relentless spread, Romans 5:12 (AB).
Alluring sin, Romans 6:7 (LB).
Purpose of law in revealing sin, Romans 7:7–12, 14.
"Sin, devilish stuff," Romans 7:13 (LB).
"Trespass," Galatians 6:1 (NASB).
Leader's sin, 1 Timothy 5:20 (CEV).
Unintentional sin, Hebrews 9:7.
Sins forgotten in mercy of salvation, Hebrews 10:17.
Sin clings closely, Hebrews 12:1 (NRSV).
Role of evil desire in causing sin, James 1:13–15.
Big sin, small sin, all sin, James 2:10.
Love of world, 1 John 2:15–17.
"Sin is lawlessness," 1 John 3:4.
"Mortal sin," 1 John 5:16 (NRSV).
Definition of sin, 1 John 5:17.
Whole world controlled by evil one, 1 John 5:19.
When evil serves God's purpose, Revelation 17:17.

SINGING
Perks for singers, Nehemiah 13:5.
Sing praise with understanding, Psalm 47:7 (KJV).
Songs to the Lord, Psalms 81:1; 95:1.
Bed time songs, Psalms 149:5.
Mountain songs, Isaiah 30:29.
Potential singing stones, Luke 19:37–40.
Inner music, 1 Corinthians 14:15.
Communicative singing, Ephesians 5:19.
Sing praise, James 5:13.

SINGLE
Self-indulgent single, Proverbs 18:1 (NRSV).
Fear of disgrace, Isaiah 4:1.
"Gift of staying single," Matthew 19:11 (CEV).

Accepting married or unmarried state, 1 Corinthians 7:32–35.

SINNER

Endless anguished conscience, Deuteronomy 28:67; Job 15:20; Ecclesiastes 2:23; Romans 2:9.
Shallow joy, Proverbs 14:13.
Good man's sense of sin, Isaiah 6:5.
Notorious, wicked, Luke 15:2 (AB).
Friend of sinners, Luke 7:39; 19:7; John 8:11; Romans 5:8.

SLANDER

False report, Exodus 23:1.
Criticism of king, 2 Samuel 6:17–23.
Mistrust of good motive, 2 Samuel 10:3.
Scourge of tongue, Job 5:21.
Concerned with error of others, Job 19:4.
Slander of many, Psalm 31:13.
Secret slander, Psalm 101:5.
Verbal attack, Psalm 109:1–3.
Let the Lord vindicate, Psalm 135:14.
Hatred and slander, Proverbs 10:18.
Destructive mouths, Proverbs 11:9.
Power of words, Isaiah 29:20–21.
Those who attack with tongues, Jeremiah 18:18; Micah 2:4.
Undercutting prophet's message, Amos 7:10.
Jesus criticized on cross, Matthew 27:39–44.
Pharisees looked for fault in Jesus, Mark 3:1–6.
False accusation of demon-possession, Luke 7:33.
Poisoning the mind, Acts 14:2.
Slandering type, Romans 1:29.
Slander no one, Titus 3:2; James 4:11–12.

SLEEP

Deep sleep, Genesis 15:12; Job 4:13; Daniel 8:18; Jonah 1:5.
Angels retired in Lot's home, Genesis 19:1–4.
Frogs disturb sleep, Exodus 8:3.
Potentially perilous sleep, 1 Samuel 26:12.
Little time for sleep, Nehemiah 4:21–23.
No blankets, Job 24:7.
Go to bed rich, awaken poor, Job 27:19 (CEV).
Companion of night creatures, Job 30:29.

Time for heart searching, Psalm 4:4.
Peaceful sleep, Psalm 4:8.
Plotting evil falling asleep, Psalm 36:4.
Presuming God sleeps, Psalm 44:23.
Songs in the night, Psalm 77:6.
As if God sleeps, Psalm 78:65.
Frogs invade rooms, Psalm 105:30.
Giving thanks at midnight, Psalm 119:62, 148.
Gift of sleep, Psalm 127:2.
Sweet sleep, Proverbs 3:24.
Lazy slumber, Proverbs 6:9–11.
Early morning religiosity, Proverbs 27:14.
Poor man sleeps better, Ecclesiastes 5:12.
Do not disturb, Song of Songs 3:5.
Short bed, narrow blankets, Isaiah 28:20.
Ivory bed, Amos 6:4.
Historic sleep, awakening, Matthew 1:24; Luke 9:32.
Sound sleep, Matthew 8:23–25 (CEV).
Gethsemane slumber, Matthew 26:36–45.
Asleep during sermon, Acts 20:7–12.

SMILE

"Something to smile about," Job 8:21 (CEV).
Smile replaces complaint, Job 9:27.

SLING SHOT

Smile on wicked schemes, Job 10:3.
Surprising smile, Job 29:24.
"That I may smile again," Psalm 39:13 (NASB, NRSV).

SOBER
Silence before the Lord, Zephaniah 1:7.
Alert and self-controlled, 1 Thessalonians 5:6; 1 Timothy 3:2.
Sober disposition, Titus 2:2, 12.

SON
Father's willingness to sacrifice son, Genesis 22:1–18.
Bless these lads, Genesis 48:16.
Favored by brothers, Deuteronomy 33:24–25.
Threat to children if commands disobeyed, Joshua 6:26.
Many sons, Judges 8:30–31.
Father's shame for immoral sons, 1 Samuel 2:22–23.
Son's influence over father, 1 Samuel 19:1–6.
Father, son together in death, 2 Samuel 1:23.
Rivalry between father, son, 2 Samuel 15:1–37.
Attitude of David toward rebellious son, 2 Samuel 18:5.
No son to carry father's name, 2 Samuel 18:18.
Father would have died in place of son, 2 Samuel 18:32–33.
Son's fame exceeds father's, 1 Kings 1:47–48.
Father's joy seeing his son become king, 1 Kings 1:47–48.
Aged father's counsel to son, 1 Kings 2:1–9.
King Solomon succeeded by son, 1 Kings 11:41–42.
Son's evil less than parents, 2 Kings 3:1–3.
Sacrifice of son, 2 Kings 16:3.
Father's righteousness refuted, 2 Kings 21:1–6.
Fate of father becomes fate of sons, Esther 9:12–14.
Neither good nor evil from father to son, Ezekiel 18:3–20.
Joy, delight to parents, Luke 1:14–15.
Obedience of child Jesus, Luke 2:41–52.
Son yet in body of ancestor, Hebrews 7:9–10.
Son received back as from dead, Hebrews 11:19.

SORCERY
Confronting magicians of Egypt, Exodus 7:6–12; 4:1–5.
Sorcery abandoned, Numbers 24:1.
Substitute for prayer, 1 Samuel 28:5–20.
False prophets foiled, Isaiah 44:25.

S

Fortune and destiny, Isaiah 65:11.
Those who prophesy lies, Jeremiah 27:9–15.
Use of magic charms, Ezekiel 13:20.
So-called men of wisdom, Daniel 2:1–4.
Failure of sorcerers, astrologers, Daniel 5:7–8.
Simon in Samaria, Acts 8:9–11.

SORROW
Embraced corpse, Genesis 50:1.
Time to conclude mourning, Genesis 50:4.
All Israel assembled to mourn Samuel, 1 Samuel 25:1.
Weeping until exhausted, 1 Samuel 30:4.
Song of lament, 2 Samuel 1:17–27.
Grief over death of son, 2 Samuel 18:19–53.
Night obliterated by sorrow, Job 3:6.
Sorrow will pass as waters gone by, Job 11:16.
Exhausting sorrow, Psalm 6:6
Night weeping, morning joy, Psalm 30:5.
Divine comfort, Psalm 34:19.
"Bread of tears," Psalm 80:5.
Sorrow of death, joy to the Lord, Psalm 116:15.
Laughter with aching heart, Proverbs 14:13.
Song for heavy heart, Proverbs 25:20.
Judgment brings righteousness, Isaiah 26:9.
Gladness, joy overcome sorrow, sighing, Isaiah 35:10.
Sorrow of disobedience, Jeremiah 3:21.
Comfort in sorrow, Jeremiah 8:18.
"Fountain of tears," Jeremiah 9:11.
Joy, gladness gone, Jeremiah 48:33.
Weeping with no one to comfort, Lamentations 1:16.
Eyes dry from weeping, Lamentations 2:11.
Joy turns to sorrow, Lamentations 5:15.
Tears of false repentance, Malachi 2:13.
Comfort for those who mourn, Matthew 5:4.
Grief of disciples, Matthew 17:22–23.
Death of Lazarus, John 11:1–44.
Grief turns to joy, John 16:20.
Counselor shares from experience, 2 Corinthians 1:3–4.
Disappearing sorrow, Philippians 2:27–28.
Sorrow at time of death, 1 Thessalonians 4:13–18.
Tears, foundation for joy, 2 Timothy 1:3–4.
Second coming will bring sorrow, Revelation 1:7.
Tears wiped away, Revelation 7:17; 21:4 (See Isaiah 25:8).

Agony caused by refusal to repent, Revelation 16:10–11.

SOUL
Eternity in human hearts, Ecclesiastes 3:11.
Spirit returns to God, Ecclesiastes 12:6–7.
Body destroyed, not soul, Matthew 10:28; 1 Corinthians 15:54.
Worth of one lost soul, Matthew 18:12–14; Luke 15:1–32.
Eternal value of soul, temporal values of life, Mark 8:35–37.
Assured immortality, John 8:51; John 11:25–26; 1 Corinthians 15:53.
Soul peace, Galatians 1:3 (AB).
Where soul and spirit meet, Hebrews 4:12 (GNB).
Assembled martyrs, Revelation 20:4.

SOUVENIR
Souvenir manna, Exodus 16:32 (CEV).
David's souvenirs from battle with Goliath, 1 Samuel 17:54.
Tears in a bottle, Psalm 56:8 (KJV).
Time to throw away, Ecclesiastes 3:6.

SPACE
Expanse of sky, Genesis 1:17 (NIV).
Ancient space flight, 2 Kings 2:11.
Space turns thinking inward, Psalm 8:3–8.
Creation proclaims God's righteousness, Psalm 50:6.
All space cannot contain God's love, Psalm 108:4–5.
Material universe vanishes, salvation endures, Isaiah 51:6.
Nest among stars, Obadiah 4.
"High above the sky," Romans 8:39 (LB).

SPIRITUALITY
Being truly holy, Numbers 16:3–7.
Yearning for the Lord, Isaiah 26:9.
Spiritual, temporal, John 8:23.
Righteousness in Christ, 1 Corinthians 1:4–9.
Status of idols, 1 Corinthians 8:4.
Fullest measure of the law, Matthew 23:23.
Experiencing God's kingdom within, Luke 17:20–21.

Keeping soul in good health, 3 John 2.
Temporal wealth, spiritual wealth, Revelation 3:15–18.

SPORTSMAN

Old Testament hunters, Genesis 10:8–9, 25:27.
Ishmael, the archer, Genesis 21:20.
Blessing upon outdoorsmen, Deuteronomy 33:18 (LB).
Setting traps for men, Jeremiah 5:26.
Men cannot outrun horses, Jeremiah 12:5.
Ready with bow, arrow, Lamentations 2:4.
Swift riding horses, Habakkuk 1:8.
Growing up in desert, Luke 1:80.
Invitation to go fishing, Luke 5:1–11.
Peter the fisherman, John 21:3–11.
Running race with endurance, Hebrews 12:1.

SPRING

Nature "burst forth," Genesis 1:11 (LB).
Seedtime, harvest, Genesis 8:22.
Time for kings to go to war, 2 Samuel 11:1.
A day in April, Nehemiah 2:1 (LB).
God at work, Psalm 65:9–13 (LB).
New growth appears, Proverbs 27:25.
Winter past, flowers appearing, Song of Songs 2:11–12.
Spring's spiritual illustration, Isaiah 61:11.
Time for birds to migrate, Jeremiah 8:7.
"Early in April," Ezekiel 40:1 (LB).
Seeds do not germinate, Joel 1:17.

STARS

Impure stars, Job 25:5 (AB).
Lighting up sky, Philippians 2:15 (GNB).

STEALING

Enemy spoils, Numbers 31:1–54.
Need for two or three witnesses, Deuteronomy 19:15.
Riches gained unjustly, Jeremiah 17:11.
Temple robbery, Romans 2:22.
Petty thievery, Titus 2:10 (AB).

STOCK MARKET

Such as playing the market, Proverbs 28:20.
"Bad investment," Ecclesiastes 5:14 (NASB).

STORM
Symbol of divine anger, 2 Samuel 22:7–16.
Tempest surrounding God, Psalm 50:3.
Refuge from storm, Isaiah 4:5–6.
Army of storm clouds, Joel 2:2 (LB).
Water surging from sky, earth, Genesis 7:11–12.
Brimstone storm, Genesis 19:24.
Storm on command, Exodus 9:23.
Giant hailstones, Joshua 10:11.
Fear of thunder, 1 Samuel 7:10.
Mighty wind, Job 1:19.
Majestic thunder, Job 37:4 (GNB).
Thick, dark clouds, Psalm 18:11 (NRSV).
Storm at sea, Psalm 107:25–30 (LB).
Judgment likened to storm, Isaiah 28:2.
Storm calmed when Jonah thrown overboard, Jonah 1:10–15.
Whirlwind invokes judgment, Nahum 1:3.
Obedient wind, waves, Matthew 8:23–27; Mark 6:45–52; Psalm 89:9.
Prelude to hurricane, Acts 27:13–14 (NIV).

STRANGER
Golden Rule toward aliens, Exodus 22:21; Leviticus 19:34.
Courtesy to foreigners, Exodus 23:9.
Fear of strangers, Numbers 13:17–33.
Stranger's ministry, Deuteronomy 18:6–8.
Misunderstood stranger's gesture, 2 Samuel 10:1–4.
Special courtesy to stranger, Ruth 2:14–18.
Identity of stranger, Mark 14:13–15.
Entering communities and homes of strangers, Luke 10:5–12.
Hospitality to recommended stranger, 1 Corinthians 16:10–11.
"Friendly to strangers," Titus 1:8 (CEV).
"Welcome strangers into your home," Hebrews 13:2 (CEV).
Fellowship with all who come to worship, James 2:1–4.
Love strangers, 1 Peter 4:9 (AB).

STREET EVANGELISM
Shout in the streets, Jeremiah 2:2 (LB).
Sermon at temple gate, Jeremiah 7:1–15.
Invitation extended to streets, Matthew 22:8–9.

STREET PEOPLE
Hospitality for stranger on street, Job 31:32.
Living on the streets, Lamentations 4:5.

STRESS
Leadership for those in stress, 1 Samuel 22:2.
Stressing circumstances, Job 1:6–22.
Aging caused by stress, Psalm 6:7.
New attitude, Psalm 40:1–3.
One who helps, sustains, Psalm 54:4.
For times of stress, a God who hears, Psalm 55:1–17.
No need for fear, Psalm 56:3–4.
Rest in God alone, Psalm 62:1–2.
Promises made under stress, Psalm 66:13–14.
Insomnia induced by stress, Psalm 77:2–6 (RSV).
Dwelling place for yearning soul, Psalm 84:1–12.
Distress, anguish, Psalm 116:3 (NRSV).
Refuge in times of anguish, Psalm 118:1–9.
The Lord on our side, Psalm 124:1–5.
Sleep a gift from the Lord, Psalm 127:2.
Bold and stout-hearted, Psalm 138:3.
When no one else cares, Psalm 142:1–7.
Cheerful heart, Proverbs 17:22; 18:14.
Prayer for strength in time of distress, Isaiah 33:2.
Renewal of strength, Isaiah 40:30–31; Isaiah 41:10.
Peace through obedience, Isaiah 48:17–18.
The Lord will guide, satisfy, strengthen, Isaiah 58:11.
Flowers in place of sorrow, Isaiah 61:1–3.
The Lord shared their distress, Isaiah 63:9.
Where to find rest for the soul, Jeremiah 6:16.
The Lord understands, gives counsel, Jeremiah 15:15–16.
Sure resource in time of trouble, Lamentations 3:19–33.
Witness in time of stress, Jonah 1:4–9.
Rest for your soul, Matthew 11:28–30.
Jesus' mastery over fear, Luke 8:22–25.
No need for stress, Luke 12:22–34.
Jesus gives light, John 8:12.
Confidence in future, stability to present, John 14:1–6.
Trusting One who gives peace, John 16:33.
Suffering strengthens faith, Romans 5:1–11.
More than conquerers, Romans 8:12–39 (Note fear, verse 15).

Generating inner peace, Philippians 4:4–7 (See Nehemiah 8:10b).
Antidote for stress, 1 Thessalonians 5:16–18.
The Lord knows what He is doing, 2 Thessalonians 1:3–5.
Restoration for those who suffer, 1 Peter 5:10.
Abundant grace and peace, 2 Peter 1:2.
Absence of stress, Revelation 21:1–5.

STUBBORN

Stiff-necked people, Exodus 32:9; 33:5; Deuteronomy 9:6.
"Stop being so stubborn," Deuteronomy 10:16 (CEV).
Presumptuously stubborn, Deuteronomy 17:12 (KJV).
Stubborn as a mule, Psalm 32:9
Rebellious cobra, Psalm 58:3–5.
Fool's opinion, Proverbs 18:2.
Refusing counsel, Proverbs 29:1.
Iron neck stubbornness, Isaiah 48:4.
Break up unplowed ground, Jeremiah 4:3.
Proud, stubborn, Jeremiah 11:8 (LB).
Stubborn hearts, Zechariah 7:11–12.
"Don't be stubborn," Hebrews 4:7 (CEV).

STUDENTS

Asking good questions, 1 Kings 10:1–3.
Lifetime study of Scriptures, Ezra 7:10 (CEV).
Habitual study, Psalm 1:2 (AB).
True wisdom comes from Scriptures, Psalm 119:97–100.
Giving heed to instruction, Proverbs 16:20.
Discernment provides knowledge, Proverbs 18:15.
Pay attention to teacher, Proverbs 23:11 (GNB).
Wisdom-loving son delights father, Proverbs 29:3.
Weary from studying, Ecclesiastes 12:12.
God-given knowledge, Daniel 1:17.
Students rank beneath teachers, Matthew 10:24.
Hearing, not understanding, Mark 4:11–12.
In-depth learning, Mark 4:34.
Willingness to learn, Luke 11:1.
Thorough knowledge of Scriptures, Acts 18:24–26.
Holy Spirit's guidance in Bible study, 1 Corinthians 2:6–16.
Folly of intellectual pride, 1 Corinthians 3:18–20.
Faith the ultimate intelligence, 1 Corinthians 3:21–23.

S

Student sharing with teacher, Galatians 6:6 (CEV).
Properly receiving the Word of God, 1 Thessalonians 2:13.
Slow learners, Hebrews 5:11–14.
Faith as sure antidote for doubt, Hebrews 11:1–3.
Take Scriptures to heart, Revelation 1:3.

STUDY

Can't sleep? Read history, Esther 6:1.
Opened eyes, Psalm 119:18.
"Nuggets of truth," Proverbs 1:6 (LB).
Do not neglect God's Word, Psalm 119:16.
Prayer for perception in Bible study, Psalms 119:18; 119:33–38.
Royal research study, Proverbs 25:2.
Excessive study, Ecclesiastes 12:12.
Motivation for study, Daniel 7:19.
Lack of study, Matthew 22:29.
Wealth, worry impair study, Mark 4:19.
Missing the point, John 5:39–40 (NRSV).
Good teaching into action, John 13:17.
Eager to study Scriptures, Acts 17:11.
Bible-centered fellowship, Acts 18:24–26.
Holy Spirit's guidance, 1 Corinthians 2:6–16 (AB).
Search for spiritual maturity, 1 Timothy 4:13.
Searching intently, 1 Peter 1:10–12.

SUBMISSION

Beaten into submission, Exodus 21:20–21.
Submission to royal authority, 1 Samuel 26:7–11.
Total submission, 1 King 20:1–6.
Woman's willing submission, Esther 4:12–16.
Satanic view of submission, Job 2:1–10.
Made pure through testing, Job 23:10.
One does not contend with God, Job 40:2.
Delayed submission, Job 42:1–9.
Revelation inspires submission, Proverbs 29:18.
Clay submitted to potter, Isaiah 45:9; 64:8.
One who suffered for us, Isaiah 53:1–7.
Pressured submission, Jeremiah 49:35.
Knowing who is the Lord, Ezekiel 6:10, 14; 7:4, 9, 27; 12:16, 20; 13:9, 23; 14:11.
Refusing submission to pagan gods, Daniel 3:8–30.
Gethsemane submission, Mark 14:36.
Willingness of Jesus to be sacrificed, John 18:1–11.

"Yielding in faith," Romans 1:5 (Berk.).
Position in life submissive to will of God, Titus 2:9–10.
Jesus' reverent submission, Hebrews 5:7 (NRSV).
Submit to God, resist Satan, James 4:7.

SUCCESS
Successful creation, Genesis 1:10, 12, 18, 21, 25.
Joseph prospered in Egypt, Genesis 39:2.
Promised success, Exodus 34:10; Deuteronomy 26:19.
Abounding with God's favor, Deuteronomy 33:23.
Shepherd boy to king, 2 Samuel 7:1–16.
Strength from God, 2 Samuel 22:33.
Success formula, 2 Chronicles 26:5.
Succeeding with God's help, Nehemiah 6:16.
Assured true success, Psalm 1:3.
Success delights guide, Psalm 37:23–24.
Success in Divine purpose, Psalm 57:2.
Giving God glory for success, Psalms 115:1; 118:23.
In-depth success, Proverbs 3:1–4.
Key to success, Proverbs 16:3; 21:30.
Emptiness of mere success, Ecclesiastes 2:4–11.
Success inequity, Ecclesiastes 8:14.
Those whom the Lord commissions achieve success, Isaiah 48:15.
Success assured whatever circumstances, Jeremiah 17:7–8.
Prosperity linked to conduct, Daniel 4:27.
Not by might nor by power, Zechariah 4:6.
Measure for greatness, Matthew 20:25–28.
Fishermen's failure turned to success, Luke 5:1–11.
Vine, fruit, John 15:1–8.
Chosen for guidance, blessing, John 15:16.
Speaking only of what Christ has done in us, Romans 15:18–19.
Success comes from God, 1 Corinthians 3:6–8.
In race, one wins; serving God, all win, 1 Corinthians 9:24–27.
Spreading fragrance of Christ, 2 Corinthians 2:14.
Let the Lord commend, 2 Corinthians 10:17–18.
Paul's commendation of Timothy, Philippians 2:19–23.
Widely reported success, 1 Thessalonians 1:8–10.
Joy and glory, 1 Thessalonians 2:17–19.
Praise to God for success in ministry, 1 Thessalonians 3:8–10.

Purpose, means of spiritual success, 2 Thessalonians 1:11–12.
Prepared by God to succeed, Hebrews 13:20–21.
Business success, certainty of death, James 1:10.
Mentality of success, 1 Peter 1:15.
Attributes of mature Christian life, 2 Peter 1:5–9.
Certainty of success in Christian life, Jude 24–25.

SUICIDE

Better off dead, Genesis 27:46.
Royal suicide on battlefield, 1 Samuel 31:1–6.
Accused of murder for abetting suicide, 2 Samuel 1:1–16.
Disgruntled suicide, 2 Samuel 17:23.
Death by arson, 1 Kings 16:18.
Dying before one's time, Ecclesiastes 7:17.
Covenant with death, Isaiah 28:15–18.
Death of Judas, Matthew 27:3–5.
Demon suicide, Luke 8:26–34.
Man who almost killed himself, Acts 16:25–28.
Assisted suicide, Jonah 1:12 (Note 1 Samuel 31:4).

SUPERIORITY

God as first priority, Genesis 1:1.
Protected from superior enemy, Exodus 14:15–31.
Measure of holiness, Numbers 16:3–7.
The God greater than numbers, Deuteronomy 20:1–4.
Superior human wisdom, 1 Kings 4:29–34.
Claiming superiority, Psalm 35:26 (GNB).
Race not to swift or strong, Ecclesiastes 9:11.
Wrong, right boasting, Jeremiah 9:23–24.
God the creator, gods who perish, Jeremiah 10:11–12.
Knowing who is the Lord, Ezekiel 6:10, 14; 7:4, 9, 27; 12:16, 20; 13:9, 23; 14:11.
All one in Christ, Galatians 3:28.
Christ superior to angels, Hebrews 1:3–4.

SUPERSTITION

Ark of Covenant for good omen, 1 Samuel 4:3.
Dangerous gods of hills, 1 Kings 20:23.
Use of incense, Jeremiah 44:18.
Use of magic charms, Ezekiel 13:18.
Disciples thought to be gods, Acts 14:11–15.
Sign of the serpent, Acts 28:3–6.

SURROGATE

Bearing child for another, Genesis 16:1–5; 21:9–11; 30:1–6.
Actual mother as surrogate, Exodus 2:1–9.
Surrogate mother among birds, Jeremiah 17:11.

SURVIVAL

People divided for protection, Genesis 32:6–8.
No graves in Egypt, Exodus 14:11.
Chance survival, 2 Samuel 8:2.
Protection against enemies of road, Ezra 8:21–23.
Survival of felled tree, Job 14:7–9.
The Lord on our side, Psalm 124:1–5.
Ask for ancient paths, Jeremiah 6:16.
Birds know seasons of migration, Jeremiah 8:7.
Empty cisterns, parched fields, Jeremiah 14:1–6.
Ten percent survival, Amos 5:3.
Contest enemy, seek peace terms, Luke 14:31–32.
Desiring food of pigs, Luke 15:16.

SYMPATHY

Historic sympathy, Exodus 2:5–6.
Delegation sent to express condolence, 2 Samuel 10:1–2.
Suspicious condolence, 2 Samuel 10:1–4.
Those at ease have contempt for others, Job 12:5.
Vain search for sympathy, Psalm 69:20.
Divine sympathy, Psalm 78:39; 103:13; Isaiah 63:9.
Sympathy put into action, Isaiah 58:7.
Help in time of need, Luke 10:33–35; Acts 20:35.
Shared sorrow, John 11:19–33.
Tears of Jesus, John 11:35.
Bearing burdens of others, Galatians 6:2; Hebrews 13:3.
Remembering another's tears, 2 Timothy 1:4.
Divine empathy, Hebrews 4:15 (See GNB).
Truest form of sympathy, Hebrews 13:3.
Sympathy from a distance, Revelation 18:10.

T

TACT

Using tact in diplomacy, Genesis 41:33–46.
Tactful comparison of accomplishments, Judges 8:2.

Tense tact, 2 Samuel 2:4–5.
Waiting for proper time to speak, Job 32:4–6.
Anger turned away by gentle words, Proverbs 15:1.
"Word spoken at right circumstances," Proverbs 25:11 (NASB).
When to speak, Ecclesiastes 3:7.
Proper time, procedure, Ecclesiastes 8:5–6.
Taught tact, Isaiah 28:26.
"A word in season," Isaiah 50:4 (KJV).
Tactful response to false prophecy, Jeremiah 28:1–17.
Speaking with wisdom, tact, Daniel 2:14 (NIV).
Wise as snakes, innocent as doves, Matthew 10:16 (CEV).
Response of Jesus to critics, Matthew 21:23–27; Mark 12:34.
Gracious words of Jesus, Luke 4:22.
Tact of Jesus with Samaritan woman, John 4:4–26.
Timely validation of ministry, Acts 23:6.
Relating to unbelievers, 2 Corinthians 2:15–16.
Avoidance of stumbling blocks, 2 Corinthians 6:3–13.
Speaking truth in love, Ephesians 4:15.
Tactful in conversation with others, Colossians 4:6.
Tact concerning debt, Philemon 18–19.
Dealing gently with those who need guidance, Hebrews 5:2.
Tact in times of duress, James 1:19–20.
Wisdom from heaven, James 3:17–18.

TALENT
Lost skill for farming, Genesis 4:9–12.
Musical talent a family tradition, Genesis 4:21.
Assumed lack of talent, Exodus 4:10–12 (See 6:30).
Talented minds, hands, Exodus 28:3; 31:3; 38:23; 1 Kings 7:14; 1 Chronicles 22:15–16; 2 Chronicles 2:13–14; 26:15.
Special gifts through Spirit of God, Exodus 31:1–5; 35:30–35.
God-given ability to produce wealth, Deuteronomy 8:18.
Elimination of blacksmiths, 1 Samuel 13:19.
Solomon multi-talented, songs, 1 Kings 4:32.
Cunning men, 1 Chronicles 22:15 (KJV).
Farmer cannot manage wild ox, Job 39:9–12.
Pen of skillful writer, Psalm 45:1.
God's blessing upon work of hands, Psalm 90:17.
Race not to swift or strong, Ecclesiastes 9:11.
Those wise in their own eyes, Isaiah 5:21.

Farmer's God-given skills, Isaiah 28:24–29.
Artist is mortal, Isaiah 44:11 (NRSV).
Skilled in doing evil, Jeremiah 4:22.
Men have talent but God is sovereign, Jeremiah 10:8–10.
Finest of young men chosen for service, Daniel 1:3–4.
Parable of talents, Matthew 25:14–30.
Those given much, those given little, Mark 4:24–25; Luke 12:48.
Neighbors did not expect divinity in Jesus, Luke 4:22–24.
Relationship between talent, God's call, Romans 11:29.
Function of body members, Romans 12:4–8; 1 Corinthians 12:14–20.
Gifts from God, 1 Corinthians 4:7.
Special talents, special tasks, Ephesians 4:7, 11–13 (LB).
Do not neglect your gift, 1 Timothy 4:14.
Fan gift of God into flame, 2 Timothy 1:6.
Holy Spirit designates gifts, Hebrews 2:4.
Prepared to succeed as believer, Hebrews 13:20–21.
Using one's gift for others' good, 1 Peter 4:10 (See AB).

TAXES

Percentage to government, Genesis 47:13–26; 1 Samuel 8:15; 2 Kings 23:35; Esther 10:1.

TAN

Twenty-five annual tons of gold, 1 Kings 10:14 (CEV).
Arrested for tax evasion, 2 Kings 17:4.
Clergy tax-free, Ezra 7:24.
Borrowing money to pay taxes, Nehemiah 5:4.
Tax revenue misused, Ecclesiastes 10:19 (AB).
Tax coin in fish mouth, Matthew 17:24–27 (Note: Jesus
    paid tax, v. 27).
Pagan, tax collector, Matthew 18:17.
Calling of tax collector, Mark 2:13–17; Luke 5:27–31.
"Tax collectors and other sinners," Mark 2:15 (CEV).
Correct procedure paying taxes, Mark 12:17.
Taxation, census, Luke 2:1–5 (See KJV).
Advice to tax collectors, Luke 3:12–13.
Give to government what is due, Luke 20:25.
Citizen's obligation, Romans 13:6–7.

TEAMWORK

Taking care of business, Deuteronomy 20:5–9.
Leadership for those in trouble, 1 Samuel 22:2.
Working diligently together, Nehemiah 4:6.
Iron sharpens iron, Proverbs 27:17.
Two better than one, Ecclesiastes 4:9–10.
Skilled crews on ships, Ezekiel 27:8–9.
Disciples sent out two-by-two, Mark 6:7.
Healing of paralytic man, Luke 5:17–26.
Set apart, laying on of hands, Acts 13:1–3.
Teamwork in reaching others, 1 Corinthians 3:6–9.
Body as unit, 1 Corinthians 12:12–30.

TEARS

Cry for help, Judges 10:14 (CEV).
Phony tears, Judges 14:11–19.
Tears of gratitude, 1 Samuel 20:41.
Fear of confessing wrong to another, 1 Samuel 24:16–17.
Weeping until exhausted, 1 Samuel 30:4; Psalm 6:6.
Altered countenance, Job 16:16.
Red-eyed from weeping, Psalm 31:9 (LB).
Weeping as part of prayer, Psalm 39:12.
"Bread of tears," Psalm 80:5.
Burdened soul-winning, Psalm 126:6.
"Fountain of tears," Jeremiah 9:1 (See LB).
Unable to shed tears, Lamentations 2:11 (LB).
Rivers of tears, Lamentations 3:48 (NRSV).
Peter cried hard, Matthew 26:75 (CEV).
Redeemer's tears, Luke 19:41.

Weeping en route to crucifixion, Luke 23:27 (CEV).
Tears of compassion, Philippians 3:18 (CEV).

TELEVISION

Suggested guidance in use of television, Proverbs 14:7
    (GNB); Matthew 6:22, 23; Romans 12:2; Ephesians
    5:15–6; Philippians 4:8; 1 Thessalonians 5:21–2.

TEMPER

Angry revenge, Deuteronomy 19:6.
"Bad tempered boor," 1 Samuel 25:25 (LB).
"Hot head," 2 Samuel 20:1 (LB).
Very angry, Nehemiah 5:6.
Divine anger, Psalm 6:1 (LB).
The Lord's momentary temper, Psalm 30:5.
The Lord slow to anger, Psalm 86:15; Nahum 1:3.
Quick temper, Proverbs 14:29.
Temper control, Proverbs 16:32.
Violent temper penalized, Proverbs 19:19 (NRSV).
Avoid angry man, Proverbs 22:24.
Furious anger, Daniel 3:19 (LB).
God's temper, Hosea 11:9 (CEV).
"Angry tempers," 2 Corinthians 12:20 (NASB).
Be slow to anger, James 1:19–20.

TEMPERANCE

Sexual restraint, 1 Samuel 21:4–5.
Led astray by alcohol, Proverbs 20:1.
Excess food, drink cause laziness, Proverbs 23:20–21.
Lingering over wine, Proverbs 23:30–33.
Best of meats, finest wine, Isaiah 25:6.
Laid low by wine, Isaiah 28:1–7.
Refusal to drink wine, Jeremiah 35:1–14.
Nazirites forced to drink wine, Amos 2:12.
Not heavy drinkers, 1 Timothy 3:3, 11 (CEV).
Drinking wine, 1 Timothy 5:23.

TEMPTATION

Tantalizing questions, Genesis 3:1 (LB).
Satanic persuasion, Genesis 3:1–6; Matthew 4:3–11;
    2 Corinthians 2:11.
Handling temptation, Genesis 4:7.
Resisting temptation, Genesis 39:6–10.
Personal responsibility in temptation, Deuteronomy
    11:16.

Visual temptation, Joshua 7:21.
Temptation refuge, Psalm 46:1 (AB).
Overtly resisting temptation, Proverbs 1:10–17.
Facility for resisting temptation, Proverbs 2:10–12, 16.
Playing with fire, Proverbs 6:27–29.
Man who pleases God escapes immorality, Ecclesiastes 7:26.
Made strong by God's power, Jeremiah 1:17–19.
Prior resolution to resist temptation, Daniel 1:8.
Temptation of Jesus, Matthew 4:1–11 (Note Holy Spirit, v. 1).
Ministering angels, Matthew 4:11.
Temptation, tempter, Matthew 18:7 (LB).
Using Scripture to confront devil, Luke 4:1–13.
One-time-only temptation, Luke 4:7 (AB).
Satanic technique, Luke 4:13.
Temptation defined, Luke 17:1 (AB).
Sin's allure, Romans 6:7 (LB).
Deliverance by faithful God, 1 Corinthians 10:13.
"Outwitted by Satan," 2 Corinthians 2:11 (NRSV).
Deny the devil, Ephesians 4:27 (GNB).
"Schemes of the devil," Ephesians 6:11 (NASB).
Shield of faith, Ephesians 6:16.
Supporting and surveying one another, 1 Thessalonians 3:5.
Resisting ungodliness and passions, Titus 2:11–12.
Jesus tempted to help those tempted, Hebrews 2:18; 4:15.
Promised deliverance, Hebrews 7:23–28.
God tempts no one, James 1:13–14.
Evil desires, 2 Peter 1:4.
Sure rescue in the Lord, 2 Peter 2:7–9.
Battleground in which Satan attacks, 1 John 2:15–17.
Work of the devil, 1 John 3:7–8.

THANKSGIVING

Harvest token, Leviticus 19:24; Deuteronomy 26:10; Proverbs 3:9–10.
Prayer after meal, Deuteronomy 8:10.
Prayer of gratitude, 2 Samuel 7:18–29.
Song of praise, 2 Samuel 22:1–51; Psalm 98:1.
Gratitude for Divine faithfulness and goodness, 1 Kings 8:14–21.
Songs of gratitude, Psalms 9:11; 33:2.
Perpetual gratitude, Psalm 35:28.
Value of sacrifice, offering, Psalm 50:23.

TERMINOLOGY

Thanking God for enduring love, Psalm 106:1.
Thanksgiving leads to witnessing, Psalm 107:1–3.
Refusing to glorify God for harvest, Jeremiah 5:24.
Gratitude to God for wisdom, Daniel 2:19–23.
Thankful for food, Joel 2:26.
Prayer of thanks before eating, John 6:11.
Key to answered prayer, Philippians 4:6.
Overflow with thankfulness, Colossians 2:6–7.
Thankful for everything, 1 Thessalonians 5:18.

THOUGHT

Wicked thought, Deuteronomy 15:9; Proverbs 15:26;
    Jeremiah 4:14; Matthew 9:4; 15:19.
Thoughts pleasing to God, Psalm 19:14.
Divine introspection, Psalm 26:2; Jeremiah 17:10.
Futile thoughts, Psalm 94:11.
Thought determines action, Proverbs 4:23 (GNB).
Warped minds, Proverbs 12:8.

Cost conscious thinking, Proverbs 23:7.
Thought control, Ecclesiastes 11:10.
Wicked thoughts, Jeremiah 4:14.
Self-evaluation, Haggai 1:5–6.
Relationship of thought and action, Romans 2:1–11.
Humility thinking, Romans 12:3.
How to have pure thoughts, Romans 13:14.
Out of one's mind, 2 Corinthians 5:13.
Things worth thinking about, Philippians 4:8.
Practice thought control, Colossians 3:1–12.

TIMING

Leave revenge to God's timing, 1 Samuel 26:1–11.
The Lord's timing, Psalm 119:126; Isaiah 49:8; 60:22.
Time for everything, Ecclesiastes 3:1–8.
Proper time, procedure, Ecclesiastes 8:5–6.
Time to prepare, time to plant, Isaiah 28:24–25.
Seeking at right time, Isaiah 55:6.
Mistake in timing, Haggai 1:2–5 (CEV).
Jesus could not die before His time, Luke 4:28–30.
Jesus offered no resistance to oppressors, Luke 22:47–53.
Time speeds by, Acts 25:13 (Berk.).
Perfect timing in Christ, Romans 5:6.

TOLERANCE

Tolerant of foreigners, Exodus 23:9 (CEV).
Unwilling to tolerate food, Numbers 11:4–6.
Tolerating ridicule, Psalm 123:3–4.
Slow to anger, great in power, Nahum 1:3.
Attitude toward lost, Matthew 9:10.
"Tolerance of Jesus for sleeping disciples," Matthew 26:37–46.
Those of differing views, Mark 9:38–39; Luke 9:49–50; Philippians 1:17–18.
Tolerating opinions of others, Romans 14:1–8.
"Put up with anything," 2 Timothy 2:10 (CEV).

TONGUE

Spreading false reports, Exodus 23:1.
Criticizing those the Lord has not denounced, Numbers 23:8.
Talk about spiritual matters, Deuteronomy 6:4–7.
Stewardship of speech, Deuteronomy 23:23.
Crushed with words, Job 19:2.

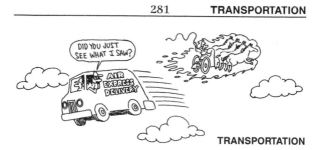

TRANSPORTATION

Disciplined tongue, Psalm 34:13; Proverbs 13:3 (See LB); 21:23.
Purity of speech, Proverbs 4:24.
Silver-tongued, Proverbs 10:20.
Words like rare jewel, Proverbs 20:15.
Word aptly spoken, Proverbs 25:11.
Vileness from every mouth, Isaiah 9:17.
Sticking out tongue, Isaiah 57:4.
Like deadly arrow, Jeremiah 9:8.
Critical tongues made silent, Luke 20:20–26.
Glossolalia caution, 1 Corinthians 14:23 (AB).
Whatever you say or do, Colossians 3:17.
Double-tongued, 1 Timothy 3:8 (NASB, NRSV).
Do not talk back, Titus 2:9.
Control tongue, control body, James 3:2 (CEV).
Guard tongue well, James 3:3–6.

TOUCH

Forbidden fruit, Genesis 3:3.
Defiling touch, Leviticus 5:2; 15:11; Isaiah 52:11; 2 Corinthians 6:17; Colossians 2:21.
Dead body touched, Numbers 19:13.
Touching Great Physician, Matthew 9:20–22 (CEV); 14:36; Mark 3:10; Luke 6:19.
Cleansing touch, Matthew 8:3.
Healing touch, Matthew 8:15; 9:29–30; Mark 7:33–35; Luke 22:51.
Touch of sight, Matthew 20:34.
Children touched by Jesus, Mark 10:13–16.

TRANSPORTATION

Transportation provided as act of love, Genesis 45:16–20.

T

Transportation for forty sons, thirty grandsons, Judges 12:14.
Chariot of fire, whirlwind, 2 Kings 2:11–12.
"Chariots of God," Psalm 68:17.
Royal palanquin, Song of Songs 3:9 (NRSV).
Intercontinental highway, Isaiah 19:23.
Mountains turned into roads, Isaiah 49:11.
Wealth to those who lived by many waters, Jeremiah 51:13.
Donkey chosen to serve Jesus, Matthew 21:1–7; Mark 11:1–7.

TRAVEL

Washing feet after journey, Genesis 18:4; 19:2.
Not traveling after sunset, Genesis 28:11.
Three days journey, Exodus 3:18.
Travelling by divine instructions, Numbers 9:23.
Prayer for protection, Numbers 10:35.
Listing journeys, Numbers 33:1–48.
Travel directions, Deuteronomy 1:2.
"Ride on white donkeys," Judges 5:10.
Travel for forty sons, thirty grandsons, Judges 12:14.
Journey with divine approval, Judges 18:6.
Early morning departure, 1 Samuel 17:20.
Day's journey, 1 Kings 19:4.
Travel energy, 1 Kings 19:7.
Unsafe to travel, 2 Chronicles 15:5.
Speed boats, Job 9:26.
Avoiding lighted pathway, Job 24:13.
Travel expands knowledge, Job 36:3.
Sleeping on high seas, Proverbs 23:34.
Safe travel, Isaiah 35:8–9.
Mountains turned into roads, Isaiah 49:11.
Crooked roads, Isaiah 59:8.
Find the good way, Jeremiah 6:16.
Divine obstruction, Hosea 2:6.
Altered travel plans, Matthew 2:12.
Nativity journey, Luke 2:1–5.
Wearisome travel, John 4:6.
Jesus avoided dangerous travel, John 7:1.
Stop over en route, Romans 15:24.
Letters of introduction, 1 Corinthians 16:3.
Care planning journey, 2 Corinthians 1:15–17.

TRUST

Remembering Egypt instead of trusting God, Exodus 16:2–3.

Exemplary leadership, 2 Kings 18:5.

Confidence against all circumstances, Job 13:15.

"I trust you completely," Psalm 28:7 (CEV).

Our times in God's hands, Psalm 31:15.

Child-like trust, Psalm 131:1–2.

Betraying confidence, Proverbs 11:13.

Kept in perfect peace, Isaiah 26:3.

Trust in the Lord rather than men, Isaiah 36:4–10.

Trust God, Isaiah 43:10 (CEV).

Confidence in the potter, Isaiah 45:9.

Trust in man, Jeremiah 17:5.

Safer to trust God than run away, Jeremiah 42:1–22.

Cannot trust best friend, Micah 7:5 (CEV).

Trust in midst of trouble, Habakkuk 3:17–18.

"Depend only on Him," Matthew 5:3 (CEV).

Needless fear in time of storm, Mark 4:35–41.

Assurance to those who trust the Lord, John 6:37.

Do not test the Lord, 1 Corinthians 10:9–10.

Trust, assurance, confidence, Hebrews 2:13 (AB).

Invisible reality, Hebrews 11:1.

Cast all cares upon the Lord, 1 Peter 5:7.

TRUTH

Scripture contains blessings and curses, Joshua 8:34.

Let God judge, Job 32:13.

Ears hear, eyes see, Job 42:5.

God's covenant never changes, Psalms 105:8–9; 111:5.

"Eternity in the heart," Ecclesiastes 3:11.

Sincere search for God, Jeremiah 29:10–14.

Faithfulness rewarded with imprisonment, Jeremiah 37:1–21.

Futile effort to suppress truth, Jeremiah 38:1–6.

Listening out of desperation, Jeremiah 38:14–28.

Truth proclaimed with boldness, Ezekiel 33:21–33.

Positive, negative result, Hosea 14:9.

Purpose of parables, Matthew 13:10–13.

Believe good news, Mark 1:14–15.

Mother of Jesus too frightened to comprehend, Mark 16:1–8.

Truth gives life, destruction, Luke 20:17–18.

Knowing truth gives freedom, John 8:32.

Doubt augmented by truth, John 8:45–47.

Spiritual blindness, spiritual sight, John 9:39–41.
Walking in light, John 12:35–36.
Response to resurrection message, Acts 17:32.
Truth declared with power, Romans 1:4.
Those who stumble over redemption, truth, Romans 9:33; 1 Corinthians 15:12–19.
From God, not man, Galatians 1:11–12.
Truth proclaimed with false motives, Philippians 1:18.
Pillar, bulwark, 1 Timothy 3:15 (NRSV).
God cannot lie, Titus 1:2; Hebrews 6:18.
"Practice the truth," 1 John 1:6 (NASB, NKJV).
Certain of truth, 1 John 2:21.
Truth, love united, 2 John 1:3, 5–6.
Love in truth, 3 John 1.

TWINS

Jacob and Esau, Genesis 25:21–26.
Obstetrical trickery, Genesis 38:27–30.
Strife before birth, Hosea 12:3.
Disciple twin, John 20:24 (Berk., CEV, LB, NRSV).

--------------------- **U** ---------------------

UFO

Unusual sights in sky, Jeremiah 10:2 (GNB).
Wheels of Ezekiel's vision, Ezekiel 1:15–21.

UNBELIEF

Making joke of truth, Genesis 17:17; 19:14.
Moses discredited, Exodus 4:1.
Blatant unbelief, Exodus 5:2.
Faith to unbelief in one generation, Judges 2:10.
Pessimism of unbelief, 2 Kings 18:29–35.
No God, no priest, no law, 2 Chronicles 15:3.
Death to unbelievers, 2 Chronicles 15:13.
Contrasting belief, unbelief, Psalm 1:1–6.
So few believe, Isaiah 53:1 (LB).
Idols in heart, Ezekiel 14:1–11.
Laughing at truth spoken by Jesus, Matthew 9:23–24.
Attributing work of God to demons, Matthew 9:34.
Hindrance to miracles, Matthew 13:58.
Requesting increased faith, John 9:24 (LB).
Unbelief faces proof, John 12:37–40.
Certain of unbelief, Acts 19:35–36.

Empty minds, darkness, Romans 1:21 (GNB).
Faith becomes nonsense, 1 Corinthians 1:18 (GNB).
Blinded by Satan, 2 Corinthians 4:1–6.
Danger of intellectual pride, 2 Timothy 3:7.
Deceiving others, deceived themselves, 2 Timothy 3:13.
Failure to combine hearing, believing, Hebrews 4:1–3.
Abandoned faith, Hebrews 6:6 (GNB).
Scoffers in last days, 2 Peter 3:3–4.
Denying that Jesus is the Christ, 1 John 2:22–23.
Those cast into lake of fire, Revelation 21:8; 22:15.

UNDERPRIVILEGED
Providing for underprivileged, Leviticus 23:22.
Inequity among citizens, Nehemiah 5:1–5.
Sons of sorceress, Isaiah 57:3.
Status of servant, Luke 17:7–10.

UNDERSTANDING
Eyes see, ears hear, Deuteronomy 29:2–4.
Purposeful comprehension, 1 Chronicles 22:12.
Seeing light in God's light, Psalm 36:9.
God-given ability to understand Scripture, Psalm 119:125.
Persistent search for understanding, Proverbs 2:1–6.
Refusal, inability to read, Isaiah 29:11–12.

UNEXPECTED

U

Those with insight understand, Daniel 12:10 (NASB).
Effect of attitudes on understanding, Matthew 13:14–15.
Childhood understanding, Luke 10:21.
Sharing Scriptural insights, Acts 18:24–26.
Seeing light, not understanding voice, Acts 22:9.
Taught by the Holy Spirit, 1 Corinthians 2:6–16.
Milk, solid food, 1 Corinthians 3:1–2.
Tolerant understanding, 1 Corinthians 11:18–19.
"Power to comprehend," Ephesians 3:18 (NRSV).
Thinking clarified, Philippians 3:15 (CEV).
Filled with knowledge of God's will, Colossians 1:9–12.
Lacking understanding, 1 Timothy 1:7 (AB).

UNFAITHFUL

Destiny set for rebellious people, Numbers 14:35.
Turning quickly to heathen gods, Judges 8:33–34.
Woman unfaithful to husband, Judges 19:1–3.
"We have broken faith," Ezra 10:2 (NRSV).
Divine disappointment, Isaiah 5:7.
Eyes, ears that do not function, Ezekiel 12:2.
Peter's unfaithfulness, Matthew 26:31–35, 69–75.
Test of faithfulness, Luke 16:12.
Unfaithful wife, James 4:4 (LB).

UNFORGIVING

Prolonged retribution, Deuteronomy 23:2–6.
Stark picture of vengeance, Psalms 58:10; 68:23.

UNITY

Wrong kind of unity, Numbers 11:4–10.
King, people united, 1 Samuel 12:14.
Heart, soul in unity, 1 Samuel 14:7.
Two becoming one in spirit, 1 Samuel 18:1–4.
Mutual love between friends, 1 Samuel 20:17.
Multitude as one, Nehemiah 8:1.
At peace with one's enemies, Proverbs 16:7.
Grains of sand hold back ocean, Jeremiah 5:22.
Two sticks become as one, Ezekiel 37:17–23.
Two in agreement, Amos 3:3.
Serving shoulder-to-shoulder, Zephaniah 3:9.
People at peace with each other, Mark 9:50.
Mark of true discipleship, John 13:34–35.
Devotion to one another, Romans 12:10.

USED

Divine call to unity, 1 Corinthians 1:10–17; 2 Corinthians 13:11; Ephesians 4:3; 1 Peter 3:8.
Unity in Christ, Ephesians 2:14.
Diversity producing unity, Ephesians 4:11–13.
Instructions on unity, Philippians 4:1–9.
United in love, Colossians 2:2.
"Try to get along," 1 Thessalonians 5:13 (CEV).
Faith held in common, Titus 1:4.

URBAN

Building first city, Genesis 4:17.
Urban development, Genesis 10:11–12.
Cities totally given to debauchery, Genesis 18:16–33.
Dynamic communities, Numbers 13:27–28; Deuteronomy 6:10–12.
Fortified cities, Deuteronomy 9:1 (AB).
Town, country, Deuteronomy 28:3.
Urban water works, 2 Chronicles 32:30.
City planning, Nehemiah 11:1.
Desolate cities, Job 15:28 (KJV).
Daybreak for city in need, Psalm 46:5.
Urban violence, Psalm 55:9–11.
Neighborhood watch, Psalm 101:8 (LB).
City government, Proverbs 31:23.
Congested cities, Isaiah 5:8.

U

Ruined city, Isaiah 17:1.
Beautiful city, Isaiah 60:15 (CEV).
Restored city, Jeremiah 30:17–18 (LB).
Vanquished city, Lamentations 2:15.
Vast city, Jonah 3:3 (RSV, LB).
Nineveh's charms, Nahum 3:4 (LB).
City built on crime, violence, Habakkuk 2:12 (CEV).
Once proud city, Zephaniah 2:14 (LB).
Violence, crime, Zephaniah 3:1 (LB).
City without boundaries, Zechariah 2:4 (CEV).
Total urban rejection, Matthew 8:34.
Heart cry for urban population, Matthew 23:37; Luke 13:34.
"Dangers in the city," 2 Corinthians 11:26 (NASB, NRSV).
New Jerusalem, Revelation 21:2, 15–27.

V

VALUES

Life, death, 2 Samuel 19:6.
Distorted values, Psalm 52:7 (KJV); Isaiah 5:20.
Evil as good, good as evil, Isaiah 5:20.
Ruined temple, luxurious homes, Haggai 1:2–3.

VANITY

Success caused pride, downfall, 2 Chronicles 26:16.
Victim of vanity, 2 Chronicles 32:24–26.
Vanity numbs realization of sin, Psalm 36:2.
Pretending to be what one is not, Proverbs 12:9; 13:7.
Vanity on display, Proverbs 21:24.
Those wise in their own eyes, Isaiah 5:21.
Pride of conqueror brought down, Jeremiah 50:11–12.
Skill in business brings vanity of heart, Ezekiel 28:4–5.
Egypt's claim of possessing the Nile, Ezekiel 29:3–5.
Vanity over wealth, self-righteousness, Hosea 12:8.
Destruction of wise men, Obadiah 8.
Seeking notice, acclaim, Luke 11:43.
Choosing place of honor, Luke 14:7–11.
High cost of flagrant vanity, Acts 12:19–23.
Danger of intellectual pride, 1 Corinthians 8:1–3.
Comparing oneself with oneself, 2 Corinthians 10:12.
Role of conceit in false doctrine, 1 Timothy 6:3–5.
Monetary wealth, wealth of good deeds, 1 Timothy 6:11–19.

VAGUE

Empty, boastful words, 2 Peter 2:18.
Pride, blasphemy, Revelation 13:5.

VEGETARIAN

Man, animals originally vegetarian, Genesis 1:29–30.
Using meat as food, Genesis 9:3.
Caution regarding eating of meat, Genesis 9:4.
Discontent over meatless diet, Numbers 11:4–6.
Greedy for meat, Numbers 11:31–34 (CEV).
Vegetable meal preferred, Proverbs 15:17.
Vegetable diet, Daniel 1:8 16.
Vegetable diet, Romans 14:2.

VICTORY

Master over sin, Genesis 4:7.
Victory song, Exodus 15:1–18.

V

Assured victory, Deuteronomy 3:2.
Yours to conquer, Joshua 8:1 (LB).
Victorious in death more than life, Judges 16:30.
"We won!" 2 Samuel 18:28 (CEV).
Resource in time of weakness, 2 Chronicles 14:11.
Certainty of God's promises, 2 Chronicles 20:17.
Victory, defeat in God's hands, 2 Chronicles 25:8.
Trusting God for deliverance, 2 Chronicles 32:1–21.
Power of God's name in time of trouble, Psalms 54:1;
   118:8–12.
God, not man, best help in time of trouble, Psalm
   60:11–12.
Key to victory over sin, Psalm 119:133.
Strength to declare God's message, Jeremiah 1:6–10,
   17–19.
Jesus responded to Satan with Scripture, Matthew 4:1–
   11.
Freedom from mastery of sin, Romans 6:14.
Nothing separates from God's love, Romans 8:37–39
   (LB).
In serving God, all may win, 1 Corinthians 9:24–27.

VOYAGE

Armor of God, Ephesians 6:10–18.
Encouraging report, 1 Thessalonians 3:6–8.
Ultimate victory over man of sin, 2 Thessalonians 2:8.
Mature Christian life, 2 Peter 1:5–9.
Deliverance from continual sin, 1 John 3:4–6.
Satan's work destroyed, 1 John 3:8.
Overcoming world through faith, 1 John 5:4.
Certainty of success in Christian life, Jude 24–25.
Satan's inevitable defeat, Revelation 12:1–9.
Rejoicing in victory over Babylon, Revelation 19:6–8.

VIRGIN

Father's evil offer of virgin daughters, Genesis 19:4–8.
Defiled virgin, Genesis 34:1–4.
Virgin spared in time of war, Numbers 31:17–18.
Plundered virgins, Deuteronomy 21:10–14.
Medical proof of virginity, Deuteronomy 22:13–19.
Sacrifice of daughter, Judges 11:30–40.
Incarnation prophesied, Isaiah 7:14; Matthew 1:22–23.
Matrimonial happiness, Isaiah 62:5.
Pregnant virgin, Matthew 1:25 (LB).
Ten virgins, Matthew 25:1–13.
No specific command, 1 Corinthians 7:25–26.
Presented to husband, 2 Corinthians 11:2–3.

VOLUNTEER

Distress, debt, discontent, 1 Samuel 22:2.
Volunteering personally, 2 Chronicles 17:16.
People volunteer freely, Psalm 110:3 (NASB).
"At his own expense," Acts 28:30 (NRSV).
Not volunteering, 1 Corinthians 9:17 (LB).

VOTE

Appointment of leader, Numbers 27:16.
Choosing right leader, Deuteronomy 17:14–15.
Trees seek king, Judges 9:7–15.
Choice of Jesus or Barabbas, Matthew 27:15–26.
Casting lots to determine God's will, Acts 1:23–26.
Agreeing in united mind and thought, 1 Corinthians 1:10.

VOW

Conditional vow, Genesis 28:20–21.
"Explicit vow," Leviticus 27:2 (NRSV).

VULTURES

SMITHERS AGAIN!

WELL, YOU KNOW WHAT THEY SAY ABOUT THE EARLY BIRD.

Keeping your word, Numbers 21:2; Deuteronomy 23:21; Ecclesiastes 5:4.
Making, keeping vows, Numbers 30:2–5.
Daughter sacrificed for vow, Judges 11:30–35.
"Sacred promise," Judges 21:1 (CEV).
Mother's promise for a son, 1 Samuel 1:11.
Keeping one's vow to God, Psalm 65:1; Ecclesiastes 5:4–5.
Think, then promise, Ecclesiastes 5:2 (CEV).
Vow to Queen of Heaven, Jeremiah 44:24–30.
Forced to break vow, Amos 2:12; Numbers 6:1–3.
Keep promises, Matthew 5:33 (CEV).
Peter vowed not to betray, Mark 14:29–31, 66–72.
Haircut in response to vow, Acts 18:18.

W

WAR
Victory assured in advance, Numbers 21:34.
Power in numbers, Numbers 22:2–4.
God greater than numbers, Deuteronomy 20:1.
Civilian and military, Deuteronomy 20:5–9.
Price of possession, Joshua 1:12–15.
Use of ambush, Joshua 8:14–29.
Apparent supremacy of enemy, Joshua 11:1–6.
Learning to wage war, Judges 3:1–2.
Those excluded from battle, Judges 12:1–3.
Surrender to power of God, 1 Samuel 14:1–14.
Futility of war, 2 Samuel 1:27.
Fortunes of war, 2 Samuel 11:25 (CEV).
Trained for battle, 2 Samuel 22:35.
Brother against brother, 2 Chronicles 11:4.

Children destined for war, Job 27:14.
God trained David for war, Psalm 18:34.
Courage in time of war, Psalm 27:3.
Those who hate peace, Psalm 120:6–7.
Time for war, Ecclesiastes 3:8.
Millennial peace among nations, Isaiah 2:4.
Awesome defeat, Isaiah 13:11–18.
Devastating statement of God's judgment, Isaiah 34:1–7.
Daring to scoff at name of the Lord, Isaiah 36:18–21.
Break bow, Jeremiah 49:35.
Coming great war against Israel, Ezekiel 38 and 39.
Plowshares to swords, Joel 3:10.
No world peace without Christ, Matthew 24:6–8; Mark 13:6–8.
Four horsemen, Revelation 6:1–6.
One fourth of earth's population destroyed, Revelation 6:8.
War in heaven, Revelation 12:7.

WARDROBE

Tunic of many colors, Genesis 37:3 (NKJV).
Widow's clothes, Genesis 38:14.
Clothes make the man, Exodus 28:2; James 2:2–3 (AB).
Prison clothes, 2 Kings 25:29.
Royal wardrobe, Esther 6:8, 15; Psalm 45:13; Acts 12:21.
Wardrobe items, Isaiah 20:2; Jeremiah 13:2.
Warm weather, warm clothes, Job 37:17.
Dressed for church, Psalm 29:2 (Berk.).
Fragrant wardrobe, Psalm 45:8.
Gold interwoven gown, Psalm 45:13.
Wearing white, Ecclesiastes 9:8.
Extreme weather concern, Ecclesiastes 11:4.
Fragrant garments, Song of Songs 4:11.
Luxurious wardrobe denied, Isaiah 3:18–24.
Elaborate robe, Isaiah 6:1.
Garments of righteousness, Isaiah 11:5.
Everyone in sackcloth, Jonah 3:5 (CEV).
Foreign wardrobe, Zephaniah 1:8.
Joshua's filthy clothes, Zechariah 3:3.
Palace wardrobe, Matthew 11:8.
Camel's hair clothing, Mark 1:6.
Wardrobe instructions, Mark 6:9.
"Swaddling clothes," Luke 2:7–12.

W

Repairing old garment, Luke 5:36.
"Dressed for action," Luke 12:35 (GNB).
Best robe, Luke 15:22.
Well-dressed rich man, Luke 16:19.
Clothed for Christian service, Ephesians 6:15 (NRSV).
"Only rags to wear," 1 Corinthians 4:11 (CEV).
Clothing wears out, Hebrews 1:11.
Corrupt wardrobe, Jude 23.
Clothing dirtied by sin, Revelation 3:4 (CEV).
Sun as a garment, Revelation 12:1.

WEALTH

Earth's wealth, Genesis 2:11–12.
Promise, warning, Deuteronomy 6:10–12.
Tainted gold, silver, Deuteronomy 7:25.
Wealth an impetus to backsliding, Deuteronomy 8:13–14; 31:20; 32:15; Psalm 62:10.
Ability to produce wealth, Deuteronomy 8:18; Ecclesiastes 5:19.
The Lord gives, takes away, 1 Samuel 2:7.
Plunder dedicated to God, 2 Samuel 8:9–12.
Solomon's great wealth, 2 Chronicles 9:22.
Great wealth, Job 1:3.
Avoid trusting wealth, Job 31:24–28; Psalm 49:5–12.
Producing wealth for others, Psalm 39:6.
Transient wealth, Psalm 49:16–20.
Growing rich by harming others, Psalm 52:7.
Greatest of all wealth, Psalm 119:14.
Barns filled, flocks abundant, Psalm 144:13.
Honor the Lord with one's wealth, Proverbs 3:9–10.
Wealth stolen by strangers, Proverbs 5:8–10.
Wisdom the truest wealth, Proverbs 8:17–19; 16:16.
Ill-gotten wealth, Proverbs 10:2.
Pretrense of wealth, Proverbs 13:7.
Greatest value, Proverbs 16:8.
Greater than gold or silver, Proverbs 16:16.
Purchase of prestige, Proverbs 18:16.
Priceless value of good name, Proverbs 22:1.
Power of money, Proverbs 22:7.
Stealing from poor, giving to rich, Proverbs 22:16.
Exhausted becoming rich, Proverbs 23:4–5.
Do not envy wicked, Proverbs 24:19–20.
Prayer of true wisdom, Proverbs 30:8–9.
Meaningless accumulation of wealth, Ecclesiastes 2:4–11.

Money alone never satisfies, Ecclesiastes 5:10.
Wealth plus happiness, Ecclesiastes 5:19–20.
Money as shelter, Ecclesiastes 7:12.
Money's presumed function, Ecclesiastes 10:19.
Mid-life loss of unjust wealth, Jeremiah 17:11; 5:27.
City of luxury brought down, Ezekiel 27:1–36; 28:1–19.
Exploiting poor for personal gain, Amos 5:11.
Gold and silver belong to God, Haggai 2:8.
Eternal wealth, Matthew 6:19–21.
Wealth a spiritual liability, 1 Timothy 6:9.
Rich man provided tomb for Jesus, Matthew 27:57–61.
Poor can inherit kingdom, Luke 6:20.
Much given, much required, Luke 12:48.
Surprised beggar, Acts 3:1–8.
Sharing spiritual and material blessings, Romans 15:26–27.
Assured wealth, 2 Corinthians 9:11.
God's grace lavished on us, Ephesians 1:7–8.
Jesus the source, Philippians 4:19.
Bring nothing into world, take nothing out, 1 Timothy 6:6–8.
Dangerous wealth, 1 Timothy 6:9–10.
Functioning wealth, 1 Timothy 6:17–19.
High position is, instead, low, James 1:10.
Eternal inheritance, 1 Peter 1:3–4.
Gold perishes, 1 Peter 1:7.
Not redeemed with silver, gold, 1 Peter 1:18–19.
True wealth, Revelation 2:9.
Temporal wealth, spiritual wealth, Revelation 3:15–18.

WEAPONS
No weapons in Israel, 1 Samuel 13:19–22.
Spiritual weapons, 1 Samuel 17:45; 2 Corinthians 10:4; Ephesians 6:17; Hebrews 4:12.
Bronze bow, 2 Samuel 22:35.
Primitive weapons, 2 Chronicles 26:10–14.
Spear, battle-axe, Psalm 35:3 (NASB).
The Lord on our side, Psalm 124:1–5.
Satisfied sword, Jeremiah 46:10.
Break bow, Jeremiah 49:35.
Arsenal of the Lord, Jeremiah 50:25.
Trusting the Lord, trusting in weapons, Luke 22:35–38.

WEATHER

WEDDING
Long delayed wedding, Genesis 29:28.
Dowry payment, Genesis 34:12; Exodus 22:16–17.
Wedding riddle, Judges 14:12–13.
Esther's great banquet, Esther 2:18.
Bridal attire, Jeremiah 2:32 (Berk.).
Bride stands at right side, Psalm 45:9 (CEV).
Arrival of bridegroom, Song of Songs 3:9–11.
Dressed like bridegroom, Isaiah 61:10.
Newlyweds disturbed, Joel 2:16.
Parable of virgins, Matthew 25:1–13.
Invited guests, John 2:1.
Site of Christ's first miracle, John 2:1–11.
No more weddings, Revelation 18:23; 19:7.
Garments of bride, Revelation 19:7–8; 21:2.
Bride of Christ, Revelation 21:9.

WELFARE
Mutual responsibility, Genesis 9:5.
Food stored for welfare, Deuteronomy 14:28–29; 26:12.
Concern for those in need, Deuteronomy 15:7–11; Job 29:16.
Harvest gleaners, Deuteronomy 24:19–21.
Welfare supplies, Deuteronomy 26:12.
Heartless attitude, Job 12:5; 22:7–9.
Eyes to blind, feet to lame, Job 29:15.
Sharing with others, Job 31:16–22.

Welfare rewarded, Psalm 41:1-3 (LB); Matthew 25:34-40; Hebrews 6:10.

Kindness to needy, Proverbs 14:21.

God loves poor people, Proverbs 14:31.

Demean poor, demean God, Proverbs 17:5.

Welfare a spiritual investment, Proverbs 19:17.

Blessing for generous man, Proverbs 22:9.

Outreach to enemy, Proverbs 25:21.

Leader oppresses poor, Proverbs 28:3.

Concern for poor rewarded, Proverbs 28:27; 31:20.

Those who cannot help themselves, Proverbs 31:8-9.

Welfare as spiritual service, Isaiah 58:6-10.

Babylonian mercy to poor, Jeremiah 39:10; 40:7-9.

Welfare for orphans and widows, Jeremiah 49:11; Zechariah 7:8-10.

Cheap value on human beings, Amos 2:6.

Responding to request for aid, Matthew 5:42.

Private welfare, Matthew 6:2-4.

Cup of cold water, Matthew 10:42.

Expensive perfume prepared Jesus for Cross, Mark 14:3-9.

Practical welfare for paralytic man, Luke 5:17-26.

Good Samaritan, Luke 10:30-37.

Altruistic welfare, Luke 14:12-14.

Surprised beggar, Acts 3:1-8.

Early Christian welfare, Acts 4:32-35.

Woman who helped the poor, Acts 9:36-42.

Generous centurion, Acts 10:1-2.

Welfare recognized by the Lord, Acts 10:4.

Reaching out to help others, Acts 11:27-30.

Share with those in need, Romans 12:13.

Church-centered welfare, Romans 15:26-27.

Seeking good of others above self, 1 Corinthians 10:24.

Greater gift than money, 1 Corinthians 13:3.

Concern of early Christians, Galatians 2:9-10.

Proper care for widows, relatives, 1 Timothy 5:3-8.

Widows on welfare, 1 Timothy 5:9-11.

Women helping women, 1 Timothy 5:16.

Share with others, Hebrews 13:16; 1 John 3:17.

Looking after those in need, James 1:27.

Proper attitude toward poor, James 2:1-8.

Faith without works, James 2:14-18.

W

WIDOW

Widows not to be exploited, Exodus 22:22.
Tithe benefits widows, Deuteronomy 26:12.
Three widows in one family, Ruth 1:1–5.
Concubine widows, 2 Samuel 20:3.
Widow threatened by creditor, 2 Kings 4:1.
Widows who do not mourn, Job 27:15.
Father to fatherless, Psalm 68:5.
Numerous widows, Jeremiah 15:8.
Priests' widows, Ezekiel 44:22.
Sorrow of young virgin, Joel 1:8.
Widow's mite, Mark 12:42–44; Luke 21:1–4.
Long years of widowhood, Luke 2:36–37.
Ministry of aged widow, Luke 2:36–38.
Caring for widows, 1 Timothy 5:3–16.
Congregational concern, James 1:27.

WIDOWER

Abraham, death of Sarah, Genesis 23:1–20.
Boaz and Ruth, Ruth 3:7–18.

WIFE

Creator's design, Genesis 2:18, 24.
Wife search, Genesis 24:14.
Husband's involvement in wife's contracts, Numbers 30:10–15.
Wiles of new bride, Judges 14:11–19.
Wife's insult, 2 Samuel 6:20 (LB).
Bossy wife, 1 Kings 21:1–16.
Favorite among many wives, 2 Chronicles 11:21.
Influence of evil wife, 2 Chronicles 21:6.
Wife's refusal to be put on display, Esther 1:9–21.
Complaining wife, Job 2:9–10.
Fruitful vine, Psalm 128:3.
Husband's crown, Proverbs 12:4.
Favor of the Lord, Proverbs 18:22 (CEV).
Woman of noble character, Proverbs 31:10–31.
Death of Ezekiel's wife, Ezekiel 24:15–27.
Joseph's enigma concerning Mary, Matthew 1:18, 19.
Pilate's wife, Matthew 27:19.
Loving husband's enemies, James 4:4 (LB).

WILD OATS

Sins of youth, Psalm 25:6–7.
Reaping what is sown, Galatians 6:7–8.

WINE
Wine used in spiritual offering, Exodus 29:40.
Abstinent priests, Leviticus 10:9.
Nazarite vow, Numbers 6:3–4.
Purchase of wine, Deuteronomy 14:26.
Wine from snake venom, Deuteronomy 32:33 (GNB).
Antidote for weariness, 2 Samuel 16:2.
Beverage of soldiers, 2 Chronicles 11:11.
Wine steward, Nehemiah 2:1.
Social consumption, Esther 1:7–8; 5:6.
Vented wineskin, Job 32:19 (Berk.).
Illustrative wine, Psalm 60:3 (GNB, LB).
Gladdened heart, Psalm 104:15.
Love of wine, fattening food, Proverbs 21:17; 23:1–2.
Wine, leadership, Proverbs 31:4.
False cheer, Ecclesiastes 2:3.
Love better than wine, Song of Songs 4:10 (KJV).
Vintage years, Isaiah 25:6.
Cup of Divine fury, Jeremiah 25:15.
"Wine flowed freely," Daniel 5:1 (LB).
Teetotalers forced to drink wine, Amos 2:12; Numbers 6:3–4.
Treacherous wine, Habakkuk 2:5 (CEV).
Fermentation of wine, Mark 2:22.
"Cheap wine," John 19:29 (CEV, NRSV).
"Juice of grapes," Mark 14:23 (AB).
Setting good example, Romans 14:21.
Digestive function, 1 Timothy 5:23.
Wine of lust, Revelation 18:3 (GNB).

WINK
Malicious wink, Psalm 35:19.
Gesture of scoundrel, Proverbs 6:12–14; 10:10.
Haughty women of Zion, Isaiah 3:16–17.
Divine wink, Acts 17:30.

WISDOM
Wise hearted, Exodus 28:3 (KJV); 35:10 (AB).
Wise behavior, 1 Samuel 18:14 (KJV).
Priority prayer for wisdom, 1 Kings 3:9–15; 4:29–34.
Reputation for wisdom, 2 Chronicles 9:23.
Need to obtain advice more than give, 2 Chronicles 10:1–8.
Wisdom's many sides, Job 11:6 (CEV).
Wisdom not inherited, Job 11:12 (LB).

Wisdom of youth, age, Job 32:4–9.
Words without knowledge, Job 38:2.
Divine supply of light, Psalm 36:9.
Wealth without wisdom, Psalm 49:20.
Pomp without insight, Psalm 49:20 (Berk.)
"How to use wisdom," Psalm 105:22 (CEV).
Fear of the Lord, Psalm 111:10.
Wisdom for study of Scriptures, Psalm 119:33–38; 97–100.
Asking God for discernment, Psalm 119:125.
Wisdom like "sweetheart," Proverbs 7:4 (LB).
Folly of lacking wisdom, Proverbs 8:32–36.
Always for the best, Proverbs 19:8 (LB).
Wisdom brightens countenance, Ecclesiastes 8:1.
Divine omniscience, Isaiah 40:13–14.
Learning of wise overthrown, Isaiah 44:25.
God's thoughts higher than ours, Isaiah 55:9.
Wisdom banished, Jeremiah 49:7 (CEV).
"Wiser than Daniel," Ezekiel 28:3.
Wisdom of trusting the Lord, Hosea 14:9.
Wise as snakes, innocent as doves, Matthew 10:16.
Greater wisdom than Solomon's, Matthew 12:42.
Truth understood by children, Luke 10:21.
Articulate wisdom, Luke 11:49 (AB).
Given wisdom in difficult time, Luke 12:11–12; 21:15.
Knowledge beyond classroom, John 7:15.
Understanding divine thoughts, 1 Corinthians 2:16 (CEV).
Wise fools, 1 Corinthians 4:10.
Eyes of heart, Ephesians 1:18–19.

Complicated wisdom, Ephesians 3:10 (AB).
"Power to comprehend," Ephesians 3:18 (NRSV).
Knowledge, insight, Philippians 1:9.
Reward of careful reflection, 2 Timothy 2:7.
We are given understanding, 1 John 5:20.

WITCHCRAFT

Witchcraft destroyed, Exodus 22:18; 2 Kings 23:24; Micah 5:12.
Abstinence from witchcraft, Leviticus 19:31; 20:6; Isaiah 8:19.
Sin of divination, 1 Samuel 15:23.
King who consulted witch, 1 Samuel 28:5–20.
Mediums consulted, Isaiah 19:3.

WOMEN

Man's helper, Genesis 2:18.
"Life giving one," Genesis 3:20 (LB).
Good-looking women, Genesis 6:1–2 (Berk.).
Husband's deceitfulness, Genesis 20:1–18; 12:10–20.
Shepherdess, Genesis 29:9.
Women without inheritance, Genesis 31:15–16.
Miriam's song of praise, Exodus 15:21.
Sold as slave but granted rights, Exodus 21:7–11.
Daughters who had no brother, Numbers 27:1–11.
Husband's involvement in wife's contracts, Numbers 30:10–15.
Death to enemy women, children, Numbers 31:7–18.
Asking special favor, Judges 1:13–15.
"Wisest ladies," Judges 5:29 (NKJV, NRSV).
Spoils for conqueror, Judges 5:30 (LB).
Demeaned by woman, Judges 9:50–55.
Woman's value degraded, Judges 19:1–30.
Kidnapping wife, Judges 21:20–21.
Change of mind, Ruth 1:8 (LB).
Short work break, Ruth 2:7.
Women strengthening Israel, Ruth 4:11.
Daughter-in-law worth seven sons, Ruth 4:13–15.
Prompt gathering of food, 1 Samuel 25:18.
David's respect for concubines, 2 Samuel 20:3.
Language of woman's heart, 1 Kings 10:2 (NKJV).
Evil woman, 1 Kings 19:1–2.
Well-to-do woman, 2 Kings 4:8 (KJV).
Mothers listed, not fathers, 2 Kings 23:31, 36; 24:8, 18.
Prophetess counseled king, 2 Chronicles 34:22–28.

W

Daughters assisted rebuilding wall, Nehemiah 3:12.
Beautiful queen refused to be put on display, Esther 1:9–
  21.
Beauty treatments, Esther 2:3, 9, 12.
Queen's influence over king, Esther 9:12.
Women's witness, Psalm 68:11 (GNB).
Boisterous woman, Proverbs 9:13 (NASB).
Blessing of good wife, Proverbs 12:4.
One upright man, no women, Ecclesiastes 7:28.
Weaker sex, Isaiah 19:16; Jeremiah 50:37; 51:30; Na-
  hum 3:13; 1 Peter 3:7.
Consistent lady, Isaiah 47:7 (KJV).
Beautiful, delicate, Jeremiah 6:2.
Queen of Heaven, Jeremiah 7:18; 44:18–19.
King, queen brought to judgment, Jeremiah 13:18.
Woman made superior to man, Jeremiah 31:22.
Fate of young women, Lamentations 3:51 (RSV).
Women prophets, Ezekiel 13:17 (CEV).
Queen's wisdom, Daniel 5:10–11.
Women command husbands, Amos 4:1.
Mary compared to shepherds, Luke 2:19–20.
Ministry of aged widow, Luke 2:36–38.
Women who traveled with Jesus, Luke 8:1–3.
Separating men, women, John 4:27.
Effectiveness of woman's testimony, John 4:39–42.
Ministry to women, Acts 16:13.
Business woman, Acts 16:13–15.
Prominent women at Thessalonica, Acts 17:4, 12.
Daughters with gift of prophecy, Acts 21:9.
Assistance to co-worker, Romans 16:2 (NASB).
Woman like mother to Paul, Romans 16:13.
Advice to unmarried women, 1 Corinthians 7:25–26.
Wife traveling with husband, 1 Corinthians 9:5.
Role of women, 1 Corinthians 11:2–16.
Women in worship, 1 Corinthians 14:33–36; 1 Timothy
  2:9–15.
Wives likened to Church, Ephesians 5:25.
Sexual desire, 1 Timothy 5:11.
Responsibility of young wives, Titus 2:3–5.
Epistle dedicated to chosen lady, 2 John 1–5.

WOMEN'S RIGHTS
Creator's plan, Genesis 3:16.
Freedom to decide marriage, Genesis 24:54–58; Num-
  bers 36:6.

Daughter sold as servant, Exodus 21:7–11.
Rights of pregnant woman, Exodus 21:22.
Father's authority over daughter, Numbers 30:3–5.
Husband's superiority over wife, Numbers 30:10–16.
Apparel worn by opposite sex, Deuteronomy 22:5.
Selfish marital relationship, Deuteronomy 22:13–19.
Women divided among spoils, Judges 5:30.
Sacrifice of daughter, Judges 11:30–40.
Substituting heterosexual for homosexual, Judges 19:22–25.
Stolen wives, Judges 21:15–23.
Woman of character, Ruth 3:1–13.
Value of woman, Ruth 4:9–12.
Beloved but barren, 1 Samuel 1:2–7.
Solomon's counsel with two mothers, 1 Kings 3:16–28.
Daughters working with fathers, Nehemiah 3:12.
Male chauvinism, Esther 1:10–22.
Daughters' inheritance, Job 42:15.
Women as home builders, Proverbs 14:1 (GNB).
Good wife's description, Proverbs 31:10.
Haughty women, Isaiah 3:16.
Self-sufficient women in need of name, Isaiah 4:1.
Women who command husbands, Amos 4:1.
Women unfit soldiers, Nahum 3:13 (See LB, RSV).
Mother chose name of son, Luke 1:59–66.
Responsibility of servant returned from fields, Luke 17:7–10.
Marriage or career, 1 Corinthians 7:34 (LB).
Relationship of woman, man, 1 Corinthians 11:3–12 (GNB, LB).
Women's questions in early church, 1 Corinthians 14:34–35.
Two quarrelling women, Philippians 4:2 (LB).
Women not to teach, 1 Timothy 2:11–12.
Relationship between husband, wife, 1 Peter 3:1–7.

WORK (Physical)
Forced to serve with rigor, Exodus 1:13–14 (KJV).
Unfairness to workers, Exodus 5:6–18.
Priest different from laity, Deuteronomy 18:1–2.
Taking care of business, Deuteronomy 20:5–9.
Concentrated work, Nehemiah 5:16.
Divine blessing upon work, Psalm 90:17.
Profitability of work, Proverbs 14:23.
Work avoided in cold weather, Proverbs 20:4 (KJV).

Strength in numbers, Proverbs 30:25.
Satisfying work, Ecclesiastes 3:13.
Working with diligence, Ecclesiastes 9:10.
Digging cistern, Jeremiah 2:13.
Avoiding Sabbath work, Jeremiah 17:21–27.

WORRY

Donkeys, people, 1 Samuel 9:3–5; 10:2.
Unnecessary fear, 1 Kings 1:50–53.
Desire for peace, security, 2 Kings 20:19.
Wrestling one's thoughts, Psalm 13:2.
Songs in night, Psalm 42:8.
No fear of bad news, Psalm 111:6.
Do not dwell on the past, Isaiah 43:18.
Non-productive worry, Matthew 6:27, 28.
Worry blinds eyes to truth, Matthew 13:22.
Life's worries, Mark 4:19.
Circumstances need not cause worry, Luke 8:22–25.
Worry about wine at wedding, John 2:1–5.
The Lord always at hand, Acts 2:25–28.
Hope when no basis for hope, Romans 4:18–22.
Paul's anxiety, Philippians 2:28.
Antidote to worry, Philippians 4:6–7.
God's best in abundance, Jude 2.

WRESTLING

Jacob's Divine encounter, Genesis 32:22–32.
Face rubbed into ground, Lamentations 3:16 (GNB).
Satan as opponent, Ephesians 6:22.

WRITING

Writing on front, back, Exodus 32:15–16.
Handwriting of God, Exodus 31:18; 32:16; Deuteronomy 10:4.
Writing on stones, Deuteronomy 27:8.
Moses as author, Deuteronomy 31:24.
Written plan, 1 Chronicles 28:19.
Early correspondence, 2 Chronicles 2:11.
Shortest short story, Ecclesiastes 9:14–15.
Deceitful theology, Jeremiah 8:8.
Book writing instructions, Jeremiah 30:2.
Danger of writing truth, Jeremiah 36:4–32.
Taking dictation, Jeremiah 36:6, 16–18.
Edible scrolls, Ezekiel 3:1–3.
Plain writing all can read, Habakkuk 2:2.

Gigantic scroll, Zechariah 5:1–2.
Attempts to record New Testament events, Luke 1:1–4.
Writing superior to speaking, 2 Corinthians 10:10.
Play on words, 2 Thessalonians 3:11.
Commanded to write, Revelation 1:10–11; 21:5.

WRONG

Unintentional sin, Leviticus 4:1–5.
Testing divine patience, Numbers 14:18.
Defiant sin, Numbers 15:30–31.
Guilt for one person's sin, Numbers 16:22.
Wrongly suspecting woman of drunkenness, 1 Samuel 1:9–16.
Limited admission of wrong, Job 34:31–33.
Wrongdoing categorized, Proverbs 6:16–19 (LB).
Pardon for nation's bloodguilt, Joel 3:12.
Accused yet admired, 1 Peter 2:12.

X

XENOPHOBIA

Sarah, Hagar, Genesis 21:8–10, 21.
Abraham's concern to find wife for Isaac, Genesis 24:1–4.
Courtesy to foreigners, Exodus 23:9.
Providing for strangers, Leviticus 23:22.
Report of spies who explored Canaan, Numbers 13:17–33.
Loaning money to foreigner, Deuteronomy 23:19–20.
Showing kindness to foreigner, Ruth 2:10.
Misunderstanding goodwill gesture, 2 Samuel 10:1–4.
No marriage to foreigners, Nehemiah 10:30.
Language confused by intermarriage, Nehemiah 13:23–27.
Hatred of Jews, Esther 3:8–15.
Do good to foreigners, Jeremiah 22:3.
Falling into foreign hands, Ezekiel 11:9.
Delivered from malicious neighbors, Ezekiel 28:24.
Ingratitude to foreigner, Luke 17:11–19.

X-RAY

Divine penetration, Hebrews 4:12.

Y

YEAR
Designed by Creator, Genesis 1:14.
Measurement of life span, Genesis 11:10–32.
First month of year, Exodus 12:2.
Lunar determination of time, Numbers 10:10.
Divine reckoning of time, Psalm 90:4.

YIELDING
Yielding to temptation, Genesis 3:6; Joshua 7:21;
1 Kings 11:4.
Foolish sins, Numbers 12:11.
Potter and clay, Isaiah 45:9; 64:8.

YOUTH
Resentment toward youth in leadership, Genesis 37:5–
11.
Youthful, prestigious Joseph, Genesis 41:41–46 (LB).
Census of men twenty or older, Numbers 26:2; 1 Chron-
icles 27:23.
Young woman's vow, Numbers 30:3–5.
Early joys of marriage, Deuteronomy 24:5.
Sacrifice only child, Judges 11:28–40.
Age variable between Boaz and Ruth, Ruth 3:10–13.
Growth in spirit, character, 1 Samuel 2:26.
Impressive young man, 1 Samuel 9:2.
Age of Saul when he became king, 1 Samuel 13:1.
Boldness of Jonathan against Philistines, 1 Samuel
14:1–14.
David chosen over older brothers, 1 Samuel 16:4–12.
Confrontation between David, Saul, 1 Samuel 17:32–
37.
Veteran soldier underrated boy, 1 Samuel 17:42.
Saul went home, David prepared for action, 1 Samuel
24:22.
Father would have died in place of son, 2 Samuel 18:32–
33.
Younger men, not elders, advise, 1 Kings 12:1–15.
Youths ridiculed Elisha's baldness, 2 Kings 2:23–24.
Sixteen-year-old king, 2 Kings 14:21–22; 2 Chronicles
26:1.
Ages of young kings, 2 Kings 21:1, 19; 23:36; 24:18;
2 Chronicles 33:1, 21; 34:1; 36:2, 5, 9, 11.
Father, inexperienced son, 1 Chronicles 22:5; 29:1.

Resisting counsel, 2 Chronicles 10:6–11.
Victim of bad influence, 2 Chronicles 13:7.
The Lord honored in early reign of young king, 2 Chronicles 17:1–4.
Good young king, 2 Chronicles 34:1–5 (LB).
Longing for younger years, Job 29:4–6.
Respect for elders, Job 32:4.
Wisdom of old, young, Job 32:4–9.
Sins of youth, Psalm 25:7.
Youthful faith, Psalm 71:5.
Afflicted from youth, Psalm 88:15.
Days of youth shortened, Psalm 89:45.
Youth's purity, Psalm 119:9.
More understanding than those older, Psalm 119:100.
Youth, old age, Proverbs 20:29.
Cautious happiness, Ecclesiastes 11:9.
Counsel to young, Ecclesiastes 12:1–7.
All have become ungodly, Isaiah 9:17.
Youth's fear of death, Isaiah 38:10–20.
Sins of youth forgotten, Isaiah 54:4 (CEV).
Why some die young, Isaiah 57:1–2 (LB).
Young at one hundred, Isaiah 65:20.
Youthful limitations, capabilities, Jeremiah 1:6–10 (LB).
Finest youth killed in battle, Jeremiah 48:15.
Youth facing problems, Lamentations 3:27 (LB).
Plight of young girls, Lamentations 3:51 (LB).
"Worth weight in gold," Lamentations 4:2 (NIV).
No youth music, Lamentations 5:14.
Young prostitutes, Ezekiel 23:2–3 (LB).
Chosen for royal service, Daniel 1:3–6.
Daniel resolved not to defile himself, Daniel 1:8–20.
Young prophesy, old dream dreams, Joel 2:28.
Attractive young men, young women, Zechariah 9:17.
Role of recent convert, 1 Timothy 3:6.
Young not to be looked down upon, 1 Timothy 4:12.
Evil desires of youth, 2 Timothy 2:22 (GNB).
Respect for those who are older, 1 Peter 5:5.
Youth overcomes evil, 1 John 2:13.

Z

ZEAL
Keep fire burning, Leviticus 6:13.
Zeal for spiritual vitality, Deuteronomy 6:4–7.

Earnestness of new priest, Deuteronomy 18:6–7.
The Lord's demands within reach, Deuteronomy 30:11.
Burning zeal, Psalm 69:9 (LB).
Do not envy sinners, Proverbs 23:17.
Zeal of the Lord, Isaiah 9:7.
Zealous for new gods, Isaiah 57:7–10 (LB).
Press on to acknowledge the Lord, Hosea 6:3.
Zealous fanatics, Matthew 23:15.
Burning, shining, John 5:35 (ASB, RSV).
Eagerness to be baptized, Acts 8:36–37.
Zealous ministry, Acts 18:24–28.
Zeal without knowledge, Romans 10:1–2.
Never lacking zeal, Romans 12:11.
Paul's former fanaticism, Galatians 1:13–14 (NRSV).
Former zeal lost, Galatians 4:15 (AB).
Ready to serve, witness, Ephesians 2:10; 6:10–20.
Never lazy, Hebrews 6:12 (CEV).
Losing first love, Revelation 2:4.

ZODIAC

Term used in astronomy, Job 9:9 (LB).

God's message in the stars, Psalm 19·1–6 (Note words "speech," "language," "voice" in the text. Then compare verses 7–13.).

ZOOLOGY

Distinction of species, Genesis 1:25; 1 Corinthians 15:39.

Naming of birds, animals, Genesis 2:20.

Solomon's expertise, 1 Kings 4:33–34.

Apes, baboons, 1 Kings 10:22.

Creature book, Isaiah 34:16 (GNB).

Z